MW00805588

Cinesonidos

THE OXFORD MUSIC / MEDIA SERIES

Daniel Goldmark, Series Editor

oxford
music/media series

Tuning In: American Narrative Television Music
Ron Rodman

Special Sound: The Creation and Legacy of the BBC Radiophonic Workshop
Louis Niebur

Seeing Through Music: Gender and Modernism in Classic Hollywood Film Scores
Peter Franklin

An Eye for Music: Popular Music and the Audiovisual Surreal
John Richardson

Playing Along: Digital Games, YouTube, and Virtual Performance
Kiri Miller

Sounding the Gallery: Video and the Rise of Art-Music
Holly Rogers

Composing for the Red Screen: Prokofiev and Soviet Film
Kevin Bartig

Saying It With Songs: Popular Music and the Coming of Sound to Hollywood Cinema
Katherine Spring

We'll Meet Again: Musical Design in the Films of Stanley Kubrick
Kate McQuiston

Occult Aesthetics: Synchronization in Sound Film
K.J. Donnelly

Sound Play: Video Games and the Musical Imagination
William Cheng

Sounding American: Hollywood, Opera, and Jazz
Jennifer Fleeger

Mismatched Women: The Siren's Song Through the Machine
Jennifer Fleeger

Robert Altman's Soundtracks: Film, Music and Sound from M*A*S*H to A Prairie Home Companion
Gayle Sherwood Magee

Back to the Fifties: Nostalgia, Hollywood Film, and Popular Music of the Seventies and Eighties
Michael D. Dwyer

The Early Film Music of Dmitry Shostakovich
Joan Titus

Making Music in Selznick's Hollywood
Nathan Platte

Hearing Haneke: The Sound Tracks of a Radical Auteur
Elsie Walker

Unlimited Replays: Video Games and Classical Music
William Gibbons

Hollywood Harmony: Musical Wonder and the Sound of Cinema
Frank Lehman

French Musical Culture and the Coming of Sound Cinema
Hannah Lewis

Theories of the Soundtrack
James Buhler

Through The Looking Glass: John Cage and Avant-Garde Film
Richard H. Brown

Sound Design is the New Score: Theory, Aesthetics, and Erotics of the Integrated Soundtrack
Danijela Kulezic-Wilson

Cinesonidos: Film Music and National Identity During Mexico's Época de oro
Jacqueline Avila

Cinesonidos

Film Music and National Identity During Mexico's Época de oro

JACQUELINE AVILA

Thanks for your support! Enjoy! Abrazos!

OXFORD
UNIVERSITY PRESS

OXFORD
UNIVERSITY PRESS

Oxford University Press is a department of the University of Oxford. It furthers
the University's objective of excellence in research, scholarship, and education
by publishing worldwide. Oxford is a registered trade mark of Oxford University
Press in the UK and certain other countries.

Published in the United States of America by Oxford University Press
198 Madison Avenue, New York, NY 10016, United States of America.

© Oxford University Press 2019

All rights reserved. No part of this publication may be reproduced, stored in
a retrieval system, or transmitted, in any form or by any means, without the
prior permission in writing of Oxford University Press, or as expressly permitted
by law, by license, or under terms agreed with the appropriate reproduction
rights organization. Inquiries concerning reproduction outside the scope of the
above should be sent to the Rights Department, Oxford University Press, at the
address above.

You must not circulate this work in any other form
and you must impose this same condition on any acquirer.

CIP data is on file at the Library of Congress
ISBN 978-0-19-067131-0 (pbk.)
ISBN 978-0-19-067130-3 (hbk.)

1 3 5 7 9 8 6 4 2

Paperback printed by Marquis, Canada
Hardback printed by Bridgeport National Bindery, Inc., United States of America

Para mi familia y para Oswaldo

Contents

Acknowledgments   ix

Introduction: Listening to the Época de Oro   1

1. The Prostitute and the Cinematic Cabaret: Musicalizing the
   "Fallen Woman" and Mexico City's Nightlife   21

2. The Salon, the Stage, and Porfirian Nostalgia   68

3. The Sounds of Indigenismo: Cultural Integration and Musical
   Exoticism in *Janitzio* (1935) and *María Candelaria* (1944)   111

4. The Singing Charro in the Comedia Ranchera: Music,
   Machismo, and the Invention of a Tradition   150

5. The Strains of the Revolution: Musicalizing the Soldadera in the
   Revolutionary Melodrama   193

Epilogue: After the Época de Oro   234

Bibliography   243
Index   263

Acknowledgments

There are many people and institutions that have helped getting this labor of love completed. First, I am profoundly grateful for the team at Oxford University Press who have helped make this book possible, especially editors Daniel Goldmark and Norm Hirschy. Daniel approached me when I was still conducting research and asked if I would consider publishing the book in this series. His encouragement and support have kept me going through all stages of development. Norm has been an amazing and understanding editor, who has guided me through this project from beginning to end. This book wouldn't have been possible without their faith in me and in my work, to which I am very thankful. I would also like to extend my sincere thanks to the whole Oxford project team for their help in marketing and in editorial assistance. I am also very grateful to the anonymous readers who provided feedback that improved the overall quality of the book.

At the University of California, Riverside, where I did my both of my graduate degrees, I would like to thank the amazing faculty that have supported my work, including Byron Adams, Walter Clark, Keith Harris, René Lysloff, Jonathan Ritter, and Deborah Wong. I was especially grateful to have worked with Leonora Saavedra. Leonora patiently listened to my ideas about cinema, music, and Mexican culture for several years, and supported my researching this difficult topic. Her guidance, both personal and professional, has helped me (and continues to help me) in so many ways.

I am profoundly grateful to mycolleagues at the University of Tennessee who have been a bedrock of support as I worked on this project. My sincere gratitude first goes to my colleagues in the musicology area, Rachel May Golden and Leslie Gay, who have been both patient and encouraging particularly during the final stages of the book. Also at the School of Music, I am indebted to Director Jeffrey Pappas, whose support has helped me considerably since beginning my career at the University of Tennessee. I would also like to thank my fellow colleagues in Latin American and Caribbean studies including Rudy Alcocer, Dawn Duke, Liliana Gonzalez, Tore Olssen, and De Ann Pedry who read samples of my chapters and provided necessary feedback. I would also like to thank all the friends that I have made in Knoxville since 2012, who have made this small town feel like home.

My work has been supported by several organizations and institutions throughout the years: the Richard E. Greenleaf Visiting Library Scholar Award (2016) from the Latin American and Iberian Institute (LAII) and University Libraries at the University of New Mexico, Albuquerque, the UC MEXUS-CONAYCT Post-Doctoral Fellowship (2014–2015) from the University of California Institute for Mexico and the United States (UC MEXUS), the Howard Mayer Brown Fellowship (2010–2011) from the American Musicological Society (AMS), the UC MEXUS Dissertation Research Grant (2009–2011) from UC MEXUS, the Dissertation Mentorship Fellowship (2008–2009) from the UC Riverside Graduate Division, the UCR Department of the Humanities and Social Sciences for supplying me with several small travel grants, and the then UC Riverside Graduate Division Dean Joseph Childers. I would also like to thank the University of Tennessee Humanities Center and the Office of Research and Engagement for providing additional support. All people and organizations believed in my research interests and my project for which I am very grateful.

In Mexico, I had the pleasure of working with several individuals and institutions who have advanced my research and influenced me in many ways. I am indebted to both the Centro Nacional de Investigación, Documentación e Información Musical Carlos Chávez (CENIDIM) and the Facultad de Música (FaM) at the Universidad Nacional Autónoma de México (UNAM) for acting as my host institutions during my fellowship years of research, doctoral, and postdoctoral. At CENIDIM, I would like to express my deepest gratitude to Eduardo Contreras Soto and Aurelio Tello, who pointed me in several directions regarding film music in Mexico, shared many sources with me, and offered their own insights on Mexican cinema. At UNAM, my sincere thanks go to Roberto Kolb Neuhaus who acted as my faculty sponsor during my postdoctoral fellowship and offered his expertise and knowledge on all things related to music in Mexican cinema. His support of my project and recognition of its importance were significant contributions to its development. At the Instituto Mexicano de Cinematogafía (IMCINE), I am indebted to Cristina Prado, who provided several sources for me to follow and gave me much needed encouragement and friendship. At the Cineteca Nacional, I would like to thank Catherine Bloch, Leopoldo Gaytán Apáez, Raul Miranda, and Dora Moreno Brizuela for offering their expertise, guidance, and encouragement. I would also like to thank the invaluable staff at the Biblioteca Nacional and Hemeroteca UNAM, the Filmoteca UNAM, Cineteca Nacional, the Biblioteca de las Artes at the Centro Nacional de las Artes (CENART), and Biblioteca Lerdo de Tejada. Their help in locating materials and their patience with my terrible (but improving) Spanish over the years encouraged me to continue with the project. Special thanks are also needed for Roberto Fiesco at Mil Nubes Cine, who expressed enthusiasm for my work and granted me permissions for several photographs in these chapters. I would also like to send special thanks to Viviana García Besne at Permanencia Voluntaria Archivo Cinematográfico for granting permissions for the photographs of Ninón Sevilla from *Víctimas del pecado* for chapter 1 and the cover of this book.

I am blessed to have so many amazing friends and colleagues who have helped me in so many ways. I would like to thank my fellow Latin Americanists, Mexicanists, and friends in music, film studies, and cultural studies who have provided much needed help, comments, feedback, encouragement, love, and laughter over the years: Lizette Alegre, Jeff and Lori Beth Beck, Rebecca Bodenheimer, Juan Arturo Brennan, Steve Bunker, Chelsea Burns, Ximena Cuevas, Guadalupe Caro Cocotle, Drew Edward Davies, Sergio de la Mora, Cesar Favila, Colin Gunckel, Laura Gutiérrez, Nancy Guy, Ray Hernández-Durán, Eduardo Herrera, Dean Hubbs, Jesús Ibarra, John Koegel, Elizabeth LeGuin, Neil Lerner, Ilana Luna, Alejandro Madrid, Ryan McCormack, Ana Alonso Minutti, Robin Moore, Mitchell Morris, Shawn and Jill Mollenhauer, Rielle Navitski, Anna Ochs, Alyson Payne, Marysol Quevedo, Jesús Ramos, Elissa Rashkin, Jake Rekedal, Jazmín Rincón, Ignacio Sánchez Prado, Stephany Slaughter, Stephanie Stallings, Robynn Stilwell, and Joan Titus. I especially would like to thank the wonderful Mara Fortes who has been an amazing friend and colleague. I am so grateful for her hospitality and her friendship during the periods I stayed in Mexico City. Many parts of this book would not be possible without her help.

Over the course of three years, I have been privileged to work with several scholars from the Phantom on Screen network: Giorgio Biancorosso, Timmy Chen, Annette Davidson, Charlotte Glenhorn, Clarice Greco, Cormac Newark, and John Snelson Our travels together, our numerous presentations, and especially our conversations have helped shaped my research and I am grateful for all the feedback and encouragement they have provided. Special thanks are also in order for those who were brave enough to read through the madness of the rough drafts. I send my love, gratitude, and apologies to León F. García Corona, Matthew J. Jones, Tony Rasmussen, and Dolores Tierney.

Your comments and suggestions have helped this project considerably (and helped cut off several thousand words). I owe a very special thanks to Susan Thomas and her family. They were my adopted family when I moved to Tennessee and my friendship with them has been one of the most important in my life. Susan has been an invaluable mentor and colleague, and one of my best friends. I am inspired by her and am so grateful for her encouragement, her critical eye, her overwhelming support, and her fight for me to succeed in this difficult field.

Special thanks go to my massive family, who are scattered throughout Mexico and the United States and who have been supportive in their own creative, often sarcastic (yet loving) ways. In Mexico, I particularly want to thank my cousin Carlos Elisea, my aunt María Ávila Nuñez (Bika), and my uncle Ángel Elisea who opened their homes to me, helped me, and put up with my antics in the early stages of research. My sincere gratitude also goes to my cousin Paulina "Rosy" Elisea, who took me on many tours of Mexico City before I officially began my research; likewise to my other cousins, aunts, and uncles in Morelia and Sahuayo for their love, support, and enthusiasm. Finally, I would like to thank my family in California, in particular my parents, Pieternella and Maximino Avila, who have encouraged me, supported me, and teased me during my academic pursuits. I would not have completed this without their love and patience.

Lastly, my special and sincere thanks go to Oswaldo Mejía Mendiola, who has been my biggest cheerleader. Oswaldo believed in the value of this project from the beginning and has offered his own expertise and advice on Mexican cinema and Mexican culture over the course of our relationship. He stuck with me through the whole process of bringing this book to life, helping me find sources, listening to my ideas, and suggesting new avenues of criticism. Even from a distance, he provided much needed support and overwhelming amounts of love and patience, especially during those times when I felt I couldn't continue. This book would not exist without his help and encouragement, his belief in me and his passion for the topic, and his unflinching love. *Te amo tanto.*

Sections of chapter 2 were previously published. I thank the University of Texas Press for granting me permission to reprint of my article "*México de mis inventos:* Salon Music, Lyric Theater, and Nostalgia in *Cine de añoranza porfiriana,*" first published in *Latin American Music Review / Revista de Música Latino Americano* 38, no. 1 (2017): 1–27.

Introduction

Listening to the *Época de Oro*

Although this book is about Mexican cinema's *época de oro*, or Golden Age (roughly 1936–1952), I begin this story in 2010. During this year, Mexico was undergoing celebratory events for the *Bicentenario* (Bicentennial) of Mexican Independence from Spanish rule (1810–1821) and *Centenario* (Centennial) of the Mexican Revolution (1910–ca. 1920).[1] Several state-sponsored institutions commemorated these national events by organizing yearlong activities that observed national heroes, symbols, and myths. These events, however, focused primarily on the Revolution, and Mexican national cinema occupied a crucial role in this project. Two of the institutions responsible for the production and distribution of Mexican cinema, the Cineteca Nacional and the Instituto Mexicano de Cinematografía (Institute of Mexican Cinematography, IMCINE), sponsored an exhibition titled "Cine y Revolución: La Revolución Mexicana vista a través del cine" ("Cinema and Revolution: The Mexican Revolution Seen through Cinema"), located at the Antiguo Colegio de San Ildefonso in downtown Mexico City. The exhibition featured screenings, photo stills, costumes, and poster art about the Revolution in cinema from Mexico's silent-film period (1896–1930) to the present. Each installation presented different conceptions of the Revolution constructed by the national film industry. Included in the exhibition was a sound installation entitled *1910* by composer and sound artist Antonio Fernández Ros, which required the museum patron to walk through a long, weaving hallway in the dark with the aid of a support railing to guide the way.

---

[1] These events included several parades, concerts, and pyrotechnic displays. Museum exhibitions throughout Mexico City devoted at least one room to nationalist works, primarily by one of the muralist painters or Frida Kahlo. New monetary coins and bills were printed and distributed as early as 2009, featuring national leaders and heroes. The film industry also produced several films that depicted narratives involving the Independence and the Revolution, including: *Hidalgo: La historia jamás contada* (*Hidalgo: The Untold Story*; 2010, dir. Antonio Serrano); *El atentado* (*The Attempt Dossier*; 2010, dir. Jorge Fons); *Chicogrande* (2010, dir. Felipe Cazals). Although not directly related to the Independence or the Revolution, *El infierno* (*Hell*; 2010, dir. Luis Estrada) offers scathing criticism concerning the hypocrisy of Calderón's drug war and the Centennial and Bicentennial celebrations.

Participants experienced a juxtaposition of sounds extracted from revolution themed films, designed to reconstruct, or reimagine, the sounds of the Revolutionary period:

> 1910 is a sound work based on film dialogues regarding the Mexican Revolution. Small sonic extracts of large number of films on this theme weave an unedited narration not so much on facts, but the meaning of the Revolution . . . the significance of the words is as important as the dramatic intention set forth by the actors; the word converts to music and the music to narration.[2]

This reimagining of the Revolutionary soundscape included gunfire, screams, explosions, and snippets of musical examples. Interwoven into this electroacoustic tapestry were *corridos*, a narrative ballad from the nineteenth century, the hybrid genre of *corrido-canciones, canciones rancheras* (ranch songs), and even fragments of orchestral underscoring (music composed for the film with a non-diegetic function). By placing the installation in the dark, Fernández Ros desired the museum patrons to not only be aware of their other physical senses when walking the pathway but also to recognize what sound and music add to film, which he defines as "a phenomenon imminently visual but with an important richness of sound."[3]

During this time, Mexico was in midst of another crucial domestic movement that was shaping the country's national identity: then President Felipe Calderón's war on the domestic drug cartels. Almost immediately after taking office in 2006, President Calderón initiated his anti-drug campaign by sending troops into Michoacán, one of the country's largest drug-trafficking states, to cease drug-related violence and dismantle the power of the drug cartels. This action began a series of exceedingly violent events that has since placed Mexico in a negative light in the world and has left the population in fear.

The preparation of the *Bicentenario* and *Centenario* celebrations ran concurrent with President Calderón's war on drugs, in a sense distracting the public from the wave of violence sweeping the country. As previously mentioned, the fight for independence from the Spanish Crown began in 1810, but it is the Revolution of 1910 that receives far more attention from

---

[2] Antonio Fernández Ros, "1910," in *Cine y Revolución: La Revolución Mexicana vista a través del cine*, ed. Roberto Garza Iturbide and Hugo Lara Chávez (Mexico City: Instituto Mexicano de Cinematografía, 2010), 123. Unless indicated, all translations are my own.

[3] Ibid.

Mexican institutions and the public. Beginning as a revolt against the almost thirty-year dictatorship of Porfirio Díaz, whose reign lasted from 1876 to 1911, the Revolution serves as a crucial historical disjuncture for Mexico for not only ending Díaz's oppressive regime, which exploited the working and lower classes while providing preferential treatment to the upper classes and foreign investors, but also igniting a new era of national identity formation. The post-Revolutionary period witnessed crucial national projects that depicted several, at times contradictory interpretations of *Mexicanidad* (Mexicanness)—the cultural identity of the Mexican people. The Revolution has come to be interpreted as a turning point, both as an event and as a process, for many exploring the development of and causes for a Mexican national identity in the twentieth century. And cinema played a significant role.

This juxtaposition of different sound clips and musical examples in Fernández Ros's sound installation recreate a Revolutionary soundscape that relies solely on cinema's varied interpretations, constructing a new conception of the Revolutionary event(s). The use of the music and sound selections in this installation led me to ask repeatedly: What role does music have in this national industry? How did music aid in constructing and/or solidifying those symbols and myths that have now become part of nationalist discourse? How persuasive are these musical choices in film? How can we discuss conceptions of nationalism—if it is indeed nationalism—through film music?

Critics and historians, such as Carlos Monsiváis, Ana M. López, Rafael Aviña, Dolores Tierney, Sergio de la Mora, Joanne Hershfield, Aurelio de los Reyes, and Jorge Ayala Blanco, among others, have examined Mexican cinema from the early half of the twentieth century as a cultural practice that evokes several contesting nationalist signifiers for the mass audience. Music has remained on the margins of such analysis, although film music works to reinforce these visual representations of national identities. The visual is continuously privileged in Mexican film studies receiving the most concentrated scholarly attention regarding questions of identity—be it social, ethnic, class, or gender—and national rhetoric.[4] However, as Fernández Ros's sound installation suggests, national myths rely on musics and sounds that the national populace would recognize to be fully persuasive. Within Mexican cinema, the continuous reiteration of symbols, myths, memories, and traditions is solidified through specific musical and aural associations.

---

[4] See, for example, Mette Hjort and Scott Mackenzie, eds., *Cinema & Nation* (London: Routledge, 2000); Rick Altman, *Film/Genre* (London: British Film Institute, 1999); Walter Murch, "Foreword," to Michel Chion, *Audio/Vision* (New York: Columbia University Press, 1990), vii–xxiv.

Nationalism, Cinema, and
the Movie-Going Audience

Nations and nationalisms are widely interpreted as modernist phenomena stemming from Europe during the eighteenth and nineteenth centuries, when industrialization and the quest for imperial expansion became dominant movements. According to Ernest Gellner, nations and nationalisms are crucial social components of modernity. The nation functions as a product of nationalism, which expresses modernity's need for "high cultures," or cultures based on a homogenous, standard, and generic education through interpellation. In an industrialized, modern society where culture, a system of similar ideas, signs, and associations, is needed to suture populations, nations and nationalisms become essential, creating mass loyalties. The recognition of one individual for another through similarities in cultural practices, in Gellner's view, builds the concept of the nation.[5]

The recognition of the "self" through symbols and myths is an important component of Eric Hobsbawm's "invented traditions," where cultural practices claim a tie to a communal past that is continuously constructed and reconstructed. The "invented traditions" in the form of repeated myths, symbols, and rituals, defined as "essentially a process of formalization and ritualization, characterized by reference to the past, if only by imposing repetition," became critical apparatus for the ruling classes to control, manipulate, and absorb the energies of the masses.[6] For Benedict Anderson, language organizes the nation through the emergence of print capitalism. In the "imagined community," books, newspapers, and other forms of media, written in the vernacular, help systematize large populations through their recognition of a common language. People in this population may exist at the same time and yet may never meet, but ideally its members will recognize each other as similar and belonging to the same group, encouraging the populace to "imagine" themselves as a nation.[7]

For these theorists, the concept of nation is, by and large, a product of modernity, and is created and disseminated through repetition and reinterpretation. While communal groupings based on the recognition of a cultural practice through invented traditions and tales of an ethnic past help to build

[5] Ernest Gellner, *Nations and Nationalism* (Oxford: Blackwell, 1983).

[6] Eric Hobsbawm, "Introduction: Inventing Traditions," in *The Invention of Tradition*, ed. Eric Hobsbawm and Terence Ranger (Cambridge: Canto, 1992), 4.

[7] Benedict Anderson, *Imagined Communities* (London: Verso, 1983), 195–97.

a nation, those—particularly those in power—desiring nationalist solidarity face a problem in figuring out how to convince the popular masses to conceive of themselves as a unified sociocultural entity.[8] In his essay, "All the People Came and Did Not Fit Onto the Screen: Notes on the Cinema Audience in Mexico," cultural critic Carlos Monsiváis argues that the movie theater, or as he frames it "The Celluloid Temple," became the nation-building space for the massive, largely Spanish illiterate, post-Revolutionary Mexican audience. Cinema was understood as a learning tool that modernized the population into homogenous social behaviors, teaching the public about their unified histories and cultural practices. Silent cinema captured the attention of some, but it was sound cinema that encouraged the weekly ritual of movie going: "The transition from silent cinema to the talkies helped to strengthen the conviction that what happens on the screen is a more real reality. It does not spurn us, but instead allows us instantaneous identification, it addresses us in the first instance, and makes us share its idea of the nation, family, and society."[9] Cinema secularized the audience and helped bring them into the modern era, functioning as a vehicle for cultural nationalism and cosmopolitanism. Popular media became a form of mediation between the shock of industrialization and "the rural and the popular urban experience, which has not been prepared in any way for this giant change." The film industry provided what was most irreplaceable to the Mexican public: "the familiar turns of phrase, the scenes of poverty, the faces-like mirrors, the adventures of melodrama, the music which is stubbornly unsophisticated."[10]

So what was this national audience watching? When discussing the movie-going experience in Mexico, we note a distinction that exists at the Mexican box office, consisting of films from Hollywood, other foreign films, and *cine mexicano*. Hollywood features at the Mexican box office made up (and still make up) the majority offered at movie theaters nationwide.[11] *Cine mexicano* refers specifically to those films produced in Mexican studios or featuring a Mexican cast and/or director. While by some scholars' estimation Mexican cinema has reached an age of neoliberalism

---

[8] Anthony D. Smith, "Images of the Nation: Cinema, Art and National Identity," in *Cinema & Nation*, ed. Mette Hjort and Scott Mackenzie (London: Routledge, 2000), 46.

[9] Carlos Monsiváis, "All the People Came and Did Not Fit onto the Screen: Notes on the Cinema Audience in Mexico," in *Mexican Cinema*, ed. Paulo Antonio Paranaguá (London: British Film Institute, 1995), 146.

[10] Ibid.

[11] Today, there are also other foreign features, particularly from Western Europe and Latin America. Hollywood films, however, maintain the dominant space.

sponsored by specific film institutions and international co-productions, *cine mexicano* as a national entity and concept still exists and has had an intriguing history.[12] The period between the 1930s to the mid-1950s is often designated by scholars, critics, and fans as Mexican cinema's *época de oro*, owing to myriad reasons: this period boasted a rising star system, the consolidation of the industry and development of the studio system, box office successes, and the creation of film genres depicting varying interpretations of Mexicanidad. Embedded in this *época de oro* is a tradition that is at once national and cosmopolitan, exhibiting several currents that reinforce an interpellation into a Mexican national aesthetic. In his work on classic Mexican cinema, Charles Ramírez Berg states that Hollywood played a significant role in the establishment of a national film practice in Mexico. When film production during the silent period was low, Hollywood features were widely screened and Mexican audiences adapted to the Hollywood method of telling stories through film. At the beginning in the 1930s, the Mexican film industry was geared toward creating a national framework, but the influences and impact of Hollywood remained considerable. The Mexican industry followed in the cinematic norms set forth by Hollywood that included a paradigm for narratives, specific shots, and shooting techniques for the engagement and suspension of time, and "a spatial system that constitutes filmic space as story space" where human bodies hold a privileged space in the frame. Berg writes:[13]

> The classical Hollywood filmmaking model, both as signifying practice and as industrial mode of production (including studio and star systems, powerful producers, well-developed distribution networks, and exhibition chains), was imitated in Mexico by the late 1930s as it embarked on what is now recognized as its cinematic Golden Age (el Cine de Oro), roughly from 1936 through 1957. Actually, most Mexican films *adopted* as well as *adapted* the Hollywood model, giving the Hollywood paradigm a decidedly Mexican inflection.[14]

---

[12] For a discussion of neoliberalism in contemporary Mexican cinema, see Ignacio Sánchez Prado, *Screening Neoliberalism: Transforming Mexican Cinema, 1988–2012* (Nashville, TN: Vanderbilt University Press, 2015).

[13] Charles Ramírez Berg, *The Classical Mexican Cinema: The Poetics of the Exceptional Golden Age Films* (Austin: University of Texas Press, 2015), 6.

[14] Ibid, 7.

It wasn't just Hollywood that had an impact on Mexican film production; other industries and their popular players were also highly influential. Soviet director Sergei Eisenstein, whose brief sojourn in Mexico took place during the early 1930s, brought with him the socialist realism approach to filmmaking and cinematography that was adapted to later create the Mexican cinematography aesthetic. Spanish director Luis Buñuel arrived in Mexico during the late 1940s and directed several significant films that became part of the national tapestry, including *Los Olvidados* (*The Young and the Damned*; 1950). Russian director Arcady Boytler contributed to the creation of several important film genres during the 1930s, including the prostitute melodrama and the *comedia ranchera* (ranch comedy). American cinematographers Jack Draper and Paul Strand pointed the lens at the Mexican population, shaping an image of the national populace. In terms of acting, several players across Latin America and Spain lent their talents to the development of the industry, including Argentinean actress Libertad Lamarque, Spanish actor and director Antonio Moreno, and Colombian actress Sofia Álvarez, just to name a few.[15] In looking at this list of influences and contributions, which is by no means exhaustive, Mexican national cinema can be interpreted as not necessarily just national but also transnational, built on cultural exchanges from across continents.

This transnationality applies to music as well. The performance of music and dance in Mexican cinema was quite ubiquitous, executed in almost every major genre shaped by the film industry. In her examination on film musicals in Mexico, Ana M. López asserts:

> Integral to the narratives, songs, rhythms and performances are typically invoked as markers of nationality and as sites for national identification. In the Mexican "Golden Age" (1930 to 1960), cinema, music and dance are constant across all "genres" but are always deployed within melodramatic narrative scenarios. At first, national rhythms are the rhythms of the "people" (rather than of individual characters) and simultaneously serve to unify the nation by providing an identity and to market the nation abroad

---

[15] On discussing the presence of Eisenstein in Mexico, see Eduardo de la Vega Alfaro, *Del muro a la pantalla: S.M. Eisenstein y el arte pictórico mexicano* (Mexico City: Instituto Mexicano de Cinematografía, 1997); and Aurelio de los Reyes, *El nacimiento de ¡Que viva México!* (Mexico City: Universidad Nacional Autómona de México, Instituto de Investigaciones Estéticas, 2006). Regarding Luis Buñuel in Mexico, see Luis Buñuel, *Mi último suspiro* (Madrid: Debolsillo Poc, 2012); regarding Paul Strand in Mexico, see James Kripper and Alfonso Morales Carrillo, *Paul Strand in Mexico* (New York: Aperture, 2010).

(therefore articulating both the pedagogical and the performative aspects of discourses of nationhood).[16]

Music, melodrama, and nation are an important trifecta in Mexican cinema during this period. Two major genres that exploit this combination are the comedia ranchera and the *cabaretera* (cabaret, night club, or dance hall genre). López claims that these genres are set within two representational spaces: the comedia ranchera is situated in the hacienda and the cabaretera in the cabaret. She further argues that while these genres are difficult to classify as film musicals, particularly in the Hollywood sense, they do "constitute the musical backbone" of Golden Age cinema. While López is correct in her assertion that music is a dominant force within the narrative of these genres and has an important role in developing the sounds of the nation, I argue that the function and power of music extends to several film genres—not just the cabaretera and the comedia ranchera but also the revolutionary melodrama, the fictional *indigenista* film (dramatic films about an indigenous population), and the *cine de añoranza porfirana* (films of Porfirian longing or nostalgia), to create and enforce meanings through a process of "cultural synchresis" (discussed later) that shapes conceptions of the nation and identity on the silver screen. The music and performers in these films transcended borders that not only helped perpetuate national meanings but also propelled new currents in musical performance and musical consumption in Mexico.

Film Music in Mexico: A Scholarly Challenge

To date, there has not been an extensive study done that focuses on the music in Mexican cinema. *Cinesonidos: Film Music and National Identity During Mexico's Época de oro* endeavors to fill this gap. I do not attempt to provide a complete history of film music in Mexico or a history of the prominent film composers. Instead, this book adds another level of critical examination to the existing scholarship on Mexican film history and criticism in this early period of filmmaking and does so from a primarily cultural perspective. What did this national ideology sound like and what factors contributed to this aural phenomenon? In discussing film music in a national film industry, the overriding emphasis is on how this music works in

---

[16] Ana M. López, "Mexico," in *The International Film Musical*, ed. Corey K. Creekmur and Linda Y. Mokdad (Edinburgh: Edinburgh University Press, 2012), 122.

collaboration with the narrative and the moving image to reflect ideologies of cultural nationalism.

Generally, any mention of film music relates to the popular song or musical genre attached to the film and how that fits with popular musical currents in Mexico. In her book, *Historia de la música popular mexicana*, musicologist Yolanda Moreno Rivas traces the development of popular and folkloric music in Mexico. Organized chronologically, Moreno Rivas's book offers several sections detailing popular genres and styles, such as the bolero, the canción ranchera, and *la música tropical* (tropical musical), which have shaped and been shaped by the film industry. She provides production, composer, and performer information, as well as explanations on performance practice and reception. This serves as an invaluable source for examining the trajectory of music in Mexican popular culture.

Other sources focus on music as a central component in the development of film genres. In her work on the comedia ranchera and the *cine campirano* (films set in the countryside), Marina Díaz López examines the cultural roots of these genres, drawing on popular theater, such as the *teatro de revistas* (theater of revues), and radio as central agents. She provides overviews of several films from the 1930s, including *Allá en el Rancho Grande* (*Over on the Big Ranch*; 1936, dir. Fernando de Fuentes), and the divisions of folkloric consumption that were intended to "rejuvenate" a traditional patrimonial society.[17] In works by Ana M. López, Joanne Hershfield, and Dolores Tierney, Afro-Cuban music and dance—in particular, the bolero and danzón—in the cabaretera genre become essential signifiers of sexuality when examining the emergence of melodrama in Mexican cinema and the changing roles of women in post-Revolutionary Mexican society.[18] For these authors, the cabaretera reflected the social and economic instabilities of the 1940s, and music functioned both as an escape valve for and a sign of these anxieties.

Popular music in Mexican cinema receives more scholarly attention than the orchestral underscoring. With the exception of modernist composer Silvestre Revueltas (1899–1940), composers writing the orchestral

---

[17] See Marina Díaz López, "El folclore invade el imaginario de la ciudad: Determinaciones regionales en el cine mexicano de los trienta," *Archivos de la Filomteca: Revista de estudios históricos sobre la imagen, segunda época* 41 (June 2002): 10–31.

[18] See Ana M. López, "Tears and Desire: Women and Melodrama in the 'Old' Mexican Cinema," in *Mediating Two Worlds: Cinematic Encounters in the Americas*, ed. John King, Ana M. López, and Manuel Alvarado (London: British Film Institute, 1993), 147–63; Ana M. López, "Of Rhythms and Borders," in *Everynight Life: Culture and Dance in Latin/o America*, ed. Celeste Praser Delgado and José Muñoz (Durham, NC: Duke University Press, 1997), 310–44; Joanne Hershfield, *Mexican Cinema/Mexican Woman* (Tucson: University of Arizona Press, 1996); Dolores Tierney, "Silver Slingbacks and Mexican Melodrama: *Danzón* and *Salón México*," *Screen* 38, no. 4 (Winter 1997): 360–71.

music for film soundtracks are typically disregarded, even admonished for not restoring to Mexican cinema what Max Steiner (1888–1971) and Erich Korngold (1897–1957) brought to Hollywood: lush, hyper-romantic orchestral scores with dramatic and memorable leitmotifs.[19] Indeed, music in Mexican cinema, and by extension in Latin America, is given very little attention in English and Spanish textbooks and histories dealing with film music, owing in part to the lack of research on the topic.[20] In his contribution to *Modern Music*, composer and critic Paul Bowles bluntly declares, "So far there have been practically no cinema composers in Mexico who have turned out actual scores. The norm has consisted of untalented arrangements of standard tripe."[21] During the 1960s, film critic and historian Emilio García Riera retrospectively jabbed several film composers in his monumental *Historia documental del cine mexicano.*[22] He uses descriptors such as "embarrassing" and "shameful" when referencing any type of underscoring.[23] Because the underscoring does not receive any acclaim, information regarding the development of the film score is scarce or does not exist at all.

The orchestral underscoring, referred to in Mexico as *música de fondo* (background music), served as a space for construction and reconstruction of musical tropes, and at times conveyed reminiscences of the classic Hollywood film score model of the 1930s, through use of heavy and lush strings and brass and thematic material associated with characters and locations.[24] Musical production, however, followed paradigms set forth by

[19] For more information on Silvestre Revueltas in the film industry, see Eduardo Contreras Soto, *Silvestre Revueltas en escena y en pantalla: la música de Silvestre Revueltas para el cine y la escena* (Mexico City: Instituto de Bellas Artes y Literatura, 2012).

[20] I discuss this absence in scholarship when teaching courses on film music. For more information, see Jacqueline Avila, "Using Latin American and Iberian Film Music: Classroom Methodologies," *Journal of Music History Pedagogy* 7, no. 2 (2017): 112–23.

[21] See Paul Bowles's "Letter from Mexico," which appeared in *Modern Music* (November–December 1941), discussed in Timothy Mangan and Irene Hermann, eds., *Paul Bowles on Music* (Berkeley: University of California Press, 2003), 48. Bowles was an author, music critic, and composer who made several contributions to *Modern Music*. In this article, Bowles states that there are only two Mexican composers who have composed, in his opinion, successful film scores: Silvestre Revueltas and Raul Lavista. Bowles also calls attention to the dire state of musical practice in Mexican radio and film.

[22] This is a multi-volume collection that provides production details, summaries, and commentaries on every Mexican film from 1929 to 1976.

[23] One particularly blatant criticism is in his entry for *Salón México* (1949; dir. Emilio Fernández). In the film, the club's owner mentions to a group of Anglo tourists that Aaron Copland visited the club and composed his work *El Salón México* shortly thereafter, which has been considered an important musical work. In the film's entry, García Riera claims Antonio Díaz Conde's film score is "inappropriate" and "in sad competition" with Copland's piece, which is not performed in the film but only mentioned. See Emilio García Riera, *Historia documental del cine mexicano,* (Guadalajara: Universidad de Guadalajara, 1993), 3:266.

[24] For more information on the classic Hollywood film score, see Kathyrn Kalinak, *Settling the Score: Music and the Classical Hollywood Film* (Madison: University of Wisconsin Press, 1992).

Hollywood music departments. According to Manuel Esperón, a composer credited for more than two hundred films and who served as sound mixer for a hundred others, the score had to be completed in twenty days after the last day of filming, in order to accommodate the dubbing and looping sessions in the playback segment of postproduction. That is, music composed after filming was completed so as to fit the film's rhythm. Esperón states, "the [music] rhythm has a very different pace from the cinematographic rhythm. Good music cannot save a badly made film."[25] The music was never recorded for commercial sale because, at that time, the recording industries were not interested in this material; the films are really the only sources where the underscoring exists.[26]

Steps have been taken to close the gap in research regarding orchestral underscoring, the música de fondo composers, and the diegetic, popular music composers. In 2005, one volume of *Cuadernos de estudios cinematográficos* (*Notebooks of Cinematographic Studies*) was published, dedicated to film music and sound treatment in Mexican cinema. The articles consist of interviews with contemporary Mexican film composers, such as Javier Álvarez and Antonio Zepeda, and explorative essays on the role of music and the composer in narrative films. This volume only examines music in contemporary Mexican cinema, however, offering readers insight into the current music departments in Mexican studios.[27] In 2009, musicologist Aurelio Tello contributed over two hundred biographical entries for the *Diccionario del Cine Iberoamericano* (*Dictionary of Iberoamerican Cinema*), which features contributions from Spain, Portugal, and Latin America. Tello's entries focus on the composers of Mexican cinema from the beginning of the 1930s to the present, and includes a select filmography along with short biographical information.

---

[25] Teresa Carvajal, "La obra de Manuel Esperón en el cine mexicano," *Bibliomúsica* 39 (Spring/Summer 1992): 39. Esperón is one of the few composers who kept a library of his film scores, which includes the orchestral underscoring and the popular diegetic music. However, in a 1989 article for *El Nacional*, Esperón states that his scores from the Golden Age were lost in a fire. See Felipe Orso, "Extraviadas las partituras que Manuel Esperón escribió para el cine mexicano," *El Nacional*, June 24, 1989.

[26] Ibid. Esperón states in this article that he doesn't know why Mexico was not like the United States in this regard, but he also remembers that the recording industry executives felt that marketing the underscoring was not good business.

[27] The one exception in this volume is José Antonio Alcaraz's article "La noche de los mayas," which details the musical elements added to the orchestral suite rather than the music from the 1939 film originally composed by Silvestre Revueltas. See José Antonio Alcaraz, "La noche de los mayas," *Cuadernos de Estudios cinematográficos* 4 (2005): 95–100.

Film Music in Mexico: Melodrama and
Cultural Synchresis

In Mexican cinema, several interpretations of "the nation" exist si-multaneously, highlighting that although one unified national identity was desirable, it was virtuously impossible to create, as the identities and narrativesconstructed on the screen were fused with transnational currents and influences. Thus, this book posits that within the process of developing a national film tradition, music has served a significant and fundamental role that has not been fully considered. The question now becomes one of how best to approach and discuss this role.

My discussion and analysis of select case studies come from the *época de oro*, beginning with Mexico's early sound period of the 1930s. This early sound period began with the premiere of the 1931 prostitute melodrama *Santa* and continued to 1936 with *Allá en el Rancho Grande*, the film that of-ficially initiated Mexico's *época de oro*, which then lasts until the mid-1950s. The popular film genres from this period have their origins in the silent era and in popular theater, especially the lyric theater tradition. Silent cinema provided much of the narrative and visual foundation for this early sound cinema, while the lyric theater tradition supplied the shaping of customs and vernacular practices and musical performance.[28] The film genres from this period represent a hybridity of these practices.

At the heart of these genres is a concentration on melodrama. Scholars such as Carlos Monsiváis, Ana M. López, Joanne Hershfield, and Andrea Noble base their examinations of Mexican melodrama on the work of literary critic Peter Brooks, who defines melodrama as "a fictional system for making sense of experience as a semantic field of force that comes into being in a world where the traditional imperatives of truth and ethics have been violently thrown into question." Brooks argues that the modern forms of melodrama, shaped by popular theater and the novel, are linked to changes and conflicts in the social and political spheres. The early literary and theatrical melodramas

---

[28] Silent film historian Aurelio de los Reyes provides some detailed history of silent-film music practice in his book *Medio siglo de cine mexicano (1896–1947)* and his essay "La música para cine mudo en México," in *La música de México*. He includes historical context for the films and primary source references describing the bands, orchestras, performers, and composers that supplied music and sound to Mexico's early cinema. Presently, this is the only source that focuses specifically on mu-sical accompaniment to silent film screenings in Mexico. See Aurelio de los Reyes, "La música para cine mudo en México," *La música de México*, ed. Julio Estrada (Mexico City: Universidad Nacional Autónoma de México, 1984), 4:85–117.

of Europe, for instance, laid out the aesthetic and thematic foundations that were carried into the cinema of the twentieth century.[29] In the case of Latin American melodrama, elements of these older forms of European melodrama were fitted into Latin America's social and cultural contexts, as well as local practices in the vernacular popular and lyric theater. In Mexico, popular theatrical practices such as the teatro de revistas, *carpas* (tent shows), and zarzuelas (Spanish language lyric theater) served as significant precursors of film development in Mexico, as several of the major players in these staged entertainments transferred their talents to the silver screen.

Mexican melodrama, according to Hershfield, has endured as a popular genre throughout the technological changes, "in part because it has served as a mediating function between older forms of narrative and the newer forces of modernity."[30] In a similar vein, Jesús Martín-Barbero argues that melodrama functions as a mediation between existing and emerging cultures, so as to address specific social and cultural needs of the changing populations and functioning as a bridge between the collective historical experience and the lives of individuals during periods of social and ideological crisis.[31] As Mexico underwent rapid modernization at the end of the nineteenth century and experienced the social and political angst of the Revolution, popular entertainments such as theater and cinema became the escape valve for the public, as well as an interpellating process for the national population.

The images, narratives, and characters depicted and constructed in these film melodramas encouraged audiences to "seek the familiar" in a specific emotional and ideological structure. Marvin d'Lugo states, "that process of mirroring by the reoccurrence of visual and musical tropes . . . transcended the verbal and seduced the popular audience into seeing its own likeness in the obsessions and desires of fictional characters."[32] Martín-Barbero outlines three mechanisms to explain how melodrama shaped the formation of a Mexican national identity. The first mechanism is the theatrical, focusing on Mexican models of gesture, linguistic expressions, and excessive emotions

---

[29] See Peter Brooks, *The Melodramatic Imagination. Balzac, Henry James: Melodrama and the Mode of Excess* (New Haven, CT: Yale University Press, 1976), 152–55.

[30] Hershfield, *Mexican Cinema/Mexican Woman*, 43.

[31] Jesús Martín-Barbero, *Communication, Culture and Hegemony: From the Media to Mediations* (London: Sage Publications, 1993), 119. See also Hershfield's discussion in *Mexican Cinema/Mexican Woman*, 43.

[32] See Marvin d'Lugo, "Luis Alcoriza; or A Certain Antimelodramatic Tendency in Mexican Cinema," in *Latin American Melodrama: Passion, Pathos, and Entertainment*, ed. Darlene J. Sadlier (Urbana: University of Illinois Press, 2009), 114–15 ; and Martín-Barbero, *Communication, Culture and Hegemony*, 114.

depicted on a dramatic stage; the second mechanism is degradation, as it was necessary for the public to recognize themselves on screen through characterizations, dramatic scenarios, and national symbols; and the third mechanism is modernization, in which sociocultural and economic changes impacted narratives. According to Martín-Barbero, "Often the mixture of images contradicted the traditional plots and brought up to date old myths, introduced customs and new models of moral behavior and gave public access to the new rebelliousness and forms of speaking."[33] Alongside the recycled and readapted narratives, and the easily recognizable characters acting and speaking in the vernacular, the music had the crucial function of crystallizing the meaning.

Music and meaning in film have received considerable attention in recent years, particularly as discussed in Amy Herzog's study of "musical moments" and even Phil Powrie's work on "the crystal-song." Both studies offer intriguing approaches to the function of linear time in film and to bodily reactions to the music performed or articulated in film, both referring to specific genres in specific cinematic traditions. While Herzog focuses on the film musical, Powrie concentrates on contemporary French cinema.[34] Here, I propose another method for discussing the music in film, one that is grounded on the cultural ramifications of a synthesis of sound, narrative, and moving image. This is especially significant when we view the Mexican film industry during this period as a crucial perpetuator of varying representations of Mexicanidad. My aim is to position the role of film music within its historical and cultural context, so as to better understand its narrative functions and associations with the nationalist symbols and messages conveyed in those film genres that have been influenced by the melodramatic forms.

Music heard, and sometimes seen, in this way does not operate as Claudia Gorbman's "unheard melody," in which she argues that the most successful film music is that which remains unnoticed by the audience.[35] Rather, music takes on a role of a "cultural suture," joining the necessary sonic associations with the representations and narratives on the screen. In other words, music makes the representation appear more real and convincing

---

[33] Martín-Barbero, *Communication, Culture and Hegemony*, 167.

[34] See Amy Herzog, *Dreams of Difference, Songs of the Same: The Musical Moment in Film* (Minneapolis: University of Minnesota Press, 2010); and Phil Powrie, *Music in Contemporary French Cinema: The Crystal-Song* (London: Palgrave Macmillan, 2017).

[35] See Claudia Gorbman, *Unheard Melodies: Narrative Film Music* (Bloomington: Indiana University Press, 1987). See also Gorbman's early article, "Narrative Film Music," *Yale French Studies* 60 (1980): 183–203.

to the audience. For example, in Mexico's prostitute melodrama, the dance music performed in cabarets, especially the danzón and the mambo, became the signature sound for desire and sexuality. Thus, the music from the cabarets and Mexico's burgeoning nightlife transferred to the cinema and quickly became associated with the prostitute archetype. In order to discuss these associations and meanings built by music, as well as the moving image and narrative, I utilize the concept of "cultural synchresis," which builds upon sound theorist Michel Chion's term "synchresis." According to Chion, synchresis is the juxtaposition of two important sound elements—synchronism and synthesis—creating "the spontaneous and irresistible weld produced between a particular auditory phenomenon and visual phenomenon when they occur at the same time."[36] Synchresis permits extemporaneous sounds to fuse with the moving image, so as to create implied meanings and contextual determinations, which with repetition establish specific psycho-physiological associations for the audience. Considered a technique of behavioral conditioning, à la Pavlov, Chion claims, "the effect of synchresis is obviously capable of being influenced, reinforced, and oriented by cultural habits."[37] With ample repetition, the synthesized moving image and sound create a sense of "mutual reinforcement," enabling the association to appear natural and logically obvious. For instance, when a door slams on the screen, we expect to hear an appropriate corresponding sound rather than a bell ringing or a dog barking.[38] This sound-event phenomenon in cinema appears to materialize naturally, and because of our expectations and experiences with sound in our own reality, it becomes a habitual tendency.

Expanding from such ambient sound events, the synchresis of music and moving image creates a relationship whereby cultural meaning is created, consumed, and understood. In Mexican national cinema, music creates and reinforces the national representations; music and meaning become coterminous. Music utilized with a specific image and at a specific moment in the narrative provides a synthesis that, when reiterated, appears to be a natural and/or a convincing occurrence. Further, this effect has embedded cultural implications that reference transnational and national relationships, understandings of history, constructions of social mores and

[36] Michel Chion, *Audio-Vision: Sound on Screen* (New York: Columbia University Press, 1994), 63.
[37] Ibid., 64.
[38] Ibid.

practices, and so on. The cultural synchresis interpreted by the eyes and ears thus creates a fixed relationship between reality and the simulacrum of reality, entering what Chion calls the audio/visual contract: spectators watch a film and unknowingly "agree" that what they see and hear is a reality.[39] In other words, the culture that is depicted visually and aurally on the screen is accepted by the audience and references in some way their own experiences.

The impact of cultural synchresis, when applied to Mexican cinema, creates *cinesonidos*, or "cinema sounds," referring to the unique makeup of sound design and music that helped shape the soundscape Mexican national cinema. This concept is indebted to the work of Sergio de la Mora and his approach in analyzing masculinities and sexual identities in Mexican cinema, entitled *cinemachismo*. Machismo, according to de la Mora, "is an ideology of heterosexual male supremacy that in Mexico gets wedded to the institutionalized post-revolutionary State apparatus, of which cinema is a crucial component."[40] His work focuses on the construction and presence of machismo and sexuality perpetuated by specific institutions through the medium of film: "Cinema is the modern technology that enables the invention, reinvention, and circulation of national models of manhood and womanhood."[41] *Cinesonidos* borrows the framework of this concept to explore how music and sound shape not just constructions of gender and sexuality but also conceptions of ethnicity, of self and other, and of official historical discourses to provide new readings and interpretations of national cinema and Mexicanidad that have previously gone unnoticed. This book investigates the myriad ways that music functions in Mexican film by examining these practices within its historical and cultural context. Although discussion of the image is a crucial component of my analysis, I concur with Neil Lerner in suggesting that films' meaning lies in the use of both the eye and the ear, which when taken together will "generate readings of the film that do not emerge when considering only visual and cinematographic elements."[42]

---

[39] See Part One, "The Audio-Visual Contract," in Chion, *Audio-Vision,* 1-138.

[40] Sergio de la Mora, *Cinemachismo: Masculinites and Sexualities in Mexican Cinema* (Austin: University of Texas Press, 2006), 7.

[41] Ibid., 3.

[42] Neil Lerner, "Preface: Listening to Fear/Listening with Fear," in *Music in the Horror Film: Listening to Fear,* ed. Neil Lerner (New York: Routledge, 2010), x.

Organization of this Book

Each chapter of *Cinesonidos* explores the music in the film genres of the silent and early sound era and their transformation during the *época de oro*. Distinct in narrative and structure, each genre exploits specific, and at times contradictory, aspects of Mexicanidad and, as such, employs different musics to concretize those recycled constructions of tropes. Throughout this turbulent period—during the Porfiriato, the Revolution, and the post-Revolutionary years—these tropes and archetypes mirrored changing perceptions of Mexicanidad that were manufactured by the state and dominated popular and transnational culture. Several social and political agencies were heavily invested in creating a unified national identity to unite a fragmented populace as a result of the Revolution. The commercial medium of film became an important tool in acquainting that diverse urban audience with the nuances of Mexican national identity, and several musics played an essential and persuasive role in that process. Indeed, in this heterogeneous environment, cinema and its music continuously reshaped the contested, fluctuating space of Mexican identity.

Chapter 1 explores perhaps the most controversial film genre in Mexican cinema: the prostitute melodrama and its subgenre, the cabaretera. I focus on how music helps construct the complex identity of the prostitute protagonist, and how that identity links to changing notions of womanhood in a modernizing society. I examine Mexico's first successful sound film *Santa* (1932, dir. Antonio Moreno) and the later sensual and exotic rumbera figure in *Víctimas del pecado* (*Victims of Sin*; 1950, dir. Emilio Fernández). I argue that music reinforces the dichotomies of the prostitute: one side that elicits empathy and the other that draws upon notions of sex and desire. The prostitute is positioned as a challenging and contradictory presence in the national imagination and national rhetoric, considered a "necessary evil" by Mexican society. This chapter examines the spaces—specifically, the brothel and the cabaret—and their featured dance music, focusing on the bolero, danzón, and rumba as significant elements in the construction of the prostitute and her association with Mexico's changing urban nightlife.

Chapter 2 explores the largely overlooked cine de añoranza porfiriana, which reconstructs, or reimagines, the Belle Époque of the Porfiriato. Conceived as homage to Mexico's turn-of-the-twentieth-century musical tradition by director Juan Bustillo Oro, these films concentrate on the misadventures and romantic misunderstandings of the Porfirian bourgeoisie and aristocracy, paying particular attention to proper social mores and the role of women in society. This genre functioned as an outlet for the post-Revolutionary middle- and upper-class audiences made anxious by the social reforms promoted by President Lázaro Cárdenas's leftist administration (1934–1940). Instead of exhibiting especially composed music for the film, the genre recycles excerpts from the *música de salon* (salon music), zarzuela, and teatro de revista traditions in order to reconstruct the Porfiriato as a light-hearted and carefree utopia, away from oppression and struggle. I assert that these films feature extensive musical performances of turn-of-the-twentieth-century music so as to convey an atmosphere of Porfirian nostalgia that relies on the presence and performance of women.

Chapter 3 targets the highly problematic and ethnically fueled fictional *indigentisa* film.[43] This chapter focuses on the approaches featured in the orchestral underscoring of two critical film examples: *Janitzio* (1935, dir. Carlos Navarro) and *María Candelaria* (1944, dir. Emilio Fernández), both of which utilize exoticist music written by modern composer and folklorist Francisco Domínguez. Developed during the post-Revolutionary period, during which several discourses advocated for the cultural integration of indigenous populations into modern Mexican society, such as those presented by anthropologists Manuel Gamio and Alfonso Caso, these fictional indigenista films communicated contradictory messages: an integrationist/nonintegrationist stance on Mexico's indigenous cultures, exhibiting the consequences of both modern penetration and communal isolation. Using Domínguez's music as a guide, this chapter explores how these films sought to represent indigenous populations and what messages were sent to the growing urban mestizo audience about these communities.

Chapter 4 analyzes Mexico's most popular film genre, the comedia ranchera, concentrating on the emergence of the singing *charro* (Mexican cowboy) figure, Mexico's most visible national symbol. A consequence of several cultural hybridizations over the course of Mexican history, the singing charro is examined as an experimental figure that became further interpellated into the post-Revolutionary national consciousness through

---

[43] Generally, the indigenista film genre is anthropological in nature. These fictional films focus on indigenous populations and themes that were perceived as important as a result of the indigenismo movement.

popular theater, radio, and film, thereby becoming a visual and aural embodiment of Mexicanidad. The comedia ranchera showcased the charro, and when sychrentized to music, developed the singing charro as a successfully exported symbol and commercial tool of Mexican identity. Select musical sequences are examined in three key films: *Allá en el Rancho Grande* (1936, dir. Fernando de Fuentes), *¡Ay Jalisco, no te rajes! (Jalisco, Don't Backslide!*; 1941, dir. Joselito Rodríguez), and *Los tres García (The Three Garcías*; 1946, dir. Ismael Rodríguez). The music in these films solidifies, or exalts, the charro's changing sense of machismo and his connections with nationalism and the nation in the face of his compatriots and foreigners.

Chapter 5 focuses on the revolutionary melodrama and the malleable and contested role of the *soldadera* (female camp follower). Concerning the revolutionary melodrama, Monsiváis states "the Mexican Revolution genre produced definitions of the epic, archetypes of the male, scenarios of fatality, and a programmatic pictorialism."[44] Building from an extensive collection of photographs and newspapers from the Revolution, the revolutionary melodrama became a complicated film genre. It began as a criticism of the armed struggle, then later turned into a romanticized narrative that perpetuated mythologies about national unity. While the films are generally dominated visually and narratively by men, music about the soldaderas are foregrounded. One of the leading examples was "La Adelita," a popular song that circulated during the Revolution, shaping the archetype of Revolutionary womanhood. Culturally identified as a corrido, "La Adelita" became, for the film industry, the anthem of the Revolution, recycled in varying ways in several films. Although the song is about a soldadera, an examination of its function in these films reveals its intimate tie to male revolutionaries rather than to the women—in effect suggesting that the only role a woman could play in the armed struggle was as soldadera. This chapter analyzes the recycled use of songs referencing the soldaderas, as appearing in three Revolutionary melodramas: *¡Vámonos con Pancho Villa! (Let's Go Pancho Villa!*; 1934, dir. Fernando de Fuentes), *La Adelita* (1938, dir. Guillermo Hernández Gómez), and *Enamorada (Woman in Love*; 1946, dir. Emilio Fernández).

---

[44] Carlos Monsiváis, "Mythologies," in *Mexican Cinema*, ed. Paulo Antonio Paranaguá (London: British Film Institute/Instituto Mexicano de Cinematografía/Consejo Nacional para la Cultura y las Artes de México, 1995), 118.

The final chapter provides an overview of the Mexican film industry after the *época de oro*, covering the 1960s through the 1980s, including the *cine de luchadores* (wrestling films) and the subgenre of the cabaretera, the *cine de ficheras* (melodramas set in a cabaret or brothel during the 1970s and 1980s). The impact of the *época de oro* continued well into the 1990s and on into the twentieth-first century, evident in several attempts to reconstruct the period or recycle the soundscape in several films. This last section explores the contemporary nostalgia felt by filmmakers and musicians for the *época de oro* and how that period and its music are remembered and reused with longing.

1

The Prostitute and the Cinematic Cabaret

Musicalizing the "Fallen Woman" and Mexico City's Nightlife

Antonio Moreno's prostitute melodrama *Santa* premiered at the Palacio Theater in Mexico City on March 30, 1932, initiating the film industry's transition into recorded, synchronized-sound cinema. Based on the 1903 bestselling novel by Federico Gamboa, the cinematic adaptation of *Santa* created quite a spectacle at its premiere. The eclectic soundscape was captured in print by the popular periodical *El Universal*:

> A portion of cars stopped at the curb already bursting with people. Noisy shouting, yelling, calls, crushing, then nudges. From time to time, the sound of a band was scattered, punctuating the strident confusion of genius. In the fragrant lobby, the harsh ink of the posters seemed more alive, harmonized with the ambient luminosity. Amidst the whine of horns, the hasty conversations, the tinkling bells, and the spirited tunes pulled from the metallic instruments, one can see, with the brilliant lightness of sparks that come from the dark, the short word that serves as the title of the popular novel.[1]

Crowds gathered to see the dramatization of the highly controversial story of a young country girl who moves to the metropolis and becomes a prostitute, a story that reflected the realities of many women living in Mexico City. This particular "fallen woman" story became a standard narrative in Mexican cinema in films set either in brothels or cabarets, locations that exuded sex through smoky spaces, "tropical" rhythms, and provocative dancing.

Santa initiated a current in the new moving picture medium that closely scrutinized social stratifications in post-Revolutionary society, particularly

---

[1] "La metamorfosis de Santa," *El Universal*, April 12, 1932.

that of the most marginalized and challenging figure: the prostitute. The prostitute in Mexican cinema and in Mexican society symbolized "sexuality and the pleasures and dangers incurred by modernity,"[2] dangerously and provocatively rubbing against Catholic indoctrinations that viewed sex solely as a means to procreate. Because of Catholicism's fervent presence in Mexico since the time of the Conquest, religious teachings became stringent rules of social conduct—particularly during the Porfiriato (1876–1911)[3]—and female sexuality was strictly contained while male promiscuity was permissible and even encouraged. Prostitution, although frowned upon by the Church as sinful and immoral, became "a 'necessary evil' that, it was believed, prevented greater problems like rape or seduction from threatening the moral order."[4] The Church therefore separated sexual pleasure from reproductive sex, and consigned women to two distinctive camps. In the first were the domestic women men have children with, but whom they do not necessarily seek for sexual pleasure (these women were not meant to experience sexual pleasure either). These were the *señoras decentes* (decent women) that society needed to exalt as "angels of the household."[5] In the other camp were the mistresses and sex workers that men visited for sexual indulgence, but with whom they would never marry or recognize children. The women in this latter category were regarded as social deviants, the immoral challengers of the conservative social norms that limited women entirely to the domestic sphere. Prostitutes were also viewed as the sole transmitters of venereal diseases, rather than the sexually active men from all social classes who pursued them and then returned to their homes and families.

Intertwined with these gender constructions is an image of Mexico City's growing urban nightlife. The spaces that the prostitute frequents, such as

[2] Sergio de la Mora, *Cinemachismo: Masculinities and Sexuality in Mexican Film* (Austin: University of Texas Press, 2006), 22.

[3] The Porfiriato refers to the dictatorship of Porfirio Díaz (1876–1911). Although Manuel González served as president from 1880 to 1884, Díaz maintained a strong hold on the government, essentially governing from behind the scenes. Politically, the Porfiriato is characterized as a period of economic expansion through the incorporation of foreign interests and industrialization (building of railroads, for example) and stability after the Reform Wars. Culturally, the Porfiriato is known for the incorporation of foreign influences, particularly French, in dress, architecture, and art. See Moisés González Navarro, *Sociedad y cultura en el porfiriato* (Mexico City: Consejo Nacional para la Cultura y las Artes, 1994).

[4] Katherine E. Bliss, *Compromised Positions: Prostitution, Public Health, and Gender Politics in Revolutionary Mexico City* (University Park: Pennsylvania State University Press, 2001), 3.

[5] See Fausto Ramírez, *Modernización y modernismo en el arte mexicano* (Mexico City: Universidad de Autónoma de México, 2008), 124–26.

brothels and cabarets, were spaces that were carefully observed and regulated by the state, which enforced the morals of the (male) dominant class through legislation and legal punishment that included the registration and medical inspection of sex workers, which I will discuss in the following section. The forced regulation and consistent exploitation of sex workers by patriarchal structures that viewed them as both a necessity for society and vice to be eradicated made them the tragic protagonists in literature, art, music, and also film.

Beginning first in the early 1930s and then continuing into the *época de oro*, the prostitute melodrama became one of the most popular film genres, reflecting the uncertainties that the post-Revolutionary public felt about modern expansion and the accompanying rise of cabaret and dance hall culture—entertainment locales that granted both promiscuity and pleasure. While perceived as a continual vice to modern Mexican society, the female prostitute became an essential yet tainted figure. Her presence in national cinema reinforced the ideological contradictions and paradoxes of female sexuality. The social pedagogy constructed by the prostitute melodrama was furthered heightened with the rise of the cabaretera, a subgenre that took place in the cabarets, where currents of popular dance music from across the Americas aurally characterized the prostitute archetype. In these films, music both represented her miserable "downfall" in society and reflected her sexuality and her abilities to seduce. She was a tragic figure that received empathy while also viewed as morally corrupt and socially tainted.

Within the prostitute melodrama and the later cabaretera subgenre, music and narrative created a compelling cultural synchresis that not only engages the character with a particular moment in the scene but also enforces and reiterates cultural associations that became part of modern Mexican society. This chapter explores the social and political doctrines, spaces, and music that shaped Mexico's nightlife culture through their representation in two emblematic films: the aforementioned prostitute melodrama *Santa* and the later cabaretera film *Víctimas del pecado* (*Victims of Sin*; 1950, dir. Emilo Fernández). Following contemporary cultural practice and social mores, these two films construct key characteristics of the prostitute protagonist, specifically concerning her inextricable association with the urban nightlife. In particular, I examine her irreconcilable split identity—she is both object of desire and focus of audience sympathy—"played" through the familiar sounds of transnational dance music.

Spaces of "Sin"

The national construction of the prostitute begins during the Porfiriato, decades before the film industry converted to recorded, synchronized sound. The Mexican Department of Public Health had attempted to regulate sex work and sexual commerce since the mid-nineteenth century with various measures intended to control the spread of venereal diseases such as syphilis and gonorrhea. The *Reglamento para el ejercicio de la prostitución 1872* (Regulation for the Practice of Prostitution 1872) required that all prostitutes, defined as "any woman over the age of fourteen who was not a virgin, who habitually had sexual relations with more than one man, and who expressed a specific desire to engage in sexual commerce,"[6] register with Mexican health authorities, focusing only on those women who were sexually active, a maneuver that exempted men from legal and medical surveillance. The regulation was based on laws initiated in Paris during the 1830s, and prostitutes were inspected for disease; special districts, called *zonas de tolerancia* (tolerance zones), or red-light districts, were portioned off for sexual activities.[7] While the law exempted any sexually active male, married and sexually active females were also excused, narrowing the focus exclusively to female sex workers. In the eyes of the government, these women were the sole spreaders of disease and venereal infections. Studies from nineteenth-century hygienists such as Luis Lara y Prado painted female sex workers as degenerates, arguing that social conditions and patriarchy did not cause prostitution, but heredity did.[8]

During the Porfiriato, police consistently patrolled specifically designated areas for sexual commerce. In order to avoid arrest and imprisonment, sex workers walked with identification and a registration card at all times. To keep the government and the customers (sometimes one and the same) content, officials organized a system for sex workers, intending to regulate and control

[6]   Bliss, *Compromised Positions*, 27–28.

[7]   The French law advocated the separation of legal and illegal prostitution practices and state-inspected bordellos. This adoption was the result of the French occupation of Mexico during the 1860s as part of an imperialist project. According to Bliss, the public health regulation was instituted when Maximilian I was emperor. The regulation strongly suggested that the spread of venereal disease was due to prostitution. During the end of the 1860s, after the French occupation ended, the law remained in place, but was refined by the Mexican department of health and sanitation. See Bliss, *Compromised Positions*, 29.

[8]   See Luis Lara y Prado, *La Prostitución en México* (Mexico City: Librería de la viuda de Ch. Bouret, 1908).

the "distribution of vice."[9] In her study on prostitution and the health and morality campaigns during the Porfiriato and Revolutionary periods, Katherine Bliss states that women were classified as *en communidad* (in community)—working in brothels where they also lived—or *aisladas* (isolated), women who made appointments to meet men at different locations. *Matronas* (matrons) and madams ran specific sites for sexual commerce, including *casas de asignación* (houses of allocation)—houses where registered prostitutes had sexual intercourse with men but did not reside—and *casas de citas* (date house), houses where unregistered women could meet and socialize with men. Mexican cultural critic and historian Salvador Novo claims that a large part of leisurely life for the Porfirian elite took place at the brothels, the casas de citas, and the casas de asignación. In these spaces, the clients were not inhibited by social and familial conventions and embraced the "expanding spirituality" of these new modes of communications that filled the room.[10]

During the Revolution, sexual commerce grew outside of zonas de tolerancia due to the population boom—particularly of single women—in effect ending the Porfiriato house-based bordellos and the reign of the matronas, displacing many sex workers. This growth encouraged the rise of a new class of businessman, who invested in hotels, cabarets, and burlesque theaters and other entertainment spaces where sexual commerce could also take place. By the 1920s and 1930s, sexual commerce became socially and geographically stratified, but did not disappear. Since zonas de tolerancia were not strictly enforced, new laws required all city hotels that permitted sex workers to register with the police and the Department of Public Health, pay a fee, and undergo regular health inspections.[11] This meant that hotel managers had to question women who entered the hotel about their marital status and business at the establishment, which often led to uncomfortable situations for both sides.

After the dismantling of the Porfirian house system, cabarets, dance halls, theaters, and bars became hot spots for men and women to dance and socialize as well as engage in sexual commerce. The popularity of these venues

---

[9] Excessive drug and alcohol use was also perceived by the Porfirian elite to be part of society's vices as a consequence to modernity. For more information, see Ricardo Pérez Montfort, Pablo Picatto, and Alberto del Castillo, *Hábitos, normas y escándalo: Prensa, criminalidad y drogas durante el porfiriato tardío* (Mexico City: Plaza y Valdés, S.A de C.V., 1997).

[10] Cited in Carlos Monsiváis, *Amor Perdido* (Mexico City: Ediciones Era, 1977), 65–66.

[11] In 1926, the Reglamento para el ejercicio de la prostitución en el D.F. (Regulation for the Practice of Prostitution in D.F.) "aimed at controlling the spread of sexually transmitted diseases and protecting Mexicans against 'harmful' foreign influences, including different forms of mass media deemed pornographic." This law remained enforced until 1940. See de la Mora, *Cinemachismo*, 36.

led many to believe that they demonstrated Mexico City's growing cosmopolitanism and modernity, linking the metropolis to other major European centers, such as Barcelona. However, according to the anti-vice activist Elías Hurtado, Barcelona housed "men's only" cabarets, functioning as markers of sophistication and modernity that Mexico had yet to reach and, in his opinion, would most likely not. In a declaration similar to the moralizing campaigns, Hurtado states that women are a necessity in Mexico City cabarets, but men should appeal to their paternal instinct to persuade these "particular" women "who dance nude in these venues" to move away from the trade and look for other occupations.[12] Journalist Eduardo Pallares, on the other hand, agrees that prostitution need to be controlled and regulated, but without the state's hypocritical and forced moralizing campaigns:

> We must persecute brothels and prostitution, but in a rational manner, without violating the constitution and falling into exaggerations of fanaticism and stupid hypocrisy, and, above all, without pretending to moralize the people with aggressive and violent measures, while the powerful bask in all kinds of pleasures. . . . When a society ostentatiously persecutes vices and immorality, it is almost certain that it is entirely corrupted.[13]

Indeed, women, particularly prostitutes and sex workers, maintained a troubled and unstable position in the eyes of the state and in modern Mexican society. As the population of Mexico City was swept up in a wave of cosmopolitanism and as women began to leave the house and enter the public sphere, a new institutionalization of male dominance and control took over. One practice that received substantial attention was the rising dancing culture in urban cabarets and dance halls.

The Cabarets, El dancing, and the Construction of the Modern Woman

Since the late 1910s, cabarets converged dance, sex, and alcohol in one location. In order to deflect complications with authorities and to avoid

[12] Elías Hurtado, "El problema de la mujer que trabaja en cabarets," *El Nacional*, October 15, 1937. Bliss provides an excellent discussion on Hurtado's stance on women in the cabarets. See also Bliss, *Compromised Positions*, 167.
[13] Eduardo Pallares, "La campaña contra la prostitución," *El Universal*, March 21, 1944.

mandatory registration and health exams, women were often hired as waitresses and/or *ficheras* in addition to continuing on with prostitution.[14] Alcohol service encouraged by female workers kept these businesses afloat. Bliss notes that certain cabarets such as the Estrella, the Adams, and the Molino Rojo took over the lots where casas de asignación once stood, insinuating that the women who worked in these new establishments most likely carried over from the past trade and catered to old clientele, placing a new mask on an old practice.[15]

Cabarets, however, were also significant social hot spots and centers for musical diffusion. The cabaret functioned as a space for men and women, particularly from the rising middle class, to enjoy dancing, leisure, and sexual commerce. These establishments also doubled as visible sites of modernization and transnational exchange, owing in part to the live music and new dance genres coming from across the Americas; this included the foxtrot, the shimmy, and the danzón. This musical and cultural exchange initiated new diversions for the middle class that moved ever farther away from the restricted salon culture and moral codes of the Porfirian period, but still raised considerable concern from more conservative and religious sectors of society.[16] Dancing became a social practice that received substantial attention in the popular press, particularly in relation to the scandals these new dances often provoked. In a 1919 article for *Revista de Revistas*, Rafael López describes the provocative closeness and intimacy involved in this social ritual of dancing:

> Couples march to the sound of music, stuck together, melted into a tightness of heroic character; the men capture the women in an all encompassing embrace as if escaping a fire where there are no firefighters; it is a wielding so solid and so decisive that it is remarkable they can detach when the orchestra is silent.[17]

This newfound closeness between couples became a heated issue. During the early 1920s, the shimmy caused considerable uproar as the dance became quickly linked to immorality and sin. In his article for *Revista de Revistas*, José D. Frias connected the "shimmie" with other communally agreed social

[14] A *fichera* is a woman who dances with patrons for pay in the form of a token, or *ficha*, at the cabarets. In addition to dancing, ficheras may provide sexual services.

[15] See Bliss, *Compromised Positions*, 167.

[16] For more information on Porfirian salon culture, see chapter 2, this volume.

[17] Rafael López, "Los cabarets en México," *El Universal Ilustrado*, May 8, 1919.

vices, such as alcohol and drugs: "I don't know the special excitation, the dia-bolically effective exertion that accompanies each piece in this genre that the dancers tenaciously request, dominated by a strong, irresistible force—liquor, wine, drugs, strong toxics—that does not stop with the rhythmic and deaf-ening noise of the infernal orchestra."[18] Frias goes on to contrast the shimmy to the "elegant and lovely" Argentinean tango, which he views as having a "plaintive and passionate" melody. The shimmy, however, emits nothing "ele-gant or friendly," and is a stain on the "barbaric custom" of dancing.[19]

The shimmy was only one such dance that became a popular practice in the development of *el dancing,* a term designating the popular dancing cul-ture emerging among the Mexico City middle class. In his book, *El "dancing" mexicano,* dance scholar Alberto Dallal argues that within the dance hall, dances, especially those once believed for the pleasure and diversion of the lower classes, were reinterpreted to fit a new and consumable context for middle-class audiences, beginning new rites and rituals disassociated from religion, now permissible within the cabaret walls.[20] El dancing was perceived as a necessity for middle-class urbanites because it enabled them to gather with members of their own social status and encouraged a new av-enue of self-expression.[21] This self-expression moved past the national level and incorporated something more cosmopolitan as Latin American music and dance practices juxtaposed with local culture and, Dallal argues, be-came devoid of class prejudice. Dances like rumbas, sambas, congos, tangos, merengues, milongas, cha-cha-chá, and the like grew to be important components of this new practice, challenging the dated codes of appropriate conduct carried over from the Porfiriato.[22] The cabaret represented a new space, almost utopian, where music and dance became important features for the changing capital.

The culture within the cabarets can best be described as frenzied as the music and clientele moved nonstop. In a 1927 article for *El Universal Ilustrado,* Juan de Ega labeled cabarets "Las nuevas academias de baile" ("the new dance academies"), which multiplied and exploited "nuestros vicios" ("our vices"). He speaks specifically about participating in el dancing partic-ularly with the ficheras: "Fifteen cents to dance one song with a woman—five

---

[18] José D. Frias, "Shimmie," *Revista de Revistas,* May 29, 1921.
[19] Ibid.
[20] Alberto Dallal, *El "dancing" mexicano* (Mexico City: Ediciones Oásis, S.A., 1982), 87.
[21] Ibid., 179.
[22] Alberto Dallal, *La danza en México: Cuarta Parte, El dancing mexicano* (Mexico City: Universidad Nacional Autónoma de México, 2010), 197–98.

minutes of dancing for each ticket . . . and if these are missing, one must go to the street." De Ega also references the popular dances taking over these new "academies" of dance at the end of the 1920s: "The danzones, the fox, the Charleston, follow one another rapidly. You can still hear the eco of one as another begins. How diligent are these musicians, right? They play like this, so tirelessly!"[23]

Although cabarets served as locales for sexual commerce, the objective of el dancing was to dance, which created new avenues for socialization, particularly for the once regarded "angels of the household." According to Dallal, el dancing provided women much more liberty in society, where dancing— along with smoking—functioned as their "first liberating act." El dancing confronted the conservative viewpoint regarding principally young women, whose primary position in society was to maintain the honor of the family by not acting in any way immoral, indecent, and/or improper.

The influence of a cosmopolitan, popular culture during the 1920s and '30s shaped women in the metropolis into what Joanne Hershfield has called *la chica moderna*, or the modern woman. Hershfield posits that the cosmopolitan traits that structured la chica moderna included cinema (Hollywood and Mexican), French fashion and makeup, and national and international magazines and advertisements. She further argues that much of the characteristics of la chica moderna is based on visual culture such as fashion as women adapted shorter skirts and shorter hair (a la 1920s-flapper culture), and also by "modern domesticity," in which this modern woman acclimatized to new household technologies.[24] In addition to Hershfield's visual construction, I suggest that la chica moderna was also shaped by the contemporary musical soundscape, which included the musical soundscape of el dancing. The social practice of el dancing allowed women to move away, however slightly, from conservative gender roles and a restrictive social class. El dancing soon became a new marker of sexual liberation and ritualized social practice of city life, and within these cabarets sexual commerce took place,

[23] Juan de Ega, "Las nuevas academias de baile se han multiplicado en esta capital desde hace tres meses," *El Universal Ilustrado*, January 1927. The author also mentions the shimmy as a popular dance in these growing establishments.

[24] Joanne Hershfield, *Imaging la chica moderna: Women, Nation, and Visual Culture in Mexico, 1917-1936* (Durham, NC: Duke University Press, 2008), 69. For a discussion on the changing perspectives of female fashion, see Perla Schwartz, ed., *Vanidad de vanidades: Moda femenina en México, siglos XIX y XX* (Mexico City: Uva Tinta Ediciones, 2013). Schwartz includes descriptions of fashion quoted in Mexican literature, including *Santa*.

furthering the association of music to urban growth, cosmopolitanism, and sexuality.

Gamboa's Aural Environment and the Silent *Santa*

In 1903, Federico Gamboa, Porfirian gentleman, journalist, and diplomat, published what is considered an exemplary novel from the Porfiriato: *Santa*. In it, Gamboa provided a voyeuristic "invitation to gaze at what is morally forbidden but socially sanctioned and a precautionary tale with a morally edifying conclusion": women who engage in sexual activities before marriage will face the ultimate punishment.[25] Taken from his experiences of Porfirian era bordello culture, Gamboa tells the story of Santa, a young woman who lives in the idyllic rural town of Chimalistac with her small family. Seduced and abandoned by the general Marcelino, Santa suffers a miscarriage and is disowned and thrown out of the house by her two older brothers and her mother. With nowhere to go, Santa travels to Mexico City and becomes the sought-after prostitute in Doña Elvira's brothel, winning the affections of El Jarameño, a Spanish bullfighter and Hipólito, the brothel's blind pianist. When living with El Jarameño, Santa, apparently unable to control herself, seduces another man, only to be discovered by El Jarameño, who also leaves her. After being passed from the high-end brothels to the lower-class houses, Santa succumbs to alcohol and illness and eventually dies.

Influenced by literary naturalism exemplified in the work of French author Èmile Zola (1840–1902) and from fellow compatriot author and politician Emilio Rabasa (1856–1930), Gamboa based *Santa* on real-life descriptions of Porfirian bordellos that he had observed and wrote about in his journals. Santa's story was inspired by his friendship with the Spanish prostitute Esperanza Gutiérrez *La Malagueña*, murdered in 1897 by María Villa *La Chiquita*.[26] According to Álvaro Vázquez Mantecón, Gamboa sought to depict reality but a reality with imposed moral limitations that corresponded with Gamboa's ideological position:

---

[25] De la Mora, *Cinemachismo*, 32.
[26] See Miguel Ángel Morales, "Santa del papel al DVD," *El Nacional*, June 5, 2004. For a discussion of the trial, see Bliss, *Compromised Positions*, 41. For more information on *La Chiquita's* life, see Rafael Sagredo Baeza, *Maria Villa (a) La Chiquita, no. 4002: Un parásito social del Porfiriato* (Mexico City: Cal y Arena, 1996). According to Álvaro Vázquez Mantecón, Gamboa began to write Santa's story in 1894 under the provisional title *El diario de una perdida* (*The Diary of a Lost Woman*). See

Morality remained present in the narrative's development, where the writer manipulated the lover's destiny, much like a moral demonstration regarding the despicable act of adultery. This point was particularly important: the fact that Gamboa saw himself as a naturalist writer did not say in any way that his writings were too committed to the exact description of the social realities of the time.[27]

In keeping with the contemporary moral order and the common conception about prostitutes, Gamboa described Santa as a passive and submissive character, a tragic victim of the harsh treatments and social paradoxes of Porfirian society yet also a destructive figure, a carrier of disease and vice, and a sinner.[28] According to Sergio de la Mora, Santa is a conflation of fear and desire, a symbol of male anxieties about female sexuality and a central emblem for Mexico's conflicted modernity and growth of Mexico City's cosmopolitan nightlife. Santa's narrative becomes a symbol for modernity's destruction of the pastoral, pre-industrial, idyllic past.[29]

The figure of the female prostitute—simultaneously glorified and tainted—served as muse for artists, writers, and composers. It was with the rise of cinema, however, that the figure of the fallen women was fully interpolated into popular culture.Fifteen years after its publication, Gamboa's *Santa* was adapted into a film directed by Luis G. Peredo and produced by Germán Camus.[30] During Mexico's silent film period (roughly 1916–1930),[31]

Álvaro Vázquez Mantecón, *Orígenes literarios de un arquetipo fílmico: adaptciones cinematográficas a Santa de Federico Gamboa* (Mexico City: Biblioteca de Ciencias Sociales y Humanidades, 2005), 29.

[27] Ibid., 27.

[28] This was just one description of Mexican womanhood in popular literature. For more information on the construction of gender in Mexican literature, see Debra A. Castillo, *Easy Women: Sex and Gender in Modern Mexican Fiction* (Minneapolis: University of Minnesota Press, 1998).

[29] De la Mora, *Cinemachismo*, 32–33.

[30] Germán Camus also produced twelve episodes based on themes presented in *El automóvil gris* (*The Grey Automobile*), entitled *La banda del automóvil* (*The Automobile* Gang) or *La dama enlutada* (*The Mourning Lady*) also directed by Ernesto Vollrath (1919). Camus began his career first as a traveling film exhibitor then moved into production with *Santa* and *Caridad* (1918). For production information on *Santa* and *Caridad*, see Aurelio de los Reyes, *Filmografía del cine mudo mexicano 1896–1920* (Mexico City: Filmoteca Nacional, 1984), 122. For more information on Germán Camus, see Federico Dávalos Orozco, *Albores del cine mexicano* (Mexico City: Clío, 1996), 32–33.

[31] The designation of this period is typically for the development of lengthier narrative films. Prior to 1916, the silent film industry specialized in actuality filming of the Revolution and short narrative films with nationalistic themes. For information about Mexican silent film pre-1916, including primary sources, see the extensive twenty-one volume collection by Juan Felipe Leal, Carlos Arturo Flores, and Eduardo Barraza, *Anales del cine en México* (Mexico City: Voyeur, 2009). The series provides the most thorough research completed on Mexican silent cinema to date. For information on Mexican silent film in 1896–1930, which includes summaries and production details, see

silent films from the United States and Europe (primarily France, Italy, and Germany) were widely screened to urban audiences, but distribution diminished as a result of World War I, which enabled Mexican film studios and filmmakers to produce and direct their own features specifically for national consumption. Borrowing from the French style of filming initiated by Georges Méliès and Italian-inspired melodramas from the turn of the twentieth century, *Santa* was the first Mexican film adapted from a novel, and the first film to deal with the controversial subject of prostitution. The film featured a cast of journalists from the periodical *El Demócrata* and included Alfonso Busson in the role of Hipólito and, from the Conservatorio Nacional de Música and student of Manuel de la Bandera's class of cinematic study and practice, Elena Sánchez Valenzuela as Santa.[32]

According to Vázquez Mantecón, the Filmoteca at the Universidad Nacional Autónoma de México (UNAM) conserved approximately one-third of the film (about thirty minutes of the original ninety). It lacks the beginning section and scenes of Santa's acclimation to the brothel. Primary source documentation, however, has helped shed light on some of the gaps in the film.[33] Peredo and Camus's *Santa* is structured as a cinematographic triptych corresponding to the three sections of Santa's life: purity, vice, and martyrdom.[34] Film scholar Federico Davalos Orozco states, "Each part was preceded by symbolic characterizations by the dancer Norka Rouskaya. Some modifications were made to the original work to mitigate its 'harsh realism.'"[35] Sánchez Valenzuela's interpretation of Santa follows theatrical practices influenced by the Italian divas Pina Menichelli and Francesca Bertini, typical from the Porfirian age, depicting a "'redeemed sinner' full

Aurelio de los Reyes, *Medio siglo de cine mexicano (1896–1947)* (Mexico City: Editorial Trillas S.A. de C.V., 1987).

[32] Dávalos Orozco, *Albores del cine mexicano*, 32.

[33] Vázquez Mantecón, *Orígenes literarios de un arquetipo fílmico*, 83.

[34] Aurelio de los Reyes notes that this copies the structure outlined in the Italian film *El fuego*. See Aurelio de los Reyes, *Cine y sociedad en México 1896–1930: Vivir de sueños* (Mexico City: Universidad Nacional Autónoma de México, 1981), 225. See also Vázquez Mantecón, *Orígenes literarios de un arquetipo fílmico*, 83.

[35] Ibid. These "symbolic attitudes" performed by Norka Rouskaya occur at the beginning of each of the three sections. At the beginning of "Virtue," Rouskaya is in a forest, dressed in white robes similar to a toga with leaves in her hair. She happily gesticulates towards the trees while lying on the grass, connecting virtue with nature. Examples from the 1918 version of *Santa* can be seen in the Special Features section of the 2001 release of *Santa* (1932, dir. Antonio Moreno) on DVD. See Antonio Moreno, *Santa* (Mexico City: Colección Filmoteca de la Universidad Nacional Autónoma de México, 2001).

of facial explosions, raised arms to the heavens, flaring and falling and unceasing anguish."[36]

Using a stationary camera, the film's still shots provide glimpses of the idyllic rural life of Chimalistac, exemplified through Rouskaya's short performances—which, according to Vázquez Mantecón, represents the "intensity of female desire"—and the modernized metropolis with images of the Paseo de la Reforma, Castillo de Chapultepec, Chapultepec Park, and the crowded city streets near Doña Elvira's bordello. In scenes involving Santa's love interest, El Jarameño, the setting changes to his cosmopolitan apartment and to the bullring. According to Aurelio de los Reyes, the film not only denounces the exploitation of prostitution and sex workers but also serves as a beginning in the formation of nationalist cinema through its depiction of various national locales.[37]

As a silent film, Peredo and Camus's *Santa* lacks the connection to music and dance culture that pervaded the bordellos. Following silent-film musical practice, the performance of musical accompaniment with the film would have certainly changed with screenings, but we know that the performed music would have consisted of popular music of the day, such as salon music or arranged excerpts from operas or zarzuelas.[38] An early poster of a screening from the Teatro María Guerrero located in the barrio La Lagunilla indicates that the Orquesta Típica "Lerdo" provided the musicalizations of the film.[39]

But while the film does not present to us any lasting musical or sonic associations, Gamboa's book does, providing readers with an idea of the contemporary soundscape. In his book, Gamboa names a few works, some

---

[36] "Santa: el cine naturalista," *Ciclo Cine Mexicano 1* (1965), courtesy of Cineteca Nacional.

[37] De los Reyes, *Medio siglo de cine mexicano*, 68–70.

[38] For more information regarding musical performance during Mexico's silent film period, see Aurelio de los Reyes, "La música para el cine mudo en México," in *La música de México, I: Historia, 4: Periodo nacionalista (1910 a 1958)*, ed. Julio Estrada (Mexico City: Universidad Nacional Autónoma de México, 1984), 85–117.

[39] This fact is confirmed in an article entitled "Historia del cine mexicano," written by José María Sánchez García for the *Cinema Reporter*. In his examination on the silent version of *Santa*, Sánchez García included reprints of articles about the films he investigated. He includes eight articles on *Santa*. In one article, he states that on Monday, July 26, 1943, a gala event honoring the Cineteca Nacional took place at the Cine Olimpia in which Peredo's *Santa* was screened. As part of the screening, musical accompaniment was provided: "Livening the function will be the Orquesta Típica "Miguel Lerdo de Tejada," in memory of maestro Lerdo, who also a quarter century ago, provided the musical adaptation of the first "Santa" in the "Olimpia" salon." See Federico Dávalos Orozco and Carlos Arturo Flores Villela, eds., *Historia del cine mexicano (1896–1929): Edición facsimilar de las crónicas de José María Sánchez García* (Mexico City: Universidad Nacional Autónoma de México, 2013), 85.

of which he suggests are original compositions by Hipólito, but he also describes the characters' interactions and involvement with the music. After Santa's introduction to the brothel, Hipólito plays a provocative *danza mexicana* entitled "Bienvenida" ("Welcome") for her:

> The so-called "Bienvenida" was, in effect, a passionate and beautiful dance, despite its despicable essence. In its first part, above all, it seemed to moan a deep pain that the chords and syncopations of the bass do not let us guess entirely; then, in the second, which is the dance, the shame and pain have faded away, dying into a smooth harmonic transition and leaving only those fiery notes that lead to closeness; the lewd and characteristic rhythm that excites and inflames. Hipólito was forced to repeat his composition up to four times in the midst of explosive applause and screaming.[40]

We, as the readers, get a sense of Hipólito's feelings for Santa through his musical performances in the brothel's salon because he dedicates most of his compositions to her, using the music as a conduit for his affections. However, when Santa approaches Hipólito and asks about his life and blindness, he recounts his story of abandonment while playing an unnamed waltz. Gamboa describes the music in fragments, which accompany Hipólito's sad story. Hipólito knows neither light nor his parents. His father abandoned him and his mother was forced to leave him at a school for the blind:

> The first part of the waltz sprang from the blind man's hands, rhythmic and voluptuous. . . . The second part of the waltz, much happier and lighter than the first part, came out of Hipólito's tobacco-yellowed fingers, which chased after it [the music] among the darker and bland keys of the piano. . . . The third part of the waltz—slow, weak, melancholic—spread through the brothel's salon.[41]

The waltz is verbally syncretized to his words, functioning almost anempathetically—music or sound performed without regard to emotion or feeling to the atmosphere—to his sad story. In the book, Hipólito plays several unnamed waltzes. Although they are performed in the brothel's

---

[40] Federico Gamboa, *Santa* (Mexico City: Fondo de Cultura Económica, 2003), 82.
[41] Ibid., 89–90.

salon, it is in this particular section that Gamboa offers musical descriptions disassociated with sexual commerce and instills feelings of empathy.

Other music, however, develops a more intimate relationship with the prostitute and the act of seduction. Gamboa isolates danzas and danzones as the music and dance par excellence when the prostitutes entertain. When Santa arrives at Doña Elvira's brothel, Gamboa describes her as timid and unable to dance. The other women in the brothel decide to teach her:

> She rarely danced because she did not have a clue about that popular waltz called "Boston," and as for the danzas and danzones, which must be danced with lewd and rhythmic swaying, an exciting mix of belly dance and old-fashioned habanera—she was not very advanced either; her house companions were just initiating her in the secrets of the dance.
>
> "You push yourself against your man a lot here, see? . . . In the first part you need to turn around a lot, see, just like we are doing, without leaving the same spot . . . and in the second part, you have to loosen your hips, as if your waist were breaking, as if, almost fainting with delight, you tried to escape the pursuit of your partner who goes after you, and you slide back and forth, and side to side."[42]

Much like the descriptions of el dancing, Gamboa offers a depiction of the couple's closeness during the dance, insinuating points of seduction and sexuality.

Music highlights the various haunts that Santa visits with the other women in the book. Gamboa refers to several dance and musical styles that were in vogue, offering his audience a descriptive earpiece for the soundscape of the Porfirian brothels and *salones de baile* (dance halls). His musical descriptions provide the reader with an aural awareness of what role music played in this conflicted landscape, furnishing a glimpse of a Mexican's self-awareness of the sonic environment at the turn of the twentieth century.

---

[42] Gamboa, *Santa*, 120. The "Boston" refers to the American waltz style, also called the Boston waltz, developed during the 1830s in Boston, Massachusetts, by Lorenzo Papatino.

Sound in Antonio Moreno's *Santa* (1931) and the Myth of Agustín Lara

Building off of the sound recording experimentation taking place in Hollywood's *The Jazz Singer* (1927, dir. Alan Crosland), the Mexican film industry utilized the Vitaphone sound-on-disc method for recording and synchronizing sound to the moving image.[43] The first acknowledged film to do this successfully in Mexico was *Más fuerte que el deber* (*Stronger than Duty*; 1929, dir. Raphael J. Sevilla). The sound-on-disc method, however, was short lived. It is difficult to ascertain which film used the sound-on-film, or optical sound, technique first in the Mexican industry, but Antonio Moreno's 1931 version of *Santa* was Mexico's first optical-sound box office success. This new version of *Santa* features a cast and production team with ties to Hollywood, including the director Antonio Moreno, the sound team of Joselito and Roberto Rodríguez, and actress Lupita Tovar.

The film's recorded and synchronized sound received little attention in the print media, perhaps owing to the novelty of the technology. This neglect comes as somewhat of surprise, since the Rodríguez brothers developed the optical sound system for the Compañía Nacional Productora de Películas. In a short article in *El Universal Ilustrado,* one author merely states that the film boasts perfect sound, better than the Spanish films screened in France and Buenos Aires.[44] An article in *Excélsior* avoids sound altogether, focusing principally on the image: "The settings were chosen appropriately and the work will give foreign spectators the opportunity to know the country side, colonial corners, ample views of the city, gaining an idea of the magnificence and originality of the great Mexican metropolis."[45] Until recently, there has been little discussion of Rodriguez's optical sound system. Scholars first

---

[43] The sound-on-disc method refers to the recording of the film's soundtrack, which includes music, sound effects, and dialogue, onto a wax cylinder or disc to be played on a gramophone at the same time as screened film. This differs from the sound-on-film or optical-sound technology, which allows for a soundtrack to be recorded directly on the film. This method was made possible through directional microphones and sound mixing in the postproduction phase of filming. For more information on film sound, see John Belton and Elisabeth Wise, eds., *Film Sound: Theory and Practice* (New York: Columbia University Press, 1985); Vincent LoBrutto, *Sound on Film: Interviews with Creators of Film Sound* (Westport, CT: Greenwood, 1994); Rick Altman, ed., *Sound Theory/Sound Practice* (London: Routledge, 1994).

[44] "Santa," *El Universal Ilustrado,* April 7, 1932. See also Carlos Noriega Hope, "Cómo se hace una película vitafónica en México," *El Universal Ilustrado,* December 10, 1931, quoted in Gustavo García and David R. Maciel, eds., *El cine mexicano a través de la crítica* (Mexico City: Dirección General de Actividades Cinematográficas, Universidad Nacional Autónoma de México, 2001), 65–68.

[45] "Gran Triunfo obtuvo anoche 'Santa,' la primera película nacional," *Excélsior*, March 31, 1932.

began to explore Rodríguez's practice in the 2000s, during the centennial cel-ebration of Gamboa's book, and in articles they describe the better fidelity of sound and lighter sound equipment.[46]

While the sound technology received some limited mention, the musical track received even less, despite its headlining performers. The film boasted two important contemporary Mexican composers, Miguel Lerdo de Tejada (1896–1941) and Agustín Lara (1897–1970). Lerdo de Tejada had consider-able experience accompanying films with his popular orchestra—as previ-ously mentioned, his orchestra accompanied the silent version of *Santa*—yet his involvement in the sound version of *Santa* is minimal.[47] His music appears in three sections: in the opening credits, during the beginning scenes set in the countryside, and at the end of the film.[48] In his entry on *Santa* in his personal diary, Federico Gamboa acknowledged the studio recording of the music: "The entire afternoon in the studios, where the music for *Santa* was synchronized, performed by the orchestra . . . by Miguel Lerdo de Tejada."[49] Agustín Lara contributed a foxtrot, a bolero, and a danzón, compositions that became important markers for the prostitute figure and the urban at-mosphere, initiating Lara's career as a film composer and the label *el flaco de oro* ("the skinny man of gold").

By the time *Santa* premiered, Lara had already reached mythical proportions in popular Mexican culture. Lara's beginnings are the stuff of urban legend. Raised in a middle-class family in the state of Veracruz, be-ginning in 1912 Lara played the piano at various sites for popular entertain-ment, including the teatro de revistas, carpas, cabarets, and brothels. He rose to fame during the 1920s, working in cabarets such as El Cinco Negro, Los

---

[46] See Ángel Morales, "Santa del Papel al DVD," 12; José de la Colina, "*Santa* ya centenaria," *Milenio Diario*, January 26, 2008. Some mentions appeared in the early 1990s as well; see José Luis Gallegos, "Pascual Ortiz Rubio, Quien Fuera Presidente de México, dio Facilidades para el Filme "Santa," *Excélsior*, November 5, 1991. In this last article, Gallegos points out that after the success of *Santa* and the optical-sound technology, President Ortiz Rubio offered a train to the Rodríguez Brothers to transport their sound equipment from the border to Mexico City.

[47] Carlos González Peña states that Lerdo de Tejada and his orchestra served as musical accom-paniment for several silent films, but does not say what pieces they performed and for what films. See Carlos González Peña, "La decadencia del teatro," *El Mundo Ilustrado*, November 17, 1912, quoted in de los Reyes, "La música en el cine mudo en México," 103. For background on Miguel Lerdo de Tejada, see Mario Talavera, *Miguel Lerdo de Tejada: Su vida pintoresca y anecdótica* (Mexico City: Editoral Compás, 1942).

[48] The music in the beginning and ending credits is Lerdo's arrangement of the canción-tema "Santa."

[49] Federico Gamboa, *Mi diario tomo VII (1920–1939)* (Mexico City: Consejo Nacional para la Cultura y las Artes, 1996), selection quoted in Gustavo García, *Viendo la luz . . . Salas de cine en la lit-erature mexicana* (Mexico City: Uva Tinta Ediciones, 2013), 83.

Héroes, La Casa de Marquesa, and El Agua Azul, where it is believed he received the scar on his face, possibly coming to the defense of a prostitute.[50] Lara soon became a popular and sought-after composer of canciones and revistas during the late 1920s, beginning with his first registered song with the Sociedad de Autores y Compositores (Society for Authors and Composers) in 1926, "La Prisionera" ("The Prisoner"). After successful performances at the popular Teatro Lírico and the Teatro Politeama, Lara performed in the inaugural program for Emilio Azcárraga's radio station XEW *La Voz de América Latina desde México* (*The Voice of Latin America from Mexico*).[51] Lara was soon offered his own radio program entitled *La hora azul* (*The Blue Hour*), which he used as a space to premiere his new music.[52]

Lara's rise to fame paralleled the mass migration from the countryside to the metropolis after the armed struggle of the Revolution displaced so many. During this transition, musicians and songwriters brought with them their regional performance styles, which found a crucial space on the popular stage and in the *canción mexicana* tradition. Lara, however, represented a more modernized and urban sound owing to his performance background, song topics, and absorption of diverse musical styles. According to Yolanda Moreno Rivas, "Lara represented the modernity of the city's new middle classes that had abandoned the provincial values determined and originated in their social class."[53] Because of the mass diffusion of radio broadcasting, Lara's show and his music reached a wide and diverse audience from all walks of life.

By the 1930s, Lara's commercial success led him to work in the new sound film industry, immediately finding a niche in films with an urban backdrop, contrasting those films set in the countryside, such as the comedia ranchera.[54] In an interview with Paco I. Taibo I, Lara explains that although he

[50] Some have claimed that the scar is a result of fighting for the Villista forces during the Revolution, acting as a pianist-spy. See Agustín Caro, "El tema de Lara," *Cine*, December 1949, p. 20.

[51] Other artists that participated in XEW's inaugural program are the police orchestra led by Miguel Lerdo de Tejada, Ana María Fernández, Néstor Mesta Chayres, Ortiz Tirado, Juan Arvizu, Josefina Chacha Aguilar, la Marimba Chiapaneca de los Hermanos Foquez and Lucha Reyes. See Yolanda Moreno Rivas, *Historia de la música popular mexicana* (Mexico City: Editorial Océano de México, 2008), 70–71; Joy Elizabeth Hayes, *Radio Nation: Communication, Popular Culture, and Nationalism in Mexico, 1920–1950* (Tucson: University of Arizona Press, 2000); José Luis Ortiz Garza, *La guerra de las ondas* (Mexico City: Editorial Planeta Mexicana, 1992).

[52] For more information on Agustín Lara's rise to fame, see Andrew Grant Wood, *Agustín Lara: A Cultural Biography* (New York: Oxford University Press, 2014).

[53] Moreno Rivas, *Historia de la música popular mexicana*, 105.

[54] In September 1932, the same year *Santa* premiered, *El Universal* printed announcements and advertisements for another Agustín Lara revista titled *Chaquiras*, written for the Compañía del Politeama.

enjoyed the folkloric ranch comedies, he would never perform in them: "It is not my genre. If you want to ask me the reason why I do not write rancheras, I will tell you it is because I am not from a ranch. I'm from the cabaret. And the cabaret is not in the hills, but in the city neighborhoods."[55] Lara's musical style, affectionately labeled as *laraismo*, or *el estilo lariano* (Laraism or Larian style), developed during a time when transnational musical genres and styles reterritorialized in the country. As a working pianist, Lara familiarized himself with the rhythmic, harmonic, and melodic structures of foxtrots, danzones, and tangos. He is most known for his boleros, which link to his past experiences in brothels and cabarets and which detail the pain of the fallen woman. These songs became a fixture in Mexican cinema particularly in those melodramatic narratives set in the cabaret, and added to Lara's romanticism.

Although his music becomes intimately linked with these spaces, Lara acknowledges the cinematic cabarets were not the establishments he has come to know so well: "Our cinema did not know the cabarets, but I did. Those that appear on screen are in between black and white."[56] Regardless, Lara became the mouthpiece for the marginalized, for unrequited love, and for the pain of loss. Oscar Leblanc paints a more quixotic and detailed portrait of the composer:

> Lara, who was the first forger of painful poems, a singer of pessimism, discovered—and this was his best bet for succeeding and obtaining popularity easily—that he only needed to become a singer of women. And because he already knew the soul of many poor, tormented women, he put in verse the vulgar details of great human pain, and became a poet rather than a musician.[57]

Lara's significance in Mexican culture and the film industry is perhaps best summed up by cultural critic Carlos Monsiváis: "Without Agustín Lara, half of Mexican cinema would not have existed."[58]

---

[55] Paco I. Taibo I. *La música de Agustín Lara en el cine* (Mexico City: Universidad Nacional Autónoma de México, 1984), 66.

[56] Ibid., 64.

[57] Oscar Leblanc, "Lara, el Larismo y las mujeres," *El Universal Ilustrado*, June 9, 1932.

[58] Macarena Quiroz Arroyo, "Sin Agustín Lara no existría la mitad del cine mexicano: Carlos Monsiváis," *Excélsior*, February 4, 1991.

Santa's Bolero

Indeed, with the song "Santa," which inaugurated Mexican sound cinema, Lara placed in the lips of the blind Hipólito a complete philosophy of the brothel that would continue for six decades.[59]

In Gamboa's novel, Hipólito dedicates waltzes, danzas, and danzones to Santa, describing the turn-of-the-century cabaret soundscape. In the 1931 recorded, sound production, however, Santa's experiences as a prostitute are syncretized with a bolero played on the piano and a danzón performed by a small New Orleans–style jazz band.[60] Santa's music in the film corresponds to the then current trends in popular music, which transfers the time period over from the novel's Porfirian atmosphere to the late 1920s or 1930s, creating an identifiable sound bridge for audiences.[61] Each musical performance, however, functions differently in the narrative and conveys different messages.

The bolero is the first, full diegetic musical work in the film and is Lara's musical introduction to national cinema. Lara did not invent the bolero, but is credited for its Mexicanization and its diffusion for mass audiences, particularly in 1929 when his bolero "Imposible" ("Impossible") premiered at the Teatro Politeama.[62] An integral part of the *canción romántica* (romantic song) tradition because of its sentimental lyrics and singing style, the

[59] Rafael Aviña, Ana Vigne-Pacheco, and Patrick Lebre, "Los ritmos populares de cine mexicano / Les Rythmes Populaires dans la Cinéma Mexicain," *Cinémas D'Amérique Latine*, no. 8 (2000): 42.

[60] There is one more bolero used in the film. According to an article in *Excélsior*, Juan Alberto Villegas contributed his bolero "Amor de Ciego" ("Blind Love"), which is played in a brief scene in which Santa is dancing around her room in Doña Elvira's brothel. Some believe that the bolero is Lara's work, but Villegas wrote to *Excélsior* to clear up the matter. Villegas does not receive credit in the film, although the article states that it was played over the radio. See "La música de Santa es de dos autores," *Excélsior*, April 16, 1932.

[61] The period shift is also evident in the characters' clothing, which mirrored fashion trends from the 1920s and 1930s, particularly the short haircuts, which may reflect the culture of *las pelonas* (Mexican flappers), urban women influenced by the short haircuts of silent film actresses and fashionistas from Hollywood and Paris. Photographs and artist conceptions on las pelonas can be seen in the popular Mexico City magazine *Revista de Revistas* from the 1920s and are associated with the foxtrot, Charleston, and jazz music. For more information on las pelonas, see Anne Rubenstein, "The War on *Las Pelonas*: Modern Women and Their Enemies, Mexico City, 1924," in *Sex in Revolution: Gender, Politics, and Power in Modern Mexico*, ed. Jocelyn Olcott, Mary Kay Vaughan, and Gabriela Cano (Durham, NC: Duke University Press, 2006), 57–80; and Guadalupe Caro Cocotle, "La música de las pelonas. Nuevas identidades femeninas del México moderno, 1920–1930," PhD dissertation, Universidad Nacional Autónoma de México.

[62] According to Federico Krafft Vera and Elena Tamargo Cordero, Lara wrote this bolero in the house of Margarita Pérez, which he calls "the best and cleanest" brothel in the neighborhood. See Federico Krafft Vera and Elena Tamargo Cordero, *Bolero: Clave del corazón* (Mexico City: Fundación Ongenerio Alejo Peralta y Díaz Ceballos, IBP, 2004), 88.

Figure 1.1 Cinquillo rhythm.

Mexican bolero derives from the Cuban bolero, a 2/4 song and dance form with Afro-Cuban influences, which included a *cinquillo* rhythmic pattern (figure 1.1), also heard in the danzón.[63]

According to Alejandro L. Madrid, the bolero arrived in Mexico gradually via maritime commerce, such as involving sugar and tobacco routes, and traveling performing troupes, such as the Compañía de Bufos Cubanos. The genre was then absorbed into Mexican musical culture primarily in the Yucatán at the turn of the century.[64]

The bolero in *estilo yucateco* (Yucatecan style) was played almost exclusively on guitars and decelerated from a fast-paced dance to a slower song style. It was in Mexico City, however, that the bolero underwent its transformation into the "urban sound of Mexico,"[65] performed in popular theater, carpas, brothels, and cabarets. In these spaces, the bolero birthed its modern melodic and lyrical characteristics—particularly, as Monsiváis notes, lyrics with testimonial and confessional value.[66] Sentimental

[63] Pablo Dueñas and Yolanda Moreno Rivas link the rhythmic structure of the Cuban bolero to Afro-Cuban contradanza and the habanera through the rhythmic cinquillo cell, which corresponds to the clave. See Pablo Dueñas, *Bolero: Historia gráfica y documental* (Mexico City: Asociación Mexicana de Estudios Fonográficos, A.C., 2005), 17; Moreno Rivas, *Historia de la música popular mexicana*, 78–129.

[64] For more information on the cultural and stylistic development of the bolero, see Alejandro L. Madrid, *Music in Mexico: Experiencing Music, Expressing Culture* (Oxford: Oxford University Press, 2013), 37–55; Dueñas, *Bolero*; Moreno Rivas, *Historia de la música popular mexicana*; María del Carmen de la Peza Casares, *El bolero y la educación sentimental en México* (Mexico City: Universidad Autónoma Metropolitana-Xochimilco, 2001); Krafft Vera and Tamargo Cordero, *Bolero: Clave del corazón*; George Torres, "The *Bolero Romántico*: From Cuban Dance to International Popular Song," in *From Tejano to Tango*, ed. Walter Aaron Clark (New York: Routledge, 2002), 151–71; Carlos Monsiváis, *Mexican Postcards* (London: Verso, 1997), 166–95. For more information on the Caribbean sugar routes, see Bernard Moitt, *Sugar, Slavery, and Society: Perspectives on the Caribbean, India, the Mascarenes, and the United States* (Gainesville: University Press of Florida, 2004); Michelle Harrison, *King Sugar: Jamiaca, the Caribbean, and the World Sugar Economy* (London: Latin American Bureau, 2001). For more information regarding the Bufos Cubanos, see Jill Lane, *Blackface Cuba* (Philadelphia: University of Pennsylvania Press, 2005); Robin Moore, *Nationalizing Blackness: Afrocubanismo and Artistic Revolution in Havana, 1920–1940* (Pittsburgh: University of Pittsburgh Press, 1997). While in Mexico in 1919, the Compañía de Bufos Cubanos performed at the Teatro Principal.

[65] Mark Pedelty, "The Bolero: The Birth, Life, and Decline of Mexican Modernity," *Latin American Music Review/Revista de Música Latino Americana* 20, no. 1 (Spring-Summer 1999): 36.

[66] Monsiváis, *Mexican Postcards*, 167.

messages of love, of its capture and loss, its confusions and torments, its outcomes joyful and tragic, overtook the bolero's narratives, both reflecting and reconfiguring the dramatic psyche of 1920s and 1930s urban Mexicans.[67] Stylistically, Lara molded the bolero to fit an urban context by changing instrumentation from strictly guitars to piano and solo voice, and relaxing the rhythmic structure by playing the verses with open arpeggios and exaggerated rubato.[68]

In *Santa*, the bolero marks an important narrative transition. Santa, newly adjusted to urban life in the brothel, enjoys a slow night with no client traffic. She sits with Hipólito and asks him to recount his life (figure 1.2). He describes how his mother abandoned him at the school for the blind, promising to see him every week, but never returning. At the end of his story, Santa asks him to play the song he wrote for her, a slow, lyrical bolero, performed on his upright piano:

> Santa,
> My Santa
> Woman that illuminated my life;
> Santa
> Be my guide
> Down this sad road of pain.[69]

An example of Michel Chion's empathetic music—music designed to instill an emotive response from the characters and/or the audience—this song creates several emotional connections with the characters.[70] Hipólito composed and performed the song, using the bolero as the channel to express his devotion to Santa and to communicate his frustration over not being able to see her, conveying a sense of longing. Hipólito's identity as the talented, blind piano player is only permissible through sound film, contrasting his

---

[67] Madrid notes that much of the sentimentality in the lyrics had to do with contemporary currents in poetry, particularly Latin American *modernista* poetry, which contributed to the cosmopolitan nature of the song genre. See Madrid, *Music in Mexico*, 41–42.

[68] Lara's bolero style of the late 1920s heard in "Imposible" from 1929 was influenced by Guty Cárdenas's bolero from 1926, "Nunca" ("Never"), which utilizes a relaxed Cuban cinquillo rhythmic cell and is in binary form. See Enrique Martín and Álvaro Vega, "La canción yucateca," in *La música en México: Panorama del siglo XX*, ed. Aurelio Tello (Mexico City: Fondo de Cultura Económica, 2010), 253–90.

[69] Moreno, *Santa*, ch. 4.

[70] Michel Chion, *Audio-Vision: Sound on Screen* (New York: Columbia University Press, 1994), 8.

Figure 1.2 Santa (Lupita Tovar) and Hipólito (Carlos Orellana), in *Santa* (1931).
Photo courtesy of Mil Nubes-Foto.

role in the silent feature. In Peredo's version, Hipólito would have appeared mute, essentially an empty vessel. Synchronized, recorded sound, in particular music, however, gives Hipólito's character life, both aurally and visually, in the narrative.

Hipólito is not only brought to life with synchronized sound but also serves as an avatar for Lara. Both are piano players in brothels and bear witness to the effects of urban growth and modernization on the moral hierarchies and belief system of Mexican society. Lara situates these experiences in the forefront of his boleros, bringing the marginalized into the spotlight, and participating in a new current of consumer culture:

> Although difficult to conceive of as nationalistic icons, Lara's boleros and their cinematic renderings also participated in the complex of Mexican nation-building . . . musically and cinematically they serve to inscribe

the prostitute and the cabaret life with which she is associated as an anti-utopian paradigm for a so-called modern Mexican life.[71]

Lara's role in the rise and popularity of the bolero and its associations with prostitution, brothels, and cabarets position him, like Hipólito, as the voice of the urban nightlife, maintaining an important role in the nation's quest for modernization.

During the bolero, the camera does not focus solely on "the point of audition"—sound accompanied with a corresponding shot. While Hipólito sings, the camera slowly pans, revealing groups of women at cocktail tables—playing cards, drinking, and/or talking. When they hear the piano introduction, they gradually stop and look at Hipólito, directing the audience's focus to the music. Their gazes create an intimate connection with the music, one that is unified in a shared longing, sadness, and understanding. Intriguingly, the center of attention is not Hipólito or even Santa but, rather, the secondary characters: the women of the brothel. The camera concentrates on Hipólito's small audience, constructing a cultural synchresis that is specifically designed to draw sympathy from the spectator. The fact that the song is about Santa and that the moving image is shared with the other women constructs a deeper association between music and image: Hipólito could have been singing about any one of them, the marginalized and ostracized women of society, which they acknowledge nonverbally through their focused attention and unflinching gazes. As the song nears its conclusion, however, the camera rests on a close-up of Santa's face as she watches Hipólito play the final chords, shifting attention back onto the protagonist. The bolero in the film is the only musical number that acquires intense focus by the characters, the gaze, and, by extension, the audience, and is the only musical example played in its entirety.

"Danzón dedicated to Santita, the most beautiful woman in Mexico"

In his novel, Gamboa repeatedly refers to the danzón as a popular musical form, performed especially at the Salón Trivoli. He describes the music, or the people's reaction to the music, as follows:

---

[71] Ana M. López, "Of Rhythms and Borders," in *Everynight Life: Culture and Dance in Latin/o America*, ed. Celeste Fraser Delgado and José Esteban Muñoz (Durham, NC: Duke University Press, 1997), 323.

The danzón explodes with the clamor of a tropical storm, the timbales and the trumpet make the windowpanes shake, striving to break them and rouse the peaceful passersby that stop and distort their faces, dilate their noses and smile, won over by the promise of these wandering and lustful harmonies. . . . The vigilant policemen in the salon look around with a sour expression and, because they cannot arrest those irreverent notes, adjust their whiskers.[72]

From this description, Gamboa associates the danzón with the tropical and the exotic, and implies that the music is a seductive, almost siren-like sound that could entice anyone merely walking by, except the police who are helpless to contain the music's seductive power.[73] Gamboa marks a strong social (and moral) distinction between those who enjoy and participate in the music and those who merely observe.

Much like the bolero, the danzón stems from Afro-Cuban origins. In their study on the roots and the changing, cultural meanings of the danzón, Alejandro L. Madrid and Robin D. Moore examine the danzón as a hybrid form, depicting a fusion of European and African musical and rhythmic elements that continued to adapt and evolve in the Caribbean and Latin America. In Cuba, the danzón emerged during the late nineteenth century as an instrumental dance genre from Matazanas, exhibiting rhythmic and stylistic influences of the contradanza and danza. Cuba's black middle class and Afro-Cuban social clubs popularized the danzón by appropriating it as a ballroom dance form that became widely popular across the island.[74] Like the bolero, the danzón was assimilated into Mexican musical and theatrical culture through transnational maritime commerce and traveling performing groups, quickly becoming a popular dance form in Veracruz and the Yucatán. The danzón eventually made its way to Mexico City and experienced its vogue in the dance halls and cabarets during the 1920s, particularly in the Salón México, popularly known as "la catedral del danzón" ("the cathedral of danzón").[75] Madrid and Moore state that "working-class Mexican

---

[72] Gamboa, *Santa*, 116.

[73] Moreno Rivas notes that in Mexico the generalized denomination of "música tropical" ("tropical music") is used to denote any music with black or Caribbean influence; Moreno Rivas, *Historia de la música popular mexiana*, 169.

[74] Moore, *Nationalizing Blackness*, 26.

[75] The danzón was also incorporated into the teatro de revista. Jesús Flores y Escalante notes that María Conesa, "La Gatita Blanca," danced the danzón "El papel de Veracruz" in the 1918 revista, *Los muchachos* by Pablo Prida and Carlos M. Ortega, with music by Manuel Castro Padilla. See

migrants who moved to the capital adopted the dance and refashioned it as a symbol of urban cosmopolitanism and modernity."[76]

The danzón is a partner dance that requires the partners to face each other in an embrace, their upper bodies fairly stationary while they move in small, circular steps from the knees down. The Cuban danzón obliges that the partners hold each other in a close yet loose embrace, which adds to its seductive character. Because of stricter customs of decorum in Mexico, the embrace there is not as close, but retains the style's subtle hip motion and the relaxation of the upper and lower body. The musical structure of the Mexican danzón introduces an easily recognizable theme, the *estribrillo,* usually in duple meter, which repeats three or more times throughout the dance. Other melodic themes occur after each *estribrillo* before arriving to the *montuno,* the final theme that ends the work and emphasizes rhythmic and torso movements.[77] During the 1920s and 1930s, the danzón was performed by an orchestra of violins, woodwinds (varies between clarinet, saxophone, and flute), horns, and the timbal, and featured the signature cinquillo rhythm.[78]

In *Santa,* the danzón follows the introduction of El Jarameño, the Spanish bullfighter deeply infatuated with Santa. In their shared scenes, Santa performs her sex-worker duties for the first time on screen. This contrasts to her earlier scenes in the brothel, where she was still the innocent country girl in modest light-colored dresses, full of fear and naiveté about her new urban surroundings. In scenes involving El Jarameño, however, she dons a low-cut, black satin dress that clings to her body; her hair is slicked back— she is unmistakably modern, fashionable, and enticing, reminiscent of the Hollywood starlets that graced the covers and entertainment pages of popular Mexico City periodicals.[79]

Jesús Flores y Escalante, *Salón México: Historia documental y gráfica del danzón en México* (Mexico City: Asociación Mexicana de Estudios Fonográficos, A.C., 2006), 192.

[76] Alejandro L. Madrid and Robin Moore, *Danzón: Circum-Caribbean Dialogues in Music and Dance* (New York: Oxford University Press, 2013), 76.

[77] See Susan Cashion, "The Mexican Danzón: Restrained Sensuality," in *Dancing Across Borders: Danzas y Bailes Mexicanos,* ed. Olga Nájera-Ramírez, Norma E. Cantú, and Brenda M. Romero (Urbana: University of Illinois Press, 2009), 237–55. See also Madrid and Moore, *Danzón,* 33–35 and 93–94.

[78] Moreno Rivas, *Historia de la música popular mexicana,* 166.

[79] *Revista de Revistas* and *El Universal Ilustrado* regularly featured photo spreads of Joan Crawford, Bette Davis, Marlene Dietrich, Mae West, Clara Bow, and Greta Garbo. *El Universal Ilustrado* also included articles entitled "Hollywood's Ugly Girls," featuring pictures and articles on those successful actresses (always in supporting roles) in Hollywood who do not fit a model of beauty. Mary Wickes was a particular favorite.

Sexual tension and seduction become quickly associated with the danzón in this scene. The outdoor patio of a mansion provides the setting where the brothel's prostitutes mingle with El Jarameño's entourage. The crowd is first entertained by a live foxtrot played by the jazz band with female vocalist, and danced by the chorus girls from the Teatro Politeama.[80] Santa uses this moment to make El Jarameño jealous by sitting away from him and casting her attention on another man. In response to her new client's request for a danzón, she describes the bodily movements of the dance, almost an exact emulation of the description detailed in Gamboa's narrative: "You have to be very close, you know? First, you must do many turns, almost without leaving the same place. And in the second part, you have to shake your hips."[81] After Santa's description, the bandleader shouts out, "Danzón dedicated to Santita, the most beautiful woman in Mexico." The jazz ensemble, composed of violins, accordions, guitars, clarinet, saxophone, trumpet, and drums, strikes up a minor-key danzón. As the music begins, Santa and her client hold each other close and proceed to dance in small circles, quickly followed by the rest of the party (figure 1.3).

The danzón plays a crucial role in demonstrating the cultural synchresis of the genre with desire and seduction. It occurs when Santa is performing her role as a lady of the evening and is clearly enjoying herself, solidifying the music's association with sexuality and even with female social liberation as she selects who she wants to dance with and when she wants to dance (and also what music they will be dancing to). In an early scene, Santa cowered in the corner, afraid to let the clientele touch her, claiming she did not know how to dance. Now, her clients ask her to teach them how to dance the danzón, indicating her experience, with all its associated meanings and loss of innocence. Here, Santa is a confident and captivating cosmopolitan woman, who titillates her clients not just with her provocative appearance but also by being coquettish and teasing them into jealousy. Strikingly, the danzón is the only musical genre that is explicitly mentioned and described by any of the film's characters. The labeling of the genre and the explanation of the movements provide a bridge for the audience to recognize what is taking place on screen. This is further enhanced when, after Santa and her client begin to dance, the camera zooms in on the band, placing the ensemble in the foreground rather than the intimate dancing taking place.

---

[80] At the time, Lara composed revistas for the Teatro Politeama and this chorus line most likely appeared in his works.

[81] Moreno, *Santa*, ch. 6.

Figure 1.3 Santa (Lupita Tovar) and unnamed client dance danzón with band in the background, in *Santa* (1931). Screen capture from film.

The bolero and danzón scenes in *Santa* initiated the intimate relationship between cinema and commercially successful music in Mexican popular culture and catapulted Lara further into the entertainment spotlight. Differing from 1930s Hollywood productions, Mexican films did not depict an elaborate musical revues but, rather, showcased more integrated and "natural" performances. In spite of this difference, music is still foregrounded and is diegetically central to the prostitute melodramas.[82]

Santa placed the consumption of popular music and the prostitute into the national spotlight. Author Luz Alba stated: "The success of 'Santa' with the public can be explained for two reasons: the popularity of the excellent novel by Don Federico Gamboa that serves as the basis for the films adaptation, and the fact that the film reflects our customs."[83] *Santa* received positive reviews when it premiered in 1932 after extensive sneak peaks in *El Universal*, which

---

[82] López, "Of Rhythms and Borders," 321.
[83] Luz Alba, "Por el mundo de las sombras que hablan," *El Universal Ilustrado*, July 21, 1932.

featured stills from the film and ads for special screenings of selected clips.[84] While some ads for the feature label the film as "the first grand national cinematic production," others stated, "It is not a wonder . . . but it is a good film."[85] The prostitute would still be scrutinized in the state's morality campaigns, but now, with the success of *Santa,* garnered a stronger presence in the national imagination, which would continue to change.

Modernization, Exoticism, and the Rumbera

One year after the premiere of *Santa,* Russian director Arcady Boytler adapted a short story by nineteenth-century French author Guy de Maupassant into a new prostitute melodrama. Following the "fallen woman" narrative, Boytler's *La mujer del puerto (The Woman of the Port;* 1933) tells the story of a socially ruined country girl who moves to an urban area and becomes a prostitute, but utilizes the social taboo of incest to push the female protagonist, Rosaura (played by Andrea Palma), to commit suicide. Following in *Santa's* musical track model, the film features the iconic ballad "La mujer del puerto"—or "Vendo placer" ("I Sell Pleasure")—composed by Manuel Esperón (1911–2011), providing an empathetic association to the prostitute in order to elicit sympathy from the audience for her current condition. Danzones in the film accompany the communal scenes in the brothel to solidify the connection between spaces of sexual commerce and the protagonist.[86] Danzones also accompany the ficheras with their clients in Adolfo Best Maugard's 1938 film *La mancha de sangre (Blood Stain),* which follows the romance of a prostitute and a poor country boy.[87] Off screen, the Department of Public Safety and the state's moralizing campaigns continued to target prostitutes and ficheras, yet removing these women from these spaces was out of the question. Some feared that if women could not work in these establishments, they would open their homes to sexual promiscuity, allowing disease and vice to spread quicker.[88]

---

[84] Special screenings for the film took place in February 1932 at the Cine Royal, Cine Lux, Cine Alcazar, and the Majestic. Ads for *Santa* in *El Universal,* February 27, 1932.

[85] Ad for *Santa* in *El Universal,* March 25, 1932.

[86] See Jacqueline Avila, "Arcady Boytler: *La mujer del puerto* (1933)," in *Clásicos de cine mexicano: 31 películas emblemáticas desde la Época de Oro hasta el presente,* ed. Christian Wehr (Frankfurt: Editorial Vervuert, 2015), 57–70. See also Jacqueline Avila, "Musicalizando la muerte en el cine mexicano durante los 1930s," *Balajú: Revista de Cultura y Comunicación* 3, no. 2 (2016): 48–60.

[87] See Jacqueline Avila and Oswaldo Mejía Mendiola, "Dance, Desire, and Cosmopolitanism: Early Danzón Performances in the 1930s Prostitute Melodrama," in *Routledge Companion to the Music and Sound of World Cinema from the First "Talkies" to the 1940s* (in press).

[88] Elías Hurtado, "El problema de la mujer que trabaja en cabarets," *El Nacional,* October 15, 1937.

During the mid- to late 1940s, the prostitute melodrama transitioned from the intimacy of the brothel to the urban cabaret, branching into the cabaretera subgenre, featuring an updated "fallen women" narrative that reflected contemporary social changes.[89] Joanne Hershfield argues that economic and social uncertainty, due to the swift and disruptive changes made during the presidential *sexenios* (six-year terms), of Manuel Ávila Camacho (1940–1946) and Miguel Alemán (1946–1952), facilitated an air of pessimism in the cabaretera film and "reflected a world consumed with anxieties of social transformation."[90] Both sexenios were characterized by rapid economic growth and modernization. Ávila Camacho allied Mexico with the United States during World War II, making Mexico dependent on foreign investments and encouraging a more capitalist-based economy.[91] Alemán's administration continued the industrialization policies of his predecessor and maintained stable relations with the United States, but also formented intense economic greed and corruption at the expense of the overall population. Social conditions for the masses grew grim as Alemán's economic policies lowered salaries and raised inflation rates, and new labor policies controlled labor for the benefit of the private sector.[92] Social and economic changes were uneven, as the upper class received the benefits at the expense of the middle and working classes.

Amid this transformation, women's roles began to shift as well. As women entered the modern work force during and after World War II, specific gender roles and conservative moral codes required revision.[93] In cinema, the cabareteras attempted to update the role of women in working-class society as they moved away from the sacred domestic space, and exemplified the cabaret as "a microcosm of the city, with its multiplicity of ethnicities, classes, and expressions of sexuality."[94] As a cultural text, the cabaretera film challenged the Porfirian moral order that the prostitute melodrama of the

---

[89] Cabaret backdrops had been utilized in Mexican cinema during the late 1930s, but the cabareteras or cine de rumberas are specifically associated with the Alemán sexenio.

[90] Joanne Hershfield, *Mexican Cinema/Mexican Woman, 1940–1950* (Tucson: University of Arizona Press, 1996), 79. For a discussion regarding economic corruption during the Ávila Camacho and Alemán sexenios, see Stephan R. Niblo, *México en los cuarenta: Modernidad y corrupción* (Mexico City: Editorial Océano de México, 2008).

[91] See ch. 2, this volume, for a discussion of the dependence on foreign investors during the Porfiriato.

[92] Susan M. Deeds, Michael C. Meyer, and William L. Sherman, *The Course of Mexican History*, 7th ed. (Oxford: Oxford University Press, 2003), 618–20.

[93] De la Mora, *Cinemachismo*, 51.

[94] Ibid., 100.

1930s had previously enforced, transforming into an emblem of a new and growing modernity.[95]

Conveying an atmosphere of excess, decadence, and even pageantry, the cabareteras showcased extended music and dance numbers and featured over-the-top tropical backdrops and links to the exotic. The cabareteras also evidenced the influx of Afro-Cuban dance music from el dancing since the 1920s, and the gradual migration of several Cuban dancers and musicians into Mexico and into the Mexican film industry.[96] The stage design and costuming further differentiated these films from the 1930s prostitute melodrama, which constructed a more subdued and natural atmosphere in the brothel/cabaret; social differences and sexuality in the 1930s onscreen cabaret were conveyed through music and dance. However, in the cabareteras, such as *Salón México* (1949, dir. Emilio Fernández) and *Aventurera* (*Adventuress*; 1952, dir. Alberto Gout), racial and social differences were portrayed in the form of hyper-exoticized music and dance cultures depicted both visually and aurally in the onscreen cabaret's performance space.

The off screen cabaret, the cabaret of actuality, served as a space for fantasy, an escape to desire, and a site for the performance of alternative identities in a (relatively) safe space. It offered evasion to the sexual repressions of home to a site where all that is forbidden and deemed immoral is normal.[97] In order to indulge in this escape from Catholic restrictions and engage in fantasy "role playing," several cabarets utilized themes, backdrops, and decorations to convey Otherness and to encourage the adoption of other identities. The popular Agua Azul, for example, featured escapist murals of international waterfalls and the Club Ba-Ba-Lú featured a tropical décor of palm trees and drums, and advertisements with characters in blackface. Other cabarets such as the Bagdad and Estambul featured Middle Eastern backdrops or featured decorations in "estilo oriental" ("oriental" or "Eastern style").[98]

The adoption of exotic places adorned the stages in the cabareteras, creating a space where the images and sounds of the Other were imported

[95] Ana M. López, "Tears and Desire: Women and Melodrama in the 'Old' Mexican Cinema," in *Mediating Two Worlds: Cinematic Encounters in the Americas*, ed. John King, Ana M. López, and Manuel Alvarado (London: British Film Institute, 1993), 159.

[96] Cuban performers in Mexico include Beny Moré, Dámaso Pérez Prado, Toña la Negra, and Rita Montaner.

[97] See Carlos Monsiváis, "Mexican Cinema: Of Myths and Demystifications," in *Mediating Two Worlds: Cinematic Encounters in the Americas*, ed. John King, Ana. M. López, and Manuel Alvarado (London: British Film Institute, 1993), 145.

[98] For more information on cabarets of the 1930s and 1940s, see Armando Jiménez, *Cabarets de antes y de ahora en la ciudad de México* (Mexico City: Plaza y Valdés Editores, 1991).

and translated into a Mexican context. In the cabareteras, Afro-Cuban culture became the most exoticized Other and a central component to this construction was the popular Afro-Cuban dance, the rumba, and its female protagonist, the rumbera. Onscreen, cabaretera rumberas typically performed stylized rumbas and other dances for audiences as part of a cabaret show, and were perceived as figures of sexist pleasure.[99] The rumbera became a controversial figure for conservative sectors of society because her body was positioned as a commercial object. Laura Gutierrez states, "The objectification of the female body happens in two different ways in the space of the cabaret: the women that occupy that space are either prostitutes (i.e., there's a monetary exchange for sex) or rumberas (i.e., the stage is reserved for the dance numbers the female dancer executes) and, at times, both."[100] The rumberas of Mexican cinema, or "Las reinas del trópico" ("The queens of the tropics"), include María Antonieta Pons, Ninón Sevilla, Amalia Aguilar, Rosa Carmina, and Meche Barba.[101] With the exception of Meche Barba, these dancers took part in the transnational move from Cuba to Mexico that permeated the period and found their niche in the film industry as rumberas.

In addition to her revealing and outrageous costumes, the rumbera exhibited her exoticness through her dance performance. Gutierrez classifies the dance sequences in cabaretera films as "momentary interruptions" in the narrative, providing a discourse that focuses on the rumbera's body and on engaging the audience, on and off the screen, in another level of escape that moves "outside the purview of the nation-state's doctrines."[102] Dancing and the focus on the female body have been controversial and risqué subjects in popular entertainment since the nineteenth century. In her discussion of the exotic in Georges Bizet's 1875 opera *Carmen*, Susan McClary asserts that Carmen's seductive dance, sexually driven by her swinging hips and

[99] Moore, *Nationalizing Blackness*, 285. An early precursor of the rumbera comes from the *tiple* (soprano) performers from the teatro de revistas and *teatro frívolo* (spicy or frivolous theater), which featured actresses who sing, dance, and act with flair, or *chispa*. The scant costuming, music, and provocative choreography allow the actresses to flaunt their figures while singing and dancing a musical number, appealing to the mass, primarily male, audiences. When burlesque shows from Paris arrived in 1925, the teatro frívolo was quick to respond with its own interpretation: *Mexican Rataplán* featuring "las primeras 'venus modernas de huarache'" ("the first 'modern Venuses wearing huaraches'") appearing nude on stage. See Edgar Ceballos, "Las abuelitas de las rumberas," *Somos: Las rumberas de cine mexicano* 10, no. 189 (November 1999): 82.

[100] Laura Gutierrez, *Performing Mexicanidad: Vendidas y cabareteras on the Transnational Stage* (Austin: University of Texas Press, 2010), 114.

[101] See Fernando Muñoz Castillo, *Las reinas del trópico* (Mexico City: Grupo Azabache, 1993).

[102] Ibid.

twisting body, is inextricably linked to the dance of the Orient, which others Carmen from the rest of the characters on stage. McClary further suggests that Carmen's depiction through sensuous dance "would not be a problem, were it not for the mind/body anxieties" evident in late nineteenth-century French culture.[103] Because of the state's past stronghold on public health campaigns and the deeply embedded Porfirian moral codes and Catholic indoctrinations that transferred into 1930s and 1940s cinema, the rumbera was a controversial and challenging figure. Unable to depict nudity or sexually promiscuous behavior owing to the scrutiny of the Legion mexicana de la decencia (Mexican Legion of Decency),[104] the rumberas executed their sexuality and exoticism through their gyrating hips, thrusting pelvis, and other provocative movements to the popularized and commercialized music imported from Latin America and the Caribbean—such as the rumba, samba, mambo, and conga—thoroughly enjoying seducing the audience on and off screen. Via exotic escapism, the rumbera as a representation of the exotic serves as a conduit for both the reinterpretation of Afro-Cuban musical cultures in Mexico and an exploration in the changing social mores.

Crossing over from the 1930s prostitute melodrama, the bolero and danzón maintain central positions within the cabaretera film, but more music and dance sequences are incorporated in order to feature the rumbera and keep apace with transformations in Mexico's contemporary music culture. This is best demonstrated in *Víctimas del pecado* (1950), the third film made by the famous team of director Emilio Fernández, cinematographer Gabriel Figueroa, and screenwriter Mauricio Magdaleno, which paints a seductive and compelling visual and aural interpretation of the urban nightlife and the position of the rumbera.[105]

---

[103] Susan McClary, *Georges Bizet Carmen* (Cambridge: Cambridge University Press, 1992), 55–56.

[104] This legion began during the 1930s to censor questionable moral material in cinema, which includes sex and drug and alcohol use. When the cabareteras became popular with moviegoers, the legion distributed material regarding the appropriate uses of cinema in society, which includes upholding morals. Although examples of their propaganda remain scare, an article in *Cinema Reporter* details some of the league's preoccupations. See "Legion mexicana de la decencia," *Cinema Reporter*, September 27, 1952. I owe special thanks to Leopoldo Gaytán Apáez at the Cineteca Nacional for sharing this information with me.

[105] Previous prostitute melodramas produced by this team include *Las abandondas* (*The Abandoned*; 1944) and *Salón México* (1948).

Víctimas del pecado (1950)

Víctimas del pecado tells the story of Violeta (Ninón Sevilla), a headlining rumbera at the Club Changoo, who adopts the prostitute Rosa's (Margarita Ceballos) baby boy. Rosa placed the baby in a garbage can in a desperate attempt to keep the affections of the baby's father, the *pachuco*-pimp, Rodolfo (Rodolfo Acosta).[106] After Violeta is forced to leave the club due to her new role as mother, she becomes a prostitute to support her adopted son, Juanito. She meets the generous and kind Don Santiago (Tito Junco), who offers her employment at his cabaret La Máquina Loca (The Crazy Machine). Violeta reprises her star status and becomes a successful dancer again. Her time there is short-lived, however, when Rodolfo returns after a stint in prison and kills Don Santiago in order to gain control over Violeta and Juanito. When Rodolfo attempts to harm Juanito, Violeta kills him and is thrown in prison while Juanito works on the streets to survive. Unlike *Santa*, Violeta does not succumb to death in the end but, instead, is surprisingly redeemed by the state solely because of her determination to be a good mother and provider for her adopted son. As de la Mora notes, with this ending, the state becomes the benevolent redeemer of prostitutes rather than marked as explicit for exploiting working mothers and sex workers.[107]

The cabarets in *Víctimas del Pecado* are the central locales where the action—physical fighting, arguments, and music and dance performance—takes place. The Club Changoo and La Máquina Loca are constructed and manipulated by Fernández and Figueroa,[108] and are culturally syncretized with different music and dances to match the social divisions of the clientele in each separate establishment: the Club Changoo uses commercialized mambos, boleros, and musical fusions to entertain a middle-class audience, and La Máquina Loca features rumbas performed by smaller ensembles for the working class.

The Club Changoo is a large, two-floor nightclub with a central dance space visible from the second story, allowing spectators to look down on to the dance floor, providing a bird's-eye view of the dancers. Figueroa's vision for the club is strikingly similar to his dance-hall construction in *Salón*

---

[106] A *pachuco* refers to a youth subculture that developed during the 1930s and 1940s in the southwestern United States, whose emblem was the zoot suit and favored jazz and swing music. For more information, see Octavio Paz, *The Labyrinth of Solitude* (New York: Grove Press, 1985), 9–28.

[107] De la Mora, *Cinemachismo*, 59.

[108] Ceri Higgins, *Gabriel Figueroa: Nuevas Perpectivas* (Mexico City: Consejo Nacional para la Cultura y las Artes, 2008), 202.

México, situated on a dark, narrow city street with neon lights. The club's name, Changoo (an exaggerated or satiric take on Changó or Shangó), refers to the most popular *orisha* in the practice of *Santería*.[109] Because of the prevalence of Catholicism in Cuba, Changó is commonly juxtaposed with, or camouflaged as, Santa Bárbara. He is able to move from one gender to another in order to comply with both interpretations of Santería practice and Catholicism. In addition to gender bending, Changó is also worshiped as the greatest drummer with his own characteristic colors, songs, rhythms, and dances, and is known his seductive nature, inherent machismo, and mastery of music and dance.[110] With the use of the name Changó, the performance of Afro-Cuban dance music, and the presence of a rumbera, the Club Changoo becomes a critical venue for experiencing the importation of Afro-Cuban culture.

The Club Changoo's headlining performers further enhance this connection. The Cuban rumbera popularly known in Mexico as "la rubia con piernas de oro" ("the blond with legs of gold"), Ninón Sevilla, stars as the blond Venus protagonist, Violeta. The Changoo's star vocalist is Rita Montaner, a Cuban-born performer and the "cultural mediator" for performing Afro-Cuban music in a "sophisticated manner."[111] Montaner plays Violeta's godmother and is responsible for finding Violeta the rumbera position. The Club Changoo's featured ensemble is the Pérez Prado Orchestra led by Cuban-born Dámaso Pérez Prado, who is credited with bringing the mambo to Mexico and for "Mexicanizing" the genre.[112] Through the incorporation of jazz-band instrumentation, experimental rhythmic elements,

---

[109] An orisha is a divine supernatural force within the Yoruba-based religion known as Santería or *Regla de Ocha*. The religion was brought over from West Africa during the slave trade in the nineteenth century, Cuba's peak period in the sugar industry and commerce. See Mercedes Cros Sandoval, *Worldview, the Orichas, and Santería: Africa to Cuba and Beyond* (Gainesville: University Press of Florida, 2006).

[110] Ibid., 229.

[111] See Moore, *Nationalizing Blackness*, 174–75. For more information regarding Rita Montaner, see Ramón Fajardo Estrada, *Rita Montaner: Testimonio de una época* (Havana: Fondo Editorial Casa de las Américas, 1997). See also Susan Thomas, *Cuban Zarzuela: Performing Race and Gender on Havana's Lyric Stage* (Urbana: University of Illinois Press, 2009).

[112] José Agustín, *Tragicomedia Mexicana I: La vida en México de 1940 a 1970*, 2nd ed. (Mexico City: Editorial Planeta Mexicana, S.A. de C.V., 2007), 94. The mambo is often defined as the sound of the Alemán administration. Mambos were frequently used in the cabaretera films in this period and also in the third-wave Mexican cinema of the 1990s. In his controversial film *La ley de herodes* (*Herod's Law*; 1994), director Luis Estrada presents a scathing look at the corruption and greed that prevailed in Mexico during Alemán's presidency. The music used to accompany the more crucial scenes depicting the exploitation and malfeasance executed by the protagonist Juan Vargas (Damián Alcázar) on the citizens of the small pueblo are mambos performed by Santiago Ojeda and his orchestra, La Orquestra del Mambo Kid.

and modern uses of dissonance, Pérez Prado and his orchestra won box office success in theaters, nightclubs, and the cinema.[113]

Violeta first appears during the first musical number of the film, "Changó."
The number begins with a close-up shot of Montaner singing from the club's
stage, then zooms out to reveal several lines of female dancers, whose faces
are obscured by dark lighting. It is not clear when the dancers entered, but as
the camera zooms out to a long shot of the dance floor, they suddenly appear
already dancing. Violeta dramatically emerges from backstage and the stage
light follows her movements. She stands out among the other dancers with her
blond hair and her ruffled dress with an open split on her left side, revealing
white bloomers and her famous shapely legs. The other dancers, all brunettes
with large bows in their hair, don a variation of Violeta's dress, but stay in the
darkness, making Violeta the focal point of the performance[114] (figure 1.4).

This scene introduces Violeta as a rumbera, not a prostitute, and as Dolores
Tierney notes, the camera places her in non-voyeuristic terms, capturing
her whole body in high angle, long shots, or *plan américain* rather than
fragments.[115] Figueroa, who was a musician in his youth, captures Violet's
seductiveness and dance abilities by focusing on her through these shots
that, when cutting from one shot to another, match the rhythmic patterns
in the percussion. This technique accentuates her dance as a spectacle. There
are occasional crosscut shots to Montaner, but the camera envelops Violeta,
offering different angles of her from several positions on the dance floor,
displaying her movements with the music.

Musically, this opening number is a synthesis of two musical practices, the
stylized ritual singing associated with Santería and mambo, making an exact
genre not easily identifiable. This interpretation of "Changó" juxtaposes a
"mambo-ized" version with high brass accompaniment performed by the
Pérez Prado orchestra during Montaner's entrance, followed by rhythmic
ostinatos played exclusively on congas, bongos, and güiro instead of the
more traditional batá drums.[116] According to David F. García, the rhythms

---

[113] Moreno Rivas, *Historia de la música popular mexicana*, 177–79.

[114] In his analysis of the Afro-Cuban music in the film, David F. Garcia points out that the large
bows these dancers wear appear to be shaped like Chango's crown, signifying his status as the king
of kings. See David F. García, "The Afro-Cuban Soundscape of Mexico City: Authenticating Spaces
of Violence and Immorality in *Salón México* and *Víctimas del pecado*," in *Screening Songs in Hispanic
and Lusophone Cinema*, ed. Lisa Shaw (Manchester: Manchester University Press, 2012), 181.

[115] Dolores Tierney, *Emilio Fernández: Pictures on the Margins* (Manchester: Manchester University
Press, 2007), 141.

[116] In the ceremonial style of *gümilere*, batá drums are traditionally used, as they are one of the
many voices of the orishas, representing the embodiment of power. For more information on *batá*

Figure 1.4 Violeta (Ninón Sevilla) during her opening number at Club Changoo, in *Víctimas del pecado* (1950). Screen capture from film.

played by the percussion are based on a traditional batá rhythm of sa-lute for Changó.[117] Because of the isolation of the percussion with the re-petitive ostinato and the chanting, a santería musical ceremony is implied. Brass instruments are not used in the ceremonial performance and chant for Changó or any other orisha, and its use here suggests a more consumer-friendly performance practice, overlapping implied ceremonial rhythms of the percussion with the familiar sounds of mambo, without moving out of the ritualistic atmosphere.

drumming and Santería worship, see Migene Gonzalez-Wippler, *Santería: African Magic in Latin America* (New York: Julien Press, 1973); Fernando Ortiz, *La música afro-cubana* (Madrid: Ediciones Jucar, 1974); John Amira and Steven Cornelius, *The Music of Santería: Traditional Rhythms of the Batá Drums* (Tempe, AZ: White Cliffs Media, 1991); Peter Manuel, *Caribbean Currents: Caribbean Music from Rumba to Reggae* (Philadelphia: Temple University Press, 1995), 19–24; Maya Roy, *Cuban Music: From Son and Rumba to the Buena Vista Social Club and Timba Cubana* (London: Latin American Bureau, 1998); Katherine J. Hagedorn, *Divine Utterances: The Performance of Afro-Cuban Santería* (Washington, DC: Smithsonian Institution Books, 2001).

[117] García, "The Afro-Cuban Soundscape of Mexico City," 181.

Montaner sings a reinterpretation of the batá chant Changó, *oba eré*, in Lucumí and in the traditional call-and-response form. From the scene, the accompanying dancers and the musicians sing the responsorial, but we, as the audience, do not see them sing at any point. A weak example of a diegetic function, communal singing can be heard before the dancers appear, reinforcing in the illusion that these women are singing. The effect elucidates an almost magical environment: the women both visually and aurally come out of nowhere. Violeta's vocal interjections are shouts of Changó while her dance invokes several movements derived from Santería dance practice— dancing in circles, moving arms back and forth while hands rest on her waist, and thrusting the hips from side to side. Her performance also reinterprets santería practice: as a symbol of male virility, Changó is usually danced by a man, rather than by a woman. In this light, Violeta embodies the gender-bending capabilities of Changó. By fusing elements from ritual practice with the modern brass fusions of the mambo, Fernández, Pérez Prado, Montaner, and Sevilla create a new consumable product while also introducing Violeta as inextricably linked as both the modern and the exotic.[118]

After Violeta's "Changó" dance scene, the Pérez Prado orchestra performs a swing number that features Rodolfo, the pachuco-pimp, dancing with one of the ficheras. As previously mentioned, the pachuco is Chicano or Mexican American male who belongs to an urban youth subculture that wears zoot suits.[119] In his role as pachuco, Rodolfo's speech—a mixture of Spanish, French, English, and Caló (a form of Spanish argot that includes words in English)—and his appearance mark him as decadent, a "repulsive emblem of the cosmopolitan dandy" and a negative representation of Mexican masculinity. De la Mora states, "his hip *pachuco* fashion style and subcultural linguistic and corporeal expressions are caricatured as narcissistic and vulgar and are marked as not Mexican."[120] In a review for the film, the critic known as V.V. illustrates this harsh interpretation of Paco:

[118] David F. García goes further, suggesting that the director Fernández and screenwriter Magdaleno featured Changó not only to convey the soundscape of the city but also to mirror Rodolfo's violent and aggressive character. Although there is no question that Rodolfo has violent proclivities, I hesitate to declare that the presence of Changó in the film is solely because of Rodolfo. The exoticization of Afro-Cuban culture in Mexican film is prominent in the cabaretera films, and in this scene the musical number, and the camera's gaze, focuses on Violeta and her performance, not necessarily Rodolfo. See García, "The Afro-Cuban Soundscape of Mexico City," 181–82.

[119] As the pachuco was a subculture in the southwest of the United States, it is likely that it crossed the borders with braceros, under a transnational agreement that temporarily imported workers, both agricultural and railway, from Mexico to the United States for relief during World War II.

[120] De la Mora, *Cinemachismo*, 57.

Something excellent that occurs in the background of *Víctimas del pecado* is that it lectures against the "small waist" type of the pachuco by others, ridiculing him by what he appears to be, disgusting, and nothing to be imitated since he is a mannish degenerate.[121]

This description highlights a major public opinion of pachucos: they were interpreted by audiences as suspicious characters owing to their cultural hybridity. Rodolfo's swing dancing in this scene reinforces this perception. Although Pérez Prado is known for his mambos, his orchestra regularly played swing and other jazz music when traveling on tour. The swing dance, however, paints a ridiculous portrait of Rodolfo, as he clumsily moves in his large zoot suit. Unlike other musical scenes at the Changoo, the swing scene is not viewed in its entirety but is cut short, providing the spectator only moments of music to audibly associate with Rodolfo.

The next major performance at the club is a mambo, which follows Violeta's rescue of Rosa's baby from the garbage bin. She brings him to the Club Changoo, much to the dismay of the club's owner, Don Gonzalo, who adamantly and violently orders the baby out and demands that Violeta perform, pushing her out on the dance floor. The mambo "La cocaleca" features Violeta dancing solo for the first time and places a brighter spotlight on the Pérez Prado Orchestra (figure 1.5). As previously mentioned, Pérez Prado is most known for his internationalization of the mambo, a genre that utilizes small, repetitive rhythmic fragments in a cyclic structure, performed by a jazz band. Alberto Dallal states:

> True to symphonic inventions, Pérez Prado's pieces induced you to move your feet and to do it in a manner that seemed to translate the innovations of the technological age into rhythm. Now the contagion occurs by itself because mambo is a functional and essential part of popular urban culture. But Pérez Prado is not only a good musician. He also knows how to capture the concerns of social groups, the changes of time and the possibilities of artistic "reclaim."[122]

Because of the cyclic and repetitive qualities of the mambo, the structure became easy for musicians to play and was infectious with crowds, developing

---

121 V. V., "Film de la semana," *Mañana*, February 10, 1951.
122 Dallal, *La danza en México*, 172.

Figure 1.5 Violeta (Ninón Sevilla) performing "La cocaleca" with the Pérez Prado Orchestra, in *Víctimas del pecado* (1950). Photo courtesy of Cinematográfica Calderón / Permanencia Voluntaria Archivo Cinematográfico.

into an essential contribution to el dancing. As a result, the mambo was a prominent and well known genre in the Mexico City cabaret scene during the 1940s and 1950s. Violeta's performance of the mambo in the film further highlights this popularity.

Much like the "Changó" scene, Violeta visually flaunts her sexuality in an elaborate, ruffled costume that exposes her torso—not her belly button— and bares both her legs. During her performance, Violeta is enthusiastic and smiling, which contrasts to her previous desperation in finding food for the crying baby, making the musical sequence an important character construction for Violeta: she is able to perform her number while she sets aside her personal feelings of distress about her new responsibility, which parallels the new struggles and challenges faced by women joining the work force. Violeta's ability to shift from mother to performer contributes to the changing perceptions of motherhood and the new roles for working women in Mexican society, another symptom of the period's modernization.

After Violeta is fired from the Club Changoo for not giving up the baby, she begins to work at La Máquina Loca, a cabaret run by the businessman Don Santiago, located near the railroad tracks by Nonoalco Bridge. This transition in location provides another vision of an urban, modernized environment in a decidedly lower-class area. Figueroa's constructed landscape contrasts to his previous cityscape compositions, particularly to the bright nightlife representation of the Club Changoo. While the Club Changoo utilizes an electric tropical façade to promote its brand, La Máquina Loca adopts the railroad as its key symbol. Since the Porfirato, the railroad was featured as an important icon, connoting an optimistic modernization.[123] Its position in the film, however, marks a significant association with urban deterioration, a symbol of the industrial modernization that characterized the Alemán period:

> The bridge and neighborhood of Nonoalco have been exploited many times in national cinema, but only now, thanks to *Víctimas del pecado*, has it acquired proper citizenship. It was a happy finding to situate the entrance of La Máquina Loca at the railroad tracks, where later the film's culminating tragedy would take place. And there, Emilio Fernández and Gabriel Figueroa obtain one of the most beautiful cinematographic images, of great poetic flavor, when the protagonist watches the trains go by from the bridge during a misty and smoky dawn that envelops her in mourning; a page from the anthology on that difficult art of directing and shooting films.[124]

The smoke from the railroads and the obscurity of the surrounding area envelop the cabaret in a murky atmosphere, exhibiting the period's dirty side of urbanization.

With a different location comes a different clientele. The Changoo catered to a middle-class crowd with performances by headlined artists. La Máquina Loca, however, serves the working class, evident in the heavy attendance of railway workers. The cabaret is a two-story space much like the Changoo, but is modestly constructed from wood and does not boast any decorative theme. It also

---

[123] Several silent films during the 1910s featured the railroad traveling across the country and utilized by revolutionaries. The presence of mobility was a great attraction in silent film, featuring trains and automobiles. For more information on the images of the railroad in Mexican silent cinema, see Ana M. López, "Early Cinema and Modernity in Latin America," *Cinema Journal* 40, no. 1 (2000): 48–78.

[124] José Antonio Rodriguez, "Modernas sombra fugitivas: Las construcciones visuales de Gabriel Figueroa," *Luna Córnea* 32 (2008): 253–54.

does not feature an illustrious orchestra or headlined performers but, rather, consists of a small percussion ensemble including congas and bongos.

After the featured dancer becomes too drunk to dance the number, Violeta takes over, reassuring Don Santiago that she used to perform it at the Club Changoo. Instead of performing in a revealing costume with ruffles and bows, Violeta wears a modern light colored dress and high heels, similar to the attire of the female protagonists from the 1930s prostitute melodramas. After Violeta quiets the cheering crowd, close-up shots enframe her as the percussion ensemble begins a rumba.

Violeta's rumba is saturated with eroticism, differing from her musical numbers at the Changoo. Tierney suggests that the eroticism of her dancing is "not necessarily figured as one of patriarchal domination," but is closely linked to Violeta's enjoyment and pleasure of dancing, which "questions the mores of Mexican bourgeois morality."[125] Here, Violeta is less restrained than in the middle-class Changoo, freeing herself from the hypocritical constraints of society. Tierney describes Violeta's dancing as freestyle and improvisatory, particularly after she invites one of the musicians to accompany her. Because Violeta, a white woman, dances with a black musician, the uncredited bongocero Jimmy Monterrey, Tierney notes that this dance scene is unusual and suggestive for this period in Mexican cinema, where questions of race in cinema generally involved indigenismo and mestizaje and virtually ignored African identity[126] (figure 1.6). Violeta's performance with Monterrey questions perceptions of race within the boundaries of current social attitudes. The pleasure and spontaneity that Violeta imparts when dancing—in addition to dancing with a black bongocero—challenges

---

[125] Tierney, *Emilio Fernández*, 141.

[126] The most utilized African identity in Mexican cinema is Afro-Cuban. Two films that receive the most attention are *Angelitos Negros* (*Little Black Angels*; 1948, dir. Joselito Rodríguez) and *Mulata* (1954, dir. Gilberto Martínez Solares) for their incorporation of blackface and the performance of Afro-Cuban music. For a summary of African identities in Mexican cinema, see Leopoldo Gaytán Apáez, "Lo negro de lo negro: La negritud a través de sus imagines cinematográficas," *Antropología: Boletín oficial del Instituto de Antropología e Historia* 89 (2011): 85–90. The author provides an overview of films that integrate Afro-Cuban and Afro-Mexican identities in Mexican cinema during the 1950s and 1960s. For discussion on the Afro-Cuban presence in Mexican film and the use of blackface, see Joanne Hershfield, "Race and Ethnicity in the Classical Cinema," in *Mexico's Cinema: A Century of Film and Filmmakers* (Wilmington: SR Books, 1991), 81–100; Marilyn Miller, "'The Soul Has No Color' But the Skin Does: *Angelitos Negros* and the Uses of Blackface on the Mexican Silver Screen, ca. 1950," in *Global Soundtrack: Worlds of Film Music*, ed. Mark Slobin (Middletown, CT: Wesleyan University Press, 2008), 241–58; Gabriela Pulido Llano, *Mulatas y negros cubanos en la escena Mexicana, 1920–1950* (Mexico City: Instituto Nacional de Antropología e Historia, 2010).

Figure 1.6 Violeta (Ninón Sevilla) and bongocero Jimmy Monterrey at La Máquina Loca, in *Víctimas del pecado* (1950). Photo courtesy of Cinematográfica Calderón / Permanencia Voluntaria Archivo Cinematográfico.

gendered notions of Mexican racial and national ideology. This rumba scene positions race, both visually and aurally, in the foreground.

Race isn't the only focal point. A closer reading of the musical context provides more insight into the association of music to place and to the prostitute/rumbera. The rumba is a dance form that is heavily grounded in the black working class of Cuba and has specific connotations to sexuality through the movements. Violeta and Monterrey's nameless character dance a *guaguancó*, a subgenre of the traditional rumba that involves a "ritualized enactment of sexual conquest"[127] (figure 1.7). The guaguancó is a fast and energetic couple dance that culminates on one movement, the *vacunao*. This movement is "an overt game of pursuit-and-capture of the female by the male . . . the couple dances at each other a few feet apart, until without warning the male makes a sudden symbolic gesture of possession at the

---

[127] Moore, *Nationalizing Blackness*, 168.

Figure 1.7 Violeta (Ninón Sevilla) and bongocero Jimmy Monterrey dance the guaguancó at La Máquina Loca, in *Víctimas del pecado* (1950). Photo courtesy of Cinematográfica Calderón / Permanencia Voluntaria Archivo Cinematográfico.

woman's genitals."[128] The male partner attempts several aggressive gestures either through moving his hand, kicking, or thrusting his pelvis, and the female, anticipating these movements, quickly covers her pelvic region, blocking her partner's intentions in an action known as *botao*.[129] Violeta and Monterrey perform these movements with improvisatory flare: Monterrey mimics a baseball player at bat, swinging at the kick that Violeta sends his way, and, at one point, Violeta drops to the floor, exposing her body and her flexibility to the cheering crowd while Don Santiago looks on, contented.[130]

It is not surprising that the rumba guaguancó is featured music for La Máquina Loca, as it was a popular form in Cuban cabaret acts since the

---

[128] Ned Sublette, *Cuba and its Music: From the First Drums to the Mambo* (Chicago: Chicago Review Press, 2004), 271.

[129] Ibid.

[130] Sevilla also executes this move in the "In the Persian Market" scene from *Aventurera*. Here, the camera keeps her in a middle shot, which enables the audience off-screen to see the audience onscreen and the performers. In *Aventurera*, the camera zooms in to an extreme close-up, allowing us to see her full body in this contorted position.

1930s.[131] The guaguancó is the most socially condemned subgenre of the rumba by the middle class and elite in Cuban society owing to "the sexual nature of its choreography and its close associations with the poorest most socially marginal Afrocubans in western areas."[132] With her extensive background in Afro-Cuban dance, Ninón Sevilla highlights the association with marginality when detailing her connection with the rumba in an interview with *Somos*:

> [T]he rumba is culture, rumba is culture because it is music of my country, of the people. The rumba was not danced by people with money, it was danced by the people. Rumba, son, danzón, punto, contrapunto, danzonete, guaracha, cumbia, cha-cha-chá, calipso, mambo. . . . I have all this inside of me.[133]

Not only does Sevilla speak of the marginality of the rumba, but also her mastery of all Cuban musics, a list that encompasses multiple social (and racial) identities, insinuating that she can move from one to another without difficulty. The use of the rumba in La Máquina Loca exercises specific cultural and social meanings associated with the working class, serving as another consequential model of modernization that differs from other cultural meanings inscribed at the Club Changoo.

Up until now in my discussion, the cultural synchresis of music to moving image in *Víctimas del pecado* has consisted of musical genres that point to readings of exoticism, sexuality, and space in order to paint the cultural symptoms of modernization in post-Revolutionary society. The music and dance sequences construct several definitions of Otherness to highlight the ubiquitous urban nightlife and Violeta's engagement with the music solidifies these meanings to the prostitute/rumbera figure, seeming to imply what is not Mexican rather than what is. To counter the figure of Violeta, the linking of Mexicanidad and masculinity is represented in the middle-class businessman and owner of La Máquina Loca, Don Santiago, who provides Violeta and her adopted son with a home and care. Contrasting with the cosmopolitan representation of Rodolfo, Don Santiago personifies a different version of modern Mexican modernity through his paternal and heroic actions and his association with the working class. Reinforcing his

---

[131] Moore, *Nationalizing Blackness*, 168.
[132] Ibid., 169.
[133] Muñoz Castillo, *Las reinas del trópico*, 163.

nationalist image, Don Santiago walks around the city with a small mariachi, his own personal minstrels, that perform the *son jalisciense* "El tren" ("The Train"),[134] functioning in part as his personal theme in a way that counters the synchresis of swing music to Rodolfo.

> Listen gentleman, the train
> That goes whistling away,
> Hear the whistles that play
> While it's on its way.[135]

La Máquina Loca is frequented by railroad workers and is located close to the tracks. Since the railroad is closely associated with the Revolution and the son jalisciense is considered a popular subgenre in the Mexican son tradition, Don Santiago becomes a carrier for revolutionist ideologies, marking him as a modern Mexican patriot.[136]

Conclusion

During the post-Revolutionary years, the state translated into law the ideas and beliefs of the ruling class concerning the sexuality and position of women. Contradictory social norms worked in favor of male desires and placed women, particularly sex workers, in restrained roles in society. Despite efforts of regulation, the state did not eradicate prostitution or control the spread of venereal diseases in Mexico City "because their reformist measures and the rhetoric of promoting a 'revolutionary morality' did not seriously address the sexual habits of men."[137] As such, the prostitute held a contradictory position as a necessity for society, but rejected by the dominant class, tainted as immoral and full of sin. Although the state attempted to unfairly control and contain sex workers and the spaces in which they worked, regulation proved to be difficult as the growth of the modern city and postwar economic hardship led to a growth in prostitution. With the rise

---

[134] In his *Historia documental del cine*, Emilio García Riera labels this son as "El trencito" ("Little Train"), but in the *Cancionero Popular Mexicano*, the son is labeled as "El tren" ("Train"). The son jalisciense is a regional son that has been labeled as the precursor to the modern mariachi.

[135] Mario Kuri-Aldana and Vicente Mendoza Martínez, *Cancionero popular mexicano*, 2nd ed. (Mexico City: Consejo Nacional de la Cultura y las Artes, 2001), 1:44.

[136] De la Mora, *Cinemachismo*, 56.

[137] Ibid., 66.

of cabaret culture at the end of the Revolution through the 1920s and into the 1940s, the burgeoning urban middle class encountered new spaces for varying forms of entertainment. With specially decorated cabarets designed to depict exotic locales and featuring new currents in transnational dance music, the population moved away from the restrictions of modern social norms within the cabaret's enclosed spaces.

The film industry represented the prostitute's position in society in several features during the 1930s and 1940s, predominantly as a tragic figure that succumbs to the consequences and challenges of modern urban society and is, in film, associated with specific music that highlights certain aspects of her identity: she is at once a figure of desire and a figure of empathy. Reflecting Porfirian social mores that transferred to the post-Revolutionary years, Antonio Moreno's *Santa* follows Gamboa's "fallen woman" with the heart of gold narrative and, keeping up to date with currents in popular music culture, utilizes the musical stylings of Agustín Lara's bolero and danzón to depict the prostitute's split identity. In *Víctimas del pecado*, the prostitute doubles as the rumbera, an empowering female figure that takes part in pleasure and seduction through dance performances that enforce her sexuality and exoticness. The bolero and danzón maintain crucial positions in the film's narrative, but rumbas and mambos are incorporated into the musical track to keep pace with changes in the cultural climate and to illustrate divisions in social class. Both films paint the prostitute as a challenging and controversial figure, but the changes in narrative—Santa dies while Violeta is redeemed by the state—and the inclusion of diegetic musical sequences reflect several transformations in society. Despite this, the prostitute/rumbera still embodied the anxieties, desires, and contradictions inherent in Mexico's growing and conflicted modernity.

2

The Salon, the Stage, and
Porfirian Nostalgia

Juan Bustillo Oro's 1939 film, *En tiempos de don Porfirio* (*In the Times of Don Porfirio*), begins with a slow zoom in on a page of the score for "Vals poético" ("Poetic Waltz") by composer Felipe Villanueva (1862–1893)[1] (figure 2.1). The zoom in is aurally accompanied with the waltz played by strings, not piano as originally composed. As the piece continues, the first page of the score turns and we see carefully transcribed musical notation. Another page turn and we see an intertitle written in elegant calligraphy that reads: "We dedicate this film to the beautiful Mexican music of the past, and to its creators, who, with beautiful melodies, grasped the spirit of the period thus making it immortal."[2] After another page turns, and the dedication turns into page after page of face sketches of nineteenth-century Mexican composers: Felipe Villanueva, Alberto Ma. Alvarado, Manuel M. Ponce, Rodolfo Campodónico, José de Jesús Martínez, Alberto de la Peña Gil, Alfredo Carrasco, Juventino Rosas, Genaro Codina, Miguel Lerdo de Tejada, Ernesto Elorduy, Delino M. Preza, Ricardo García de Arellano, Ricardo Castro, and J. Peredes Enríquez. Following this, the credits roll and a story begins that is set at the end of the nineteenth century, during the reigning years of Mexican dictator Porfirio Díaz, known historically and culturally as the Porfiriato (1876–1911).

The *cine de añoranza porfiriana* (films or cinema of Porfirian longing) uses the Porfiriato as the principal setting for narratives of romantic misunderstandings, comedic sketches, and musical performance. Produced at the tail end of the 1930s, the genre was a latecomer to the already established cinematic genres, such the revolutionary melodrama, the prostitute

---

[1] This chapter first appeared as "*México de mis inventos:* Salon Music, Lyric Theater, and Nostalgia in *Cine de añoranza porfiriana,*" in *Latin American Music Review/Revista de Música Latino Americana* 38, no. 1 (2017): 1–27. Copyright © 2017 by the University of Texas. All rights reserved.

[2] Juan Bustillo Oro, dir., *En tiempos de don Porfirio*, DVD, ch. 1, (1939; Mexico City: Laguna Films, 2007).

Figure 2.1 Cover of score for "Vals poético" by Felipe Villanueva, in *En tiempos de don Porfirio* (1939). Screen capture from film.

melodrama, the comedia ranchera, and the fictional indigenista film. The film industry was not unaccustomed to producing films that were historically based, having explored the Conquest and the Wars of Independence with vigor and without heeding historical accuracy. However, during the mid-1930s, filmmakers reexamined historical events that were still fresh in the nation's memory: the Porfiriato and the Revolution.

Although operating with different goals, the cine de añoranza porfiriana and the revolutionary melodrama reinterpret, or reimagine, specific periods in history for the national audience of the post-Revolutionary era. In her suggestive chapter on the revolutionary melodrama, Andrea Noble argues that advances in audiovisual technology helped reinforce new approaches to (or understandings of) the Revolution in cinema. She introduces the concept of "moving memory" in order to describe the consequences of these specific audiovisual relationships in films about the armed struggle. Her study focuses on Carmen Toscano's documentary *Memorias de un mexicano* (*Memories of a Mexican*; 1950), which consists of newsreels and footage from the Revolution filmed by Toscano's father director, Salvador Toscano, edited with newly synchronized music and sound that presented the Revolution as a unified event.[3] Noble states:

> For the revolution to function within the post-revolutionary political and cultural imaginary as the desired unifying, foundational narrative of identity, it therefore had to be remembered and thereby *reinvented* as what it was not: a unified struggle propelled by a set of coherent aim and ideals.[4]

The cine de añoranza porfiriana functions in a similar way. Rather than unveil the period's corruption, the genre paints a moving portrait of the Porfirian elite, the upper class that enjoyed the spoils of Porfirian culture, the Belle Époque, when anything foreign, particularly French or Spanish—fashion, food, art, architecture, music—was in vogue.

In examining the trajectory of films set during the Porfiriato, it is evident that the era was not portrayed as a complicated and corrupted dictatorship swayed by foreign interests, nor as an era of massive industrialization and economic growth. The cinematic Porfiriato was imagined and conveyed as a simpler, easier era for the bourgeoisie, far away from the post-Revolutionary social and political instability and institutional revolution of the 1920s and 1930s. In one of the few examples of scholarship discussing the genre, film scholar Jorge Ayala Blanco states:

> We are in a world of fantasy, of determined, enviable, compassionate, reactionary, languid Porfirian longing. It was an evocation, full of the kindness and the gentleness of 1900, of the best times gone by, but not too remote and salvageable.[5]

What Ayala Blanco fails to address is that producers of the genre were especially focused on portraying the female bourgeoisie—a reserved and restricted class preoccupied with marrying well and maintaining high social status through strict, traditional, and religious social decorum and manners. In her work on gender in modernity, Rita Felski defines nostalgia as a

---

[3] For more information regarding Salvador Toscano and *Memorias de un mexicano*, see Pablo Ortiz Monasterio, *Fragmentos: Narración cinematográfica compilada y arreglada por Salvador Toscano, 1900–1930* (Mexico City: Instituto Mexicano de Cinematografía, 2010).

[4] Andrea Noble, *Mexican National Cinema* (London: Routledge, 2005), 53.

[5] Jorge Ayala Blanco, *La aventura del cine mexicano: En la época de oro y después* (Mexico City: Editorial Grijalbo, 1993), 37.

formative theme during the modern period, "understood as a mourning of an idealized past . . . also an age of yearning for an imaginary edenic condition that has been lost."[6] Porfirian nostalgia in cinema concentrated on women's positions, the act of coupling, and a longing to return to Porfirian society, all of which were emphasized through music. Rather than relying on originally composed music, the world of fantasy and the Porfirian longing that Ayala Blanco speaks of is featured in already composed works and excerpts from the música de salon, zarzuela, and teatro de revistas traditions, all of which were vital practices of nineteenth-century Mexican musical culture and contributed to the Porfirian soundscape, strategically situated in the film in accordance with historical performance practice.

As the opening sequence in Bustillo Oro's *En tiempos de don Porfirio* demonstrates, music played a key role in establishing and solidifying the appropriate style of the period. A closer examination of music's functions in these films, however, reveals that the musical performances instilled a culture synchresis that shaped a utopian atmosphere instigated by middle- and upper-class nostalgia during the social and political agitation of the post-Revolutionary years. Intriguingly, the performed works reference both the developing romantic narratives and the social contradictions of Porfirian culture, particularly concerning gender roles, social mores, and conceptions of decency, directed specifically toward the behavior and position of women in Porfirian society. This fashions these films as intriguing musical and cultural texts for the nostalgic reconstruction—or invention— of the Porfiriato.

The Porfiriato: Corruption, Modernization, and Cosmopolitanism

As previously mentioned, historical dramas focusing on the Conquest, the Independence, the Reform period, and yes, the Revolution, were a part of Mexico's cinematic tradition during the 1930s and 1940s,[7] but the Porfiriato as a film genre, at first glance, is somewhat of an anomaly, given the position of the dictatorship in Mexican history. Positive and negative gazes have

---

[6] Rita Felski, *The Gender of Modernity* (Cambridge, MA: Harvard University Press, 1995), 40.
[7] For more information on these historical themes in Mexican film, see Ángel Miguel, ed., *La ficción de la historia: El siglo XIX en el cine mexicano* (Mexico City: Cineteca Nacional, 2010).

defined the epoch. The positive gaze interprets the Porfiriato as a period of industrialization, economic growth, political stability, and supposed peace and prosperity, while the negative gaze characterizes the era as a period of abject conservatism, unapologetic greed, and brutal economic exploitation. When Díaz first obtained presidential power in 1876, he inherited an empty treasury and massive foreign debt owing to several domestic and international wars and ongoing political instability since Independence.[8] Díaz's primary concern was to change Mexico's image with foreign investors—particularly from the United States and Western Europe—whose capital Díaz believed would stimulate the manufacturing, mining, and agricultural sectors of Mexican society. Potential investors would be more inclined to invest in Mexico if order, stability, and firmness were implemented in the political and social arenas. As a result, he embraced the positivist ideology of Order and Progress.[9] Campaigning on the platform of "no re-election," after his first term in office, Díaz stepped down from the presidency and his handpicked successor, Manuel González (1833–1893) stepped up. This interregnum presidency reeked of corruption, as González granted land favors to the United States and select European countries and ran Mexico into substantial debt.[10] At the end of his term in 1884, Díaz was happily reelected to office and did not step down until 1911.

Díaz immediately continued his initial campaign commitments of economic reform and improving Mexico's image abroad. As he consolidated his political power, Mexico entered a period of sustained modern growth through rapid industrialization, with steam, water, and electric power and new hydraulic and hydroelectric-generating stations. Improvements in transportation led by the railroad boom and the founding of the Mexican Central Railroad Company (backed by investors from Boston) connected the city with the countryside and stretched across the country. Health and sanitation improved when the British firm S. Pearson and Son arrived in Mexico to help the drainage problem, and lights were installed on city streets by U.S., Canadian, German, and English firms.[11] Much of the nation's business was conducted in Mexico City, as Díaz centralized political and social power.

---

[8] The Wars of Independence took place between 1810 and 1821.

[9] See Susan M. Deeds, Michael C. Meyer, and William L. Sherman, *The Course of Mexican History*, 7th ed. (Oxford: Oxford University Press, 2003), 415.

[10] Friedrich Katz, "The Liberal Republic and the Porfiriato, 1867–1910," in *Mexico Since Independence*, ed. Leslie Bethell (Cambridge: Cambridge University Press, 1991), 73–74.

[11] See the discussion of Porfirian modernization in Deeds et al., *The Course of Mexican History*, 421–23.

Foreign businessmen and merchants maintained the most power, at the expense of national citizenry.[12] Other industries such as oil received ample attention from British and U.S. investors, who competed to exploit Mexican petroleum resources.

Modernization and the prevalent harmony of the period, however, came by force, violence, and intimidation to the lower working classes, the disenfranchised, and the indigenous populations. Díaz's infamous guard, the *rurales*, was an important enforcement tool during the *pax porfiriana* (Porfirian peace).[13] Indigenous slaves labored in henequen plantations in the Yucatán, where Mayan and deported Yaquis of Sonora were beaten into submission and forced to work. Muckraking socialist John Kenneth Turner provides accounts of the slave conditions in his exposé *Barbarous Mexico*, claiming that Mexico's peace and prosperity were in fact superficial. While the gross national product climbed and seduced foreign investors, the standard of living for the majority of the Mexican population was catastrophically poor and declining.[14] The hacienda system, in place since the colonial period, was consistently abused by Díaz's regime, particularly when the railroad boom pushed up land values and foreign seizure was greatly encouraged. Rural Mexicans bore the cost of the rapid rises in modernization through fear from the rurales, exploitations by the *hacendados* (owners of the hacienda), and the continued confiscation of land by the government and foreign industries.[15]

Growth in commerce and industry, at the expense of the lower classes, flourished in Mexico and gave rise to new, growing consumer cultures, diverse lifestyles, and social stratification. This social class hierarchy expanded to foster a small bourgeoisie or middle class, which included skilled artisans, government bureaucrats, and other professional men, who were now able to move their families from smaller residences in poorer neighborhoods to larger apartment homes off the more popular boulevards, becoming, according to Moisés Gonzaléz Navarro, the nucleus model of the nation.[16]

---

[12] Michael Johns, *The City of Mexico in the Age of Díaz* (Austin: University of Texas Press, 1997), 16.
[13] The rurales were not solely a Porfirian invention. This police force had been in implementation since Benito Juárez was in power (1858–1864). See Paul J. Vanderwood, *Los rurales mexicanos* (Mexico City: Fondo de Cultura Económica, 1981).
[14] See John Kenneth Turner, *Barbarous Mexico* (Austin: University of Texas Press, 1969). See also Manuel Balbas, *Recuerdos del Yaqui: Principales episodios durante la campaña de 1899 a 1901* (Mexico City: Sociedad de Edición y Librería Franco Americana, 1927).
[15] Ibid.
[16] Moisés González Navarro, *Sociedad y cultura en el porfiriato* (Mexico City: Consejo Nacional para la Cultura y las Artes, 1994), 146. On the middle class in Mexico, see also Juan Díaz Covarrubias, *Obras completas* (Mexico City: Universidad Nacional Autónoma de México, 1959), 327–97.

The wealthy, perceiving themselves to be the pillar of civilization, enjoyed the pleasures of the Porfirian regime with all things foreign, as Mexico City transformed into a vibrant cosmopolitan center. The architecture of fin-de-siècle Paris became the prominent construction model and the popular Paseo de la Reforma was renovated to match the Champs-Elysées. Fashion was either imported directly from Paris or designed to match French couture, and parks, such as the popular Alameda, were renovated and turned into large, lush public gardens, suitable for leisurely afternoon strolls by the upper classes.[17] Michael Johns posits that one was able to view "the look of Europe in the streets of Mexico."[18] New consumer cultures burgeoned as retail and department stores, such as El Palacio de Hierro, opened its doors to sell goods from around the world. In his study on consumerism during the Porfiriato, Steve Bunker states, "Foreign and domestic observers referred to the stores, the plate-glass windows, and the advertising as shorthand for the modern cosmopolitanism of Mexico City and the nation's progress."[19] In addition to the construction of public buildings and parks, certain venues became popular haunts for the upper class, such as the Casino Español, a variety of French- and Swiss-inspired cafés located on the popular boulevard Plateros, and the illustrious Jockey Club, which, according to William H. Beezely, was an elite association for high-society men and women and a popular venue for Díaz's celebrations, including his presidential inaugural ball and several of his birthday parties.[20]

The Porfirian elite appeared to live within a well-furnished bubble that strongly maintained a separation between themselves and the lower classes. After continued corruption, oppression, and fraudulent reelections (despite having campaigned on a "no reelection" platform), an armed uprising in 1910 fueled by ex-presidential candidate Francisco I. Madero brought down the Díaz regime and the culture of the Porfiriato. The Revolution marked ten years of civil and political unrest in which all social strata witnessed

---

[17] Johns, *The City of Mexico in the Age of Díaz*, 23–24. See also Charles Flandrau, *Viva Mexico!* (London: Elan Books, 1982); and Edith O'Shaughnessy, *Diplomatic Days* (New York: Harper and Brothers, 1911).

[18] Johns, *The City of Mexico in the Age of Díaz*, 17.

[19] Steve Bunker, *Creating Mexican Consumer Culture in the Age of Porfirio Díaz* (Albuquerque: University of New Mexico Press, 2012), 14.

[20] William H. Beezely, *Judas at the Jockey Club and Other Episodes of Porfirian Mexico* (Lincoln: University of Nebraska Press, 1987), 3–12. See also González Navarro, *Sociedad y cultura en el porfiriato*.

the burning and destruction of the Porfirian era. The period also marked the increased violence for the demands addressed in the Constitution of 1917: sweeping agrarian reform that gave sequestered land back to the people; liberation and equality for the lower classes, particularly those in slave labor; a separation of Church and state; and progressive labor codes designed to protect the worker.

The 1930s marked a reassessment of the Revolution and its ideals after the social and political reforms of the Constitution of 1917 had gone virtually untouched by the interim presidents of the 1920s and early 1930s.[21] The sexenio of President Lázaro Cardenás (1934–1940) initiated new pursuits to remedy that which previous presidents had ignored. First on his agenda was maintaining constant contact with the population. He traveled to different parts of Mexico, meeting with delegates of workers, listening patiently to their problems and concerns, and he put into effect the agrarian reform that had long gone ignored, distributing 49 million acres of land by the end of his term.[22] Cárdenas also strengthened the labor movement, favoring complete state control over the unions, and enforcing carefully organized propaganda campaigns intended to organize, unify, and regulate. Arturo Anguiano states,

> In every work place he visited, in every meeting where he spoke to workers, he insisted again and again, to the point of exhaustion, on the need for workers to organize. This would be the president's transcendental preoccupation, his obsession, and it would lead Cárdenas to become the most important propagandist and the leading promoter of the mobilization of the working masses.[23]

In addition to the "mass politics" to provoke mobilization, Cárdenas nationalized the oil industries, constructing the government oil company, Petróleos Mexicanos (PEMEX), and removing foreign interests from Mexico,

---

[21] During this period, the presidential line was as follows: Plutarco Elías Calles (1924–1928), Emilio Portes Gil (1928–1930), Pascual Ortiz Rubio (1930–1932), and Abelardo L. Rodríguez (1932–1934). The period from 1928 to 1934 was known as the Maximato, named after Elías Calles, who acted as the de facto president when the other three presidents were in office. When Cárdenas took the presidency, he expelled Elías Calles from Mexico.

[22] Alan Knight, "The Rise and Fall of Cardenismo, c. 1940–1946," in *Mexico Since Independence*, ed. Leslie Bethell (Cambridge: Cambridge University Press, 1991), 249–50.

[23] Arturo Anguiano, "Cárdenas and the Masses," in *The Mexico Reader: History, Culture, Politics*, ed. Gilbert M. Joseph and Timothy J. Henderson (Durham, NC: Duke University Press, 2002), 458. For further reading on society during the Cárdenas sexenio, see Salvador Novo, *La vida en México en el periodo presidencial de Lázaro Cárdenas* (Mexico City: Empresas Editoriales, S.A., 1964).

creating economic independence for Mexicans—specifically, as journalist Francisco Martínez de la Vez states, for the Mexican worker.[24] This led to further opposition from dominant groups and the right wing.[25]

Cárdenas's leftist leanings in government, or *cardenismo*, carried out many of the objectives put forth by the Constitution of 1917 and placed him in a mythicized and romanticized position in Mexican history and popular folklore, much to the dissatisfaction of the middle and upper classes, who had been the prime beneficiaries of Mexico's capitalist growth. Cárdenas placed the working class in the national spotlight, implementing socialist reforms in labor, education, and land use for their benefit. Nora Hamilton notes that preferential treatment shifted from the middle and upper class to the working class, polarizing these groups even more. The Cárdenas government, however, had gone as far as it could in restructuring Mexican society within the existing capitalist constraints, and toward the end of his administration, he lost steam.[26] Many of the new policies and programs suffered a great deal of revenue decline, resulting in economic difficulties, leading many wealthy Mexicans, already fearful of the establishment of a communist state, and foreign capitalists to look elsewhere for lucrative investments.[27] It was in this heated climate of social and economic instability that the Porfiriato was remembered with longing by the insecure upper class.

Porfirio Díaz and the Porfiriato on the Stage and the Silent Screen

Porfirio Díaz was not a stranger to celluloid; in fact, he can be considered Mexico's first national film celebrity. In 1896, the Lumière brothers sent

[24] When Cárdenas became president, sixteen foreign companies controlled 98% of the petroleum industry. See Nora Hamilton, *The Limits to Autonomy: Post-Revolutionary Mexico* (Princeton, NJ: Princeton University Press, 1982), 220–22; and Francisco Martínez de la Vez, "El petroleo: pasión y triunfo de México," *Hoy*, February 24, 1951.

[25] Internationally, Cárdenas fully supported the socialist Republican struggle during the Spanish Civil War (1936–1939), sending aid and materials to the Republicans and granting asylum to those escaping General Francisco Franco's fascism regime, much to the chagrin of more conservative Mexicans who did not want to open the borders to refugees.

[26] Hamilton, *The Limits to Autonomy*, 240.

[27] For more information on the effects of cardenismo, see Enrique Krauze, *El sexenio de Lázaro Cárdenas* (Mexico City: Clío, 2000); Carlos Alvear Acevedo, *Lázaro Cárdenas: El hombre y el mito* (Mexico City: Ediciones Promesa S.A., 1986); Albert L. Michaels, "The Crisis of Cardenismo," *Journal of Latin American Studies* 2, no. 1 (May 1970): 51–79; Roberto Blanco Moheno, *Cardenismo* (Mexico City: Libro Mex Editores, 1963).

two representatives, Claude Ferdinand Bon Bernard and Gabriel Veyre, to Mexico with the cinematographe apparatus and a few samples of actuality films.[28] The Frenchmen received a warm welcome from Chapultepec Castle, where the first screening took place, away from the press and the public and in front of Díaz and a selection of his closest friends. The technology proved to be a great success, initially perceived as a crucial apparatus in the national journey toward progress. Díaz encouraged the Lumière workers to film as much of Mexico as they deemed fit, and subtlety suggested they film him as well. The filming of Díaz was entirely for vanity's sake. The consequences, however, had political advantages: by screening his image across the country, the films gave the Mexican population a chance to see their president for the first time.[29] Silent film scholar Juan Felipe Leal states:

> The reception of the images of Don Porfirio by the Mexican public, screened by the Lumière workers on Plateros, Espíritu Santo, and later, in the city of Guadalajara, confirmed the certainty of the General's judgment: the film exhibition of his image was a privileged way of asserting his power. Cinema would unveil his figure to the most remote places as the Republic failed to do so many times before by means of propaganda. Many met Don Porfirio for the first time thanks to his cinematographic presence.[30]

Those who could afford the admission to a screening site were introduced to the Porfiriato through the moving images of Díaz mounted on a horse in Chapultepec Park, riding a buggy from Chapultepec Castle to the National Palace, walking with his ministers, and enjoying his social Belle Époque.[31] At the outbreak of the Revolution, silent film production documented the varying sides of the armed struggle, and images of the Porfiriato disappeared after Díaz's exile. The last film to capture the dictator's era was *Las fiestas del Centenario* (*The Centennial Celebrations*; 1910), which depicted the lush and expensive festivities of the 1910 centennial.[32]

---

[28] Actuality films are non-fiction films that use real footage of people, events, places, and things. These films are considered the precursors to documentary films.

[29] See Aurelio de los Reyes, *Los orígenes del cine en México (1896–1900)*, 3rd ed. (Mexico City: Fondo de Cultura Económica, 2013), 165–80.

[30] Juan Felipe Leal, Carlos Arturo Flores, and Eduardo Barraza, *Anales del cine en México, 1895–1911; Vol. 2, 1896: El vitascopio y el cinematógrafo en México*, 2nd ed. (Mexico City: D. R. Voyeur, 2006), 47.

[31] Aurelio De los Reyes, *Medio Siglo de Cine Mexicano (1896–1947)* (Mexico City: Editorial Trillas, 1987), 27.

[32] For more information on the Centennial celebrations of 1910, see Rafael Tovar y de Teresa, *El último brindis de Don Porfirio 1910: Los festejos del Centenario* (Mexico City: Santillana Ediciones Generales, S.A. de C.V., 2012).

In addition to cinema, the Porfiriato became a popular backdrop in the teatro de revistas. The stage offered the Mexican public an opportunity to see interpretations of current political and social events in the form of entertainment, and the revistas were a popular practice that focused squarely on political criticism and satire. The revistas, derived from the Spanish zarzuela, consisted of *cuadros,* or scenes, which used burlesque and satire to address contemporary social and political issues, poking fun at governmental officials and the current state of society.[33] In addition to the revistas, other staged genres received ample attention: the upper and middle classes were entertained by the *teatro culto* (cultured theater) of foreign plays, Spanish zarzuelas, and operas, and the working and lower classes were entertained by the *teatro popular,* a theatrical culture influenced by puppet theater, the circus, and other popular staged spectacles.[34]

Although the staged entertainment at the turn of the century often criticized the dictator and his government, it was not until the end of the 1930s that the Porfiriato became a popular and fashionable theatrical backdrop. According to theater scholar John Nomland, the first instance of Porfirian nostalgia appeared in the 1938 one-act revista *En tiempos de don Porfirio* by Carlos Ortega, Pablo Prida, and Francisco Benítez, with music by Federico Ruíz and Manuel Castro Padilla. He states:

> It is a happy and fun revue that contrasts the material aspects of present day civilization with the "good old days." Beneath the luxurious costumes and the good humor, some serious social themes are mentioned. It is interesting that every one of the four plays by Ortega and Prida written during

---

[33] The teatro de revistas was an especially important public spectacle during the Revolution, as developments in the armed struggle and criticism of political and revolutionary leaders was put on the stage. See Leonora Saavedra, "Urban Music in the Mexican Revolution," paper read at the national meeting for the Society for Ethnomusicology, Columbus, OH, 2007; Alejandro Ortiz Bullé Goyri, "Orígenes y desarollo del teatro de revistas en México (1896–1953)," in *Un siglo de teatro en México,* ed. David Olguín (Mexico City: Fondo de Cultura Económica, 2011), 40–53; Jacqueline Avila, "Juxtaposing *teatro de revista* and *cine*: Music in the 1930s *comedia ranchera,*" *Journal of Film Music* 5, nos. 1–2 (2012): 119–24.

[34] For more information on popular theater during the Porfiriato and Revolution, see Susan E. Bryan, "Teatro popular y sociedad durante el Porfiriato," *Historia Mexicana* 33, no. 1 (July–September 1983): 130–69; Armando de María y Campos, *El teatro de género chico en la revolución mexicana* (Mexico City: Biblioteca del Instituto Nacional de Estudios Históricos de la Revolución Mexicana, 1956); Luis Reyes de la Maza, *El teatro en México durante el porfirismo,* vols. *I–III* (Mexico City: Universidad Nacional Autónoma de México, 1968). For more information on the teatro de revista, see the earlier citations, this chapter, and Pablo Dueñas, *Las divas en el teatro de revista mexicano* (Mexico City: Asociación Mexicana de Estudios Fonográficos, 1994); and *El país de las tandas: teatro de revista, 1900–1940* (Mexico City: Museo Nacional de Culturas Populares, 1984).

the thirties ... depicts the same attitude towards the current unhappy situation and a nostalgic fondness for the tranquility of yesteryear.[35]

Labeled the first in a cycle of "revistas de evocación" (evocative revistas), this revista introduced a musical structure that not only helped to solidify the time period but also hinted at nostalgia for a lost era. In his autobiography, Pablo Prida describes the revista's music: "While the whole revista was very enjoyable, it culminated in the final scene in which the numbers from the most successful zarzuelas of yesteryear were performed."[36] Music of the past reinforced this inclination toward nostalgia to a high degree—so much so that these numbers were the primary draw for audiences yearning for those "good old days."

The revista's revival of the Porfiriato led to further installments of the Porfirian past through screenings of *Las fiestas del Centenario* and performances of the following theatrical works with nostalgic titles: *Recordar es vivir* (*Remembering Is Living*; 1938), *Aquellos 35 años* (*Those 35 Years*; 1938), and *Parece que fue Ayer* (*It Feels like It Was Yesterday*; 1938). The Porfirian spectacles premiered at the Teatro Lírico in Mexico City, a 1920–30s hot spot for political theater, and all events were well attended.[37] According to theater scholar and critic Armando de María y Campos, these productions featured the figure of Díaz, but the playwrights took great care in his representation: "The authors had the good sense not to make this character speak, limiting themselves to make him appear, solemn, martial, and, in truth, imposing, at the end of each of the revues."[38] The revistas relied on a simple narrative structure set during the Porfiriato that poked fun at contemporary social and political issues, complemented with musical works—specifically popular zarzuela melodies that evoked the Porfirian soundscape. The film genre built on this successful structure, but with some variation.

---

[35] John Nomland, *Teatro mexicano contemporáneo 1900–1950* (Mexico City: Ediciones del Instituto Nacional de Bellas Artes, Departamento de Literatura, 1967), 159–60.

[36] This review first appeared in the periodical *El Redondel*. Pablo Prida Santacilla, *Y se levanta el telón: Mi vida dentro del teatro* (Mexico City: Ediciones Botas, 1960), 264–65. Pablo Prida also notes that the cast for the revista included María Conesa, Amelia Wilhelmy, Gloria Marín, Joaquín Pardavé, Alfonso Torres, and Fernando Soler, among others.

[37] Armando de María y Campos writes that the Teatro Lírico was very popular for politically themed revues. Famous theater performer Roberto Soto began a season of revistas políticas in 1935 in which Cárdenas's politics inspired many of the skits. See de María y Campos, *El teatro de género chico en la revolución mexicana*, 363–80.

[38] Ibid., 378. De María y Campos also mentions that Don Porfirio was played by David Martínez in all these productions.

The Porfirian Utopia: *En tiempos de don Porfirio* (1939)

> *En tiempos de don Porfirio*: a brilliant depiction of past times, which were the best of times. A masterpiece of Mexican cinema.[39]

Juan Bustillo Oro, a lawyer turned theater and film director and esteemed member of high society, also shared Ortega and Prida's fondness of the Porfirian era. During the late 1930s, Bustillo Oro approached producer Jesús Grovas, from Producciones Grovas, to make a film with a turn-of-the-century atmosphere, specifically the Porfiriato.[40] Grovas adamantly declined the proposal, assuming no one would be interested in the era, but after witnessing the success of the Porfirian revistas in the theater, he finally gave the go ahead in 1939.

In the film version of *En tiempos de don Porfirio*, writer Humberto Gómez Landero and Bustillo Oro spin a complicated and romantic fable centered on the rich pseudo-bohemian gentleman Don Francisco de la Torre (Fernando Soler), described as "a fin-de-siècle gentleman, a rundown, good drinker, unrepentant gambler, womanizer, and a man of invulnerable good humor."[41] Don Francisco misses his wedding owing to a night of card playing and drinking with Don Rodrigo Rodríguez Eje (Joaquín Pardavé) at Orizaba's Gran Casino. When attempting to seek amends from his fiancée Carlota's (Aurora Walker) family the following morning, he is thrown out of the house with the promise he will never see her again. Carlota, pregnant with Don Francisco's child, sails to Paris and marries her uncle in an effort to save her reputation, leaving Don Francisco behind.

Carlota, now a widow, returns to Mexico with her and Don Francisco's daughter Carmen (Marina Tamayo) and the servant Chloe (Dolores Camarillo) just as Porfirio Díaz is inaugurated as president for the second time, in 1884. Chloe seeks out Don Francisco to tell him of their return, and together they devise ways in which Don Francisco can visit his daughter. When Carmen is older, Carlota, wanting Carmen to marry into

---

[39] Advertisement from *Hoy* (1940).

[40] By 1939, Juan Bustillo Oro had worked at Producciones Grovas for some years, making a series of films for the company, including: *Amapola del camino* (*Poppy of the Road*; 1937); *Huapango* (1937); *Las tías de las muchachas* (*The Aunts of Girls*; 1939); *Cada loco con su tema* (*To Each His Own*; 1938) and *Caballo y caballo* (*Horse and Horse*; 1939). See Emilio García Riera, *Historia del cine mexicano* (Mexico City: Consejo Nacional de Fomento Educativo, 1986), 110–11.

[41] Juan Bustillo Oro, *Vida cinematográfica* (Mexico City: Cineteca Nacional, 1984), 181.

a proper family, decides to arrange her marriage to the rich yet ridiculous Don Rodrigo. The problem, however, is that she has fallen in love with Don Francisco's godson Fernando Villanueva (Emilio Tuero), presenting the film's central dilemma. In order to woo and seduce Carmen, Fernando consistently sings waltzes, danzas, and serenades, much to the displeasure and discomfort of Carlota and Don Rodrigo. Through careful and hilarious scheming on the part of Don Francisco and Fernando to break the engagement, Carmen and Fernando eventually become engaged, as do Don Francisco and Carlota. The film ends with the happy couples at last in each other's arms.

As previously mentioned, the cine de añoranza porfiriana is typically not discussed in Mexican film history or criticism, perhaps because the genre does not portray the nationalist representations that other film genres during the 1930s tended to depict, or because the goals of the film were drastically different from others. Coming at the end of the 1930s, the era of the Porfiriato represents the opposite of cardenismo, and in that realization, the cine de añoranza porfiriana stood contrary to the revolutionary melodrama, offering a different sort of escape for audiences, but for a specific type of audience. Both Jorge Ayala Blanco and Jaime Contreras Soto suggest that the genre is the result of the social unease felt by the middle and upper classes during the Cárdenas sexenio, leading into Manuel Ávila Camacho's term in office. Contreras Soto explicitly states:

> It is useful to note that the Cárdenas regime (1934–1940) introduced the cine revolucionario as a subgenre, leading it to the best results. From there, the supporting base of the national film industry arose. For Ávila Camacho, the past situations created by *cardenismo* had to be pacified by means of the now famous return to the past, a time whose calmness could promise not just economic stability, which is assumed, but also—and this was the most important—social stability.[42]

It would be erroneous to imply that the cine de añoranza porfiriana did not exhibit an atmosphere of anxiety owing to social tensions of the period, but Bustillo Oro's fundamental vision was to make a film that specifically showcased the music of that time, stating succinctly: "I imagined a film

---

[42] Jaime Contreras Soto, "El cine de ambiente porfiriano," in *Revista Filmoteca: El cine y la revolución mexicana,* ed. Manuel Gonzáles Casanova (Mexico City: Filmoteca Universidad Nacional Autónoma de México, 1989), 41.

that had an important space for Mexican music for that era."[43] Bustillo Oro collaborated with Castro Padilla and Gómez Landero to select the musical numbers, initially entitling the film project "Melodías de antaño" ("Melodies of Yesteryear"),[44] although Grovas claimed that the era was "deader than the melodies."[45]

But the melodies of the Porfiriato were anything but dead. The musical traditions at the end of nineteenth century included a mixture of stage works by Mexican and European composers and selections from the música de salón tradition. Italian *bel canto*, French grand opera, Spanish and Mexican zarzuelas, and the *género chico* (short lyrical plays in one act) were popular in Mexico during the post-Independence years.[46] Rather than feature large-scale staged works, *En tiempos de don Porfirio* presents lighter and simpler danzas and waltzes, rearranged by German-born film composer Max Urban.[47]

Much like many of the cultural aspects of the Porfiriato already mentioned, the música de salón tradition exhibits foreign influences in compositional technique and form. In her study of Mexican popular music, musicologist Yolanda Moreno Rivas states:

> Other forms of foreign origin found their place in the country, acclimated and transformed following the particular feeling of national composers. Included in this group, in particular, are the dance forms; the polka of Czechoslovakian origin, the Polish mazurka and redova, the Viennese waltz, the schottische or chotís and the gallop.[48]

Mexican composers of the nineteenth century absorbed these forms and transformed the genres to fit their own tastes. Moreno Rivas points to the line dividing the popular music and the *música culta* (cultured music) as tenuous

---

[43] Bustillo Oro, *Vida cinematográfica*, 179.

[44] This title became the subtitle or secondary title for *En tiempos de don Porfirio*.

[45] Bustillo Oro, *Vida cinematográfica*, 180.

[46] For more information on opera in Mexico, see Gloria Carmona, *La música de México: Periodo de la independencia a la revolución (1810 a 1910)*, ed. Julio Estrada (Mexico City: Universidad Nacional Autónoma de México, 1984). See also Armando de María y Campos, *Angela Perlata: Un ruiseñor mexicano* (Mexico City: Ediciones Xochitl, 1944).

[47] Max Urban (1882–1959) began his career in Mexico as a popular composer for revistas and the radio. His popularity grew during the 1930s when he entered the film industry, beginning with the 1933 prostitute melodrama *La mujer del puerto* (*The Woman of the Port*; dir. Arcady Boytler). In *En tiempo de don Porfirio*, Urban arranges many of the piano works for orchestral performance, performed both diegetically and non-diegetically.

[48] Yolanda Moreno Rivas, *Historia de la música popular mexicana* (Mexico City: Editorial Océano de México, 2008), 21.

at best, as composers from all social classes and education composed and/or performed these genres.[49] Waltzes and danzas were especially popular and easy to perform owing to their melodic simplicity and repetitive rhythmic structure. During the Porfiriato, these works were generally performed in the salon or drawing room, the location for controlling the social and private interactions for those in attendance. Musical performance and courtship were inseparable during this period, giving young ladies in particular the opportunity to show off their musical abilities.[50] Although European romantic compositions—specifically character pieces and lied—were also fashionable during the Porfiriato, Bustillo Oro chose to exhibit the Mexican música de salón tradition in his film, providing the necessary period association, or, as Bustillo Oro points out, the appropriate *style*:

> **Vals poético** by Villanueva; **Club Verde** by Campodónico; **Galán incógnito**, by I do not know who, for Joaquín Pardavé; **Adiós** de Carrasco; **Altiva** by Rica and Castellot; **Tristes jardines** by Chucho Martínez; **Serenata mexicana** by Manuel M. Ponce; **Amor** by Villanueva; **Recuerdo** by Alvarado; a fusion of children's playing songs; the theme for the flower offering by little girls to the Virgin Mary and the ditties for "posadas" that occur before Christmas. You hear all of these in the movie and, although all are not rigorously from the nineteenth century, it is in *the appropriate style*.[51]

In order to further execute "the appropriate style," Bustillo Oro, Jesús Corona, and Max Urban incorporated the musical performances in a way that would be considered a "normal" or "natural" part of the environment. To do this, diegetic performances take place in venues meant to reflect the performance practice of the period: large ballrooms, salons, and—a requisite for cinematic romance—below a young lady's balcony. In the film, performances occur in scenes of comedic relief and in scenes of romance, which at times are one in the same.

---

[49] Yolanda Moreno Rivas, "Los estilos nacionalistas en la música culta: aculturación de las formas populares," in *El nacionalismo y el arte mexicano (IX Coloquio de historia del arte)*, ed. Instituto de Investigaciones Estéticas (Mexico City: Universidad Nacional Autónoma de México, 1986), 39.

[50] Ricardo Miranda, "La seducción y sus pautas," *Artes de México: Música de la Independencia a la Revolución* 97 (2010): 16.

[51] Bustillo Oro, *Vida cinematográfica*, 182–83; my emphasis.

The crucial figure for comedic relief is Don Rodrigo Rodríguez Eje, played by the crowd-pleasing theatrical performer Joaquín Pardavé.[52] Pardavé commonly played characters that express their nervousness in awkward ways and are often the butt of jokes, which in *En tiempos de don Porfirio* are brought about in scenes concerning his engagement to Carmen. As a foil, Fernando Villanueva serves as the conduit for romance through his performance of all serenades and waltzes.

The fusion of theatrical comedy and musical performance occurs in an early scene involving Carmen, Don Rodrigo, and Carlota, sitting together in Carlota's salon in an attempt for the couple to get to know each other in the presence of a chaperon. However, they look and act bored, each yawning in turn, comically mickey-moused by muted brass glissandi. Carlota and Don Rodrigo engage in an awkward conversation, which shapes Don Rodrigo as a nervous and rather inelegant sort of fellow, much to the frustration and impatience of Carlota. Reminiscent of theatrical practice, the quick back and forth dialogue between the characters creates a humorous atmosphere as Don Rodrigo consistently misunderstands Carlota's comments and explanations, which end up offending her. The conversation is interrupted by Fernando's sudden whistling, who, in a romantic gesture, waits beneath the balcony outside for Carmen. The whistling elevates Don Rodrigo's nervousness as he desperately tries to ignore it and focuses his attention onto the piano on the other side of the room. To distract from Fernando's persistent and frustrated whistling, Carmen nervously recommends that Don Rodrigo perform a duet with her, offering a natural transition to musical performance. Don Rodrigo's choice is a *soneto* (sonnet), a bouncy poetic song in duple meter entitled "El galán incógnito" ("The Gentleman Incognito"), a popular song from the 1862 zarzuela by the same name written by Ricardo de la Vega, with music by Cristóbal Oudrid. Carmen, at the piano, plays a few measures before Don Rodrigo, who after clearing his throat and coughing, enters:

> One dark night
> an incognito suitor
> crossed the central streets
> and underneath a classic Gothic window
> Tuned his lyre and thus sang:

[52] For more information on the career of Joaquín Pardavé, see Josefina Estrada, *Joaquín Pardavé: El señor del espectáculo*, vols. I–III (Mexico City: Clío, 1996); Jorge Carrasco Vázquez, *Joaquín Pardavé: Un actor vuelto leyenda* (Mexico City: Grupo Editorial Tomo, S.A. de C.V., 2004).

> "Pure lady, with an angelic face
> Who sleeps on white sheets
> Wake up and listen to me
> That in my chants
> You will hear my brief sighs."
> The beautiful sylph heard his songs,
> Snuggled between the sheets,
> And said "Heavens, it is a bat!
> Romantic singer, I will not open for you!"[53]

As Carmen plays the introductory measures on the piano, we in the audience hear, but do not see, an orchestra take over the accompaniment (figure 2.2).

After Don Rodrigo finishes the last copla, the camera abruptly cuts to Fernando, who, waiting impatiently and angrily outside, interjects a copla into Don Rodrigo's song:

> Unknown rival with a squalid voice
> Ridiculous old man that sings over there
> Take your music and leave quickly
> Carmencita is not for you![54]

Here the scene moves into a fantasy realm. Although Fernando is standing outside, below the balcony, he can hear all the music performed as if he were in the same room. There is no spatial difference between the sound in the salon and the sound on the street. Carmen, Don Rodrigo, and Carlota all hear Fernando's aggressive stanza as well. We initially see Fernando intensely singing the first line of the stanza. When he begins the second line, the shot cuts to Carmen and Don Rodrigo listening nervously, then cuts to Carlota as Fernando begins to sing the stanza's third line. By the time he reaches the fourth line, the camera returns to a medium shot of Fernando looking up toward the salon's window, as he cadences dramatically. Fernando perceives Don Rodrigo's song as a threat and rushes to defend Carmen or, rather, to claim what he feels is his. His actions are bold, backed up by the orchestral accompaniment, which continues even when Carmen stops playing,

---

[53] Bustillo Oro, *En tiempos de don Porfirio*, ch. 5.
[54] Ibid.

Figure 2.2 Carmen (Marina Tamayo) and Don Rodrigo (Joaquín Pardavé) performing "El galán incognito" in *En tiempos de don Porfirio* (1939). Screen capture from film.

eliminating any notions that she was in control of the music. Carmen attempts to brush off Fernando's singing and performs the sentimental and lush canción mexicana "Altiva" ("Haughty") by L. de J. Castellot Jr. and A. de Rocca. When she begins to play, the camera cuts to a medium shot of her face throwing glances from the score to the balcony window, suggesting that she is performing the work for Fernando. Fernando, in turn, begins to sing the romantic lyrics set to a habanera rhythm. His sudden entrance causes Carmen to physically stop playing while the off-screen accompaniment continues, encouraging Fernando to likewise carry on:

> If my lips have never heard,
> the simplest phrase of love,
> rather than see me poorly understood
> I muffled the cries from the heart.[55]

[55] Ibid.

Many elements are at work in this scene that relate to character develop-ment, emotive atmosphere, and the realm of fantasy. Despite Carmen's re-quest for a romantic "waltz or danza," Don Rodrigo chooses an old-fashioned soneto that describes a singer intent on serenading his love interest, but she perceives him to be a bat (or, rather, vile thing) and would prefer to stay in her bed rather than listen to his romantic song. The soneto's content and Don Rodrigo's over-the-top gestures—dramatically clearing his throat, plucking an invisible lyre, and nervously laughing when he hears Fernando's copla—emphasize his ridiculousness, positioning Don Rodrigo as antithet-ical to the dreamy Fernando. This performance can be read intertextually as Carmen's own rejection of him as well, as Carmen is visually more enamored of Fernando. After this performance, it becomes clear Don Rodrigo will not be able to win Carmen's heart, and we, as the audience, prefer as much. Fernando, becoming defensive about Carmen, delivers his pithy comeback, then challenges Don Rodrigo's "romantic" performance with a velvety inter-pretation of "Altiva" that acts as an invitation to Carmen's affections.

The sudden aural presence of the orchestra and the lack of spatial depth between Fernando, who is standing below the balcony, and Don Rodrigo and Carmen, who are on the second floor of the house, are another matter. The orchestral accompaniment functions on a border of diegetic and non-diegetic categorizations, creating another cinematic dimension. This transi-tion enters what Robynn J. Stilwell terms the "fantastical gap": the liminal space between what we hear and what we see that falls into the realm of fan-tasy. It is the process of crossing from one part of the geographical sound-scape to another, challenging original notions of film sound taxonomy so that identifying what is the diegetic and the non-diegetic becomes uncertain. This liminal space, Stilwell argues, is "a space of power and transformation, of inversion and the uncanny, of making strange in order to make sense."[56] In this particular scene, orchestral accompaniment in the guise of piano ac-companiment enhances the emotional atmosphere that otherwise would have not been accomplished by piano alone. The orchestral sound becomes a necessity to these performances, heightening the expectations of the musical culture and the social exchanges within the Porfirian salon, negotiating be-tween the musical practices of the past and contemporary times.

---

[56] Robynn J. Stilwell, "The Fantastical Gap Between Diegetic and Nondiegetic," in *Beyond the Soundtrack: Representing Music in Cinema*, ed. Daniel Goldmark, Lawrence Kramer, and Richard Leppert (Berkeley: University of California Press, 2007), 186.

This orchestral sound from the fantastical gap has a persistent presence in the film's musical sequences, further implying that the use of solo piano is not quite enough for the desired effect. This requires a rearrangement of several musical selections and reinterprets música de salón performance practice for the sake of the narrative. The off-screen orchestra operates as a tool of transcendence for the audience and provides necessary emotive elements to scenes, which revolve around love and longing. For example, when Don Francisco discovers Fernando and Carmen's love, he decides that it is up to him to break the engagement between Don Rodrigo and his daughter. As part of his schemes, he invites both Fernando and Don Rodrigo over to discuss "how" Don Rodrigo should win Carmen's affections. Don Francisco and Fernando suggest a serenade for Carmen, but to be performed by Fernando, not Don Rodrigo. Initially, Don Rodrigo proposes an encore performance of "El galán incógnito," but Don Francisco, a self-defined connoisseur of music, prefers the popular danza "Adíos . . . !" ("Goodbye . . . !") by Alfredo Carrasco. The light melody in A major with descending fourths makes frequent appearances in the Urban's underscoring when Carmen and Don Francisco are together, sharing tender and affectionate moments. During the performance, the rich orchestral sound accompanies Fernando while Don Francisco stares at a photograph of Carmen with regret and sadness over the years lost. The lyrics speak to Don Francisco's deep, albeit unspoken desire to admit to Carmen that he is her father: "Your eyes / are the light of my love."[57] Fernando plays on an upright piano, but when the camera focuses on Don Francisco, the orchestral sound sweeps in and reinforces Don Francisco's state of melancholy.

Throughout the film, Don Francisco devises several schemes for separating Carmen and Don Rodrigo, including getting Don Rodrigo drunk in order to miss his own wedding. Don Francisco also successfully convinces Don Rodrigo that when he was drunk, he insulted, slapped, and challenged Fernando to a duel. Don Rodrigo arrives at the duel site, pistol in hand, but when the moment presents itself, he flees back to his estate, tail between his legs, thus terminating the engagement with Carmen. After Don Rodrigo's abrupt disappearance, Don Francisco, Fernando, Carlota, and Carmen are reunited in the field. Here, Fernando and Carmen declare their love for each other in front of Carlota. Moved, Don Francisco proposes again to Carlota, hoping to marry her not so

[57] Mario Kuri-Aldana and Vicente Mendoza Martínez, *Cancionero popular mexicano*, 2nd ed. (Mexico City: Consejo Nacional de la Cultura y las Artes, 2001), 1:98–99.

much for love as so that Carmen can call him father in front of others respect-
fully and with dignity. The film ends with Don Francisco and Carlota walking
away arm and arm, finally contented with the turn of events. The lingering
moral of the film is that love, money, and status will prevail.

The musical performances in *En tiempos de don Porfirio* represent the crucial position the repertoire played in the construction of a Porfirian atmosphere. The majority of the performances take place in the salon or parlor,
preserving the intimate qualities and functions of the space. But unlike the
standard practice of women performing in the salon, the film features the
performances of men—specifically Fernando Villanueva and Don Rodrigo,
in pursuit of Carmen's affections. The focus on the men comes as no coinci-
dence. Sergio de la Mora notes that Mexican cinema constructed "nationalist
models of manhood and womanhood, a gendered patriotic affect" during
this period.[58] Archetypes of the male, especially prominent in the 1930s revolutionary melodrama and the musical comedia ranchera, became models
of heroism, while women were consistently placed on the sidelines. While
at times an active performer, Carmen's role in the film doubles as receiver/
audience, as the off-screen orchestra typically takes over her piano accompaniment. Although Carmen is seemingly cast to the margins by the camera's
gaze, she is, however, the intended audience, as the performances are meant
to seduce (or persuade) her in a particular way, through either romantic love
(as is the case with Fernando and Don Rodrigo) or paternal love (with Don
Pancho). While it would appear that the men maintain the stronger power
dynamic in these musical performances, it is Carmen's presence, as the figure
of desire, that provides the impetus for these performances.

Much like the revistas de evocación, *En tiempo de don Porfirio* was a grand
success with critics and audiences, breaking box office records its first week.
Grovas's initial hypothesis that the period was "deader than the music," and
that the film would be a flop at the box office, was in fact not accurate. A critic
from *La Prensa* states:

The immortal music, the brilliant wit and perfumed romanticism of those
years are revived on screen with exquisite taste and pleasant inspiration.
This film opens a bright path for Mexican cinema.[59]

---

[58] Sergio de la Mora, *Cinemachismo: Masculinities and Sexuality in Mexican Cinema* (Austin:
University of Texas Press, 2006), 143.
[59] "Cartel del Teatro Alameda," *La Prensa*, April 3, 1940.

A luminous path, indeed. Bustillo Oro's film premiered on April 4, 1940, at the beautiful Teatro Alameda in Mexico City to a full house.[60] The nostalgic film about the Porfirian upper classes was also intended and initially screened for the small, present-day insecure upper classes. Emilio García Riera states,

> The great welcoming of this film by an audience that paid two pesos a seat for three weeks of screening at the Alameda (a fact without precedents at this time) established the film as the most ambitious and successful work by Bustillo Oro up to that point. The invocation of Don Porfirio in the title (who only appears in the film as a simple reference to the era and as a "sticky mess" imposed on Bustillo by the producer Grovas) favorably predisposed an entire middle class, eager to find nostalgic refuge at the movies.[61]

After its three-week run at the Teatro Alameda, the film moved to the more affordable and popular cine Encanto, which catered to the working classes.[62] Advertisements and articles about the film filled the pages of *El Universal* and *Cinema Reporter*, more so than any other film from the period. Full-page ads were taken, providing letters from the spectators, expressing their delight and enthusiasm for the film. Surprisingly, President Cárdenas also sent a letter to Producciones Grovas, congratulating the company on elevating the artistic prestige of the country.[63]

En tiempo de don Porfirio initiated a wave of cultural activity that attempted to capture the nostalgia of the Porfiriato. At the time of the film's premiere, the popular company Cerveceria Cuauhtémoc S.A. sponsored the Fiesta de Traje (Costume Party) in Chapultepec Park. The festivities included a performance of *música de ayer* (yesterday's music) by XEW's Juan Garrido and his orchestra, the revista *¡Ay, qué tiempos señor don Simón!* (*Oh, What Times Don Simón!*) starring Joaquín Pardavé and Amelia Wilhelmy,[64] a parade of Porfirian-era fashion, a performance of musical selections from *En tiempos de don Porfirio* by Emilio Tuero, and as the grand finale, cancan dancers: "The

---

[60] Francisco H. Alfaro and Alejandra Ochoa state that the theater is supposed to be a simulacrum of a city street with fashioned streetlights and wooden furniture. Because of the design, the theater has been deemed as having nationalist qualities. Upper-class theaters tended to be elaborately decorated according to a theme. See Francisco H. Alfaro and Alejandra Ochoa, *La república de los cines* (Mexico City: Clío, 1998), 36–37.

[61] Emilio García Riera, *Historia documental del cine mexicano*, (Guadalajara: Universidad de Guadalajara, 1993), 2:130.

[62] "*En tiempos de don Porfirio,* un legítimo triunfo," *Cinema Reporter*, February 9, 1940.

[63] "Homenaje a la gran película mexicana *En tiempos de don Porfirio,*" *El Universal*, April 6, 1940.

[64] This would later become a film directed by Julio Bracho.

most sensational and rowdy dance of Paris of the last century."[65] In conjunction with the festival, *El Universal Ilustrado* dedicated several articles to a reexamination of Díaz and his time as dictator. Writer Alfonso Junco traces Díaz's rise to power and his goals for modernization, stating that Díaz's main goal was "to establish and solidify channels for work and peace." His actions as the nation's leader, therefore, should not be exaggerated. He ends his two-part article with a glowing assessment of the dictator:

> The errors and defects of the Porfirian regime are for us a warning and a lesson. The exceptional, honest and patriotic man who organized peace, order, and material grandeur in Mexico, who held in his hand, for three decades, the enthusiasm of his fellow countrymen, will inconvertibly maintain an illustrious position in our history. Vain is anyone who wants to deify him; unjust is anyone who speaks of him without respect.[66]

Porfirian nostalgia became a national box office success and initiated a trend that continued—and thrived—during the next presidential administration.

México de mis inventos: The Porfiriato of the 1940s

Directly following Cárdenas was the sexenio of Manuel Ávila Camacho (1940–1946), who opposed the leftist currents of cardenismo and adopted a more conservative stance that catered to the "neglected" middle classes. Ávila Camacho boasted military experience and gradually ascended the ranks. Although he fought in the Revolution, the reforms that resulted from the armed struggle did not enter his campaign. When asked about his beliefs, Ávila Camacho responded "soy creyente" ("I am a believer"), bringing the Catholic Church back in full force to the social and political sphere and providing a new direction for Mexican leaders in the post-Revolutionary years: "Throughout his ruling, his government continued to support and subsidize religious activities that past presidents would have opposed."[67] Once in office, Ávila Camacho was eager to introduce new programs while filtering out the old, mirroring the growing anti-communist sentiment of the middle

---

[65] Advertisements for "Fiesta de Traje," *El Universal*, Espectáculos, April 14, 1940.
[66] Alfonso Junco, "Don Porfirio y su Obra," *El Universal*, April 13, 1940.
[67] Stephen R. Niblo, *México en los cuarenta: Modernidad y corrupción* (Mexico City: Editorial Océano de México, 2008), 96.

and upper classes. This new conservatism—labeled *avilacamachismo*—slowed down land distribution, made changes in the educational programs, and promoted conservative philosophies and leadership in the unions. The radical social reforms of the Revolution and of cardenismo were replaced with moderate capitalism, featuring a focus on industrialization and modernization. The middle class increased in size and power, and became the favored class over the lower-class laborers and farmers, once again leading to a widening economic gap between the social classes.[68] Above all, Ávila Camacho advocated for family, religion, and national culture, rejecting communism and class struggle.[69]

The Mexican film industry benefited from this new conservatism and concentration on capitalist enterprises. Because of the upsurge in industrialization, which led to a population boom, urban-based films increased from 57% from 1937 to 1940 to 76% by 1941, whereas films set in the rural countryside decreased from 43% in 1940 to 24% by 1941.[70] Also on the rise were historical films specifically based on Mexican history, which included the Porfirian films. National history became a central cinematic milieu, serving as smokescreens that either glorified the filmed period or criticized contemporary society. One particular change was the role of women in Mexican society. When Mexico entered World War II in 1942,[71] women entered the workforce, and while ávilacamachismo attempted to preserve conservative strongholds on the position of women, the modernization brought about by the period opened new avenues for women that had previously been closed.

Cinema was one space in which these new roles were questioned and criticized. *En tiempos de don Porfirio* initiated a specific narrative that focused on romance, comedy, and to a lesser extent, social decorum and morality. Propriety drove Carlota to marry her uncle in order to hide her illegitimate

---

[68] Virginia B. Derr, "The Rise of the Middle-Class Tradition in Mexican Art," *Journal of Inter-American Studies* 3, no. 3 (1961): 388.

[69] Knight, "The Rise and Fall of Cardenismo," 298–302.

[70] Emilio García Riera, *Breve Historia del cine mexicano: Primer siglo, 1897–1997* (Mexico City: Instituto Mexicano de Cinematografía, 1998), 124.

[71] On May 22, 1942, Ávila Camacho declared war on the Axis powers after German submarines attacked two of Mexico's oil tankers in the Gulf of Mexico. Mexico's joining the war improved relations with the United States, and the Mexican film industry benefited tremendously from the alliance. The United States sent money, film stock, and equipment to aid the developing industry, which helped further Mexico's position as the leading Spanish-language film industry during the 1940s. This is discussed more in chapter 4. For more information on the relationship between the United States and the Mexican film industry during the war, see Francisco Peredo Castro, *Cine y propaganda para Latinoamérica: México y Estados Unidos en la encrucijada de los años cuarenta*, 2nd ed. (Mexico City: Universidad Nacional Autónoma de México, 2011.).

child and her need to solidify a proper marriage for Carmen. Propriety, however, is given momentary attention in comparison to Don Francisco's antics with Don Rodrigo, and Fernando's swoony waltzes and serenades. Morality, decency, and social codes, however, become central concerns in the 1940s Porfirian utopia.

Musically speaking, the Porfiriato of the 1940s moved away from the simple and sentimental waltzes and danzas from Bustillo Oro's construction and engaged with more elaborate theatrical spectacles. Musical excerpts and performances were selected to exploit the Porfirian conceptions of morality and decency, which were resurrected and called into question owing to Ávila Camacho's conservatism. In the cine de añoranza porfiriana of the 1940s, this exploitation is exhibited in excerpts from zarzuelas, género chico, and revistas—entertainment within the entertainment that featured cancan dancers, choreographed communal dances, and songs with risqué and suggestive lyrics. These entertainments served as conduits for evoking lasciviousness, immorality, and indecency in a society that considers these behaviors taboo.

Building on the buzz of *En tiempos de don Porfirio*, director Julio Bracho (1909–1978) released *¡Ay, qué tiempos señor don Simón!* in 1941, which borrowed several narrative elements from Bustillo Oro's successful script, but with some variation.[72] *¡Ay, qué tiempos señor don Simón!* is a romantic comedy about the comic misunderstandings of the widow Inés (Mapy Cortés), her new soldier love interest Miguel (Arturo de Córdova), and the socially important yet slightly unrefined Don Simón (Joaquín Pardavé, reprising his role from the revista). The conflict occurs when Inés has suspicions of Miguel's fidelity. Inés and her friend Beatriz (Anita Blanch) sneak into a "gentlemen only" theater and discover that he is romantically involved with the famous *tiple* (soprano or female chorus line singer) Coco Anchondo. Inés, distraught, decides to end her relationship with Miguel.

As a consequence of her indiscretion of entering a "gentlemen only" theater, the Liga de Defensores de las Buenas Costumbres (League for the Defense of Good Customs) decides to throw her out of their elite organization. Don Simón, the president of the league, is, however, smitten with Inés and asks for her hand in marriage at a social soirée, which Inés considers but only to make ex-lover Miguel jealous. Threatened with losing Inés, Miguel

---

[72] For more information on Julio Bracho, see Jesús Ibarra, *Los Bracho: Tres generaciones de cine mexicano* (Mexico City: Universidad Nacional Autónoma de México, 2006).

makes several attempts to win her back, ultimately challenging Don Simón to a gentlemen's duel. Through a series of rather comical and absurd obstacles, the film ends with Inés and Miguel happily back in each other's arms and rejoicing in the revelation that Miguel is Don Simón's lost son.

The film's major performances take place at the theater. In the opening sequence, Inés and Beatriz ride to the Teatro los Héroes in a carriage, and an extreme close-up of the theater's playbill shows the list of varieties: "The indulgent tiple Coco Anchodo and 30 chorus girls in Los Tiempos Actuales, a spectacle for gentlemen only."[73] After causing a scandal amid the confused male workers at the theater, Inés and Beatriz sit in a box and watch the revue, on the lookout for Miguel. On stage is a chorus line of cancan dancers performing as the male audience eagerly devours them with their eyes (figure 2.3). The film's cinematographer, the distinguished Gabriel Figueroa, takes every liberty with camera positions and angles to capture the provocative and suggestive movements of the dancers to the fast and rhythmic music. He utilizes extreme close-ups and middle shots of the petticoats, white ruffled bloomers, garters, and black stockings of the dancers, who are high kicking and circling their shapely calves in the air.[74] The more daring shots are from an angle down stage looking up, as if sitting in the front row, allowing the onscreen (and off-screen) spectator to see the contours of the thighs and the extent to which the dancers extend their legs. Capturing the dancers from this particular angle also provides the spectator with momentary glimpses of the women's crotches, daintily covered by the embellished undergarments. The images are quite playful, shocking, and enticing for the male audience, which demands an encore performance.

These provocative sequences feature a quotation from Jacques Offenbach's famous cancan gallop from the operetta *Orphée aux enfers* (*Orpheus in the Underworld*) and an arrangement that also features a rather coquettish and popular Porfirian song entitled "Algo más también" ("Something Else as Well") detailing secrets that are much too naughty to repeat:[75]

[73] Julio Bracho, dir., *¡Ay, qué tiempos señor don Simón!*, DVD, ch. 1 (1941; México City: Televisa S.A. de C.V., 2008).

[74] The high kick in cancan dancing is known as a *battement*. The midair circular movement of the calf is known as the *rond de jambe*. The *port d'armes* requires the dancer to turn on one leg while holding the other vertically by the ankle. Cartwheels are also a popular movement in the tradition. For more information on the cancan, see Arthur Moss, *Cancan and Barcarolle: The Life and Times of Jacques Offenbach* (Westport, CT: Greenwood, 1975); and David Price, *Cancan!* (London: Cygnus Arts, 1998).

[75] Armando de María y Campos notes that this song was especially popular in 1907. See *El teatro de género chico en la revolución mexicana*, 378.

> If your boyfriend is deceiving you,
> avenge yourself!
> Wax up his mustache
> when he is sleeping.
> And there is something more
> That is difficult to say
> And there is something more
> That you cannot repeat.[76]

The song speaks and even foreshadows Inés's situation. Her motive for entering the theater is to discover if Miguel is cheating on her with one of the dancers. She spies him from her box seat, ogling Coco and, from their secret looks, knows of the indiscretion. Her suspicions are confirmed when she sees Miguel standing in the wings of the stage, waiting for Coco to finish her number. They share a passionate kiss and Inés, mortified, leaves the theater promptly and plots her revenge

The cancan scene exhibits discrepancies in Porfirian social codes particularly in regard to gender roles. Already a scandalous dance in its homeland of France, the cancan in Mexico becomes a site of sexual indulgence and cosmopolitanism, and its presence in the film functions as an escapist and satirical response to the conservatism and ridged social norms that permeated Porfirian society, and by extension the conservative Ávila Camacho sexenio. It is also a terrific moment in the film to display social and cultural contradictions and hypocrisies. As Inés and Beatriz enter the Teatro los Héroes, they are immediately recognized by the passing Méndez sisters, Caritina Méndez (Consuelo Guerrero de Luna) and Adelaida Méndez (Dolores Camarillo), elite members of the League for the Defense of Good Customs and strangely dressed in identical clothes. Upon seeing the two women walk into the theater, they whisper disapprovingly to each other and agree that they will bring up this lapse of judgment at the league's next meeting, faulting the women for having the audacity to enter a private space for males, even though that space is deemed suitable for dances considered indecent and scandalous. When Inés and Beatriz are inside the theater, Beatrice worries about being caught by the league, but Inés does not share her concern because she spots the president of the league, Don Simón, staring

---

[76] Bracho, *¡Ay, qué tiempos señor don Simón!*, ch. 1. I would like to give special thanks to Jesús Ibarra for helping me translate these lyrics.

Figure 2.3 Cancan with tiples, in *¡Ay, qué tiempos señor don Simón!* (1941). Screen capture from film.

greedily through his binoculars at the dancers on stage. Through a cross cut, it is clear that Don Simón has fixed his binoculars on Coco and her exposed lower half. This scene unveils the contradictory standards implemented by men and women of "good society."

The popularity of the cancan and the development of "men's only" entertainment establishments were two of the consequences from Mexico's transition into modernization. As examined in chapter 1, the Porfiriato's currents of rapid modernization gave rise to sexual commerce and special locations for this practice. The growth of brothels and other venues of entertainment during the Porfiriato conflicted with Catholic notions of moral transgression. Women of assumed proper upbringing, however, did not move in these circles, which explained why Inés was frowned upon after entering the men-only theater. The theaters did not strictly operate as brothels but, rather, the "gentlemen only" performance in the film addresses and reveals the sexual mores and social taboos of the period. Similar to the rumbera in the cabaretera genre, the exploitation of women envisaged through the cancan in the film takes the place of lascivious behavior in the brothel. According to dance scholar Maya Ramos Smith, the cancan was based on spontaneity and its scandalousness was "characterized by complete freedom of inventive choreography, extroverted attitude, exhibitionism, eroticism."[77] Sexual promiscuity is strongly implied not only by the suggestive cancan dancing but also in Miguel's actions with the dancer Coco. As she backs away, moving into the wings of the stage, he seductively kisses her exposed shoulder before kissing her fully on the mouth. Sex is insinuated, and this is enough to raise red flags of impropriety. But it is not the indiscretion of Miguel or even the wolf-like leering of Don Simón that is scrutinized with dissatisfaction; it is Inés's behavior for daring to venture into a male entertainment space that receives judgment and criticism.

As the champions of proper and respectable social mores, the League of the Defense of Good Customs mirrors the Catholic Church–driven Liga de la decencia mentioned in chapter 1. Headed by first lady Soledad Orozco de Ávila Camacho in the 1940s, the league reached the peak of its influence during the Ávila Camacho sexenio, intending to revive conservative Catholic values. Their good deeds included covering up nude statues and censorship of songs they viewed to be erotic or indecent.[78] In terms of cinema, the league was inspired by the 1936 *Vigilanti Cura*, the Vatican's official statement on the burgeoning film industry. The Vatican banned kissing, semi-nudity, and any hints of erotic behavior, believing that cinema was a tool for education and should be used for moral means.[79]

The entertainment within the entertainment in the film moves away from the sugary sentimentality conveyed in Bustillo Oro's cinematic interpretation. Portrayed in the same utopian atmosphere as its predecessor and exhibiting that upper-class nostalgia, *¡Ay, qué tiempos señor don Simón!* suggests, and even promotes, a sense of artificiality for the period. Rather than relying on música de salón for its goals, the film features

---

[77] Maya Ramos Smith, *Teatro musical y danza en el México de la belle époque (1867–1910)* (México City: Universidad Autónoma Metropolitana y Grupo Editorial Gaceta, 1995), 32. For more information on the cancan in Mexico, see Luis Reyes de la Maza, *Circo, maroma y teatro, 1819–1910* (Mexico City: Universidad Nacional Autónoma de México, 1985); and Anna Ochs, "Opera in Contention: Social Conflict in Late Nineteenth Century Mexico City," PhD diss., University of North Carolina, 2011, pp. 164–76.

[78] This included several songs by Agustín Lara.

[79] Included on the Vatican's censor list was Walt Disney's animated feature *Snow White and the Seven Dwarfs* (1937). The Church believed it indecent and immoral that a young woman should live in household with seven men. See Jesús Flores y Escalante, "La Liga de la Decencia," *Relatos e Historias en México* 1, no. 11 (2009): 71–76.

staged spectacles and conveys a sense of the ridiculous, which is exploited by Pardavé's Don Simón. The final confrontation between Inés, Miguel, and Don Simón takes place at the theater during three featured sainetes:[80] *La golondrina* (*The Swallow*), *Abre tus alas* (*Spread Your Wings*), and *El mundo comedia es* (*The Comedy World Is*). In attempting to thwart Miguel, Don Simón, dressed in an absurd disguise of an oversized suit and fake beard, wanders on stage by accident and is forced to lip-sync the last act of the sainete, reinterpreting a dramatic moment featuring a duel into a comedic one, and in a sense poking fun at the ridiculousness of not just the situation but the Porfiriato as well.[81]

The inclusion of Porfirian stage works continued in *México de mis recuerdos* (*Mexico of My Memories*; 1944, dir. Juan Bustillo Oro). Now following Bracho's lead, Bustillo Oro focuses on social etiquette and the impropriety of women, but also frames the Porfiriato using historical references. True to nostalgic form, *México de mis recuerdos* begins as a flashback with a voiceover narrative. These early moments capture present-day Mexico City, full of traffic, crowds on the sidewalk, and street noises. The narrator disappointingly describes this Mexico, which is perhaps 1944, as modern with new buildings and congested and loud streets: "No es el México de viejos . . . el México de mis recuerdos" ("This is not the old Mexico . . . the Mexico that I remember").[82] In a scene fade, the film transports back to the Porfiriato, visually depicted in the Alameda, the Teatro Principal, and the beautiful Jockey Club. Instead of the modernized sounds of congestion, the nostalgic sounds of the "pregones populares de la época" ("popular street cries of the era") are heard, sung by a variety of street vendors, offering the first yet brief glimpse of the working class in a film set during the Porfiriato.

The initial catalyst in *México de mis recuerdos* is a waltz. Upon hearing the waltz "Carmen" at a ball, Don Porfirio (Antonio R. Frausto, who is reprising his role from *En tiempos de don Porfirio*) and his wife Doña Carmen (Virigina Zurí) become enamored with the music and must know the composer. They turn to a passing soldier for information, who explains that the waltz, popular in Mexico, is named after the president's wife and composed by Jesús Flores (also popularly known as Don Chucho, played by Fernando Soler),

---

[80]   A sainete is a comic play in one act that features music and skits.

[81]   Contreras Soto, "El cine de ambiente porfiriano," 43–44.

[82]   Juan Bustillo Oro, dir., *México de mis recuerdos*, DVD, ch. 1 (1944; Mexico City: Zima Entertainment, 2008).

much to Díaz's surprise and contentment; he knows Chucho Flores from "way back when."[83] Wanting to thank Flores for a beautiful waltz, Díaz asks his cultural secretary Susanito Peñafiel y Somellera (Joaquín Pardavé) to track down Flores and give him a piano.

Here, the neglected component of the cine de añoranza porfiriana, Porfirio Díaz, becomes visible. As previously mentioned, the figure of Díaz played relatively small and insignificant roles in the revistas, typically portrayed as a simple and "imposing" man. In *En tiempos de don Porfirio*, his small appearance serves as nothing more than a transition point in the narrative, and in *¡Ay, qué tiempos señor don Simón!* he does not make an appearance at all. In 1944, however, Bustillo Oro revived Díaz's image stating, "Don Porfirio was an inseparable part of the ambient background. That is how I received him impartially. I do not exalt him; I simply used him. And I used him as a legitimate figure of comedy."[84] Don Porfirio's role, however, surpasses the role of comedy. Bustillo Oro did not want to exalt Díaz, but Díaz's role and his actions construct him as the principal figure of moral order in the film. His actions and decisions sway the people around him to his way of thinking. He is able to forgive any indiscretion. (This point will be discussed later.)

Although at the outset the film focused on Don Chucho and his musical talents, *México de mis recuerdos* actually concentrates on two members of the upper class as they struggle with societal expectations, familial obligations, and their own sexual desire: Rosario Medina, a high-society orphan (Sofía Álvarez), and Pablo Flores (Luis Aldás), a proud Porfirian gentleman with proclivities for drinking and womanizing (and who is also Don Chucho's son—although this fact is kept from Pablo for much of the film). Several different parties attempt to throw them together: Pablo's conservative spinster aunts—Gertrudis (Mimí Derba), Cuquita (María Luisa Serrano), and Blandina (Conchita Arcos)—as well as Don Chucho, and Susanito. Integral to Rosario and Pablo's coupling are musical performances in two prominent spaces: the salon—much like *En tiempos de don Porfirio*—and the theatrical stage, each of which is saturated with specific social codes that the music and the performances exploit. Also essential is that the coupling—and the film—relies on the performances of women.

---

[83] The waltz is entitled "Carmen" and is dedicated to Porfirio Díaz's wife Carmen Romero, but is composed by Juventino Rosas (1868–1894). Bustillo Oro places an intertitle at the film's beginning stating that although Rosas composed the waltz, for the purposes of the film, the character Jesús Flores will be the composer of the work.

[84] Bustillo Oro, *Vida cinematográfica*, 214.

Although Rosario is the intended match for Pablo and is described by the aunts as a "moral, decent, and Christian young woman," Pablo has no interest in her, preferring instead to cast his attention onto the tiples performing in the revistas and the zarzuelas. Despite his wanton tendencies, the aunts are convinced that Rosario can make a gentleman of him with patience, careful attention, and her musical talent. Typical for a young woman in elite society, Rosario has been educated in piano and voice, and utilizes her abilities to entertain in the salon. It is here that we are introduced to Rosario and Pablo, hosted by Pablo's aunts, who represent proper Porfirian moral and social order.

Despite Rosario's efforts, the salon scene begins as an anti-courtship scene, as Pablo remains indifferent to Rosario's performance. She begins by playing the challenging *Vals capricho* by Ricardo Castro, a complicated and technically challenging waltz that makes use of the full register of the keyboard. Rosario, however, stops abruptly as Pablo visibly ignores her. Undeterred, Rosario makes another musical attempt. Knowing that he enjoys zarzuelas, Rosario performs the romanza "Al espejo al salir me miré" ("In the Mirror, upon Leaving, I Gazed at Myself"), from the Spanish zarzuela *La viejecita* (*The Little, Old Woman*) by Manuel Fernández Caballero. In "Al espejo al salir me miré," the zarzuela's alcoholic protagonist, Carlos, who is really a man dressed as an older woman, enters a ball, where many are appalled to see "her" owing to "her" age and appearance. He dons the disguise in order to see his ladylove without confronting her disapproving family, who view him as a good-for-nothing. In order to be in character, Rosario dresses up like an old woman with glasses, hunched over a cane, shaking and coughing while singing a romance about the old lady's past love affairs, as Pablo watches in growing frustration (figure 2.4). The performance is confined to the intimacy of the salon, with the piano as the sole accompaniment, but as Rosario sings, the off-camera orchestra magically enters, accentuating the theatrical quality of the performance and transitioning into a realm of fantasy: [85]

> I looked at myself in the mirror before I left,
> And asked the mirror for advice,
> And the mirror told me: "Yes, go.
> If you enjoy yourself, it is good for you."[86]

[85] Miranda states that music from the theater and opera were also altered for the piano in the form of transcriptions and fantasies. See Miranda, "La seducción y sus pautas," 21.

[86] Bustillo Oro, *México de mis recuerdos*, ch. 4.

Figure 2.4 Rosario (Sofía Álvarez) attempts to seduce by singing the romanza "Al espejo al salir me miré," in *México de mis recuerdos* (1944). Screen capture from film.

This scene paints an unattractive portrait of Pablo, who is visually bored and annoyed, and it contrasts dramatically to the romantic Fernando in *En tiempo de don Porfirio*; Pablo does not contribute any music, or any creative energy, to the romantic plot. The scene comments more on Rosario and the period's social position of music and musical performance. After her performance, the aunts express their delight and press Rosario to name the work. When they learn that it is from a Spanish zarzuela, their initial enthusiasm disappears, replaced by horrified alarm. Although described by Rosario as "a very pretty and very moral zarzuela," Gertrudis, ironically played by the prominent zarzuela and film actress Mimí Derba, sternly declares: "there are no moral zarzuelas."[87] Spanish zarzuelas were highly popular and well

[87] Mimí Derba's role is intended to be comical in this film because she was a well-recognized diva from the *revista mexicana*. Derba began her career in theater starring in zarzuelas during the turn of the century, wanting to follow in the steps of Virgina Fábregas and Esperanza Iris. She began as a second tiple for a zarzuela company before making her professional debut at the Teatro Lírico in the zarzuela by Carlos Arniches, *El cabo primero* (*The End First*). She later joined the Compañía Teatral Mexicana and performed in the revista *Las musas del país* (*The Muses of the Country*), by

attended during the Porfiriato, specifically those conveying themes of love, romance, and social misunderstandings, yet they often contained double meanings that, although enjoyed by the public, were regarded as lowbrow.[88] Performers, although held in high esteem by the public, were not considered moral or descent, particularly those performing in the revistas and zarzuelas de género chico.[89] Because the Porfirian upper classes sought to ascend the social and economic ladder, performing in theater was viewed as a social faux pas. Despite her efforts, Rosario's musical selection and her performance succeed in bringing her down socially in the eyes of Porfirian conservatives.

After the salon scene, the musical setting switches to the stage. The film's central theatrical location is the Teatro Principal,[90] the most prominent theater during the end of the Porfiriato and the theater most frequented by the Mexican elite. Run by the famous Hermanas Moriones, the Teatro Principal was deemed responsible for creating an erudite public with Spanish zarzuelas mainly performed by Spanish companies. Pablo Dueñas notes that national artists were accepted, but Mexican works were "highly supervised" because of the hesitancy to include elements of vernacular culture, deemed to be in questionable taste.[91]

José F. Elizondo. Derba eventually found her way into the silent cinema, becoming an important figure in Mexico's early studio Azteca Films. Her debut in sound film was in 1931 as Doña Elvira in Antonio Moreno's *Santa*. For more information on Mimí Derba, see Ángel Miguel, *Mimí Derba* (Mexico City: Filmoteca Universidad Nacional Autónoma de México, 2000). See also Armando de María y Campos, *Frivolerías* (Mexico City: Imprenta Nacional, 1919); Manuel Haro, "Teatros," *La Semana Ilustrada*, July 3, 1912; Diego de Miranda, "La semana teatral," *Novedades*, November 27, 1912; Armando de María y Campos, "Adiós de Mimí Derba," *Hoy*, July 9, 1938.

[88]   The zarzuela structure leads to the development of the *género chico*, which takes the model of the larger zarzuela, but condenses it into one act. See Moreno Rivas, *Historia de la música popular mexicana*, 56.

[89]   *Zarzuelas de género grande* (longer zarzuelas) were moral and conservative while the zarzuelas de género chico were more popular in nature. Also, zarzuelas performed in the afternoon and at matinee times were more suitable for women and children versus evening performances, which became more sexual and risqué. For more information on zarzuelas, see Emilio García Carretero, *Historia del Teatro de la zarzuela de Madrid* (Madrid: Fundación de la Zarzuela Española, 2003–2005); Christopher Webber, *The Zarzuela Companion* (Lanham, MD: Scarecrow, 2002); Janet L. Sturman, *Zarzuela: Spanish Operetta, American Stage* (Urbana: University of Illinois Press, 2000); For information on the Cuban zarzuela, see Susan Thomas, *Cuban Zarzuela: Performing Race and Gender on Havana's Lyric Stage* (Urbana: University of Illinois Press, 2009).

[90]   At the turn of the century, the Teatro Principal was one the most important theater featuring prominent zarzuelas and operettas. Other theaters include Teatro Lírico, Arbeu, Virginia Fábregas, Esperanza Iris, and Renacimiento. Owners Genara and Romualda Moriones inherited the Teatro Principal after their husbands passed away. Their new ownership inaugurated an era of creativity and explorations of new theatrical forms. The Principal became a central space for performances of the género chico. For more information on the Teatro Principal, see Manuel Mañón, *Historia de Teatro Principal de México* (Mexico City: Editorial Cultura, 2009 [1932]); Haro, "Teatro," *La Semana Ilustrada*, 1912; Armando de María y Campos, *Las Tandas del Principal* (Mexico City: Editorial Diana, 1989); Gabriela Pulido Llano, "Empresarias y tandas," *Bicentenario* 2, no. 6 (2009): 14–21.

[91]   Dueñas, *Las divas en el teatro de revista mexicano*, 45.

One work that broke with the Spanish influence was the revista *Chin Chun Chan*, written by Rafael Medina and José F. Elizondo, with music by Luis G. Jordá.[92] The revista is about mistaken identity in which a fed-up husband disguises himself in order to escape his wife, only to be confused for a Chinese dignitary at a lush hotel. *México de mis recuerdos* takes the grand premiere of *Chin Chun Chan* at the Teatro Principal—April 9, 1904—as a jumping-off point to expose Pablo's fantasies of sexual desire. After leaving his aunt's parlor, Pablo, Don Chucho, and Susanito attend the premiere performance at the Teatro Principal, where Pablo sees the object of his affection: the tiple Adelina Roca (Tana Devodier). This scene provides the film's first on-stage performance: the telephone excerpt from the revista's third section of scene 3.[93] This sequence features Adelina and the chorus describing the new technology of the telephone. They detail the electric currents felt by members of the opposite sex when communicating with each other through the "pushing of a button," a metaphor for describing the attraction (or electric current) felt when touching someone you desire. The lyrics, singing, and dancing are suggestive, using the telephone, which—imitating the costuming from the 1904 production—is strangely attached to the chorus's torso and serves as a conduit for attraction and seduction: "You already know how to touch the button / Oh, what a peculiar sensation!"[94] (figure 2.5). While Adelina sings the evocative lyrics, she openly flirts with Pablo, waving and winking at him from the stage, while another one of Adelina's admirers looks on in jealousy.[95]

This short segment completes two specific functions. First, it demonstrates the importance of the theater in Porfirian modern life, highlighting Mexico's first national revista. Its inclusion in the film is a testament to a vital moment in Mexican musical history: the break from Spanish lyric theater for something considered more homegrown.[96] This scene also illustrates the heterosexual male appetite for tiples and female theater performers. This attention

[92] For an analysis on *Chin Chun Chan,* see Jacqueline Avila, "*Chin Chun Chan:* The Zarzuela as an Ethnic and Technological Farce," in *Oxford Research Encyclopedia of Latin American History,* February 2018 https://oxfordre.com/latinamericanhistory/view/10.1093/acrefore/9780199366439.001.0001/acrefore-9780199366439-e-514.See also Janet Sturman's in-depth analysis and reading in *The Course of Mexican Music* (New York: Routledge, 2016), 167–75.

[93] In the revista, the scene is labeled "Cuadro Tecero, escena III."

[94] Rafeal Medina and José F. Elizondo, *Chin Chun Chan: Conflicto chino en un acto* (Mexico City: Medina y Comp. Impresores, 1904), 55.

[95] The female roles in the cine de añoranza porfiriana were described as follows: "A romantic period when women still did not drink liquor or smoke and make love behind the grating of their windows"; see "El Pisaverde y la bella," *El Universal,* April 3, 1940.

[96] The Porfirian film *Yo bailé con don Porfirio* (*I Danced with Don Porfirio*; 1942, dir. Gilberto Martínez Solares) uses excerpts from this revista as well.

Figure 2.5 Adelina (Tana Devodier) and the modern telephone in the revista *Chin Chun Chan*, in *México de mis recuerdos* (1944). Screen capture from film.

and admiration comes as no surprise as at the turn of the century, the actress was viewed as sign and symptom of modernization, particularly as women ventured outside the domestic sphere into public spaces.[97] Rita Felski argues that at the end of the nineteenth century, the actress, much like the prostitute, was perceived as a " 'figure of public pleasure' whose deployment of cosmetics and costume bore witness to the artificial and commodified forms of contemporary female sexuality."[98] She was the object, spectacle, and commodity of desire and pleasure for the heterosexual male, who watched—and listened to—her in hopes of obtaining her. Adelina's performance and her repertoire attest to this, as she openly flirts with one man while being viewed, and even pursued, by others.

---

[97] Fausto Ramírez, *Modernización y modernismo en el arte mexicano* (Mexico City: Universidad Nacional Autónoma de México, 2008), 119.

[98] Felski, *The Gender of Modernity*, 19.

At this point, the film has constructed two female character types: the decent, reserved, Christian woman (exemplified by Rosario and to a lesser extent the aunts) and the extroverted and sexy stage performer (Adelina). According to Bustillo Oro, Pablo would only be interested in Rosario if she was: "an extremely beautiful and worldly woman."[99] Although feeling slighted by Pablo's rude behavior, Rosario endeavors to win his affection by changing herself to become his desire. She transforms into the Argentinean comedic tiple Clementina Arriaga. She slips on form-fitting, dark-colored gowns, rearranges her hair with elaborate hats, and adopts an exaggerated Argentinean accent. In order to successfully pull off the scheme, Rosario needs to debut as Clementina at the Teatro Principal, and with the help of Don Chucho and Susanito, she secures an audition.

Clementina performs "La maquinista del amor" ("The Machinist of Love") from Rafael Gómez Calleja's 1908 Spanish zarzuela Las bribonas (The Imposters). In this zarzuela, the protagonist, Margharite, leads a traveling revista company that is heavily scrutinized by the conservative sectors in a small Spanish town—specifically a group of older women popularly known as the beatas (devout or pious women). In order to attract spectators, and the affection of the town's wandering-eyed married mayor, Margharite disguises herself as a "woman of sin" through implied sexual liaisons with her lover (really her husband, disguised in blackface). Christopher Webber argues that Las bribonas questions the idea of established morality as everyone in the production—the mayor, Margharite, her husband, and even the conservative beatas—wear masks, disguising themselves as people they are not in an attempt to keep up appearances and maintain their place in society.[100]

The zarzuela mirrors parts of the film's narrative, focusing on Rosario's donning of the Clementina mask to win over the object of her affection at the moral expense of her own beatas (the conservative aunts). Her performance of "La maquinista del amor" is nothing short of coquettish, fitting for the music-hall atmosphere of the excerpt. Singing about being ogled by men in Paris who follow her like a train, men in costume—a sportsman, a French soldier, a corporal, an Englishman, a modernist, a Turk, an old man, and a

---

[99] Bustillo Oro, Vida cinematográfica, 67.
[100] Christopher Webber, "The Alcalde, the Negro and la bribona: género ínfirmo zarzuela, 1900–1910," in De la zarzuela al cine: los medios de comunicación populares y su traducción de la voz marginal, ed. Max Doppelbauer and Kathrin Sartingen (München: Martin Meidenbauer, 2010), 71–73.

Figure 2.6 Rosario/Clementina (Sofía Álvarez) and the male chorus line in "La maquinista del amor," in *México de mis recuerdos* (1944). Screen capture from film.

French bricklayer—surround Clementina, pursuing her happily and with persistence (figure 2.6):

> I am the machinist of love
> A train that moves along happily,
> Asking for a free route
> Without seeing that it may be best to derail.[101]

The flirtatious performance projects another image of Rosario, one that contrasts with her previous position as the "decent woman" performing in the salon. In order to entice Pablo, she changes her demeanor, her appearance, and especially her repertoire to fit his desires, ultimately ignoring the fact that he initially considered her to be an unattractive bore. When Pablo sees Clementina at the audition, he is immediately smitten: he sees her as

---

[101] Rafael Calleja, *Las bribonas: Zarzuela in One Act* (Madrid: Madrid Instituto Compultense de Ciencias Musicales, 2007), 52–53.

the woman he wants to marry. After a series of successful performances at the Teatro Principal, Rosario reveals her identity to Pablo and admonishes him for treating "decent women" terribly. Unable, however, to overcome her feelings for him, Rosario accepts Pablo's marriage proposal, much to the newly found disapproval of the aunts, who believe she has lost her good reputation owing to her affiliation with the stage. They change their mind, however, when they realize *el señor presidente* Don Porfirio will be presiding as the godfather of Pablo and Rosario's wedding. Rosario and Pablo are soon married with the blessing of Don Porfirio—right before he is ousted by the Revolution. In the end, Rosario played to the desires of Pablo and at the same time recovered her reputation, but only through her close social association with Don Porfirio.

Díaz's ability to quickly persuade the aunts and to secure Rosario's social standing is not that surprising. During his dictatorship, Díaz consistently offered opportunities for advancement to the bourgeoisie in order to dissuade any type of conflict. All the characters of *México de mis recuerdos* benefited from Díaz's rule and looked to him as the patriarchal leader. Unlike the other Porfiriato films examined here, certain social issues and historical references surfaced that burst the utopian bubble. In an early scene, the 1892 presidential candidate Nicolás Zúñiga y Miranda (Max Langler) visits Don Chucho's residence as the "picturesque and safe candidate," serving as a reminder of the election fraud committed by the Díaz political machine.[102] The film also references the beginning of the Revolution, which sent Díaz into exile. During these final scenes, people riot in the streets, calling for Díaz's departure. In the end, a rousing crowd cheers as a defeated and teary-eyed Díaz boards the boat in the port of Veracruz en route to France. Don Chucho, Rosario, Pablo, and Susanito watch their Díaz depart, showing their own tears of sadness and disappointment, not so much for the absence of their leader as an end to their way of life. The film ends with Don Chucho's final words: "Death to a Mexico so another could be born. Slowly the Mexico that I remembered began to weaken."[103]

Much like *En tiempos de don Porfirio, México de mis recuerdos* received considerable attention from the press. Advertisements for the film featured cartoons comparing the caricatures of the Porfiriato with those of the present day. One such cartoon compares a Porfirian cancan dancer with the current

---

[102] García Riera, *Historia documental del cine mexicano*, 3:96.
[103] Bustillo Oro, *México de mis recuerdos*, ch. 12.

Figure 2.7 Cartoon advertisement for *México de mis recuerdos*, as it appeared in
El Universal, March 17, 1944.

rumbera, stating: "Past: our grandparents, yesterday, went crazy over an inch
of skin that was uncovered by fabric! Present: the grandsons, today, despair
when an inch of fabric covers the skin!"[104] (figure 2.7).

Porfirian nostalgia once again took over as articles detailed popular
Porfirian cultural practices that were still in existence. One article in particular examined the organ grinders of the city, using *México de mis recuerdos* as
a natural transition to the topic, describing the still existing specimen of the
Porfiriato, actively performing on the streets yet not as respected as they once
were.[105] Reviews also captured the utopianism of the cinematic Porfiriato,
proclaiming that it to be a *faithful* reproduction of the period:

---

[104] Advertisement for *México de mis recuerdos, El Universal*, March 17, 1944.
[105] See "'Sobre las olas,' una de la piezas más en boga cuando los organilleros reinaban," *El Universal*,
March 28, 1944.

"México de mis recuerdos" is a story that relates to anyone's parents or grandparents because it is a faithful reproduction of national life from four decades or half a century ago. It is Mexico of the time, with their typical customs, with their distinguished men of national politics, in poetry, in music, in the theater and, in general, in all aspects of society in the years prior to 1910, so contrasting and so romantic.[106]

México de mis recuerdos helped orient audiences to a new interpretation of the Porfiriato that was based on older forms of nostalgia. The public adored the film and by extension what they thought the period represented, exploited particularly by the film's strategic choice of music.

Conclusion

The cine de añoranza porfiriana continued to be a fashionable film genre during the beginning of the 1940s, with other films that included *Yo bailé con don Porfirio* (*I Dance with Don Porfirio*; 1942, dir. Gilberto Martínez Solares) and *El globo de Cantolla* (*The Globe of Cantolla*; 1943, dir. Gilberto Martínez Solares). When Miguel Alemán took over the presidency in 1946, the Porfiriato films phased out, taken over by other genres such as the more popular and exotic cabareteras and gangster films that achieved box office success.[107] While its popularity was short-lived, the cine de añoranza porfiriana provided an intriguing reinterpretation of a turbulent period in Mexican political, social, and cultural history. Mexico's música de salón and turn-of-the-century lyric theater shaped the cine de añoranza porfiriana with a rich selection of works that, when reinterpreted for the films, not only sonically syncretized the epoch on screen and provided nostalgic interpretations of the period but also reinforced conservative gender constructions.

In *En tiempos de don Porfirio, ¡Ay, qué tiempos señor don Simón!*, and *México de mis recuerdos*, we see and hear the musical works taken out of their historical context, reinterpreted to reinforce specific aspects of the film's narrative, which included social mores and gender roles. *En tiempos de don*

---

[106] "Sofía Alvarez y J. Pardavé en una graciosa escena de 'México de mis recuerdos,'" *El Universal*, April 1, 1944.

[107] Juan Bustillo Oro made a few attempts to resurrect the genre in *Las tandas del Principal* (1949), a 1963 remake of *México de mis recuerdos*, and *Los valses venían de Viena y los niños de París* (*The Waltzes Came from Vienna and the Children from Paris*; 1966).

Porfirio utilized waltzes, danzas, and serenades to depict an atmosphere of romance for the upper class. The male characters in the film exclusively perform the musical numbers, showcasing their talent while pushing the female characters strategically out of the spotlight. Romance and seduction through musical performance became the central concern, but only male characters maintain control. *¡Ay, qué tiempos señor don Simón!* and *México de mis recuerdos* referenced the Porfirian theatrical works, the entertainment within the entertainment, to address questionable social behaviors. *¡Ay, qué tiempos señor don Simón!* featured the risqué cancan and provocative lyrics to highlight Porfirian (and contemporary) society's hypocritical stance on the social expectations of women. In *México de mis recurdos*, the selected excerpts from Spanish zarzuelas and Mexican revistas featured characters disguising or masking themselves to fit into society. These narratives are then disguised in the film's comedic narrative about a woman disguising herself in order to win over the man she wants to marry (and supposedly loves) in order to advance socially. While political instability was intentionally left out of the films, the narratives focused on social decorum as unchanging and unflinching, where women received the most scrutiny.

Given the drastic changes with the leftist current of cardenismo at the end of the 1930s and the conservative modernization of ávilacamachismo of the early 1940s, the need for cultural and social stability in the form of the cinematic Porfiriato was only a temporary distraction from the contemporary unease. This need allowed the cine de añoranza porfiriana to reinvent a lost era of Porfirian social organization and customs where musical performance became an essential practice that defined the period to the national audience in more ways than one.

3

The Sounds of Indigenismo

Cultural Integration and Musical Exoticism in *Janitzio* (1935) and *María Candelaria* (1944)

The prostitute melodrama provided one glimpse into the Mexico's modernized, urban life, but during the 1930s, the most utilized backdrop for Mexican cinema was the countryside. The comedias rancheras, the revolutionary melodrama, and the fictional indigenista film—melodramatic films about indigenous populations—were all set in an idyllic countryside. All three film genres also reimagined or reinterpreted significant aspects of Mexican history and culture that either contradicted or affirmed national discourse during the post-Revolutionary years. However, the fictional indigenista films offered an intriguing challenge for filmmakers: How best to represent Mexico's diverse indigenous cultures?

During the first half of the twentieth century, leading anthropologists, cultural critics, and members of the state produced several ideological discourses about Mexico's indigenous populations. The majority of these sources advocated for the cultural integration of these communities into modernized Mexican society in an act termed "mestizoizing," or mixing. This process, it was believed, not only was key to the mutual survival of both indigenous and mestizo populations but also served as a uniform nationalist ideology, particularly after the chaotic years of the Revolution. Integration was nothing new in Mexico, but it marked a change from the exclusionist and oppressive methods undertaken by the elite during the era of the Porfiriato. Instead of a biologically orientated mestizaje, which required racial mixing or miscegenation, cultural mestizaje was encouraged. As a tool for mass communication, cinema held a unique position in representing indigenous cultures; it reified and homogenized specific populations for the dominantly urban mestizo audience who searched for any semblance of an indigenous heritage they could claim as their own. But national cinema presented an ambivalent message: it neither fully promoted nor discouraged integrationist procedures through the constructions of indigeneity on screen.

Within these representations, music and sound played a crucial role in not just providing changes in emotive atmosphere, such as lush orchestral swells for romantic scenes and pulsing ostinati for dramatic moments, but also in aurally depicting specific components of the supposed indigenous experience—specifically their isolation and even their oppression. In a sense, music and sound persuaded the audience that the peoples depicted on screen were in fact real. In his writing on film music, ethnomusicologist Mark Slobin states, "every film is ethnographic, and every soundtrack acts like an ethnomusicologist. . . . Placing people in motion means you have to construct an integrated and logical society, music and all."[1] Slobin's study concentrates on the development of film music paradigms during Hollywood's studio era, examining the film score of the 1930s as "an effective technical and aesthetic practice" and as a cultural text that contributes to the film's narrative. The composer, Slobin argues, acts as an implied narrator, organizing "musical materials to describe how a human community lives" through diegetic and nondiegetic music. While the diegetic music supplies an aural stamp of association between place and the musical practices lived on screen, the orchestral underscoring adds crucial messages from outside the space of action. However, in tandem they construct the sonorous signature of the onscreen society: "the interplay of source and score can be very complicated. Together they structure a musical ethnography."[2] While Slobin's work focuses on Hollywood film music, his concept does apply to the film scores of the 1930s and 1940s fictional indigenista films, which exploited several musical practices and compositional approaches to enforce an explicit cultural synchresis of Otherness with the onscreen indigenous population.

Discussing the musicalization of indigenous communities in cinema is a challenging undertaking, as *indigenismo* was not just a critical component of nationalist ideology but also a prominent cultural and social movement that attempted to vindicate (select) indigenous cultures and practices to a growing mestizo society. This vindication took place in the fields of the visual arts, music, and cinema, articulating contradictory messages that had lasting effects. Beginning first with an examination on the anthropological discourses of indigenismo that favored cultural integration, this chapter

---

[1] Mark Slobin, "The Steiner Superculture," in *Global Soundtracks: Worlds of Film Music*, ed. Mark Slobin (Middletown, CT: Wesleyan University Press, 2008), 4.

[2] Ibid., 5.

explores the visual and musical currents and signifiers that shaped the fictional indigenista film genre to reflect contemporary social anxieties and changing conceptions of indigenous populations for mestizo audiences. The representation of indigenous populations in the visual arts and in the film work of Soviet director Sergei Eisenstein (1898–1948) had a significant impact on how they were visually and even narratively constructed on screen. New currents in Mexican music that focused on building a national aesthetic added to this construction, supplying musical accompaniment that reinforced the carefully structured yet problematic representations. I concentrate on two renowned examples of the fictional indigentista film genre from the 1930s and 1940s: *Janitzio* (1935, dir. Carlos Navaro) and *María Candelaria* (1944, dir. Emilio Fernández). Both films focus on indigenous populations and their experience with suffering and oppression, both social and cultural. However, both feature similar narratives with similar outcomes and similar music composed by composer and folklorist Francisco Domínguez, implying that although the concentration is on these populations—two different communities of people at two different time periods—the common belief was that they were one and the same. While the indigenous populations portrayed were not homogenous, the films were in effect a device that generated a sense of homogeneity on the silver screen.

Integrating the Indigenous

After the armed struggle of the Revolution, Mexico experienced a reconstructionist period as the country sought to rebuild shattered structures from the last era. Intellectuals and artists desired to forge a new national consciousness, attempting to push the ideologies of the Revolution to the forefront. The large indigenous populations had represented a problem for the intellectuals of the Porfiriato, who rooted an austere Mexican national identity in pre-Columbian cultures. The present indigenous populace and their dismal circumstances did not align with preconceived notions of a noble indigenous lineage and did not conform to contemporary societal expectations. After the dismantling of the Porfirian regime, the indigenismo movement attempted to provide solutions for unifying the Mexican people and for a consolidated national identity. One possible solution was the integration of these populations into the growing mestizo populace, but the approaches differed. The integration project of the pre-Revolutionary years attempted to exterminate the populations, not through ethnic cleansing but through miscegenation.

Intellectuals such as José Vasconcelos (1882–1959) and Andrés Enríquez Molina (1865–1940) proposed a process of mestizaje focused on racial categorization. In *Los grandes problemas nacionales* (*The Great National Problems*; 1909), Enríquez Molina asserts mestizos represent an evolutionary paragon while the indigenous people are on the lowest rung, reflected in what he believed to be their submissive and taciturn character.[3] His equates mestizaje with nationhood, arguing that the continuation of the mestizo as the dominant race is the fundamental base for the country's progress.[4] In a similar vein, Vasconcelos argues that mestizaje produced grander civilizations and a race superior to others. Through racial mixing, the inferior traits of the indigenous would be replaced by superior traits of the mestizo. Moving away from this process, anthropologists Manuel Gamio (1883–1960) and Alfonso Caso (1883–1946) proposed cultural mestizaje as a route toward integrating indigenous populations into the modernized country's way of thinking and behaving.

Manuel Gamio was one of the champion indigenistas who believed indigenous populations could be westernized and, with a unifying language and culture, would help construct a homogenous nation. In *Forjando Patria* (*Forging Homeland*), Gamio argues that indigenous populations remain misunderstood in modern society owing primarily to a lack of communication.[5] In order to resolve this issue, knowledge about the Amerindian needed to be obtained by the dominant society before attempting to gradually and persuasively integrate. He argues that because the Amerindian is misunderstood, it is not only he or she who should undergo transformation but also the mestizo. The Amerindian should be mestizo-ized and the mestizo, to create a national synthesis, should be "Indianized": "To incorporate the Indian we cannot pretend to 'Europeanize' them by force; on the contrary, we should 'Indianize' ourselves somewhat, in order to present already diluted with theirs, which then will not be exotic, cruel, bitter, and incompressible to them."[6] He further argues that this process, however, does not belong in the hands of the government

---

[3] Andrés Molina Enríquez, *Los grandes problemas nacionales y otros textos (1911–1919)*, rev. ed. (Mexico City: Ediciones Era, 1978), 419.

[4] Ibid.

[5] Manuel Gamio, *Forjando Patria*, 2nd ed. (Mexico City: Editorial Porrua, S.A., 1960), 25.

[6] Ibid., 96. Gamio and the other integrationists utilize the term *el indio* or Indian in their discussions. I use it here to refer to their specific language in their writings.

or sociologist, and that it is specifically destined for the anthropologist, who requires guidelines and perspectives devoid of prejudices.[7]

In speaking specifically of the indigenous populations' capabilities to integrate, Gamio asserts their intellectual aptitudes are comparable to any other race, including white Europeans, capable for progress and acting neither inferior nor superior. Through continued education, the timidity felt by the indigenous communities would eventually disappear, replaced by a newfound confidence, but it was important to study and understand them in order to create the necessary apparatuses for integration. Through his calcification of cultural characteristics, Gamio determines through scientific methods what of their material and intellectual life they should retain, what are those elements and attributes that are useful and beneficial, and what needs to be substituted to establish a modern, unified society.[8] While the integrationists supported a change in the indigenous populations' approaches to production and property to match those of modern society, artistic culture was one area they agreed should remain untouched, as their art practices formed an important part of a visual Mexican culture.[9] Gamio urged present-day artists in Mexico to seek inspiration in the indigenous arts for their own works:

> The artistic features, which are perhaps what is the most valuable in the cultural heritage of native America, need to flourish spontaneously, as far away from the influence of their European counterparts as possible: inspired as they have been for thousands of years, in the lavish American nature and interpreting their inexhaustible beauty in the manner of their own traditional spirit, one that we do not know is more aesthetic than religious or vice versa.[10]

The value of the indigenous populations was placed squarely on the preservation of their artistic heritage as long as they didn't have any influence from or were impacted by European cultures. For Gamio, this represented a true national spirit, ready for absorption or appropriation into modern works.

[7] Ibid., 25.

[8] See Manuel Gamio, "Calificación de características culturales de los grupos indígenas," *América Indígena* 2, no. 4 (October 1942): 19–22.

[9] Indigenous populations believed in collective property, communal farming, and the use of their own traditional technologies standing in contrast to modernized society, which sought private property and western technology. See Guillermo Bonfil Batalla, *México profundo: Una civilización negada*, 3rd ed. (Mexico City: Random House Mondadori, 2008).

[10] Gamio, "Calificación de características culturales de los grupos indígenas," 22.

Another supporter of indigenismo, Alfonso Caso, advocated for cultural integration, but looked specifically on indigenous communities as a whole and not the individual, proposing a new definition of the indigenous that relied on cultural terms. According to Caso, a community is indigenous if it feels that it is indigenous, whatever its social and cultural construction.[11] The individual who believes himself to be indigenous is indigenous, but if he is part of a community that "lacks the sentiment" of being indigenous, he cannot be considered as such.[12] This definition necessitates self-identification based on a particular set of criteria, yet this becomes problematic. Identification was assigned to these populations from the outside, something that had already been established at the time of the Conquest: when they arrived, Spanish conquerors grouped and labeled the indigenous populations, ignoring whatever name, label, or signifier they had called themselves. By Caso's definition, self-identification relied on the recognition of similarities in cultural practices, rather than solely biological makeup, but this identification was most likely a negative determinant imposed on the communities based on other prejudices and external idiosyncrasies. This identified grouping only furthered the contrast with the mestizo population.[13] For Caso, the culture of the indigenous remained problematic and required penetration of useful elements and characteristics from "nuestro pueblos mestizos y blancos" ("our mestizo and white population").[14]

Although widely promoted, these integrationists did not acknowledge the negative repercussions this integration might foment. It was optimistically assumed that through mestizaje, the indigenous populace would be better off in a modern culture rather than in their own, and that they would be eager to abandon their old way of life. This view did not take into consideration any of the difficulties that would surface as a consequence of the acculturation process, as it was thought "the positive aspects of Indian culture could be preserved" while the negative expunged.[15] This was of course a precarious view, since agreement as to what should remain and what should go would need to

---

[11] Alfonso Caso, "Definición del indio y lo indio," *América Indígena* 8, no. 4 (1948): 238–47 cited in Alfonso Caso, *La comunidad indígena* (Mexico City: Secretaría de Educación Pública, 1971), 89–90.

[12] Alan Knight, "Racism, Revolution, and *Indigenismo*: Mexico, 1910–1940," in *The Idea of Race in Latin America, 1870–1940*, ed. Richard Graham (Austin: University of Texas Press, 1990), 75.

[13] Ibid.

[14] Alfonso Caso, *La comunidad indígena*, 91–93. See also Alfonso Caso, "La protección de las Artes Populares," *América Indígena* 2, no. 3 (July 1942): 25–29.

[15] Knight, "Racism, Revolution, and *Indigenismo*," 86.

be reached, but indigenous groups were not consulted in these decisions.[16] The numerous indigenous populations were objects of indigenismo rather than its producers, and discourses originating from the outside attempted to integrate them into modern society with the goals of instituting a common, unified, national indigenous heritage through a reevaluation of their existence.[17]

Representing the Indigenous

In the process of mestizaje, visual representations of the indigenous in the media were constructed and repeatedly reconstructed to fit specific social and political needs. Although agrarian reform and rural integration to educate select indigenous populations were well underway during the 1920s and 1930s, particularly during the sexenio of Lázaro Cárdenas (1934–1940), the indigenous populace still had a weak voice in social and political spheres, as needs to valorize and redeem indigenous cultures pervaded the official ideology. Perceptions of their inferiority in society persisted, and these populations continued to be perceived as detrimental communities with poor education and hygiene, who did speak the national language. Ricardo Pérez Montfort acknowledges the contradiction particularly when indigenous populations were exalted in politics and in popular culture: "on one side they were viewed as strange and distant, an inherited colonial point of view, but on the other side they were identified as a root of 'our most authentic specificity.'"[18]

Although it was agreed that the negative elements of the indigenous be discarded during the process of mestizaje, the arts were one area that Gamio and Caso contended should remain untouched or, rather, should not be dissolved. According to Caso, popular art is not exclusively indigenous or exclusively European; popular art is a Mexican art because of the slow intervention of European ideas within an indigenous practice.[19] In 1921, as part of the Centennial celebrations,[20] the Centennial Committee organized

---

[16] For example, Caso states the positive values of indigenous groups are communal labor, obligation of services, respect to their natural authorities, and popular art. See Caso, *La comunidad indígena*, 105.

[17] Knight, "Racism, Revolution, and *Indigenismo*," 75.

[18] Ricardo Peréz Montfort, *Estampas de nacionalismo popular mexicano: Ensayos sobre cultura popular y nacionalismo* (Mexico City: Centro de Investigaciones y Estudios Superiores en Antropología Social, 1994), 161.

[19] Caso, "La protección de las artes populares," 25.

[20] The Centennial celebrations took place in 1910, still during the Díaz regime. However, this celebration was particularly extravagant, with golden carriages and added pomp. In order to receive

events designed to showcase *arte popular* (popular art). The Exhibition of Popular Arts was one such event, envisioned by artists Jorge Eniso (1879–1969), Roberto Montenegro (1885–1968), and Dr. Atl (Gerardo Murillo, 1875–1964) as a central space to display examples of regional and indigenous arts. The samples included shawls, furniture, blankets, paintings, pottery, toys, and any type of ceramic, which were individually photographed and included in a catalog organized and written by Dr. Atl, who claimed, "the most Mexican of Mexico [are] the popular arts":

> The artistic and industrial manifestations of the pure indigenous races and the mixed or intermediate races, present—contrary to what happens in those social groups that are ethnically similar to Europeans—very marked uniformity of method, of perseverance, and do really constitute a true national culture.[21]

Dr. Atl's commentary attempted to move away from comparisons to Europe and a European value system in order to shape a unified national culture based on an indigenous and mestizo foundation.

In addition to celebrations and public events, the visual representation of indigenous cultures and their valor, nobility, and suffering became some of the many themes undertaken by the Mexican muralist school. Two years after Vasconcelos became the minister of public education, he commissioned prominent artists Diego Rivera (1887–1957), David Alfaro Siqueiros (1896–1974), and José Clemente Orozco (1883–1949) to paint murals on the walls of the Escuela Nacional Preparatoria in Mexico City.[22] Under Vasconcelos's patronage, the goal of the muralist project was to present the ideologies of the Revolution in a manner that would be accessible to the primarily illiterate Spanish-speaking masses. The artists, however, branched out in several directions, incorporating their own political beliefs despite receiving animosity from the public. The depiction of the indigenous populace spanned centuries, from the pre-Conquest utopia to

---

foreign guests and to show that Mexico was a modern and cosmopolitan country, Díaz ordered that any persons on the street be sequestered in order to "beautify" the city.

[21] Gerardo Murillo, *Las artes populares en México* (Mexico City: Secretaría de Industria, Comercio y Trabajo, 1922), 15.

[22] Rivera, Orozco, and Siqueiros are the most well known muralists because of Vasconcelos's commission. However, many national and international artists came into the muralist orbit, including Jean Charlot (1898–1979), Fermín Revueltas (1901–1935), Roberto Montenegro (1885–1968), Fanny Rabel (1922–2008), and Dr. Atl himself.

Porfirian oppression, to present-day isolation and solitude. When Rivera, Orozco, and Siqueiros, known as "los tres grandes" ("the three giants") began working, their art exhibited influences from religious Italian frescoes of the Renaissance, inspired either by sojourns to Italy or from the teachings of Dr. Atl.[23] Each artist incorporated modern currents into his work during the 1920s.[24] Although paintings exalting and exoticizing the indigenous stem back to the eighteenth century in works by José de Ibarra (1688–1756), the muralist movement garnered the most attention for providing not only varying representations of indigenous populations but also severe class distinctions, scathing interpretations of Mexican history, and several examples of oppression, depicting what cultural critic Carlos Monsiváis has referred to as the myths and mythomanias, the didactics and aesthetics of Mexican culture.[25]

Cinema offered another expression of nationalist rhetoric regarding indigenous cultures. Despite Mexican silent film's partiality to French-style actualities, documentary short films, and newsreels, narrative films featuring indigenous populations and themes (many pre-Conquest explorations), such as *Tepeyac* (1917, dir. José Manuel Ramos and Carlos E. González), *Tabaré* (1918, dir. Luis Lezama), *Cuauhtémoc* (1919, dir. Manuel de la Bandera, 1919), and *De raza azteca* (*Of the Aztec Race*; 1921, dir. Miguel Contreras Torres), portrayed the indigenous to reflect various characteristics described by critics as "pure," "savage," "beautiful," "moral," "spiritual," "nervous,"

[23] Although regarded as a post-Revolutionary art movement, the Mexican muralist tradition reaches back before the outbreak of the Revolution. Celebrated painter of Mexican landscapes and panoramas Dr. Atl, who played a crucial role in the Exhibition of Popular Arts, was the first to urge "the government to invite artists to decorate the walls of public buildings." After Dr. Atl returned from his European travels in 1903, he encouraged his young students to study the frescoes of the Italian Renaissance because he believed they reflected spiritualism and spontaneous energy, which he concluded should be the driving force behind Mexican modernism, but it was not until the 1920s that his proposals were taken seriously. For more information on Dr. Atl and his work prior to the muralist movement, see Beatriz Espejo, *Dr. Atl: El paisaje como pasión* (Mexico City: Fondo Editorial de la Plástica Mexicana, 1994); Edward Lucie-Smith, *Latin American Art of the 20th Century*, 2nd ed. (New York: Thames & Hudson, 2004), 24; Alma Lilia Roura, *Dr. Atl: Paisaje de hielo y fuego* (Mexico City: Consejo Nacional para la Cultura y las Artes, 1999); Arturo Casado Navarro, *Gerardo Murillo, el Dr. Atl* (Mexico City: Universidad Nacional Autónoma de México, 1984).

[24] Rivera utilized Cubist techniques and influences from European painters such as Cézanne, Ingres, Renoir, and Gauguin to depict the flora and fauna of Mexico and pre-Columbian narrative reliefs. Similar to Rivera, Siqueiros was inspired by Italian Renaissance murals and, while in Europe, was influenced by modern French art and Italian futurism. Orozco, on the other hand, did not travel through Europe, but with Dr. Atl's guidance, was seduced by Italian frescoes and symbolism. See Lucie-Smith, *Latin American Art of the 20th Century*, 49–68.

[25] Carlos Monsiváis, "Notas sobre la cultura mexicana en el siglo XX," in *Historia general de México*, ed. Centro de Estudios Históricos (Mexico City: El Colegio de México, 2000), 993.

"romantic," and "reserved." The early film companies, such as Popocatépetl Films, Aztlán Films, Quetzal Films, and La Azteca Films,[26] also nodded toward a nationalist current that attempted to discover (or rediscover) roots in pre-Columbian cultures.[27] But it was not until the 1930s that the filming of the indigenous soared with the arrival of foreign filmmakers and innovations in recorded sound technology. Questionably held as the pioneer and "founding father" of Mexican cinematography, Soviet director Sergei Eisenstein provided a hybrid yet essentialist vision of Mexico, in a sense "teaching" Mexicans and others how to see and understand their country.

The Foreign Eye and Fictional Ethnography: Sergei Eisenstein and ¡Que viva México!

Eisenstein arrived in Mexico from Hollywood in 1930, after a failed attempt to direct a new film for Paramount Studios. With the financial support of liberal novelist Upton Sinclair and his wealthy wife Mary Craig Sinclair, Eisenstein set out to direct a film about Mexico. Owing to ideological conflicts with Sinclair and financial difficulties, Eisenstein did not complete the film during his lifetime.[28] With the editorial skills of Eisenstein's co-writer Grigori Aleksandrov and his crew, Eisenstein's film was edited and produced and, with the passage of time, reached mythic proportions in Mexican film history and criticism, placing the Soviet filmmaker at the top of the Mexican cinematographic hierarchy.

Eisenstein's depictions of Mexican cultures and indigenous people were not something particularly new. In his study of Eisenstein in Mexico and the birth of *¡Que viva México!*, Aurelio de los Reyes acknowledges several sources that aided in Eisenstein's construction, the majority of which consisted of foreign travel books and magazines, the artistic achievements of the muralist school, and his personal relationships with Mexican visual

---

[26] La Azteca Films was the first company to initiate a national film industry. It was established in 1917 by zarzuela diva and writer Mimí Derba and experimental photographer and exhibiter Enrique Rosas. The initial goal was to produce films of national interest, using historic themes that depicted Mexican customs. For more information, see Federico Dávalos Orozco, *Albores del cine mexicano* (Mexico City: Clío, 1996), 30–31.

[27] Aurelio de los Reyes, *Medio siglo de cine mexicano (1896–1947)* (Mexico City: Editorial Trillas, S.A de C.V., 1987), 70–72.

[28] In an article for *El Universal Ilustrado*, Sinclair indicated that the project created animosity between him and Eisenstein because of Eisenstein's persistent need to spread socialist theory. See "Upton Sinclair nos habla del caso Eisenstein," *El Universal Ilustrado*, January 12, 1933.

artists. Of the most important was Anita Brenner's *Idols Behind Altars*, which detailed ceremonies, popular art, dances, paintings, and artisanal objects that greatly inspired Eisenstein.[29] Also influential was his lengthy tour of the renovated National Museum of Anthropology, where he studied "indigenous civilizations" and traces of Tenochtitlán.[30] With Rivera as his principal guide, Eisenstein visited the murals of the National Palace and Hernán Cortés's house in Cuernavaca, and viewed the collected folk and indigenous art in Rivera's own home.[31] European magazines such as *Kölnische Illustrierte* (*Cologne Magazines*) featured sections on *Día de muertos* (Day of the Dead), whose images of the festivities and popular artist José Guadalupe Posada's art were included in the final section of Eisenstein's film. Also inspiring were Ernest Gruening's *Mexico and Its Heritage*, Carleton Beals's *Mexican Labyrinth*, and the magazine on folk arts edited by Frances Toor, *Mexican Folkways.*[32]

Eisenstein was welcomed to Mexico with practically open arms by Mexico's circle of vanguard artists, principally the muralists. Sharing the political ideologies of the muralists, which sought to exhibit the oppressed worker and lower classes, Eisenstein embarked on a project that perpetuated the Revolutionist ideologies that so many rallied behind. The Mexican government granted him permission to make his film on the agreement that he would be guided by appointed figures from the Ministry of Public Education, including Adolfo Best Maugard, Gabriel Fernández Ledesma, and Roberto Montenegro, in order for the director to not be persuaded by stereotypes and clichés.[33] The inclusion of the folkloric archetypes and the influence of the Mexican artists involved in the nationalist projects had a remarkable impact on Eisenstein's socialist realist, ethnographic technique. By presenting his narrative with this approach, Eisenstein placed himself, an outsider with

[29] Aurelio de los Reyes notes that Diego Rivera was a close friend of Anita Brenner and most likely gave the book to Eisenstein. However, in his study on the impact of muralismo on Eisenstein's film, Eduardo de la Vega Alfaro claims that Odo Stadé, an employee from a Hollywood bookstore, introduced Eisenstein to the book. According to de la Vega Alfaro, Stadé was a Villista, a follower of revolutionary leader Pancho Villa, during the Revolution and he recommended several books on Mexican culture to Eisenstein, enticing his interest more. See Aurelio de los Reyes, *El nacimiento de ¡Que viva México!* (Mexico City: Universidad Nacional Autónoma de México, 2006), 133; Eduardo de la Vega Alfaro, *Del muro a la pantalla: S.M. Eisenstein y el arte pictórico mexicano* (Mexico City: Instituto Mexicano de Cinematografía, 1997), 34.

[30] Tenochtitlán was the capital city of the Aztec empire, located in the central part of present-day Mexico City. This city was built in the middle of Lake Texcoco and remained as such until conquest by the Spanish in 1521.

[31] Ibid.

[32] De los Reyes, *Medio siglo de cine mexicano*, 99.

[33] Andrea Noble, *Mexican National Cinema* (London: Routledge, 2005), 130.

artistic informants, on an equal level with the Mexican audience, who were considered outsiders, as well.

Eisenstein's edited film is divided into seven episodes or novellas, each dedicated to an artist who inspired Eisenstein, envisaging the project as a "cinematic mural," a mural in movement.[34] The prologue, influenced by David Alfaro Siqueiros's work *Entierro de un obrero* (*Burial of a Worker*), is set in the Yucatán and includes still images that juxtapose the ancient Mayan past with the Mayan of the present. The argument made was that the traditions of the Mayans have not changed. "Conquest" depicts the Spanish and Catholic traditions mixing with indigenous traditions and customs, creating a type of folk-Catholicism. In "Sandunga," Eisenstein focuses on indigenous life unaffected by the Spanish through the protagonists Conception and Abundio, using softened images of the pair laying in the sun and gathering flowers, so as to imply the simplicity and purity of indigenous life. In "Fiesta," Eisenstein turns to the art of Francisco de Goya to signify a traditional bullfight, highlighting Spanish cultural fusion in Mexican life. His most famous episode, "Maguey," takes place in a *pulque*-producing hacienda in Hidalgo during the beginning of the Revolution, and depicts an uprising at the hacienda to foreshadow the armed struggle. Inspired by the later frescoes of Rivera, Eisenstein uses hard, contrasting images, full of aggression and violence. The episode "Soldadera" is based on the work of Orozco, representing scenes of the armed struggle of the Revolution, but it remains unfinished. Finally, the epilogue takes the audience to present-day urban Mexico, with images of old traditions mingling with modernized landscapes, implying a sense of continuity. Emphasizing the theme of renewal, Eisenstein portrays images of *Día de muertos* with *calaveras* (skeletons) inspired by Posada's prints.[35]

¡Que viva México! receives considerable scholarly attention yet commentators are puzzled as to how to classify the film: Was it a "narrative or documentary film, a treatise on film form, or is it a type of ethnography?"[36] The film uses a variety of filming techniques, from distinctive camera movements and shots to the use of non-actors. Eisenstein's style of social-realist silent cinema, exemplified in *Battleship Potemkin* (1926) and

[34] For more information on the influence of the muralist school on Eisenstein, see de la Vega Alfaro, *Del muro a la pantalla*, 45–72.

[35] For a description of the novellas, see Harry M. Geduld and Ronald Gottesman, eds., *Sergei Eisenstein and Upton Sinclair: The Making and Unmaking of Que viva Mexico!* (Bloomington: Indiana University Press, 1970); Noble, *Mexican National Cinema*, 123–46.

[36] Ibid., 128.

October (1927), and his desire to portray Mexico, characterize the film as an experimental project incorporating many of Eisenstein's ideas on film form that borders on pseudo-documentary with a fictional narrative structure.[37] In the incomplete autograph draft that Eisenstein sent to Upton Sinclair before filming in 1931, it becomes evident what Eisenstein has in mind for "the Mexican picture." His outline reflects a rich tapestry of folkloric Mexico, depicted through artisanal objects such as the sarape, Mayan statues, "Death day," fiestas, Aztecs, Tehuantepec, Catholicism, and paganism. Eisenstein's approach is best summed up in his first paragraph, where he identifies the sarape as a bridge that links all Mexicans:

A Sarape is the striped blanket that the Mexican indio, the Mexican charro, the everyday Mexican wears. And the Sarape could be the symbol of Mexico. So striped and violently contrasting are the cultures in Mexico running next to each other and at the same time being centuries away. No plot, no whole story could run through this Sarape without being false or artificial.[38]

The imagery that Eisenstein weaves through this description shapes his understanding of Mexico and its population, indigenous and all. The sarape, a colorful blanket worn predominantly by females, connects the major national symbols of Mexico: the indigenous and the charro. Eisenstein also refers to a barbarism or brutality alive in Mexico, using the colors of the sarape that "violently" contrast so as to illustrate this fact and pointing out that Mexico lives concurrently with the traditions of the past.

Eisenstein's cinematic collage illustrates the stereotypes of a folkloric yet oppressed indigenous population based on foreign perceptions and the plastic arts, establishing what some scholars call the "Mexican aesthetic" in national cinema. This aesthetic produced a specific image of indigenous cultures. Pérez Montfort states:

Indeed his foreign gaze supplied the images of Indians with many stereotypical characteristics such as the sombrero, the sarape, the white

---

[37] For more information on Eisenstein's ideas regarding film form, see Sergei Eisenstein, *The Film Sense* (New York: Harcourt Brace Jovanovich, 1947).

[38] Sergei Eisenstein, "Rough Outline of the Mexican Picture," in *Sergei Eisenstein and Upton Sinclair: The Making and Unmaking of Que Viva Mexico!*, ed. Harry M. Geduld and Ronald Gottesman (Bloomington: Indiana University Press, 1970), xxvii.

undergarment, huaraches, brown complexion, etc. Although he represented the contemporary Indian with great solemnity, he also fell into certain folklorism.[39]

Eisenstein's experimental use of the camera and the blurred definition of the film's genre create a social-justice framework that Mexican directors and cinematographers emulated during the 1930s. The preoccupation with indigenous culture carried into the early sound period with films such as *Janitzio* (1935, dir. Carlos Navarro), *Redes* (*Nets*; 1935, dir. Emilio Gómez Muriel), *La india bonita* (*The Pretty Indian Girl*; 1938, dir. Antonio Helú), *La rosa de Xochimilco* (*The Rose of Xochimilco*; 1938, dir. Carlos Véjar), *El indio* (*The Indian*; 1939, dir. Armando Vargas de la Maza), and *La noche de los mayas* (*The Night of the Mayas*; 1939, dir. Chano Ureta), and continued into the 1940s, but with some variation. Several of the fictional indigenista films were attempts by the directors and producers to create a pseudo-ethnographic cinema of indigenous cultures, yet referred to several folkloric qualities of the communities in almost exploitative terms. *Janitzio* and its remake, *María Candelaria*, are two examples of the industry's approach to presenting indigenous cultures within these parameters, and both do so visually and aurally.

Francisco Domínguez: Folklorist and Film Composer

Janitzio and *María Candelaria* feature underscoring by Francisco Domínguez, composer and folklorist. During the 1940s, Domínguez was one of Emilio Fernández's leading composers, receiving his start with *Janitzio* and continuing with box office successes such as *Flor silvestre* (*Wild Flower*; 1943, dir. Emilio Fernández) and *¡Que lindo es Michoacán!* (*How Beautiful Is Michoacán*; 1943, dir. Ismael Rodríguez).[40] Domínguez worked in several film genres, including comedias rancheras and urban melodramas, making him one of the more versatile film composers of the period. Before venturing into the film industry, however, Domínguez's musical pursuits during the 1920s and 1930s involved the study of vernacular and indigenous musics in

---

[39] Pérez Montfort, *Estampas del nacionalismo popular mexicano*, 173.
[40] Fernández's other favorite composer was Antonio Díaz Conde. His scores were featured in the urban and prostitute melodramas of the 1940s and 1950s.

Mexico—projects with the emerging avant-garde movement Estridentismo and the national school of dance, and the quest for Mexican musical nationalism. Information on Domínguez is scarce, but bits and pieces have been recovered to provide a glimpse into the composer's ideologies and endeavors, and how those impacted his film scores.[41]

Considerable research on Domínguez focuses on his contributions to the post-Revolutionary pursuit of musical nationalism during the 1920s, both as a folklorist and as a composer. As part of a list of educational programs and fieldwork assignments from the Ministry of Public Education, Domínguez was contracted in 1923 to study and catalogue vernacular music in the state of Michoacán. The finished product, a monograph entitled *Album de Michoacán*, features musical transcriptions of sones, jarabes, corridos, and canciones abajeñas for solo piano or piano and voice. In the monograph's "notas preliminares" (preliminary notes), Domínguez explains that the melodies included in the monograph represent the diverse regions of the state: "Lake region [which includes Lake Pátzcuaro], highlands [mountainous region] and the lowlands [hot lands], as a homage to the genius of the ignored mestizo and indigenous Tarascan composers."[42] Domínguez also provides contextual information on some of the collected melodies, generally remarking on unique musical characteristics and providing folkloric descriptions to color the reader's understanding of the songs. He ends his note with a summation of the music:

> This music is characterized by its simplicity and its healthy joy; its melodies are spontaneous and inspired and its harmonization is based on a diatonic musical system. Despite this, the music conserves strong aboriginal roots in its melodic turns, its cadences, and its combined rhythms.[43]

Domínguez's transcriptions of the melodies fit within the paradigms of Western art music, with time signatures in 2/4, 3/4, 4/4, and 6/8, in primarily major keys with lyrics in Spanish.

---

[41] See the following music encyclopedia entries on Domínguez: Gabriel Pareyón, *Diccionario enciclopédico de música en México* (Guadalajara: Secretaría de Cultura de Jalisco, 1995), 1:189; Aurelio Tello, "Francisco Domínguez," in *Diccionario del Cine Iberoamericano*, vol. 3, ed. Emilio Casares Rodicio (Madrid: Sociedad General de Autores y Editores, 2011), 320. See also the following sources on his involvement in dance: Alma Rosa Cortés González, *60 Aniversario de la Escuela Nacional de Danza Nellie y Gloria Campobello* (Mexico City: Instituto Nacional de Bellas Artes, 1992); Margarita Tortajada Quiroz, *Danza y poder* (Mexico City: Instituto Nacional de Bellas Artes, 1995), 124 n16.

[42] Francisco Domínguez, *Album musical de Michoacán* (Mexico City: Secretaria de Educación Publica, 1923), 3.

[43] Ibid.

In 1926, Domínguez's fieldwork in Michoacán aided his participation in the Estridentista theatrical work *El Teatro Mexicano del Murciélago* (*Mexican Theater of the Bat*), a joint project that brought together theater director Luis Quintanilla, painter Carlos González, and folk composer Nicolás Bartolo Juárez.[44] Inspired by Russian variety shows that combine folklore and popular culture with avant-garde aesthetics, the *El Teatro Mexicano del Murciélago* featured folk dances and "comic representations of modern urban life," incorporating folkloric numbers and popular representations of emerging national figures such as the charro. The music and dances of Michoacán made up several acts of the production, and as Elissa Rashkin notes, to some extent resembled the Noche Mexicana (Mexican Evening) spectacles of the early 1920s, but were much more inventive.[45] Unfortunately, the musical scores of these stage performances have not been found, but it is important to note that because of Domínguez's musical background and fieldwork experience in the rural areas of Michoacán, he was considered a suitable composer for these stage works.[46] Although not strictly a recognized member of the Estridentista movement, his participation in these performances leads me to believe that his personal ideologies on music and art, much like the movement's, rejected strict academic and Western European paradigms in pursuit of something more experimental and more homegrown.

Domínguez's ideology of musical nationalism was made apparent through his participation in the First National Congress of Music, on September 5, 1926. The First National Congress of Music was the first time Mexican

[44] Estridentismo (Stridentism) was an avant-garde movement in Mexico during the 1920s, represented by poets Manuel Maples Arce, Germán List Arzubide, and Salvador Gallardo, as well as painters Fermín Revueltas, Ramón Alva de la Canal, and Jean Charlot. Following the influence of the Dada movement in Europe, the estridentistas rejected the academy and encouraged new approaches to modernism through use of technological media such as radio and cinema, printed prose, and plays with a focus on Mexican popular culture. Although it lost its momentum at the end of the 1920s with members leaving Mexico, the movement nevertheless retained an influence in Mexican art during the 1930s. For more information, see Elissa Rashkin, *The Stridentist Movement in Mexico: The Avant-Garde and Cultural Change in the 1920s* (Lanham, MD: Lexington Books, 2009); Luis Mario Schneider, ed., *El estridentismo: México 1921-1927* (Mexico City: Instituto de Investigaciones Estéticas, Universidad Nacional Autónoma de México, 1985).

[45] Noche Mexicana was a festival or garden party in Chapultepec Park in 1921, held to commemorate the Centennial of Independence. The festival was modeled after regional fairs and featured several examples of popular and regional culture. See Rashkin, *The Stridentist Movement in Mexico*, 103; and Rick A. López, "The Noche Mexicana and Popular Arts," in *The Eagle and the Virgin: Nation and Cultural Revolution in Mexico, 1920-1940*, ed. Mary Kay Vaughan and Stephen E. Lewis (Durham, NC: Duke University Press, 2006), 23–42.

[46] In 1925, Domínguez composed for the revista *La revista es mía*, with Alvaro Pruneda. Their song "La Catarina" is featured and sung by the tiple Chucha Camacho. See Armando de María y Campos, *Crónicas de teatro de "Hoy"* (Mexico City: Ediciones Botas, 1941), 40.

musicians, composers, performers, musicologists, critics, and educators met to discuss musical matters. Topics for debate at this meeting ranged from issues of national music, folklore, and the state of musical affairs in the post-Revolutionary society, taking the form of presentations of papers that were then discussed and evaluated during the eight-day meeting.[47] Leonora Saavedra notes that the congress had three main groups of participants: the *tradicionalistas* (traditionalists), an older generation of composers who did not feel the desire to move away from the late Romantic, European style and felt little need to search for a national style of composition; the *evolutionistas* (evolutionists), composers following the path of Julián Carrillo and his work on microtonalism; and the participants interested in folk music, to which Domínguez belonged.[48] In his paper entitled "Nuevas orientaciones sobre el folk-lore mexicano" ("New Orientations in Mexican Folklore"), Domínguez adamantly suggests that Mexican composers move away from the European art-music tradition, criticizing arrangers of popular music and blaming Manuel M. Ponce for the aesthetic injury caused on folk music.[49] Domínguez, who had been a student of Carrillo's at the Conservatorio Nacional de Música and was the only musician at the time to conduct fieldwork on folk music in Mexico, insisted that the young composers concentrate on Mexico's folkloric and regional musics, heavily emphasizing the need for these individuals to do fieldwork, transcribe, and publish this music. Incorporating the melodies in their own music would mold a Mexican musical nationalism and move away from a European model. His paper was rejected.

Although examples of Domínguez's compositions are scarce, it can be deduced whether he incorporated his ideologies in his musical and folkloric undertakings.[50] During the 1930s, Domínguez became heavily involved in Mexico's dance culture, the Escuela Nacional de Danza (National School of

---

[47] For more information on the First National Congress of Music in 1926, see Alejandro L. Madrid, *The Sounds of the Modern Nation: Music, Culture, and Ideas in Post-Revolutionary Mexico* (Philadelphia: Temple University Press, 2009), 112–37; Alejandro L. Madrid, "The Sounds of the Nation: Visions of Modernity and tradition in Mexico's First National Congress," *Hispanic American Historical Review* 86, no. 4 (2006): 681–706; Leonora Saavedra, "Of Selves and Others: Historiography, Ideology, and the Politics of Modern Mexican Music," PhD diss., University of Pittsburgh, 2001.

[48] Saavedra, "Of Selves and Others," 181–84.

[49] In an essay for *Revista de Revistas* entitled "La música y la canción mexicana," Ponce advocates for the appropriation of the popular canción by Western art music in order to elevate the music to reach the cultural elite and bourgeoisie. Saavedra notes that, upon a closer reading of the article, Ponce saw himself as the composer with high enough status to succeed in that endeavor. For a discussion of Ponce's article and his work with the canción, see Saavedra, "Of Selves and Others," 19–27.

[50] Recordings of musical arrangements by Francisco Domínguez are located at the Museo de Culturas Populares in Mexico City. This collection includes *Ay cocol, Costumbres Yaquis, El palomo,*

Dance) and the Escuela de Plástica Dinámica (School of Dynamic Plastic Arts).[51] According to several theater programs, Domínguez composed ballet and dance music with regional and folkloric themes, such as *Tierra* (*Earth*), *La danza de los Malinches* (*The Dance of the Malinches*), and *La virgen y las fieras* (*The Virgin and the Beasts*).[52] Domínguez helped develop the curriculum at the Escuela Nacional de Danza, particularly in indigenous and folkloric dance, and in 1935 he was appointed the school's director. He continued his collaborations and involvement with the school into the 1940s, composing and arranging music for performances of Mexico's top contemporary dancers, including José Limón, Nelly and Gloria Campobello, and Yol-Izma.[53] In conjunction with the Escuela Nacional de Danza, Domínguez continued to work for the Ministry of Public Education, publishing several essays and transcriptions of music from several regions across Mexico.[54]

Owing to Domínguez's involvement with the Ministry of Education and his work with the dancers, he was hired as the composer for Carlos Navarro's *Janitzio*. How he came to be hired for that film is unknown, but he may have become acquainted with actor and photographer Luis Márquez Romay, who also became the film's screenwriter. In 1922, Márquez enrolled in film workshops sponsored by the Ministry of Public Education "to save the visual memory of the ministry's activities."[55] The following year, he accompanied ethnographers on the "Misiones Culturales" (Cultural Missions) to Janitzio, in marvel over the local folklore particularly the celebration of *Día de muertos*.[56] According to the entry in Emilio García Riera's *Historia documental del cine mexicano*, Márquez states:

El capire, and a recording featuring Yucateca singer Guty Cárdenas accompanied by the Orquesta Madriguera.

[51]   Tortajada Quiroz, *Danza y poder*, 64.

[52]   Tortajada Quiroz also lists the following works composed by Domínguez during the 1930s, which received support from Lázaro Cárdenas: *El vaso de dios, Ofrendas y danza ritual, Simiente, Xochiquétzal, Yohualnepantla, Amarándecua, 30–30*, and *El quinto sol* or *Sacrificio gladiatorio*; ibid., 124n16.

[53]   Yol-Izma was especially known for her folkloric and indigenous dances. Domínguez provided music for several of her dance performances, such as *Coqueta* and *Danza tehuana* (1929); *Danza antigua tarasca, La promesa, La siembre*, and *Danza michoacana* (1932). See César Delgado Martínez and Julio C. Villalva Jiménez, *Yol-Izma: La danzarina de las leyendas* (Mexico City: Escenología A.C., 1996), 189–96.

[54]   His contributions for the Ministry of Education's folkloric investigations of Mexico during the 1930s include: Chalma, Estado de México (1931); Música Yaqui, México DF (1931); Jilotepec, Estado de México (1931); Tepoztlán, Morelos (1933); Huixquilucan, Estado de México (1933); Regiones de los Yaquis, Seris y Mayos Sonora (1933); San Juan de los Lagos, Jalisco (1934); Chiapas (1934); San Pedro Tlachichilco, Hidalgo (1934); Tepoztlán, Morelos (1937).

[55]   Aurelio de los Reyes, "Luis Márquez y el cine," *Alquimia* 4, no. 10 (2000): 34.

[56]   Ernesto Peñaloza Méndez, "De luces y sombra," *Luna Córnea* 32 (2008): 216.

I visited the island of Janitzio for the first time in 1923; they celebrated the famous night of the dead, which is not known in Mexico City. Afterward, Rafael Saavedra and Carlos González did the Teatro del Murciélago where they presented diverse typical aspects of Michoacán; this is a how they learned about the Danza de los Moros, the Viejitos, the night of the dead in Mexico City.[57]

It is possible that Domínguez and Márquez worked together or at least were acquainted during this trip. Regardless of whether they met or not, though, Domínguez became the film's composer. Surprisingly, he did not incorporate his musical ideologies from the First National Congress of Music into his film score; instead, he went a different, more exoticist route.

Janitzio: The Fictional Ethnography?

Janitzio tells the story of star-crossed lovers who suffer first at the hands of an outsider, then through the intolerance of their own community. The romance between the fisherman Zirahuén (Emilio Fernández) and Eréndira (María Teresa Orozco) is challenged due to the alleged tradition of the Purépecha people of Janitzio: if a native female has sexual relations with an outsider, that female will be considered impure (figure 3.1). Because impurity was considered an insult to the Purépecha populations, she and her lover must be punished by death, their bodies thrown into Lake Pátzcuaro. Zirahuén and Eréndira's romance is cut short when a corrupt businessman, Manuel Moreno (Gilberto González), takes over the fish market on the island and buys the people's catch for much lower than what he sells. When Zirahuén confronts him, they fight and Zirahuén is subsequently arrested and thrown in prison. In order to negotiate his release, Eréndira agrees to go away with Moreno to Pátzcuaro. After Zirahuén is freed, he discovers her infidelity and considers her to be impure. Although Zirahuén eventually accepts her, their people do not and she is stoned to death. Zirahuén, heartbroken, carries her body into the lake until they both disappear under the water, bringing the film to a tragic end.

---

[57] From Raquel Tibol, "México en la cultura," Supplement in *Excélsior,* January 1, 1956 quoted in Emilio García Riera, *Historia documental del cine mexicano* (Guadalajara: Universidad de Guadalajara, 1993), 1:154. See also de los Reyes, "Luis Márquez y el cine," 33–38.

Figure 3.1 The star-crossed lovers Zirahuén (Emilio Fernández) and Eréndira (María Teresa Orozco) in *Janitzio* (1935). Photo courtesy of Mil Nubes-Foto.

In keeping with the model of ethnographic film, parts of the narrative, in particular the description of the Purépecha's traditions, are supposedly based on accounts collected by Luis Márquez Romay during his sojourn in Janitzio, although this is exaggerated. As Dolores Tierney notes, "there are several sequences where plot development or behavior is explained for a diegetic white audience (who stands in for a non-diegetic white audience)."[58] While not extracted specifically from Purépecha culture, the story is a juxtaposition of elements from two narratives: the punishment handed out to Eréndira is reminiscent of an Old Testament passage from Deuteronomy[59] and Zirahuén's carrying her lifeless body to her final resting place is similar

---

[58] Dolores Tierney, *Emilio Fernández: Pictures in the Margins* (Manchester: Manchester University Press, 2007), 79.

[59] Deuteronomy 22:23–24 states: "If within the city a man comes upon a maiden who is betrothed, and has relations with her, you shall bring them both out to the gate of the city and there stone them to death." Stoning is a common punishment for moral infractions in the Bible.

to the legend of Iztaccíhuatl and Popocatépetl.[60] When filming began in 1933, Janitzio and Pátzcuaro had received ample attention not just from the Ministry of Public Education but also from *El Universal Ilustrado*, which featured photo spreads of the island and the people—in particular Janitzio's picturesque butterfly fishing nets and the island's *Día de muertos* festivities.[61]

Prior to *Janitzio*, Fernández was part of a circle of Mexican actors, producers, and directors working in Hollywood. Upon returning to Mexico, these individuals incorporated techniques and representations learned in Hollywood to early Mexican cinema, which included alternative models of the "primitive Other."[62] According to García Riera, *Janitzio* gave Fernández an opportunity to proudly display his athletic torso while wearing a small white undergarment, strategically fashioned to look like a loincloth, stating, "*Janitzio* was a tribute to the *Tarzan* style imposed in the era of films with Johnny Weissmuller, a style that exalted the innocent sensuality of the 'primitive.'"[63] Zirahuén is captured majestically by Jack Draper's Eisensteinian-influenced cinematography against medium shots of the butterfly nets and the establishing shots of the island, marketing him as an attractive and essentialist specimen of Mexican indigeneity.[64] Advertisements in the periodical *El Universal* describe the film as "A great Mexican film; the perfume of a legend teeming with romance and tragedy,"[65] and "a film with very Mexican customs."[66] What music helped to reinforce these decided Mexican customs?

Straddling the silent and sound periods, *Jantizio* relies predominantly on music to propel the narrative and provide adequate environmental and emotional cues. The underscoring stands in for limited dialogue and, as such,

---

[60] According to Aztec legend, Iztaccíhuatl was a princess who fell in love with the warrior Popocatépetl, and they planned to marry. When Popocatépetl went to war, Iztaccíhuatl was told he had died. Upon receiving the news, Iztaccíhuatl died of grief. When Popocatépetl returned, he was dismayed to discover his love had died. He carried her body outside of Tenochtitlán and remained at her grave. Seeing this display, the gods covered them both with snow and turned them into mountains. Popocatépetl was transformed into a volcano, erupting and sending ash onto the city in his rage, and Iztaccíhualt remained a snow-capped mountain that resembles a woman sleeping. See Guadalupe García Miranda, ed., *Artes de México: Los dos volcanes: Popocatépetl e Iztaccíhuatl* 73 (Mexico City: Artes de México, 2006).

[61] *El Universal Ilustrado* featured weekly photo spreads of and articles on several locations in Michoacán from January through March 1933. The film, however, was not mentioned in the articles.

[62] Also in Hollywood with Fernández were Lupita Tovar, Dolores del Río, Ramón Novarro, director Carlos Navarro, actor and director Antonio Moreno, and the sound engineers Los Hermanos Rodríguez.

[63] Emilio García Riera, *Emilio Fernández, 1904-1986* (Guadalajara: Universidad de Guadalajara, Centro de Investigaciones e Enseñanza Cinematográficas, 1987), 19.

[64] For an analysis of the visual construction of Fernández as Zirahuén, see Tierney, *Emilio Fernández*, 48-72.

[65] "Un gran película mexicana," *El Universal*, September 28, 1935.

[66] Ibid.

acts in the manner of the silent film's compiled score.[67] This is evident in the introductory six-minute sequence that depicts several changes in mood, location, and character situation, yet has no dialogue. This sequence quotes the principal theme and then moves into a series of major key folkloric-like melodies performed primarily by woodwinds, moving in parallel thirds, reminiscent of a canción. While these melodies provide important environmental cues, it is the principal theme that is repeatedly used during the film's more dramatic scenes.

Domínguez begins the film with the principal theme based on an A minor descending pentatonic scale. This theme contains heavy articulations, emphasized by the low brass and, at other times, the upper woodwinds. In film music, the use of pentatonic and modal scales to signify the Other was standard practice, particularly in silent-film music anthologies that contained collections of music associated with moods, actions, locations, and ethnicity. Claudia Gorbman argues that musical stereotypes for the exotic Other, notably any indigenous archetype, "descend from a Euro-American all-purpose shorthand for representing primitive or exotic peoples. Musical representations of Turks, Chinese, Scots, and generic peasants since the late eighteenth century have tended toward pentatonicism, rhythmic repetitiveness, and open fourths and fifths."[68] Gorbman proposes a binary representation of the Hollywood Indian archetype featured in westerns. They are represented either as bloodthirsty marauders, represented by rhythmic, repetitive drumming figures, typically the Scotch snap, or as romanticized and noble, depicted with lush melodies in a legato style.[69]

---

[67] For more information on compiled scores for silent films, see Claudia Gorbman, *Unheard Melodies: Narrative Film Music* (Bloomington: Indiana University Press, 1987); Kathryn Kalinak, *Settling the Score: Music and the Classical Hollywood Film Score* (Madison: University of Wisconsin Press, 1992); Martin Miller Marks, *Music in the Silent Film: Contexts and Case Studies, 1895–1924* (New York: Oxford University Press, 1997); James Wierzbicki, *Film Music: A History* (New York: Routledge, 2009).

[68] Claudia Gorbman, "Scoring the Indian: Music in the Liberal Western," in *Western Music and Its Others: Difference, Representation, and Appropriation in Music*, ed. Georgina Born and David Hesmondhalgh (Berkeley: University of California Press, 2000), 236. For a source on scoring the Indian archetype in film and popular theater, see also Michael V. Pisani, "'I'm an Indian Too': Creating Native American Identities in Nineteenth- and Early Twentieth-Century Music," in *The Exotic in Western Music*, ed. Jonathan Bellman (Boston: Northeastern University Press, 1998), 218–57.

[69] Repetitive percussive ostinati and the Scotch snap are not found in the underscoring for the fictional indigenista films of the 1930s and 1940s. However, Silvestre Revueltas utilized this rhythmic figure in his work *Cuauhnáhuac* (1931). Saavedra points out that Revueltas's past experiences in the silent-film houses of San Antonio and Mobile may have been influential for Revueltas's stereotypical signifier of the Amerindian. The silent-film music anthology *Sam Fox Moving Picture Music* by J. S. Zamecnik features a section entitled "Indian Music" that depicts a similar rhythmic pattern. See Saavedra, "Of Selves and Others," 257–58.

The Hollywood western, however, cannot strictly be compared to the fictional indigenista film because representations of the Amerindian are distinct. Mexican cinema did not portray indigenous populations as antagonistic or violent but, rather, exalted them, featuring him or her (typically him) as noble and heroic, but also at times oppressed and struggling. Music in the indigenista films developed, or borrowed from, the rising Mexican musical nationalism when composers such as Carlos Chávez looked to the Amerindian for inspiration in uncovering a national identity, appropriating current indigenous melodies for their own music.[70] Regardless of ideology and personal beliefs, film music representing indigenous cultures followed in the then current art-music trends, marking film music as another area in which composers could illustrate a representation of the indigenous, but now with the visual crutch of the screen.[71] In her study of the politics of modern Mexican music and national musical projects, Leonora Saavedra examines the state of research regarding music in indigenous communities in Mexico at the end of the nineteenth and into the early twentieth centuries, and how composers approached the Indian topos in their works. During the 1920s, composers, such as Chávez, Antonio Gomezanda, and Manuel M. Ponce, adopted Western art-music signifiers for the exoticized Other to represent the indigenous. The Acadmia de Investigación de la Música Popular within the Conservatorio Nacional de Música was one space where the exploration of pentatonicism in pre-Columbian music took place. An influential source for this period is René and Marguerite d'Harcourt's study *La Musique des Incas et ses survivances* (*The Music of the Incas and its Survival*; 1925), in which "the authors collected and transcribed Peruvian folk music, which they presented as the authentic surviving Inca music because it was based—as all primitive musics of the world were said to be—on pentatonic collections." Saavedra further asserts:

> The identification of the pentatonic with the Indian is based on the evolutionist assumption, widely held in European scholarship and not exclusive

---

[70] Chávez provides the best example of this with his composition *Sinfonía India* (1935), which features two Seri melodies transcribed by Domínguez, "I Coos" and "Jime Eke," from his trips to the Yaqui, Seri, and Mayo regions in 1933; see Ibid., 305.

[71] Saavedra observes that the music intended to depict the Aztec as Other was extended to incorporate the contemporary indigenous populations, although this is not made explicit. In sound cinema of the 1930s, the indigenista films did not depict a pre-Columbian population but, rather, the present-day indigenous experience, leaving the pre-Columbian traditions to silent film. One exception is *El signo de la muerte* (*The Sign of Death*; 1939, dir. Chano Ureta) starring Mario Moreno ("Cantinflas"). During the 1940s, more films featuring pre-Columbian cultures, particularly the Aztecs, surfaced, retelling the story of Juan Diego and the sighting of the Virgin of Guadalupe, such as *La virgen morena* (*The Brown Skinned Virgin*; 1942, dir. Gabriel Soria).

to the d'Harcourts, that all musical cultures pass through a series of steps similar to the developmental steps of human beings (infancy, adolescence, maturity, etc.). According to this view, in "primitive" cultures music is pentatonic, and only by "progressing" do cultures "progress" in their music to the use of heptatonic and diatonic scales.[72]

The use of the pentatonic paradigm, as Saavedra argues, is an example of the European value system applied to represent other cultures, furthering the contention that "Mexican scholars and composers internalized a European conception of the non-European as primitive, took this conception as their point of departure, [and] concluded that ancient Mexican music must have been primitive."[73] As previously stated, Domínguez was surrounded by several composers who incorporated this framework in their own music, and he was associated with those who were the most influential in music from his participation in the First National Congress of Music. Although Domínguez argued for young composers to conduct fieldwork and use the transcribed melodies as the basis for their own compositions to represent national identity, Domínguez fell into the Western European paradigm of representing the Other for the film's theme. The film presents the Purépecha people on Janitzio as oppressed by modern society, struggling to cling to their traditions when a white, modern outsider shakes the balance. This struggle is aurally syncretized by this exoticized principal theme. Its articulation in the film occurs in several scenes, each of which strategically amplifies the conditions of the Purépecha people, either foreshadowing tragedy or solidifying social injustice.

As previously stated, the film begins with little to no dialogue, allowing the music to function as the dominant sonic source. The theme repeats while images of the fishermen in their boats with the butterfly nets appear, pulling in their catch. The goal of this sequence is the ethnographic portrayal of the island's idyllic way of life. We in the audience see the labor involved in bringing in the catch through extreme close-ups on the fish in the nets and choppy tracking shots of the fishermen in their canoes and rowboats.

A component of the ethnographical paradigm is the continued education of the outsider audience through explanations of the onscreen society. The mouthpiece for this education is the learned, mestizo character Don Pablo

---

[72] Ibid., 235–36.
[73] Ibid., 237.

(Max Langler), who explains the customs of the island to Moreno and, by extension, to the broader audience. Don Pablo instructs Moreno about the tradition of outsiders having relations with the inhabitants, but also describes the consequences when another village is caught trespassing on Purépecha territory. He explains that since the time of the Conquest, Páztcuaro waters belonged to the people of Janitzio. Any other villagers who fish in "their" lake are violating the time-honored code, and the Purépecha have the right to defend themselves. The penetration of their territorial waters is construed as an injustice, as their tradition and way of life are under attack, and the principal theme returns full force in order to accentuate this fact.

After the opening musical sequence, the theme returns when Zirahuén and the other fishermen on the island witness Moreno lower the prices of their catch (figure 3.2). During a long shot of the fishermen collectively reading the announcement of the lowered prices, the oboe and flute quote the antecedent section of the theme in unison, which is then followed by the consequent with full orchestra, at a slow tempo and legato. More articulated weight is placed on the triplets at the beginning of the theme, emphasizing

Figure 3.2 Sign indicating the lower price for the catch, in *Janitzio* (1935). Screen capture from film.

the heavy atmosphere of despair. The theme repeats six times, accompanying a sequence of images of the fishermen and Zirahuén, throwing concerned and resentful glances at Moreno as he walks through the town. The weighted descent of the theme, moving from upper woodwinds to lower strings, its darkened tone color, the minor key, and the slower tempo reiterate the injustice of the situation, providing no movement toward a positive closure.

This scene mirrors circumstances in the current political and social sphere of the 1930s. The Revolution attempted to dismantle the oppressive structures of the Porfiriato, particularly in regard to treatment of the lower and working classes, and the weakening of the national bourgeoisie. During the Maximato, however, Mexico gravitated to capitalist development, allowing many of the dominant groups from the Porfiriato, such as commercial landowners and industrialists, to reinstate themselves in the new economic system. While the working classes were brought into the national political life as a consequence of the Revolution and the Constitution of 1917, the post-Revolutionary central government sought to control the population rather than respond to them, intent on preserving their economic model. Labor laws were limited and the working class found the objectives for which they fought for were not met.[74] By the 1930s, changes were underway, particularly during the Lázaro Cárdenas sexenio, which established alliances with the working and lower class.

Moving away from the ethnographical approach and more into the realm of fiction, the theme also foreshadows tragedy, which is most prominent at the film's end. When Janitzio's adversaries take revenge on Zirahuén by stabbing him, he is taken back to Janitzio to recover. Eréndira, worried, returns to Janitizo in a canoe in order to search for him, knowing her life is danger by returning. She is quickly spotted by her rival Tacha, who then rings a large bell in the village center to inform the villagers that Eréndira has returned. Once told, the villagers come out of their homes and shops with lit torches, intent on punishing Eréndira for disobeying the island's tradition. The theme is quoted in entirety several times legato during this sequence, moving from low brass to high woodwinds, to full orchestra, and provides a sorrowful accompaniment to Zirahuén and Eréndira's situation before being replaced by faster, rhythmic music that is intended to emphasize the panic of the chase. The torch-bearing crowd corners Zirahuén and

---

[74] Nora Hamilton, *The Limits of State Autonomy: Post-Revolutionary Mexico* (Princeton, NJ: Princeton University Press, 1982), 98–103.

Eréndira. Seeing no clear escape, Eréndira sacrifices herself when the crowd begins to throw stones at the couple.[75]

Dominguez's theme is not the only representative piece of music in the film, but it is the most utilized. Other melodies are used to accompany the various moods and emphasize specific situations that contain stylistic characteristics similar to the music of the region as transcribed in Domínguez's monograph on the music of Michoacán. Domínguez supplies one song in the film baring similarities to a *pirékua*, a lyrical Purépecha canción typically in 3/4 or 6/8, with romantic text, to correspond with Zirahuén and Eréndira's romance. Played by guitars and clarinet, and sung by a male vocalist, the canción offers the necessary regional association that the underscoring does not provide. The canción is brief and is delicately introduced as diegetic music, lending a hint of tenderness to the blossoming relationship and providing a hint of authenticity to the portrayal of the onscreen culture:[76] "Now you do not remember / That I was your first love."[77] The inclusion of this melody is similar to Silvestre Revueltas's 1933 work *Janitzio,* which features several signifiers of the folkloric and popular. Revueltas's *Janitzio* is composed in an ABA form and exhibits an intended pirékua played in parallel thirds by oboes in the A sections. In addition to studying and transcribing melodies from the Janitzio and Pátzcuaro regions, it is likely that Domínguez was influenced by Revueltas's work for his own film score.[78] According to *Revista de Revistas,* the Orquesta Sinfoníca de México, which performed Revueltas's *Janitzio* in December 1933, played Domínguez's score for the film's musical track in 1935.[79]

---

[75] See also Jacqueline Avila, "Musicalizando la muerte en el cine mexicano durante los 1930s," *Balajú: Revista de Cultura y Comunicación* 3, no. 2 (2016): 48–60.

[76] Slobin, "The Steiner Superculture," 20.

[77] Peñaloza Méndez, "De luces y sombra," 218.

[78] For more information of the Revueltas's *Janitzio,* see Roberto Kolb Neuhaus, "*Janitzio,* ¿música de tarjeta postal? La retórica de un albur musical de Silvestre Revueltas," working paper, Universidad Nacional Autónoma de México, 2006. For a cinematic analysis of the work, see Jacqueline Avila, "The Influence of the Cinematic in the Music of Silvestre Revueltas," master's thesis, University of California, Riverside, 2007.

[79] See Hugo del Mar, "Luces y Sombras del Cine Nacional," *Revista de Revistas,* July 28, 1935, p. 4. Del Mar states that the orchestra is directed by Revueltas, but does not mention whether Revueltas himself conducted Domínguez's underscoring. According to another entry from *Revista de Revistas,* filming for *Janitzio* began in November 1934. It is possible that Domínguez attended the performance of *Janitzio* in 1933 and became aware of Revueltas's technique with mestizo musical elements. For his orchestral work, Carlos Chávez, who in 1931 was then director of the Conservatorio Nacional de Música, encouraged Revueltas to study the music of Pátzcuaro. Saavedra notes, however, that it is not known if Revueltas completed the trip. See Saavedra, "Of Selves and Others," 267.

Janitzio was applauded in several periodicals for depicting "lo más mexicano" ("the most Mexican") and is considered the industry's first anthropological attempt:

> "Janitzio," the Mexican film that has triumphed on its own merits and for its high documentary value, provides in each one of its scenes landscapes that will impress with their beauty, and regional types of indisputable authenticity, revealing to the world the unsuspected national treasures and the intense artistic temperament of the natives from the Michoacán region.[80]

The fictional ethnographical structure of the film concurs with Gamio's argument that modern society should seek to understand the cultures of indigenous populations in order to successfully integrate them. Several of the contributors to the film's development, including the screenwriter Marquéz and the composer Domínguez, completed research and conducted fieldwork with the community presented on screen. The film, however, does not encourage cultural integration, as modern society is portrayed as oppressive, corrupt, and racist and the Purépecha are seen as isolationist and resistant.

María Candelaria and Recycled Narratives

By the early 1940s, the representation of the indigenous and discourses of indigenismo lessened as a consequence to the modernization and industrialization that characterized President Manuel Ávila Camacho's administration (1940–1946). Many of the social and labor reforms initiated by Cárdenas desisted or came to a halt. Rural education programs that promoted integration and social transformation continued, but began to copy the methods of their urban counterparts in their attempts to assimilate the indigenous populations into modern Mexican society as quickly as possible. The agrarian reform initiated by Cárdenas stopped as the new administration shifted toward a more capitalist paradigm focused on obtaining foreign capital; and the Catholic Church, which had been distanced from Mexican society through the separation of Church and state in the Constitution of 1917 and the Cristero rebellion, surfaced again as an important conservative voice.[81] Daily

---

[80] "Auténticos Pescadores del lago de Pátzcuaro," *El Universal*, October 6, 1935.

[81] The Cristero rebellion arose when Calles enforced the anticlerical articles of the Constitution of 1917. He first ended religious processions, then deported priests and nuns and closed churches

life for Mexicans was changing and the preoccupations of the government moved away from the revalorization of indigenous populations and toward the modernization of the nation.

In 1944, the indigenous became a film protagonist once again when *Janitzio* actor-turned-director Emilio Fernández teamed up with cinematographer Gabriel Figueroa, screenwriter Mauricio Magdaleno, and Francisco Domínguez for the new indigenista film, *María Candelaria*.[82] Unlike *Janitzio*, this film maintains a more coveted place in popular culture, considered to be the most important national film for exhibiting a crucial representation of Mexicanidad for national and international audiences.[83] In this film, Fernández attempts to capture the beauty and simplicity of the indigenous by transplanting the *Janitzio* narrative to the idyllic floating gardens of Xochimilco, with two representative faces of Mexico's rising star system, Dolores del Río and Pedro Armendáriz, termed by Monsiváis as "the mythic couple of Mexican cinema." According to reviews in *Excélsior* from January 25, 1944, the film was considered "a masterpiece of national cinema," acknowledging Fernández as a national talent and genius.[84]

Set in 1909, a year before the Revolution, *María Candelaria* tells the tragic story of the young indigenous woman, María Candelaria, and the circumstances leading to her death. María Candelaria (Dolores del Río) and her fiancé Lorenzo Rafael (Pedro Armendáriz) live slightly outside of

and convents. In 1926, the archbishop declared a strike against ceremonies and reactions turned violent and bloody, particularly in Michoacán, Jalisco, Puebla, Oaxaca, Zacatecas, and Nayarit. Fighting lasted until 1929, when the new presidential elections took place. See David C. Bailey, *Viva Cristo Rey: The Cristero Rebellion and the Church–State Conflict in Mexico* (Austin: University of Texas Press, 1974); Susan M. Deeds, Michael C. Meyer and William L. Sherman, *The Course of Mexican History*, 7th ed. (Oxford: Oxford University Press, 2003), 565–68.

[82] Screenwriter Magdaleno did not want to write the screenplay for the film, believing the narrative to be poor and in bad taste. In addition to successful screenwriting, Magdaleno is a highly regarded novelist concerned with indigenous themes. In his work *El resplandor* (*The Glow*), he details the inequalities and injustices suffered by indigenous communities after the Revolution. See Eugenia Meyer, *Cuadernos de la Cineteca Nacional: Testimonios para la historia del cine mexicano* (Mexico City: Cineteca Nacional, 1976), 3:29.

[83] This fact is based on a study entitled "Revisión del Cine Mexicano," completed in December 1990–February 1991 by famed anthropologist Nestor García Canclini, presented in his book *Los nuevos espectadores: Cine, televisión y video en México* (Mexico City: Consejo Nacional para la Cultura y las Artes, 1994). The study consisted of questions regarding the state of Mexican national cinema up to the present period, being particularly mindful of spectatorship during the 1940s and 1950s. Participants were asked to list three films they considered important to national cinema. Of the selected films, *María Candelaria* was ranked the highest, with 20% of the participants' votes. Also, *María Candelaria* was an entry in the Cannes International Film Festival and received the Grand Prix, the first time a Mexican film had won the prestigious prize.

[84] "Una obra maestra del cine nacional es la película *María Candelaria*," *Excélsior*, January 25, 1944.

Xochimilco, ostracized by their people because María Candelaria's mother was a prostitute (figure 3.3). As a result, María is forbidden to sell her flowers in the village. Aside from her village's hostility, María Candelaria is consistently subjugated by the mestizo businessman, Don Damián (Miguel Inclán), who claims that she owes him money, but is in actuality resentful because she declines his sexual advances. Don Damián is an unusual character that mediates relations with the state on behalf of the indigenous populace; he runs the local drug store and is in charge of distributing quinine to the people, but

Figure 3.3 María Candelaria (Dolores del Río) and Lorenzo Rafael (Pedro Armandáriz), in *María Candelaria* (1944). Photo courtesy of Mil Nubes-Foto.

only does so as he sees fit. Because of his position and because he is mestizo, he occupies a higher social status, designing his own identity with a black charro suit and speaking of the uselessness of the indigenous community. Joanne Hershfield points out that "Don Damián articulates the state's paternalistic attitude towards the Indians, who were generally considered to be like children, incapable of taking care of themselves," yet it is unclear if she is speaking about the 1909 state or the 1940s state.[85]

María Candelaria and Lorenzo Rafael want to marry, but through several unfortunate episodes—Don Damien killing their prize pig and refusing quinine to María Candelaria after she contracts malaria, and Lorenzo Rafael's imprisonment for stealing the quinine and a wedding dress for his betrothed—the marriage date is postponed. In order for María Candelaria to negotiate Lorenzo's release, she agrees to pose for a portrait for a nameless criollo painter, who is in awe of her indigenous visage and labels her "the essence of Mexico." After painting her face, he is forced to use another model to complete the portrait because María Candelaria refuses to remove her clothes for the nude painting. One of the villagers of Xochimilco catches a glimpse of the completed portrait and informs the rest of the village. Seeking revenge on María Candelaria for shaking the balance of their way of life and their purity, María Candelaria is stoned to death. Lorenzo Rafael, escaped from prison, places her lifeless body in a canoe, and they drift through the canals of Xochimilco at the film's end.

María Candelaria tells a story of the hostility and persecution the protagonist and her fiancé suffer at the hands of her community as a consequence of rigid moral customs, paralleling the supposed Purépecha legends proposed in *Jantizio*. In order to complement the similarities in narrative, Domínguez utilizes the thematic material from *Janitzio* to reinforce its cinematic associations with oppression and social injustice. It is important to note, however, that *Janitzio's* theme is the only music material that is reused, not the whole score. While Domínguez utilizes an exoticist theme in conjunction with vernacular-influenced music to provide an adequate cultural synchresis in *Janitzio*, in *María Candelaria*, Domínguez resorts to other essentialist signifiers that further Fernández's goal of rooting national identity in Mexico's pre-Columbian heritage. This is most illustrative in the opening

---

[85] Joanne Hershfield, *Mexican Cinema/Mexican Woman, 1940–1950* (Tucson: University of Arizona Press, 1996), 55.

scene of the film: a montage of close-up shots of pre-Columbian statues, concluding with a close-up of a contemporary indigenous woman standing next to an Aztec stone statue with defined cheekbones and a stately facial expression. Placing this woman next to the statue links an imagined past with the present, implying that the traditions of the pre-Columbian past (summed up here in artifacts and facial features) are still alive. This sequence is sonically represented with an implied indigenous melody based on a pentatonic scale, repeated twice by flute, rattles, and marimba, and eighth-note ostinato figure performed by percussion. Hershfield astutely observes that this particular sequence is almost identical to Sergei Eisenstein's scene in his prologue to ¡Que viva México!, but rather than operating as a homage, it reenforces the bridge between past and present indigeneity that Fernández attempts to make. Tierney concurs, suggesting these opening shots further embody this idea of continuity between pre-Columbian indigenous cultures and contemporary ones, thereby following the paradigms of the indigenismo project.[86]

Regardless of time period, the Janitzio theme is utilized again, and this time to a greater extent, appearing in María Candelaria more than ten times. It is not entirely known, however, why Domínguez chose to reuse the theme in this film, but in terms of film music practice in Mexico at this time, it was common for film composers to recycle some, if not all, their scores, due to severe time constraints, funding issues, or problems with studio orchestras. By 1943, Domínguez had composed original music for four films, including Soy puro mexicano (I'm a Pure Mexican; 1942) and Flor silvestre (Wild Flower; 1943), both directed by Emilo Fernández, and Doña Bárbara (1943), directed by Fernando de Fuentes. The reuse of the Janitzio theme may be the result of a heavy workload or time restraints, but after watching the complete, edited version of the film, Domínguez may have recognized the borrowed narrative and chose to recycle his past theme, reorchestrated and bursting with studio polish, for moments that reflected identical conditions of oppression and injustice. The music reinforcing these particular aspects of the narrative links the two films, as well as past and present approaches to cinematic indigenismo.

---

[86] Tierney, Emilio Fernández, 81–82. This sequence is also replicated in a 1942 Office of the Coordinator of Inter-American Affairs (OCIAA) travelogue entitled Yucatán, which superimposes the image of a present-day Mayan male with a statue of an Olmec head, indicating visually once again that the ancient past is still alive particularly in the facial features of present day inhabitants of the Yucatán.

Functioning differently from *Janitzio*, which did not associate the theme to a specific character, the theme in *María Candelaria* amplifies the circumstances surrounding María Candelaria, and not the other characters. The film and the music focus on her, her actions, and her village's actions against her. María Candelaria becomes a key symbol in the film, an icon that synthesizes the nation with the indigenous through the portrait painted of her by the nameless painter, who describes her as an "Indian of pure Mexican race, a princess meant to judge the conquistadors." Domínguez's theme reinforces her significance in three crucial scenes that construct an intimate tie with María Candelaria and the oppression and intolerance that she suffers from her community rather than from the outside.

Intending to sell her flowers in an early scene to pay for a debt set by the film's villain Don Damián, María Candelaria floats through the canals in a canoe, singing her *pregón* (street cry) in a high soprano register, more reminiscent of a singer trained in the art-music tradition than in a folkloric singing style. Construing her attempt to sell in the village as insubordination, the entire village gathers gradually, creating a blockade (figure 3.4). As she moves closer to them in the water, the diegetic pregón transitions into the non-diegetic theme in low woodwinds, gradually includes more instrumentation and crescendos, creating a separation between the villagers and herself. The theme, coupled visually with a long shot of the villagers' faces, turns into a declamatory wall of sound, enforcing the notion that she is not welcome and establishing a strong sense of persecution, placing María Candelaria and the villagers on opposing ends until Lorenzo Rafael calls out to her and tells her to go home

Rather than just marking the scene as "oppression in action," the theme functions here in two ways. When María Candelaria paddles toward the villagers, the camera, through cut shots, gradually zooms back out to provide a wider view of the surroundings, making clear that the entire village is present and not letting her pass. Musically, the theme is repeated at a slower tempo and softer dynamic, but with each cut, it becomes faster and louder, accentuating the expansion of space and people within the diegesis. The theme still functions as that of oppression and does so in conjunction with the camera's wide-ranging gaze. After María Candelaria stops rowing and confronts the villagers, extreme close-up shots reveal the villagers' expressions of anger and blatant intolerance, in contrast to María Candelaria's visage of desperation and defeat. The theme's texture thins from full orchestra to individual woodwinds, narrowing that cinematic space

Figure 3.4 María Candelaria (Dolores del Río) versus the pueblo of Xochimilco, in *María Candelaria* (1944). Screen capture from film.

and becoming much more intimate. At this point, the theme transitions to reflect María Candelaria's despair, almost rhythmically sighing with her, accentuating the deep weight of each breath. This music reinforces María Candelaria's emotions and functions not only as marker of oppression but also as a physical indication of her desperation and loss.

In a later scene, Lorenzo Rafael is thrown in prison for stealing the quinine and the wedding dress from Don Damián, leading to María Candelaria's decision to pose for the painter. After the portrait is completed—with María Candelaria's face on another model's nude body—a resident of Xochimilco recognizes the naked María Candelaria in the portrait. As she rushes back to Xochimilco to the tell the villagers, the theme accompanies her, one restatement for each cut shot of a new location and with new instrumentation, which foreshadows the violence that will soon take place. When the villagers reach the studio, they see the portrait and are astonished and upset, claiming that María Candelaria has embarrassed the village of Xochimilco and must be thrown out of her garden home. To emphasize their anger, the theme is quoted several times with mounting dynamics and quicker tempi, articulated by the brass in a bombastic manner. Because of the consistency of the theme, coupled with the actions of mounting anger, the theme foreshadows tragedy, similar to *Janitzio*. However, because of its dramatic manner and its consistent presence underneath the dialogue, the theme also fuels the people's anger, siding with them in their antagonism and hatred for María Candelaria.

The next scene pays homage to the climactic ending of *Janitzio*. After leaving the studio, the camera cuts to a close-up of a woman ringing the village's bell, bringing the pueblo together. Much as in *Janitzio*, the bell ringer in *María Candelaria* is the jealous rival who intends on getting rid of María Candelaria by any means possible. The bell calls the people out of their homes, a lynch mob with torches mobilizing to punish María Candelaria. When at the studio, the people agree to throw her out of the village, but with their rapid mobilization and use of torches, it is evident that they intend to kill her. Here, the theme is quoted at several points during the chase, but is also present in a varied form, primarily with repetitive, static eighth notes. María Candelaria runs along the sides of the canals in a panic, followed closely by the torch-bearing mob. Cornered, she cowers against a wall; she does not sacrifice herself as Eréndira did, but she repeats over and over "I did nothing wrong." Lorenzo Rafael reaches her too late; the mob has stoned her and the theme-quoted tutti seals her fate. The film ends with Lorenzo Rafael taking María Candelaria's body in his canoe down the Canal de los muertos (Canal of the Dead) with the final tutti restatement of the theme.

Instead of functioning as a social commentary film on the state of the indigenous populations and the plight of the worker, *María Candelaria* operates more as a melodrama and does not exhibit any reference to other musics in its underscoring. While Domínguez utilized the principal theme from *Janitzio* in *María Candelaria*, he did not incorporate the other music from the film. *María Candelaria* does not feature a working scene, as *Janitzio* and Paul Strand's film *Redes* did with corresponding folk like music, nor does it feature a romantic diegetic canción for the two lovers.[87]

---

[87] Although not strictly classified as an indigenista film, *Redes* exhibits strong similarities visually and musically to *Janitzio*, but the narratives are slightly different: *Janitzio* is a story of star-crossed lovers in Michoacán with a score composed by Domínguez, whereas *Redes* details the uprising that takes place in the small village of Alvarado in the eastern coastal state of Veracruz and features music by Silvestre Revueltas. Both films, however, focus on the plight of the disenfranchised at the hands of a corrupt, capitalist businessman who takes advantage of the fishermen in several ways. The music for each film features a theme solidifying the present oppression felt by the fishing community, folkloric

While at the time considered a prize of the national film industry and having received accolades at Cannes for being an exemplary model of Mexican cinema, the film is not without its criticism, particularly from the nation's prominent artists. In a 1944 interview with the popular film magazine *Novelas de la Pantalla*, Diego Rivera called the film a complete failure. He pointed out the film's many shortcomings, accusing the actors and crew of not conducting proper research into any of the indigenous populations of Xochimilco, relying instead on stereotypes:

> And our actors, living a half hour from Xochimilco, did not bother to visit the city to hear the live voice of the Indians that live there, nor did the cameramen have the good sense to photograph the morning *tianguis*, preferring to do scenes in a more conventional place, full of stalls, unreaslistic and absurd that I have never seen before.[88]

In her study of Emilio Fernández, Tierney also points out that Xochimilco was an odd choice as a filming location. Showing this community so close to the city center, rather than the middle of Lake Pátzcuaro as with *Janitzio*, "suggests *indígena* assimilation." But because it is set prior to the Revolution and "highlighted as a non-modern, peripheral space," it seems remote and isolated to the 1940s audience.[89]

Other critics were more verbally antagonistic about the film. In a review written by critic Efraín Huerta, he states that *María Candelaria* occupies the worst position in Mexican national cinema. Huerta agrees with Rivera in stating that the film did no justice to any Mexican indigenous community, particularly concerning the cinematic village's conservative and over-the-top reaction to María Candelaria's portrait. He, along with author, playwright, and cultural critic Salvador Novo, create a list of reasons explaining why the film is mediocre and terrible. His third reason states:

---

elements accompanying scenes of successful fishing and the quaintness of the village, and dissonant and abrasive variations on the principal theme in scenes of physical conflict. Although *Redes* was filmed before *Janitzio*, it premiered after; yet both films present a powerful response to the current social and political climate. *Janitzio* premiered on September 28, 1935, and *Redes* premiered on July 16, 1936. For more information on Revueltas's score for *Redes*, see Eduardo Contreras Soto, *Silvestre Revueltas en escena y en pantalla: La música del compositor en el cine, el teatro y la danza* (Mexico City: Consejo Nacional para la Cultura y las Artes, Instituto Nacional de Bellas Artes, 2012); José Luis Castillo and Roberto Kolb Neuhaus, eds., *Silvestre Revueltas edición crítica: Redes (1935)* (Mexico City: Universidad Nacional Autónoma de México, 2009); Avila, "The Influence of the Cinematic."

[88] Díaz Ruanova, "Diego Rivera contra todos," *Novelas de la Pantalla*, February 1944.

[89] Tierney, *Emilio Fernández*, 82.

The pueblo's reaction (better said the mass pueblo) of Xochimilco are also the people lower than the bottom and slaves. There is in this a total lack of knowledge of the aborigines and the mestizos of Xochimilco.[90]

Novo and Huerta comment that the narrative, which they describe as *bobo* (stupid) and *ramplón* (vulgar or common), is a repetition of *Janitzio*. Not many critics or scholars comment on the reuse of the musical material, although there are some mentions. The positive review printed in *Excélsior* makes the connection, but with wrong details:

> It has been a while, we do not remember the date, that we admired a Mexican film entitled "Janitzio" and for the first time the praiseworthy work of Emilio Fernández caught our attention as well as the music of the great maestro Silvestre Revueltas, which, of course, was quite different from the monotonous and expression-lacking music we face constantly in our film works.[91]

Despite harsh criticisms and obvious flaws in the narrative and representation of indigenous culture, the film was a success with audiences and continued the so-called Mexican aesthetic in cinema. Fernández's representation of the indigenous, labeled by Adela Fernández as *indias fernandianas* (Fernadian Indians), was based on several cinematic constructions. However, in 1948, Fernández directed *Maclovia*, starring María Félix and Pedro Armendáriz, which recycled the *Janitzio* and *María Candelaria* narrative once again, but used music by Antonio Díaz Conde. The regurgitation of the narrative and its representations indicate that despite flaws, inaccuracies, and constructions based on outside influences, this was one of the most recognized, and popular, constructions of indigenous culture on the silver screen.

---

[90] Efraín Huerta, "Cine," *Esto*, February 3, 1944.
[91] "Una obra maestra del cine nacional es la película *María Candelaria*," *Excélsior*, January 25, 1944. Although music is rarely mentioned, some sources have indicated that either Fernando Domínguez or Silvestre Revueltas composed the film's music.

Conclusion

Although filmed in two different time periods during different social and political climates, *Janitzio* and *María Candelaria* share a similar narrative with similar music to convey similar messages. The integrationist discourses of Gamio and Caso not only advocated teaching the indigenous people how to function in a modernized, Western society but also encouraged that the indigenous populations be understood rather than marginalized and culturally integrated into modern society. Written specifically for a modern mestizo audience and not necessarily an indigenous one, the films attempt to introduce the modern spectator to rural indigenous culture. Ironically, however, the societies on screen are isolationist, unready to be penetrated by modernity or anything outside of their sphere, contradicting the intentions of indigenismo. Changes in this life balance end with tragic consequences within the communities. *Janitzio,* however, delivered other messages regarding social justice and the position of the oppressed worker, not just the indigenous populace, in modern society. *María Candelaria* attempted to identify the modern audience with indigenous communities and show that much of the oppression and negative impact they felt is not so much a consequence of modern society as it is created by the indigenous community itself, therefore the society would be better off on its own.

In imagining a society on screen, Mark Slobin argues that the composer must include music that logically fits with the construction. In doing so, the composer describes how the community lives, creating a musical ethnography for the time period. The repetitive use of the thematic material in both *Janitzio* and *María Candelaria* suggests that the oppression and injustice suffered by the represented indigenous populations is absolute, that the indigenous experience is in a constant state of severity, caused either by an outsider or by those in the community, or both. Domínguez held an influential position as the composer for the emerging national cinema as modern audiences flocked to the theater, where the symbols of the nation were constructed and consistently repeated. Those who investigated these communities further controlled the images and representations in cinema, and Domínguez, as the composer and folklorist, supplied the necessary aural association to guide the audience through these similar narratives. Using exoticist frameworks, Domínguez resorted to a familiar musical construction of the indigenous Other that conforms to then current visual and aural representations, adding to the developing problematic constructions of national identity and cultural integration that were dominating the period.

4

The Singing Charro in the
Comedia Ranchera

Music, Machismo, and the Invention of a Tradition

Chapter 2 explored the utopian escape of the cine de añoranza porfiriana for middle- and upper-class audiences, eager to dismiss any hint of social and economic instability for the safety and security of an imagined Mexico constructed during the Porfiriato. While this escape proved popular with audiences—evidenced by the weekly publicity coverage—the cine de añoranza porfiriana targeted a specific demographic, which limited the industry's repeated use of the genre (only thirteen films were produced during the 1940s). The search for utopia, however, was not confined to the cinematic depiction of the Porfirian bourgeoisie and their social bubble; it extended to the countryside, and specifically to Mexico's central valley haciendas, which were large portions of land converted into self-sufficient agricultural estates. During the early 1930s, films categorized as *cine campirano* (country films) utilized a country backdrop that was shaped as a rural paradise. The central character in these films was the charro, the Mexican horseman dressed in a short jacket, fitted pants with chaps, and wearing a wide-brimmed sombrero.

In films such as *Mano a mano* (*Hand to Hand*; 1932, dir. Arcady Boytler), *Revolución: La sombra de Pancho Villa* (*Revolution: The Shadow of Pancho Villa*; 1933, dir. Miguel Contreras Torres), *La calandria* (1933, dir. Fernando de Fuentes), and *Cielito lindo* (*Beautiful Little Sky*; 1936, dir. Robert Quigley), the charro became the protagonist in narratives set in the time of the nineteenth-century hacienda system and during the armed struggle of the Revolution. His rich history begins during Mexico's *virreinato*, serving as a highly esteemed and decorated horseman who worked in haciendas and ranches and was devoted to *charrería*, the practice of horsemanship.[1] When

---

[1] The *virreinato*, or viceroyalty, refers to the period roughly 1531 to 1821, when Spain conquered and settled Mexico, then known as New Spain. After its conquest, Spain established the seat of the first viceroyalties in what is now Mexico City.

theater, radio, and the silver screen appropriated the charro as a popular archetype, he quickly became the nation's most emblematic and musical figure. Cinema, however, was the major conduit for transmitting both his visual and his aural construction:

> Charro movies projected the image of a Mexico removed from its historical or temporal context, tightly bound to tradition and to the social and moral order dictated by religion. The inhabitants of this imaginary Mexico were rustic, heroic, respectful of honor and customs, and prepared to exhibit at any given moment their courage, virility and machismo, as well as their arrogance, friendliness, and singing ability.[2]

The "charro movies" mentioned here refer to the regional folkloric film genre, the comedia ranchera. Film historian Rafael Aviña describes the genre as an inoffensive way of mythifying the provinces and country life, exhibiting embellishments of Mexican traditional symbols or, as he terms it, *mexiquitos* (little Mexicos):

> The comedia ranchera is an example of an exaggerated Mexican cinema, like tequila and its fierce machos. Its universe is one of mezcal and mariachi, of the earthenware pots and papel picado, of the charro hats, the blankets, the decorated braids and the repertory of regional costumes; the songs of the mariachi, the indigenous songs, and the popular coplas, which are refined antecedents to the vulgar albur.[3]

This description paints a colorful folkloric moving collage, but it only scratches the surface. Beginning with Fernando de Fuentes's *Allá en el Rancho Grande* (*Over on the Big Ranch*; 1936), the comedia ranchera reimagines rural life during the hacienda system with the aid of canciones performed exclusively by the charro protagonist. This charro is constructed as the epitome

---

[2] Tania Carreño King, "I Am Mexican, I Come from an Untamed Land," in *Artes de México: Charrería*, ed. Margarita de Orellana (Mexico City: Artes de México, 2000), 92.

[3] Rafael Aviña, *Una mirada insólita: Temas y géneros del cine mexicano* (Mexico City: Editorial Oceano de Mexico, S.A. de C. V., 2004), 152. The *papel picado* is a popular type of ornament made of colorful paper, pierced to create silhouettes. An *albur* refers to a form of word play that is interpreted as sexual puns or jokes. Albures are usually coded as masculine in nature and refer to homosexuality and phallic imagery. For discussions on the albur in Mexican culture, see Samuel Ramos, *Profile of Man and Culture in Mexico*, rev. ed. (Austin: University of Texas Press, 1962); and Octavio Paz, *The Labryrinth of Solitude*, rev. ed. (New York: Grove Press, 1985).

of machismo—the strong and excessive sense of virility and masculinity—
that occupied a contested space in Mexican identity politics during the twentieth century. Premiering during the sexenio of Lázaro Cárdenas and at the
beginning of his agrarian reform campaigns at the end of the 1930s, *Allá en el
Rancho Grande*, it was believed, provided a conservative reading of the countryside and the hacienda system that moved contrary to the administration's
leftist leanings and intentions.[4] As part of the conservative social discourse,
the charro soon became interpellated by the film industry and the state
as both a symbol of a more traditional bygone period and the paramount
symbol of Mexican masculinity.

The charro and the comedia ranchera, however, can be read and understood as more than just conservative responses to contemporary politics. The
comedia ranchera operates as a portrayal of cultural hybridization where, as
defined by Nestor García Canclini, several facets of popular cultural systems
intersect, constructing new cultural spaces for interpretation.[5] The film genre
consolidated several popular cultural elements and entertainment practices
into one medium, while also exhibiting the changing perceptions of Mexican
masculinity and contemporary musical practices through its singing-charro
protagonist. Throughout the genre's trajectory during the first half of the
twentieth century, music in the form of manifesto-like songs and strategic
underscoring corresponded to social and cultural anxieties taking place in
Mexico's post-Revolutionary years. The end result molded a tradition that
solidified Mexican identity as primarily masculine and macho, and traditional yet modern.

I analyze the singing charro and the comedia ranchera not with the intention of concentrating on picturesque representations of folklore on
screen but, rather, considering both as experimental products stemming
from a specific sociocultural context, functioning as vehicles of cultural and
musical hybridization and as conduits for the changing representations of
Mexicanidad. I focus on three acclaimed comedia rancheras that premiered
during the *época de oro*, all featuring a pivotal singing charro protagonist
that synthesized a conception of machismo with music. The films discussed

---

[4] For more information on the agrarian reform during the Cárdena's administration, see Tore
C. Olsson, *Agrarian Crossings: Reformers and the Remaking of the U.S. and Mexican Countryside*
(Princeton, NJ: Princeton University Press, 2017). For information on the synthesis of politics and
Mexican cinema, see Carlos Monsiváis, *Pedro Infante: Las leyes del querer* (Mexico City: Santillana
Ediciones Generales, S.A. de C.V., 2008).

[5] Néstor García Canclini, *Hybrid Cultures: Strategies for Entering and Leaving Modernity*
(Minneapolis: University of Minnesota Press, 1995), xxv.

are: *Allá en el Rancho Grande, ¡Ay Jalisco, no te rajes!* (*Jalisco, Don't Backslide!*; 1941, dir. Joselito Rodríguez), and *Los tres García* (*The Three Garcías*; 1947, dir. Ismael Rodríguez). The hybrid elements of past theatrical practice, contemporary musical currents, and sociocultural and political context have shaped both the comedia ranchera and the singing charro as successfully constructed national and commercial tools of and for Mexican identity.

Constructing El Charro: From Its Origins to the Twentieth Century

The film industry did not create the charro; it did, however, catapult him as one of the most important invented traditions of Mexican popular culture. Sound cinema during the *época de oro* characterizes the charro as a forceful singer, a heavy drinker, a fighter, a womanizer, and an embodiment of machismo,[6] but the charro outside the diegesis began as a quite different entity. Visually, the charro is recognized by his traditional clothing, which underwent a process of acculturation through criollo, Spanish (typically Anadulsian), Arab, and mestizo influences. This attire consistently included a short coat, fitted pants and/or chaps, a wide, low-crowned hat, and spurs. Writers and investigators of charros and charrería point to the horseman of the virreinato as the antecedent of the twentieth-century charro, representing a time when Spanish conquistadors and settlers brought horses with them on their expeditions to the New World and, with them, a tradition of horsemanship that suited Spanish rural culture.[7] For the Spaniards, the charro became a symbol of their conquistador identity; for the mestizo, criollo, and indigenous populations trained in these practices, this symbol was an "ascent in the social hierarchy and their psychological identification with the members of the dominant class."[8]

---

[6] See Paz, *The Labyrinth of Solitude*, 29–46.

[7] For more information on charros and charrería, see Siboney Obscura Gutiérrez, "La comedia ranchera y la construcción del estereotipo del charro cantante en el cine mexicano de los treinta e inicio de los cuarenta," master's thesis, Universidad Nacional Autónoma de México, 2003, pp. 17–47; Tania Carreño King, *El charro: La construcción de un estereotipo nacional 1920–1940* (Mexico City: Instituto Nacional de Estudios Históricos de la Revolución Mexicana, 2000); Kathleen Mullen Sands, *Charrería mexicana: An Equestrian Folk Tradition* (Tucson: University of Arizona Press, 1993); Octavio Chávez, *La charrería: Tradición mexicana* (Mexico City: Instituto Mexiquense de Cultura, 1991); José Valero Silva, *El libro de la charrería* (Mexico City: Gráficas Montealbán, 1989); James Norman, *Charro: Mexican Horsemen* (New York: G.P. Putnam's Sons, 1969); D. Carlos Rincon Gallardo, *El libro del charro mexicano*, 3rd ed. (Mexico City: Editorial Porrua, S.A., 1960); Luis Inclán, *El libro de las charrerías* (Mexico City: Librería Porrúa, 1940).

[8] María Elena Franco, "Charrería, recurso turístico de México," master's thesis, Autonomous University of Nayarit, Mexico, 1990, p. 22, cited in Mullen Sands, *Charrería mexicana*, 39.

During the dictatorship of Porfirio Díaz, the rurales (countryside police) wore a charro-style uniform consisting of gray suits with white piping and a striped insignia as they rode through rural areas on horses. The charro, as a regal symbol of Mexican horsemanship, was now associated with the oppression and injustice of the Porfiriato.[9] Another important rural setting for the charro was the hacienda. Since the colonial period, the hacienda had dominated life in the countryside, and during the Díaz regime, the forced labor and oppression suffered by the indigenous and mestizo populations grew worse.[10] During periods of economic expansion, particularly when railroad construction pushed up land values and the land was redistributed to benefit foreign investors, the haciendas grew at the expense of the working and lower classes. At the head of each hacienda was the hacendado, often in the form of a charro, who worked with or oversaw others who practiced charrería, such as the foreman and the *vaqueros* (cowboys) and managed the daily workings of the hacienda.[11] For haciendas with cattle, the branding, gelding, and trimming seasons were times for celebrations, and the working charros of the estate would perform the tasks sometimes in front of an audience of neighbors, the hacienda owner's extended family, and friends.[12] Olga Nájera-Ramírez states that the hacienda was a space that presented a localized social structure, which reflected the class, gender, and ethnic differences in Mexican society. The male hacendado protected and ruled over his wife, children, and employees. Next in line were the foreman and managers, then the vaqueros and field workers. Social relationships became capitalistic, and masculinized authority and class power were intimately correlated.[13]

---

[9] José Cisneros, *Riders Across the Centuries: Horsemen of the Spanish Borderlands* (El Paso: Texas Western Press, 1984), 176; Inclán, *El libro de las charrerías*; Mullen Sands, *Charrería mexicana*, 64.

[10] For more information regarding the hacienda system in Mexico, see Giselia von Wobeser, *La formación de la hacienda en la época colonial* (Mexico City: Instituto de Investigaciones Históricas, Universidad Nacional Autónoma de México, 1989); Enrique Semo, *Historia de la cuestión agraria mexicana; Vol. 1: El siglo de la hacienda 1800–1900)* (Mexico City: Siglo XXI-CEHAM, 1988); François Chevalier, *La formación de los latifundios en México* (Mexico City: Fondo de Cultura Económica, 1976).

[11] See Olga Nájera-Ramírez, "Engendering Nationalism: Identity, Discourse, and the Mexican Charro," *Anthropology Quarterly* 67, no. 1 (1994): 3.

[12] Alfonso Rincón Gallardo, "En la hacienda de antaño," in *Artes de México: Charrería*, ed. Margarita de Orellana (Mexico City: Artes de México, 2000), 28.

[13] Nájera-Ramírez, "Engendering Nationalism," 3. See also the works by Luis Inclán, who provides first-hand experience of life on the hacienda. In his novel *Astucias*, Inclán glorifies the charro as a cowboy hero helping those in distress, preferring action to words. Charros have a code of conduct, are chivalrous to women, and treat enemies fairly. See Luis Inclán, *Astucias* (Mexico City: Imprenta Universitaria, 1945).

The Revolution added new symbolism to the charro through the contemporary fighters Emiliano Zapata and Pancho Villa, who led ranchers, vaqueros, and field workers into battle. Zapata and Villa were known to be effective leaders against the government troops because of their knowledge the terrain in their respective regions (Villa to the north, Zapata to the south). Because charrería was taken up by many from all social strata, the hacendado charro, associated with the political and professional classes, was placed in opposition to other charros from the lower and working classes; in battle, charro would face charro.[14]

At the end of the Revolution, many charros left the defunct haciendas and worked on smaller and independent ranches throughout the country, demonstrating their skills at local festivals and rodeos. The closed haciendas, however, left many without employment, and with a mass migration of rural workers to the metropolis, many charros found that their horsemanship skills were not a necessity for city life. Charrería was modified to fit their new situation and location, "detached from the work practices and environment of the countryside."[15] The labor of the past soon became a popular spectacle in the metropolis, allowing the urban elite to boast about successfully modernizing the rural masses.[16]

During the 1910s and 1920s, both the Hollywood and the Mexican silent film industries appropriated the charro as a popular stock character, but their respective interpretations proved to be drastically different. Hollywood's version shined a negative light on the Mexican national in charro clothing, repeatedly depicting him as a villain, thief, and rapist. This negative interpretation of a national icon had lasting effects on the Mexican populace, prompting Mexican filmmakers to counter the representation by incorporating the charro into their own films, transitioning him into a multi-pronged construction of the charro as a national symbol.

---

[14] Rincón Gallardo, "En la hacienda de antaño," 30.

[15] Ibid.

[16] With this modernization of the charro in the urban setting came the development of the Charro Association of Jalisco and the National Association of Charros, both of which sought to preserve the traditions and customs of charrería in the urban setting. Carlos Rincón Gallardo also noticed the popularity of charrería in the urban landscape and wrote a book, almost a "how to" guide for amateur enthusiasts, called *El libro del charro mexicano.* See Mullen Sands, *Charrería mexicana,* 74; Nájera-Ramírez, "Engendering Nationalism," 5; Rincón Gallardo, *El libro del charro mexicano,* 121.

Representations of the cinematic charro in a folkloric landscape began as early as 1917. In the film *Barranca trágica* (*Tragic Ravine*), director Manuel de la Bandera incorporates several elements considered "national":

> Our own national flavor is in the "rodeos" with their "charros" and in the "cockfights" with their variegated and picturesque competition; there is no need for the ubiquitous and monotonous theme of the indispensable Indian or the blunt "pelado"; its scenes are full of great color.[17]

In April 1921, the same year as the Centennial celebrations, director Miguel Contreras Torres premiered his film *El caporal* (*The Caporal*), which "was based on the life in a hacienda and revolved around a character, a caporal, which, although not called a charro, already foreshadowed the films set in the country that exalted the virtues of the charro."[18] The charro also made appearances in other important features, such as *Triste crepúsculo* (*Sad Twilight*; 1917, dir. Manuel de la Bandera), *Santa* (1918, dir. Luis G. Peredo), *En la hacienda* (*At the Hacienda*; 1922, dir. Ernesto Vollrath),[19] *El águila y el nopal* (*The Eagle and the Cactus*; 1929, dir. Miguel Contreras Torres), and *La boda de Rosario* (*Rosario's Wedding*; 1929, dir Gustavo Sáenz de Sicilia).[20] Once sound films were developed, the charro followed the interpretations set forth by practices in the teatro de revistas, which helped form the visual and aural paradigms that became a major part of the comedia ranchera film genre.[21]

---

[17] "Barranca trágica," *El Universal*, December 16, 1917. See also Carreño King, *El charro*, 46. The *pelado* is a raggedy, poor man from the slums symbolizing the plight of the working and lower classes. He was a common fixture in the teatro de revista that was transferred into cinema during the late 1930s. The most well-known pelado in Mexican popular culture is Mario Moreno ("Cantinflas") (1911–1993).

[18] Aurelio de los Reyes, "El nacionalismo en el cine 1920–1930: búsqueda de una nueva simbología," in *El nacionalismo y el arte mexicano* (IX Coloquio de Historia del Arte, ed. Instituto de Investigaciones Estéticas (Mexico City: Universidad Nacional Autónoma de México, 1986), 284.

[19] At the beginning of 1922, a Mexico City newspaper organized a vote for the best film of 1921. *En la hacienda* received the first-place spot, with 485 votes. The film is also based on the 1907 zarzuela, written by Federico Carlos Kegel and with music by Roberto Contreras.

[20] For specific summaries and production details on Mexican silent films, see Aurelio de los Reyes, *Filmografía del cine mudo mexicano, 1896–1920* (Mexico City: Filmoteca Universidad Nacional Autónoma de México, 1986); *Filmografía del cine mudo mexicano; Vol. 2: 1920–1924* (Mexico City: Filmoteca Universidad Nacional Autónoma de México, 1994); Aurelio de los Reyes, *Filmografía del cine mudo mexicano; Vol. 3: 1924–1931* (Mexico City: Filmoteca Universidad Nacional Autónoma de México, 2000).

[21] Jacqueline Avila and Sergio de la Mora, "Fernando de Fuentes: *Allá en el Rancho Grande* (1936)," in *Clásicos del cine mexicano: 31 películas emblemáticas desde el Época do Oro hasta el presente*, ed. Christian Wehr (Frankfurt: Editorial Vervuert, 2015), 127

Teatro de Revistas, the Canción Mexicana, and the Canción Ranchera

As mentioned in chapter 2, the teatro de revista is a satirical theatrical genre derived from the Spanish zarzuela, combining social analysis, political commentary, and burlesque.[22] Theatrical storylines and backdrops were borrowed from the revistas and were adapted for the structural development of silent and sound cinema, molding a cinematic practice with strong theatrical origins. The actors, directors, playwrights, and composers who crossed over from stage to screen kept their fingers on the popular pulse of the nation: [23]

During and after the Revolution, the stage became a forum for the consolidation of national symbols and for the circulation of political and social criticism. Here, regional customs and practices, such as dance and music, were swapped and synthesized among traveling performers and companies.[24] The charro became a crucial figure that underwent experimentation and hybridization, eventually becoming the embodiment of rural Mexico and was linked to political and class interests.[25] In addition to the growing popularity of the charrerías in the urban landscape, the charro and also the *china poblana* (women wearing the traditional Chinese Pueblan attire) were common fixtures in revistas such as *Chin Chun Chan* (1908), *Las musas del país* (*The Muses of the Country*; 1913), *México lindo* (*Beautiful Mexico*), *Del rancho a la capital* (*From the Ranch to the Capital*; 1919), *Cielito lindo* (1922), and Carlos M. Ortega y Pablo Prida's *Las cuatro milpas* (*The Four Cornfields*; 1927).[26]

---

[22] Leonora Saavedra, "Urban Music in the Mexican Revolution," paper read at the National Meeting for the Society of Ethnomusicology, Columbus, Ohio 2007.

[23] Some actors include: Joaquín Pardavé, Marío Moreno ("Cantinflas"), Mimí Derba, Lupe Rivas Cacho, Leopoldo ("El Cuatezón") Beristáin, Lucina Joya, and Alfonso ("Pompín") Iglesias. Composers include Manuel Castro Padilla, Agustín Lara, Federico Ruiz, and Lorenzo Barcelata. Playwrights include Guz Aguila and Pablo Prida.

[24] It is important to note that the revistas were not just spaces for the depiction of the rural countryside. In her article "Manuel M. Ponce y los músicos populares," Leonora Saavedra notes that the revistas were sites for staging several interpretations of daily life, such as urban life, that the Mexican public recognized. See Leonora Saavedra, "Manuel M. Ponce y los músicos populares," *Heterofonía* 143 (July–December 2010): 51–84.

[25] Obscura Gutiérrez, "La comedia ranchera y el estereotipo del charro," 72. See also Ricardo Pérez Montfort, *Estampas de nacionalismo popular mexicano: Ensayos sobre cultura popular y nacionalismo* (Mexico City: Centro de Investigaciones y Estudios Superiores en Antropología Social, 1994), 123.

[26] Saavedra, "Manuel M. Ponce y los músicos populares," 68–72. For an analysis of the depiction of race, ethnicity, and class in *Chin Chun Chan*, see Jacqueline Avila, "*Chin Chun Chan*: The Zarzuela as an Ethnic and Technological Farce," in *Oxford Research Encyclopedia for Latin American History*, ed. William Beezley (February 2018) https://oxfordre.com/latinamericanhistory/view/10.1093/acrefore/9780199366439.001.0001/acrefore-9780199366439-e-514<<<REFC>>>. For more information regarding the political and social messages in *Las cuatro milpas*, see Armando de María y Campos, *El teatro de género chico en la revolución mexicana* (Mexico City: Impreso en los Talleres

The use of theatrical ingredients in the early days of sound cinema occurred for several reasons, one of which concerned reaching the mass audience. The overlap of revista practices into sound film provided an easy and nonintimidating way to entice audiences to accept the moving medium and to fill up the theaters. For the comedia ranchera and other examples of musical rural comedies during the 1930s, the synthesized revista also provided a popular and well-known narrative framework.[27] The development of the film genre, however, depended on music, because the protagonist and the impact characters (except the antagonist) sang. Music performed by mariachis dressed in full *trajes de charro* (charro suits) became one of the genre's musical and visual signifiers during the 1940s, but the comedia ranchera's diegetic musical track is much more musically diverse, including originally composed canciones mexicanas and canciones rancheras.[28]

The canción ranchera from the 1920s was a different style from that performed by the now standard mariachi ensemble of strings and trumpets.[29] Early instrumentation consisted of a piano and a string orchestra or winds. A precursor to the ranchera, known as the *canción campirana* (country song), underwent several stylistic juxtapositions when it was transferred to the new

Gráficos de la Nación, 1956), 298–300. For information regarding *En la hacienda* (1907), see Antonio Magaña Esquivel, *Medio siglo de teatro mexicano (1900–1961)* (Mexico City: Instituto Nacional de Bellas Artes, 1964), 11–12.

[27] An example of this is the 1907 zarzuela *En la hacienda*, by Federico Kegel, which Ernesto Vallah adapted for the silent screen in 1922 and which later was readapted by Guz Aguila and Fernando de Fuentes for the sound film in 1936, *Allá en el Rancho Grande*. Aurelio de los Reyes notes that the music for the zarzuela was performed for the screening of Vallah's silent version, played by Miguel Lerdo de Tejada and his orchestra. See Aurelio de los Reyes, "La música en el cine mudo in México," in *La música de México*, vol. 4, ed. Julio Estrada (Mexico City: Universidad Nacional Autónoma de México, 1984), 109. For a discussion of the impact of *En la hacienda* on the comedia ranchera, see Jacqueline Avila, "Juxtaposing *teatro de revista* and *cine*: Music in 1930s *comedia ranchera*," *Journal of Film Music* 5, nos. 1–2 (2012): 119–24.

[28] Avila and de la Mora, "Fernando de Fuentes," 129.

[29] The mariachi ensemble has evolved from the nineteenth century, from smaller ensembles of indigenous musicians from the western states of Jalisco. The standardized ensemble makeup was not formalized until there was mass migration of rural musicians to the urban centers (mainly Mexico City). Moreno Rivas marks 1927 as a key year for the mariachi, with the establishment of the Mariachi Marmolejo. By the 1930s, with the help of radio, the mariachi became a popular ensemble. In 1934, Silvestre Vargas arrived to Mexico City with his group, the Mariachi Vargas, with new instrumentation: violins, harp, guitarra sexta, vihuela, and the guitarrón de golpe (or the tololoche). The trumpet was added later, but a definitive explanation as to its presence is not known. Some speculate that the trumpet sound was an added modification for the newly recorded sound technology or an imitation of a Cuban ensemble, Septeto Típico Habanero, which featured trumpets in their music. Through the 1930s and the 1940s, the standardized or modern mariachi ensemble continued to develop, complete with charro attire. The repertoire consisted primarily of sones, but later broadened to the canción romantica, waltzes, popular dances, and more. See Yolanda Moreno Rivas, *Historia de la música popular mexicana* (Mexico City: Editorial Océano de México, S.A. de C.V., 2008), 133–34. See also Daniel Sheehy, *Mariachi Music in America: Expressing Music, Expressing Culture* (New York: Oxford University Press, 2006).

city setting through experimentation in instrumentation (specifically the addition of the trumpet), the incorporation of different rhythmic patterns, and a more polished and commercialized sound; yet the music still hinted at the countryside through its thematic and lyrical content. Some examples include the nostalgic style in "Canción Mixteca" ("Mixteca Song"; 1916) by José López Alavés, and arrangements of "La pajarera" ("The Birdhouse"; 1917), "El desterrado" ("The Banished"; 1917), and "La borrachita" ("The Drunk Girl"; 1918) by Ignacio Fernández Esperón "Tata Nacho."[30]

The canción ranchera and the canción mexicana became musical staples in the teatro de revista, performed as interludes between the scenes, or *cuadros,* and often having nothing to do with the narrative of the revista itself. These performances helped transmit the music to the wide urban audience who frequented the theater. Radio also contributed greatly to the nationwide diffusion of the canción mexicana during the 1920s. The migration of populations from the countryside to the urban centers supported the influx of regional musics. By 1930, the largest radio broadcasting system in Mexico was born: XEW, "The Voice of Latin America from Mexico," reaching a larger Mexican and Latin American audience than any other radio signal. A crucial part of the XEW programming was its musical variety programs, helping new and upcoming artists perform to larger audiences and encouraging more musicians to travel to the city.[31]

As previously mentioned, the canción ranchera was not solely dependent on the mariachi ensemble but, rather, was a gradual acculturation of regional and metropolitan hybridity. One essential feature was the singing style. The vocal technique associated with both the canción mexicana and the canción ranchera is often traced back to the Italian *bel canto* tradition from the nineteenth century, when Italian opera was in vogue in Mexico City. The canción ranchera, however, acquired a unique approach. Labeled as the *estilo bravío* (forceful singing), this expressive singing required an emphasized use of the chest and diaphragm to project the sound to a larger audience. The effect is often raspy, commanding, and aggressive, but damages the larynx if done

---

[30] Moreno Rivas lists four titles from the 1920s that fit this description: "Adiós Mariquita Linda" ("Goodbye Lovely Mariquita"; 1925) by Marco Antonio Jiménez; "La negra noche" ("The Black Night"; 1926) by Emilio D. Uranga; "Allá en el Rancho Grande" (1927), an arrangement by Silvano Ramos; and "El limoncito" ("The Little Lime"; 1928), an arrangement by Alfonso Esparza Oteo. Saavedra states that Tata Nacho published his arrangements, which acquired popularity through oral transmission before its publication in 1920 and 1921. See Moreno Rivas, *Historia de la música popular mexicana,* 135; Saavedra, "Manuel M. Ponce y los músicos populares," 57–58; and Jesús Jáuregui, *El mariachi* (Mexico City: Santillana Ediciones Generales, S.A. de C.V., 2007), 99–133.

[31] Obscura Gutiérrez, "La comedia ranchera y la construcción del charro," 77.

without proper warming up, hence differing greatly from the more lyrical and amorous canción romantica tradition.[32] The estilo bravío was a common feature in cinema and on the radio during the 1940s, especially featuring the renowned ranchera singer Lucha Reyes (1906–1944).

In early sound cinema, both canciones quickly synthesized with the figure of the charro and established close associations with machismo. This synchresis of image, gender, attitude, and music is not surprising, as the canción mexicana has been intimately tied to Mexican masculinity, written essentially from a male point of view. In a 1936 article in *El Universal Ilustrado*, the author mysteriously known only as "A.F.B." compares the masculine sounds of popular theater composer Jorge del Moral with the effeminate lyrics and sounds of Agustín Lara, arguing that canciones are inherently masculine, and therefore purely Mexican:

> The truly popular Mexican canciones are gendered masculine. . . . The authors that have muddled with the national character of the Mexican canción have turned away from masculine flavor, from savoring the machoness of our sones. That is why, in a strict sense, they have not written popular Mexican music.[33]

As already discussed, the charro was perceived as a respected and noble figure who embodied masculine dominance, particularly as the charro hacendado at the end of the nineteenth century. Synchronized sound synthesized the music specific to the charro and highlighted several crucial traits: "other characteristics of the cinematic charro include be[ing] argumentative and [the] lead, as a logical consequence, and to sing forcefully and accentuate machismo."[34] The juxtaposition of all these attributes would be introduced on the silver screen in 1936, with *Allá en el Rancho Grande*.

The "Bum": Fernando de Fuentes's *Allá en el Rancho Grande* (1936)

Although Antonio Moreno's *Santa* was the first recorded synchronized-sound film that gained box office success, *Allá en el Rancho Grande* is

---

[32] Moreno Rivas, *Historia de la música popular mexicana*, 136.
[33] A.F.B., "El mundo y la canción mexicana," *El Universal Ilustrado*, July 7, 1936.
[34] De los Reyes, "El nacionalismo en el cine," 287–88.

repeatedly considered the first successful venture by the Mexican film industry during the 1930s, for the following reasons: (1) it provides a folkloric collage of rural life, which many identify as a reflection of an "authentic
Mexico"; (2) it is the first Mexican film to receive international accolades;[35]
(3) it is a film genre that successfully branched off of Hollywood genres,
demonstrating something that was inherently "Mexican";[36] (4) it catapulted
advertising interests through the diffusion and performance of the canción
ranchera; and (5) it painted a positive and desirable image of Mexicanidad,
articulated through the macho singing charro that challenged Hollywood's
stereotypes of Mexican masculinity.

Much like Sergei Eisenstein's 1931 *¡Que viva México!*, *Allá en el Rancho
Grande* maintains a luminous position in Mexican film history, as well as in
the national imagination. Although several films during the 1930s utilized a
rural backdrop and illustrated hacienda life, *Allá en el Rancho Grande* provided the audience with a friendly juxtaposition of folkloric images and
popular music set to a melodramatic narrative. It also propelled the image
of the charro as a desirable figure for self-identity that countered problematic representations of the indigenous that had been perpetuated in the silent
and early sound cinema, as well as in literature, the visual arts, and music
(see chapter 3). The charro exemplified the combination of musical ability,
European features, and sexual charisma.[37]

Produced during the presidential sexenio of Lázaro Cárdenas, the film is
consistently labeled by Mexican film historians and film critics as an example
of conservative sentiments objecting the *reforma agraria* (agrarian reform),
or land reform initiatives that returned previously confiscated land to the
Mexican population. The rapid redistribution of sizable communally farmed
lands, or *ejidos*, produced substantial protests from Mexico's conservative
sector, some of whose members believed that dismantling the hacienda
represented a dismantling of Mexico. Because *Allá en el Rancho Grande* is set
on a hacienda in Jalisco, the film is acknowledged as a conservative response
to those social, political, and economic changes in the Mexican countryside,
functioning almost as an exaltation of the hacienda rather than a rebuke of
it. The film is also criticized for blatantly evading the topic of the Revolution

---

[35] The film received an award for Best Cinematography in Venice's Mostra International Film
Festival in 1938. This award is the first international award received by Mexican cinema.

[36] One common comparison that Mexican film scholars make to the comedias rancheras is to the
Will Rogers and Gene Autry musical westerns from the 1930s.

[37] Tim Mitchell, *Intoxicating Identities: Alcohol's Power in Mexican History and Culture*
(New York: Routledge, 2004), 149.

and avoiding social conflict and class struggle, and instead constructing a lost rural utopia, an escape for the middle- and upper-class movie-going audience. Film historian Emilio García Riera states:

> This flight signifies the recovery of a happy and idyllic universe that the urban bourgeoisie wanted to believe existed: the bucolic arcadia whose myth the Revolution destroyed ruthlessly. But if you already know that the Mexican countryside is not that, that in 1936 the Agrarian Reform is a real fact, the myth of the blessed hacienda is jealously felt by a film in which class content advises the rejection of reality.[38]

While there is no question that the rural backdrop presented in *Allá en el Rancho Grande*, and by extension other films set in the countryside that came later, such as *Así es mi tierra* (*This Is My Land*; 1937, dir. Arcady Boytler) and *Bajo el cielo* (*Under the Sky*; 1937, dir. Fernando de Fuentes), conveys a sense of nostalgia, I believe the film does not carry as much conservative weight as most argue. Because it was produced during Cárdenas's turbulent administration, the film assumes a certain amount of social and historical obligation in the eyes of film historians and critics; this is due in part to director Fernando de Fuentes's Revolution film trilogy, which examines the questionable consequences of the Revolution and its key players (see chapter 5).[39] However, *Allá en el Rancho Grande* employs several elements that channel a narrow conservative interpretation into a wider reflection of the urban experience for newly arrived rural migrants to the metropolis, who perhaps are eager for any semblance of the home they recently left behind.

At Rancho Grande

When Don Rosendo, the fair and generous hacendado of Rancho Grande, passes away in 1936, his son Felipe (René Cardona) inherits the hacienda and, as the new hacendado, Felipe appoints his close childhood friend, José Francisco (played by the international singing sensation Tito Guízar) as

---

[38] Emilio García Riera, *Historia del cine mexicano* (Mexico City: Consejo Nacional de Fomento Educativo, 1986), 85.

[39] Fernando de Fuentes's Revolution trilogy includes *El prisionero trece* (1933), *El compadre Mendoza* (1934), and *¡Vámonos con Pancho Villa!* (1936). The latter was filmed before *Allá en el Rancho Grande*, but premiered after.

Figure 4.1 The sweethearts of Rancho Grande, Cruz (Ester Fernández) and José Francisco (Tito Guízar), in *Allá en el Rancho Grande* (1936). Photo courtesy of Mil Nubes-Foto.

the ranch's foreman. José Francisco and his sister Eulalia are orphans from Rancho Chico left in the care of Rancho Grande's washerwoman, Angela (Emma Roldán), and her comically drunk husband, Florentino (Carlos López "Chaflán"). José Francisco falls in love with Cruz (Esther Fernández), Angela's Cinderella-like servant adorned in rebozos and braids, who reciprocates José Francisco's affections[40] (figure 4.1). Cruz, however, catches the eye of two other men: Martín (Lorenzo Barcelata), another worker on Rancho Grande aiming to become the foreman, and Felipe, who is already engaged to the upper-class Margarita. Although Cruz is devoted to José Francisco, it is this love triangle that causes the most friction and drives the narrative.

[40] Emilio García Riera, *Fernando de Fuentes (1894–1958)* (Mexico City: Cineteca Nacional, 1984), 135.

When we examine race and ethnicity in Mexican national cinema, particularly the comedia ranchera, the cinematic charro becomes a challenging figure. Joanne Hershfield contends that the comedia ranchera romanticizes the discourse of *hispanismo*, an ideology exalting the Euro-Spanish heritage, which is visually localized in the charro and his glorification of machismo. She further argues that the hacendado, the state, and paternalism are aligned, where the hacienda functions as a symbol of the country and the charro hacendado preserves the structures of the feudal system. Narrowing her focus to the charros of Rancho Grande, Hershfield defines the charro as "a symbol of Hispanic masculinity, light-skinned, handsome, and respectful of the 'inherent' divisions within Mexican society."[41] The charro's physical appearance in film confronts the representations of charros of actuality: they were not only Hispanic white-skinned men but also many came from various ethnic backgrounds and were trained in the longstanding tradition of charrería. However, criollo hacendados were typical fixtures in the hacienda system during the eighteenth and nineteenth centuries, visually portrayed in paintings by Ernesto Icaza (1866–1935) as white-skinned, elaborately dressed horsemen. René Cardona, who plays the charro hacendado Felipe in *Allá en el Rancho Grande*, confirms this description: "Fernando de Fuentes immediately hired me to play the boss at Rancho Grande. He said 'Look, the bosses of Jalisco are like you, white with blue eyes, and for this movie that I am going to film, I need a boss like that. I will give you the script to read.'"[42] De Fuentes was looking for a specific image of a charro hacendado that matched past representations.

Allá en el Rancho Grande is singled out as a problematic example of racial tensions in this essentialist portrayal, although discourses on Mexican identity formation at the time questioned or challenged different aspects of racial and ethnic makeup (see chapter 3). In cinema, several films featured characters with those physical characteristics that Hershfield designates as "challenging" to the comedia ranchera schema. The fictional indigenista films such as *La noche de los mayas* (*The Night of the Mayans*; 1939, dir. Chano Ureta) and *Maria Candelaria* (1944, dir. Emilio Fernández) featured white-skinned actors as the indigenous protagonists, reserving the secondary and

[41] Joanne Hershfield, "Race and Ethnicity in the Classical Cinema," in *Mexico's Cinema: A Century of Film and Filmmakers*, ed. Joanne Hershfield and David R. Maciel (Wilmington: SR Books, 1999), 90–91.

[42] Elena Rico, "Anatomía de un éxito loco: *Allá en el Rancho Grande*," *Contenido* 157 (June 1976): 20–56, quoted in García Riera, *Fernando de Fuentes*, 48.

minor roles for darker-skinned mestizo and indigenous actors and extras.[43] In an interview with the periodical *Contenido*, the film's cinematographer Gabriel Figueroa explains that "before *Rancho Grande*, the producers were scared to 'take out the Indians in the films, and they generally considered these images would be 'denigrating for Mexico.'"[44] Sergio de la Mora states that despite past efforts to exalt the mestizo body, evident in the eroticiza-tion of the mestizo male in Eisenstein's *¡Que viva México!* and artist Adolfo Best Maugard's film *Humanidad* (*Humanity*; 1934), whiteness was a crucial element for the mass audience and was imagined to be more beautiful and acceptable than brown skin.[45] This practice was also the norm in the heg-emonic Hollywood industry, as many white-skinned Mexican actors and actresses found success during the silent period, either playing an acceptable interpretation of the exotic Other or advantageously passing and performing as European.[46] Keeping this in mind, *Allá en el Rancho Grande* should not be construed more problematic than other films, since "the *ranchero* comedies were neither more or less racist than other cultural products."[47]

While hispanismo is visually privileged in the charro (and by exten-sion, other supporting characters), the mestizo becomes aurally present in the film's diegetic music. As previously mentioned, the development of the comedia ranchera as a film genre paralleled the growth in radio and sound-recording technology, making sound cinema an important stage for up-and-coming singers and performers. With the mixing of the urban and rural cultures during the post-Revolutionary years, the public became addicted to the nostalgia encoded or encapsulated in songs and in the film narratives that were woven around these performances.[48] The music is an example of cultural mestizaje, a mixing of the regional and the urban, and is a crucial synchresis for the development of a consistently changing hybrid popular culture. Marina Díaz López states, "The music is a crucial element to use in the processes of mestizaje and to the foundation of a local popular culture be-cause it needs an environment to run on. . . . [T]he mestizo culture is reflected

---

[43] For an analysis of the visual whitening that takes place in *Maria Candelaria*, see Dolores Tierney's wonderful examination in *Emilio Fernández: Pictures in the Margins* (Manchester: Manchester University Press, 2007), 73–103.

[44] García Riera, *Fernando de Fuentes*, 45.

[45] Sergio de la Mora, *Cinemachismo: Masculinities and Sexuality in Mexican Film* (Austin: University of Texas Press, 2006), 86.

[46] Mexican actors in Hollywood include Dolores del Río, Ramón Navarro, Lupita Tovar, Lupe Vélez, Antonio Moreno, and Emilio Fernández.

[47] Mitchell, *Intoxicated Identities*, 151.

[48] Ibid., 150.

in the music and, at the same time, the agrarian culture."[49] The film's diegetic music is consistently put into the category of "the folkloric," along with the presence of artisanal crafts and sarapes, but the canciones and their strategic performance in the narrative mark the presence of the contemporary mestizo culture that Díaz López points out. The music operates as a function of daily life and as the dominant musical practice of the people who live in and interact in that environment.

The film's composer is the Veracruz-born Lorenzo Barcelata (1898–1943), who demonstrated at a young age his talent for playing the guitar and writing songs. While working for the government during his period of civil service in 1925, he began several small groups, such as the Cuarteto Regional and Los Ruiseñores Tampiqueños, during which time he experimented and "modified" the canción campirana. With the full economic and moral support of the governor of Tamualipas, Emilio Portes Gil, Barcelata rechristened his group Los Trovadores Tamaulipecos (consisting of Barcelata, lyricist Ernesto Cortázar, José Agustín Ramírez, and Carlos Peña) in 1929, which led to an eventual contract with XEW for performing regional music.[50]

Barcelata's success with Los Trovadores Tamaulipecos, his international hit "María Elena," and his later position as artistic director of XEFO led to his involvement in *Allá en el Rancho Grande*, aiding in the "jaliscazo" ("Jalisco-izing") of Mexican cinema.[51] Barcelata and lyricist Cortázar composed and arranged several songs for the film, which are placed strategically in the film's narrative as musical interludes during scenes, reflecting the sketch formula in the revistas, and he included other popular songs, constructing the necessary sounds for the rural backdrop. All performances are situated in specific spaces: at home (hacienda), in a private garden (below a balcony), in a cantina, and at a *palenque* (an arena used for cockfighting).

In the film's first musical scene, the servant Cruz sings "Canción Mixteca" by the Oaxacan composer José López Alavés (1889–1974). She performs the canción in a high soprano register while ironing, encouraged by the drunken, self-described communist Florentino, who accompanies her with open

---

[49] Marina Díaz López, "El folclore invade el imaginario de la ciudad: Determinaciones regionales en el cine mexicano de los trienta," *Archivos de la Filmoteca: Revista de estudios históricos sobre la imagen, segunda época* 41 (June 2002): 16.

[50] Pablo Dueñas, "El trovador de sotavento: Lorenzo Barcelata," *Relatos e historias en México* 2, no. 18 (2010): 68–69. For more information on Lorenzo Barcelata, see Mario Kuri-Aldana and Vicente Mendoza Martínez, *Cancionero popular mexicano*, 2nd ed. (Mexico City: Consejo Nacional para la Cultura y las Artes, 2001), 2:438–50.

[51] Dueñas, "El trovador de sotavento: Lorenzo Barcelata," 70.

arpeggios on guitar. The song, written as a relaxed waltz, is slow and wistful, detailing the recollection of a lost homeland: "How far I am from the land I am from / Intense nostalgia invades my thinking." The "Mixteca" refers to the indigenous people who inhabited parts of Oaxaca, Guerrero, and Puebla. This region is also near where the composer grew up, before he moved to Mexico City during the Revolution. Perhaps the nostalgia conveyed in the song speaks to the composer's personal feelings about being so far from his home, paralleling those who left their place of birth to look for a new way of life in Mexico City or other urban areas after the armed struggle. In the film, the nostalgia felt for the "land of their birth" is transferred to the hacienda in Jalisco, reinforcing the idea of an idyllic land and furthering the mythical status of Jalisco.

Aside from articulating the longing for a lost countryside, this canción is an example of rural simplicity juxtaposed with urban influences, and portrays hints of the música de salón tradition through the fluidity of the melodic line and waltz-like tempo. The canción has a simple and static melodic line that stays within the interval of a fifth. In the film, Cruz supplies her own ritardandos and fermatas, particularly during the last line of the first verse, describing her need to cry, and the first two lines of the next verse, referencing the lost homeland, which compels her to sigh: "And when I see myself so alone and sad as a leaf in the wind / I want to cry, I want to die of grief!"[52] The first line of the second verse, "Oh, earth of the sun! I long to see you," reaches its climax as the melody outlines an ascending major triad settling on the octave tonic with the word *sol* (sun), then gradually descending to mimic the sounds of her sighs. While singing, Cruz continues to iron clothing without hesitation, reinforcing this music as part of her daily life. As Cruz finishes the last verse, Martín, dressed in a charro suit, enters the scene and accompanies her for the remaining lines of the last verse, implying that this is a popular and familiar song at Rancho Grande.

[52] Fernando de Fuentes, dir., *Allá en el Rancho Grande*, DVD, ch. 4 (1936; Mexico City: Cinemateca, 2007). The song's lyrics are also included in Kuri-Aldana and Mendoza Martínez, *Cancionero Popular Mexicano*, 2:97. López Alavés grew up in Huajuapan de Léon, in Oaxaca, and moved to Mexico City in 1906 to study music at the Conservatorio Nacional de Música, where he worked with Rafael J. Tello and Julián Carrillo. In 1917, he submitted the song to the First Canción Mexicana Competition sponsored by *El Universal*. The song won first prize, while second place went to the canción "La apasionada." See Simón Tapia Colman, *Música y musicos en México* (Mexico City: Panorama Editorial, 1991), 76–77.

Serenades and Accolades

The film's serenade and cockfighting scenes feature several musical performances that detail the most folkloric events of daily life and reinforce class and gender divisions among the characters. José Francisco and Martín are rivals, but they come together in solidarity to sing at Don Felipe's request: to perform a serenade at the gated window of his girlfriend, Margarita. This romantic performance begins with a brief and lyrical quotation of the popular "Las mañanitas,"[53] then transitions to "Amanecer ranchero" ("Ranch Dawn"), sung by José Francisco and Martín in parallel thirds and sixths, an archetype of the canción mexicana. As they sing, the camera zooms in for a close-up of José Francisco and Martín, with a momentary cross cut to the dark, seemingly vacant window. The first half of the song conveys the nostalgia for a homeland described in the "Canción Mixteca," detailing the sadness of being in a distant location and separated from a love that remained there. The second half of the song transitions to a faster tempo, bringing in the full ensemble for the chorus: "How sad is the life / that cries for a love / My fields, my flowers / are dying without sunshine."[54] During this performance, José Francisco and Martín appear to sing toward a different audience: Martín gazes toward the direction of Margarita's window while José Francisco stares straight ahead, perhaps at the wall or at Don Felipe, which disassociates him from the serenade. After a pause, Don Felipe requests José Francisco sing the canción romántica, "Por ti aprendí a querer" ("For You, I Learned to Love"), accompanied by Martín on guitar, which is more specific to Felipe's supposed affection for Margarita: "Come to my arms that wait just for you / For you, ideal woman, only for you am I happy."[55] In an interview with the Cineteca Nacional, cinematographer Gabriel Figueroa describes the scene as follows:

> José Francisco and Martín play the guitar and sing very well, in such a way that Felipe uses them to perform a serenade for his girlfriend Margarita. The two peones wear beautiful charro suits and sarapes as José Francisco sings "Por ti aprendí a querer" ("For You I Learned to Love") while the boss covers his face with his braided sombrero to kiss his beloved who receives him on the balcony.[56]

---

[53] "Las mañanitas" is traditionally a birthday song performed in the early hours of the morning.
[54] De Fuentes, *Allá en el Rancho Grande*, ch. 5.
[55] Ibid.
[56] Eugenia Meyer, *Cuadernos de la Cineteca Nacional: Testimonios para la historia de cine mexicano* (Mexico City: Cineteca Nacional, 1976), 3:45.

As Felipe kisses Margarita, José Francisco, Martín, and their ensemble turn around to allow the lovers privacy and accompany them with "un vals moderno" ("a modern waltz"). They promptly begin an arrangement of Juventino Rosas's "Sobre las olas" ("Over the Waves"), a waltz from the end of the nineteenth century. It is an odd choice for "un vals moderno," but an easily recognizable one for Mexicans and, by extension, for international audiences.

While the live performance and the collage of musical numbers are meant to be romantic gestures from Felipe to Margarita, the social hierarchy on the hacienda is laid out: José Francisco and Martín are hired to perform while Felipe looks on, insinuating that these charros can provide something the charro hacendado cannot. The privilege of singing is not given to Don Felipe, only to his employee charros, which socially and sonically separates Don Felipe from the other characters. The performance also isolates Margarita. Although the serenade was meant for Margarita, the scene places her on the farthest side of the frame, the gaze centering on the men. She is only introduced into the scene after all the performances are over, emerging out to the window to validate Felipe's successful romantic conquest. Her dialogue is kept to a minimum as Felipe tells her he will come back in the morning to ask her father for permission to marry in a month. Margarita agrees to everything Felipe says and remains seated behind the gated window, protected, shielded, and separated from the cohort of singing charros. Felipe's stern decision-making and Margarita's fast acceptance characterize the music of the serenade as a series of hypnotic, siren-like songs, subduing the object of affection into an affirming submission. The serenade functions here not as a crucial tool in understanding the love and relationship between Margarita and Felipe but, rather, more as a space for observing the romantic and seductive methods and capacities of the singing charros.

The next musically significant scene takes place at the cockfight between rival haciendas, Real Minero and Rancho Grande. Before the actual competition begins, the crowd of charros, china poblanas, and the Anglo American, or gringo archetype, Pete, is entertained by a series of performers, beginning with the "cancioneros del alma nacional" ("singers with national soul").[57] The Trio Murciélago and the Trio Tariácuri enter the center of the palenque

---

[57] Gringo is a term referring to individuals born in the United States or an Anglo American. According to popular folklore, it was used as a derogatory term during the U.S. invasion of Mexico in the 19th century. While still sometimes derogatory, it is now used to "represent behavior and attitudes Latinos consider to be American." See the "Gringo," *Urban Dictionary*, March 5, 2005. https://www.urbandictionary.com/define.php?term=gringo

with chairs, facing each other in a confrontational line up and surrounding a *tarima,* a wooden floor for dancing. Each performer places one leg on a chair to play his guitar and launches into what Alex E. Chávez has labeled "huapango-esque" songs arranged by Barcelata that display the conquest of a woman.[58]

Dressed in white charro suits with sarapes draped over their shoulders, the first trio begins with "Lucha María," which describes a womanizing charro as a game cock who wants a beautiful lady to sit next to him so that he may flirt with her: "Take out your stool, Lucha María, sit here / I want to see you sitting next to me during the fair."[59] The trio sings in unison with rich, velvety harmonies, displaying vocal inflexions specific to the canción style, such as slight descending glissandi at the end of each phrase. During their performance, the camera zooms in to an extreme close-up of the trio's hands, focusing on their rapid strumming techniques and virtuosity as they accelerate the tempo to the conclusion. To contrast, the other trio, dressed in black suits also with sarapes draped over one shoulder, play "Presumida" ("Vain Woman"), which colorfully describes a man leaving the vain love of his life. The strength in this trio lies principally in their technique and strumming patterns. Their performance is longer than the other trio's owing to a lengthy guitar introduction rather than an acceleration of tempi. In addition to extreme close-ups, the camera crosscuts to show several angles of the musicians, placing a spotlight on the emerging trio performance style.[60] Moreno Rivas traces the origins of the musical trio to the popular ensemble of the Teatro Lírico, the Trio Garnica-Ascencio in 1927 and to Lorenzo Barcelata's group Los Trovadores Tamaulipecos, who "added to the vocal ensemble the almost virtuosic use of the guitar, which came from the harp playing style in the huapango."[61] Presented in this scene are not necessarily displays of traditional or nostalgic music, although there are lyrical references to nature and leaving "the love of their life." Instead, different methods of performance practice that embrace a machismo aesthetic are introduced: it is confrontational, relying on increasing elaborate technique to claim superiority over the other, performing songs detailing female conquest yet colored with

---

[58] Alex E. Chávez, *Sounds of Crossing: Music, Migration, and the Aural Poetics of Huapango Arribeño* (Durham, NC: Duke University Press, 2017), 38.

[59] De Fuentes, *Allá en el Rancho Grande,* ch. 6.

[60] The era of the trio typically began with the debut of the trio Los Panchos in 1948. See Moreno Rivas, *Historia de la música popular mexicana,* 122.

[61] Ibid. For more information regarding the trio, see "Trio Garnica-Ascencio," *El Universal Ilustrado,* July 7, 1927.

Figure 4.2 Cultural nationalism in action. Emilio Fernández and Olga Falcón perform the *Jarabe tapatío* in *Allá en el Rancho Grande* (1936). Screen capture from film.

references of nature, and a concentrated focus by the camera on the male performers. The cultural synchresis here exhibits a musical duel of sorts with no declared winner; both groups show off for each other and vie for audience approval, exhibiting an idealized version of machismo.

After the trio challenge, the musicians group together and move to the side of the tarima, leaving it empty for two dancers, Olga Falcón and Emilio Fernández, dressed in china poblana and traje de charro, respectively, who perform the *jarabe tapatío*[62] (figure 4.2). The piece is broken into three sections. Falcón and Fernández perform the first part of the jarabe, which

---

[62] The jarabe is a dance style with Spanish origins that focuses on the rhythmic movement of the feet called *zapateado*. During the eighteenth and early part of the nineteenth century, the dance was deemed inappropriate and was banned by the viceroyalities, but it was later adopted by insurgents during the War of Independence. The jarabe was also included in performances of the género chico and revistas during the nineteenth and early twentieth centuries. Its incorporation as a symbol of nationhood was accelerated after Russian ballerina Anna Pavlova included an *en pointe* performance of the jarabe tapitío for the revista *Fantasía Mexicana* in 1919. During the 1920s, Minister of Public Education José Vasconcelos included the dance in the Mexican dance school curriculum. For a history on the jarabe, see Gabriel Saldavar, *El jarabe: Baile popular mexicano* (Puebla: Lecturas Históricas de Puebla, 1987).

transitions to an arrangement of a traditional jarabe in triple meter "El atole," describing a popular corn-based drink consumed with tamales. During the dance, the camera crosscuts to close-ups of select members of the audience, who express admiration, pleasure, and delight. After an extreme close-up of Falcón's feet dancing on Fernández's sombrero, the music returns to the final section of the jarabe tapatío. Considered the national dance of Mexico after the Revolutionary years, the performance of the jarabe tapatío provides the most recognizable representation of Mexican nationalism, described by *Variety* magazine in December 1936 as "a routine that shines with its authenticity."[63]

After the performance, the charros in the crowd break out in *gritos,* the symbolic cry associated with charros. The camera cuts to two extreme close-ups of charros and their version of the grito before resting on the Anglo American character Pete, from Denver, Colorado (Clifford Carr), who manages to yell out a pathetic and unmanly "Whoopee, whoopee!" before placing the wrong end of his cigar in his mouth in a gesture of buffoonery. Pete's "Whoopee" reinforces and even elevates the machismo of the charro's grito. The mixture of trio performances and the dance performance of the jarabe tapatío at a cockfight with an audience of charros, chinas poblanas, and, to subtly contrast, an Anglo or gringo stereotype, stop the narrative to demonstrate several performative examples of Mexican cultural identity. Together, these elements offer the most visual and audible representation of Mexicanidad.

Music and Machismo in the Cantina

As previously mentioned, an important signifier for the charro is an embodiment of machismo. In the film, this has already been demonstrated in past musical scenes, but reaches its culmination in two important scenes after the cockfight. First, nonmusically with Felipe at the Casa Grande, then musically in the cantina after José Francisco wins a big race against Rancho Chico. Although he is engaged to Margarita, Felipe's desire for Cruz is too strong for him to bear, and he concocts a plan to buy Cruz from Angela so he can rape her. His plan is foiled, however, when Cruz suffers a severe asthma attack and faints after fighting off Felipe's advances. When she wakes up, she declares that she is in love with José Francisco and does not want to be considered a

---

[63] Edga, "Allá en el Rancho Grande," *Variety*, December 2, 1936, quoted in García Riera, *Fernando de Fuentes*, 38.

"ruined woman." Felipe takes pity on her and walks her back to her home, un-aware that his night guards watched them leave together. The men interpret Felipe's macho actions as just another sexual conquest by their womanizing boss, but Cruz, in their eyes, has committed an unforgiveable indiscretion and is now tainted.

José Francisco's performance of machismo occurs at the local cantina, one of the select locations that Carlos Monsiváis labels as a mythical space for Mexican cinema. Here, "men build up their virility and prepare their physical decline, fatal decisions are taken and the ballads (*rancheras*) ring out like hymns to self destruction."[64] In the throes of celebrating a successful race whose award money will allow José Francisco to finally marry Cruz, the cantina men request that he perform "Rancho Grande." Not capable of passing up an opportunity to perform, or to show off, José Francisco grabs a guitar and launches into a communal version of "Allá en el Rancho Grande" (figure 4.3). This collective performance generates an atmosphere of mas-culine and nationalistic camaraderie as all the men in the cantina know and sing along with the chorus, interjecting their own strategically placed gritos and catcalls.

On the surface, this song does not necessarily emote macho sensibilities, but its adoption as the film's title song does. A standard practice in Mexican cinema during the 1930s and especially in the 1940s was the utilization of popular songs for film titles that fed the growing consumer culture.[65] For this film, the anonymous song "Allá en el Rancho Grande"[66] was used, but the original film title was *Cruz*, after a Guz Aguila story. According to García

---

[64] Carlos Monsiváis, "Mexican Cinema: Of Myths and Mystification," in *Mediating Two Worlds: Cinematic Encounters in the Americas*, ed. John King, Ana López, and Manuel Alvarado (London: British Film Institute, 1993), 145.

[65] *Santa* (1932) was the first film that utilized a popular song that functioned as the musical theme.

[66] The authorship of the song "Allá en el Rancho Grande" is questionable. In the film and in the writings of Emilio García Riera, and in Yolanda Moreno Rivas's *Historia de la música popular mexicana*, the song's origin is labeled as "anonymous." The *Cancionero popular mexicano, tomo uno*, gives lyric credit to Juan D. del Moral with music by Emilio D. Uranga. However, the article "Escandalazo a propósito de una cinta ya estrenada: *Allá en el Rancho Grande* es del señor Silvano R. Ramos," from October 9, 1936, in *La Prensa*, gives credit to Silvano Ramos, who supposedly composed the song in 1915, but did not received the copyright for it in Mexico. In hearings on the case Marks v. Stasny, Ramos declared the song was his original work and that the song is included under the category "Vaqueros of the Southwest" in John and Alan Lomax's *American Ballads and Folk Songs*, published in 1934, with Ramos indicated as the composer. Opposing arguments in-dicate that the song was a part of Mexican folk culture and not copyrightable. For a summary on the court preceedings and outcome, see GW Law Blogs, *Music Copyright Infringement Resource*, Marks v. Stasny 1 F.R.D. 720 (S.D.N.Y) https://blogs.law.gwu.edu/mcir/case/marks-v-stasny/ For the 1934 version of the song, see John Lomax and Alan Lomax, *American Ballads and Folks Songs* (New York: Macmillan, 1934), 361.

Figure 4.3 José Francisco (Tito Guízar) singing "Rancho Grande" at a cantina in *Allá en el Rancho Grande* (1936). Photo courtesy of Mil Nubes-Foto.

Riera, Tito Guízar and Lorenzo Barcelata objected to *Cruz* as the film's title and proposed that it be titled after the song that made Guízar famous in the United States, "Allá en el Rancho Grande."[67] In "Anatomía de un éxito loco: *Allá en el Rancho Grande*," Guízar states that when he first read the script, he agreed with Barcelata that the initial title was wrong for the film and suggested that the title be changed: "We proposed to Don Fernando that the film should be titled *El Rancho Grande* and we sang the song that he did not know. It was not popular until I sang it a lot in the United States."[68] In an interview with René Cardona, however, he implies that the title change was Cardona's idea, not Guízar's:

> I thought the story was very interesting and likeable. It was first called *Crucita*. One morning I was eating breakfast at a café on Reforma with

[67] García Riera, *Fernando de Fuentes*, 42.

[68] Elena Rico, "Anatomía de un éxito loco: *Allá en el Rancho Grande*," *Contenido* 157 (June 1976): 20–56 quoted in García Riera, *Fernando de Fuentes*, 47.

Fernando de Fuentes and Guz Aguila, the author, and we decided, all three of us, that we did not like the title *Crucita*. In those moments someone was playing the song "El Rancho Grande" and it occurred to me to say: "Ok, well 'Allá en el Rancho Grande would be a good title.' Fernando told me: "You know, I was also thinking that" and like that, in the end, the title stayed *Allá en el Rancho Grande* and *Crucita* was discarded.[69]

Had *Cruz* (or *Crucita*) remained as the film's title, the focus would have changed from the popular song, the location, and the inherent masculine pride of the charros to a female protagonist, who does not receive much attention in the film other than as an object that is sold and fought over by José Francisco, Martín, and Felipe: she exists in the film for the charros' amusement. José Vera states that had this been the title, however, the ending would have been quite different as well:

I suppose that the writer Gus Aguila, one of the good poets (according to Cardona), conceived of the ending as follows: near the end of the film, Crucita crosses at the moment that the boss and the foreman shoot for her love, she falls dead, face down and with a shadow of a cross on her back. It should be noted that the story was modified at the request of the singing actor's wife who recommended to De Fuentes to add a happy ending rather than a tragic ending.[70]

This new conclusion, however, does not imply that Cruz would secure a more centralized role in the narrative. This alternate ending follows patterns set forth by another developing genre, the prostitute melodrama, in killing the female character to stabilize the status quo (see chapter 1). Cruz's presence upsets the balance at the hacienda and becomes the cause for the feuding among the charros. She must therefore be removed from the environment for social harmony to exist once again.

"Allá en el Rancho Grande" segues into a *huapango retachado* (huapango challenge), a song style that moves away from the ranchera tradition and which functions here as the confrontation, in form of performed coplas,

<hr />

[69] Ibid., 48.
[70] José Vera, "El 'Bum' empezó hace 50 años: "*Allá en el Rancho Grande*, Mostró al mundo por primera vez nuestra vida de campo: Parte II," *El Sol de México*, June 11, 1986.

between José Francisco and Martín over the supposed indiscretion committed by Cruz. Here, machismo pride is elevated:

> This scene is very important because it summarizes a crucial element in understanding the ways in which the macho stereotype is constructed: the nationalistic exaltation is materialized in a hymn that only the men in the bar sing, which follows, like an explicit manner of celebration, the fight between the two men for the love of a woman, who lives as a spectacle for everyone.[71]

This performance is an example not only of musical talent but also of quick thinking and wit. The strophic coplas begin as playfully poking at one another, but both men gradually devise ways to subtlety insult each other's character. Martín pushes José Francisco further by insulting Cruz in his last verse, insinuating she gave her love away (meaning her body) to another:

> It is worth more losing
> and keep your honor well
> You must not share
> The woman that you love;
> If I lose I take revenge
> And Cruz is my passion
> For a stallion
> To the boss, I will not exchange.[72]

Everyone in the cantina except José Francisco knows that Cruz was alone with Don Felipe and, because of this, they conclude that she is now tainted and unwanted. After the secret is out, José Francisco rushes to the house to confront her.

When José Francisco discovers that Felipe bought his fiancée, he challenges Felipe to a physical, not a musical, duel. Here, the utopian social division that scholars argue exists in the film is broken as the employee stands up to the hacendado, singing charro against non-singing charro, traditional Mexico against the influx of modernity. Tim Mitchell suggests that

---

[71]   Díaz López, "El folclore invade el imaginaro de la ciudad," 15.
[72]   De Fuentes, *Allá en el Rancho Grande*, ch. 8.

this action challenges the criticism that all comedia ranchera charros sided against the Cárdenas's land reform policies when they were perhaps in favor of them:

> Far from being a reactionary rebuke to *cardenismo*, therefore, musical comedies that portrayed charismatic *charros* standing up to evil landowners provided fantasmatic support for it. Keeping the people focused on the old love-hate relationship with the hacienda was the best possible smokescreen for a land distribution plan that either failed miserably or turned the state itself into what Krauze calls 'a new and all encompassing hacendado.'[73]

Felipe is not depicted in the film as a positive or desired charro figure; he does not perform in any musical numbers, which casts him as an Other, apart from the rest of the players, and he exercises his privilege by buying what he wants whenever he wants. The film does not exalt the hacendando but, rather, demonizes him, providing "tactical support for the governmental dream of liberating peons from the hacienda system."[74]

The singing charro prevails. Don Felipe explains what happened with Doña Angela and Cruz, emphasizing that if he had known that José Francisco and Cruz were together, he would have never made advances toward her, implying that if Cruz were in fact unattached, those advances would be so-cially tolerated and accepted despite her protests. José Francisco decides to believe Felipe and he welcomes Cruz back to him with open arms, declaring that they must now find a new place to live because of this unfortunate sit-uation. This further implies that although Cruz did not do anything to il-licit Felipe's behavior, she is still considered tainted. José Francisco, however, remains loyal to her. Angela, on the other hand, is beaten by her husband Florentino for her wrongdoing and apologizes to José Francisco for selling Cruz (but does not apologize directly to Cruz). Cruz receives the most mal-treatment while Felipe comes out of the situation practically unscathed. In the end, José Francisco marries Cruz, Felipe marries Margarita, and Florentino and Angela remarry in a mass wedding, bringing the film to a happy close.

Allá en el Rancho Grande was not meant to appeal to the rural audience but, rather, to an urban audience that had recently migrated to the city from the countryside and which had feelings of nostalgia. Much like many of

---

[73] Mitchell, *Intoxicated Identities*, 153.
[74] Ibid., 152.

the revistas with country backdrops, *Allá en el Rancho Grande* presents an urban interpretation of the rural for the urban dweller. And these audiences recognized the construction as a faithful depiction: "*Allá en el Rancho Grande* is an exciting and attractive theme that has all the flavor of the Mexican land, our customs, and much originality and which, with a sturdy stroke, exposes the firmness of Mexican character."[75] This perception crossed into the Mexican diaspora communities in the United States, as well. In a review from the Los Angeles Spanish-language newspaper *La Opinión*, an anonymous source states:

> At last we see a film with a faithful reflection of Mexican life in the countryside. We were already tired of watching films that were mediocre manifestations under the title of "Mexican" that did not carry a new message to the spirit of the North Americans. This "Allá en el Rancho Grande" is one of those works that prestiges and exalts Mexico to the foreigner.[76]

Thus, *Allá en el Rancho Grande* quickly became one of the most important visual and aural signifiers of Mexicanidad during this turbulent period, recognized as representing the "true Mexico" not just for Mexicans but also for international audiences. The film industry, then, faced the challenge of how to continue this trend of commercial and national success in the years to come.

Performing the Archetype: Jorge Negrete in ¡Ay Jalisco, no te rajes! (1941)

Although *Allá en el Rancho Grande* became an important celluloid signifier of and for Mexican identity by placing the singing charro in the national spotlight, Tito Guízar did not become the "face of Mexican machismo." In a review of the film, critic Fidel Murillo states,

> Speaking plainly and from the point of view of the acting, the only one that came off not as sharp is Tito Guízar. But whatever his faults, they pale when

---

75 "Allá en el Rancho Grande," *El Cine Gráfico*, October 11, 1936.
76 "Ruidoso éxito de la película 'Rancho Grande,'" *La Opinión*, February 24, 1937.

we hear him sing. The public would have enjoyed a more vigorously mas-culine type.[77]

Consistently referred to as the "happy charro" or, as Moreno Rivas puts it, the "charro rosa" ("pink charro"), Guízar did not stay long in Mexico, moving instead to the United States to pursue a career in Hollywood films and U.S. radio. The singing charro archetype, however, was recycled in *Guadalajara* (1936, dir. Agustín Jiménez), starring Pepe Guízar and in the folkloric tapestry *Así es mi tierra* (*This Is My Land*; 1937, dir. Arcady Boytler), but it was not until 1941 that the popular figure achieved an appropriate level of "machismo-ness" that resonated with the movie-going and radio-listening audience. During the *época de oro*, two rising stars became Mexican cinema's epitome of the national charro: Pedro Infante and Jorge Negrete. Infante won major acclaim with the Mexican public and became known as "the Golden Boy" of the film industry, particularly for his comedias rancheras of the late 1940s.[78] Enrique Serna and Carlos Monsiváis, however, argue that Negrete embodied the full representation of the singing charro and Mexican mascu-linity, especially in his pistol-swinging performance in *¡Ay Jalisco, no te rajes!* (1941, dir. Joselito Rodríguez).

Set in rural Jalisco during the post-Revolutionary years, the film follows the "gentleman gunman" and outlaw, Salvador Pérez Gómez (Negrete), who lost his parents by a hired assassin and seeks to avenge their deaths. In the midst of tracking down the killers, Salvador meets and falls in love with the beautiful and modern Carmela (Gloria Marín), who bashfully returns his affections. Carmela, however, is fighting off advances from the mayor's son, the smug anti-charro Felipe, who attempts to coerce Carmela into mar-rying him to save her father's ranch. After Salvador returns from a trip to Guadalajara, where he successfully and skillfully killed a group of men in-volved in his parents' murder, he is stunned to find Carmela engaged to Felipe. The engagement, however, is short-lived; Salvador wins a horse race against Felipe, and Felipe's father, the ringleader of Salvador's parents' murder, is shot to death. Once the revenge killing ends, Salvador and Carmela ride off to-gether to get married.

[77] Fidel Murillo, "Una Opinión sobre 'Allá en el Rancho Grande,'" *La Opinión*, January 18, 1937.
[78] For more information on the popularity of Pedro Infante in Mexican national cinema, see Jorge V. Carrasco, *Pedro Infante, Estrella de Cine* (Mexico City: Grupo Editorial Tomo, 2005); de la Mora, *Cinemachsimo*, 68–104; Anne Rubenstein, "Bodies, Cities, Cinema: Pedro Infante's Death as Political Spectacle," in *Fragments of a Golden Age: The Politics of Culture in Mexico Since 1940*, ed. Gilbert M. Joseph, Anne Rubenstein, and Eric Zolov (Durham, NC: Duke University Press, 2001), 199–233.

¡Ay Jalisco, no te rajes! elevated Negrete's star status and magnified the image of the pueblo in a way that *Allá en el Rancho Grande* did not—as a demonstration that the pueblo, and not just the feudal haciendas, could also be visually and aurally elegant, particularly in the hands and vocal stylings of Negrete. However, Negrete was not enthusiastic about participating in the film, at first turning the role down and repeatedly calling the film a "churro."[79] The comedia ranchera became a drastic transition for Negrete; his previous film experiences included several historic period films, including *El cementario de las aguilas* (*The Graveyard of Eagles*; 1938, dir. Luis Lezama) and *Perjura* (*Perjurer,* 1938, dir. Raphael J. Sevilla), and rural musical comedies such as *Juan sin miedo* (*Juan Without Fear*; 1939, dir. Juan José Segura).[80] The comedias rancheras, however, were something that he adamantly wanted to stay away from because he hated the traje de charro and did not want to subject himself to singing rancheras, a musical genre he did not particularly enjoy. Trained as an operatic baritone, Negrete studied privately with José Pierson during the 1920s, deciding early on in his career to not waste his talent in *tonadillas* (short, satirical musical comedies) or any type of popular or, as he termed it, kitsch entertainment. The occasional performances on the radio for XETR and his later contract with XEW were only placeholders until he was able to win a position in a national or international opera company. This was evident in his selected repertoire for XETR, which consisted of romanzas, arias, and serenatas.[81] After some performances with Roberto Soto's theatrical company at the Teatro Lírico and successful performances in New York, Negrete turned to cinema.[82]

Despite Negrete's negative proclivities regarding the rancheras, he became a sensation and pushed the canción ranchera in new directions. The molding of Negrete as the macho singing charro was largely the result of the *¡Ay Jalisco, no te rajes!* composer, Manuel Esperón, and the lyricist, Ernesto

[79] Enrique Serna, *Jorge el bueno: La vida de Jorge Negrete* (Mexico City: Clío, 1993), 1:45. Churros refer to the films that are formulaic and are produced rapidly. Anne Rubenstein states, "Viewers began to refer to many movies made in Mexico as *churros* as early as 1950, comparing them to the machine-made crullers (ring-shaped, deep-fried cake) for sale on many city street corners: Like churros, Mexican movies were no nourishing, rapidly made, soon forgotten, identical to one another and cheap." Negrete's comment about the film being a churro indicates that this term was used much earlier than 1950. See Andrea Noble, *Mexican National Cinema* (London: Routledge, 2005), 16–17; and Anne Rubenstein, "Mass Media and Popular Culture in the Post Revolutionary Era," in *The Oxford History of Mexico*, ed. M. C. Meyer and W. H. Beezley (New York: Oxford University Press, 2000), 665.

[80] In *Juan sin miedo*, Jorge Negrete plays a secondary character and does not sing any rancheras.

[81] Carlos Bravo Fernández, "La vida del Jorge Negrete," *Cine Mundial*, November 7, 1954.

[82] See advertisements for the Compañía de Roberto Soto, *El Universal*, 1927.

Cortázar, considered the most successful composer and lyricist team of the 1930s and 1940s. Both men were credited, along with Barcelata, for developing the sounds of the charro. Negrete's baritone voice was already well positioned to sing rancheras as a result of his opera training and his performance experience singing canción mexicana for radio programs. Esperón shares this memory of Negrete singing a ranchera for the first time:

> The first meeting that I had with him was very disagreeable. . . . He sang things with a Cuban style and sang romances, but not rancheras. . . . I composed the music for the songs while Ernesto Cortázar wrote the lyrics. Jorge arrived, listened to the pieces, got mad and told me he was not a mariachi. As a result, he balled up a piece of paper and threw it under the piano and left. That was our first meeting as composer and performer. Later on, he came back because he had to fulfill the contract. At first, he sang because he had to, but just as he began to do so, and realized things were going well, he started to get excited, then he tried really hard and the result is what I had imagined: success. He apologized and a twelve-year relationship was born that ended with his death in 1953.[83]

Differing from Tito Guízar, Negrete's voice was more dominant and powerful, and did not display an excessive use of vibrato and portamento. To sum up Negrete's musical education, Serna states that while Pierson taught Negrete to sing opera, it was Esperón that taught him to sing the canción ranchera.[84] Negrete and his smooth and powerful voice soon became one of the major embodiments of the charro during the 1940s.

And while Esperón provided the sound, Cortázar provided the lyrics. In *¡Ay Jalisco, no te rajes!*, Negrete's Salvador participates in several activities linked to machismo: gambling, herding cattle, tequila drinking, horse racing, and attending cockfights. His conversations with other characters also aid in this construction of machismo through statements such as "I will kill my parent's murderers like dogs." He refuses help from anyone, stating he could do it himself, and any man who begs for his life instead of picking up a gun to defend himself is a coward. His musical sequences were also declamations of his macho pride: "In great measure Cortázar fabricated the bullying image of

[83] "Hicieron Historia en el Siglo XX; Manuel Esperón," *Excélsior*, July 23, 1999.
[84] Serna, *Jorge el bueno*, 49. See also"La música está de luto con la partida de Manuel Esperón," *Imagen Diario*, February 14, 2011.

Jorge. In some of his lyrics, the macho with the pistol on his belt is an object of narcissistic adoration."[85] This comes out especially in the coplas of confrontation scene against the antagonist Felipe, which exhibits similarities to the huapango retachado in *Allá en el Rancho Grande*. After performing a serenade for Carmela at her window, Salvador is challenged to coplas by Felipe and his men, who are all dressed in cosmopolitan two-piece suits. Salvador performs the first copla, while Felipe passes the guitar to one of his friends, ordering him to sing in his place and to make his comeback "muy macho" ("very macho"). Felipe's cosmopolitanism, modernity, and his unwillingness to sing, even for his love interest, make Salvador appear much more desirable and strengthens the charro's levels of machismo.

In terms of music, the film features several original songs written by Esperón and Cortázar, including the title song "¡Ay Jalisco, no te rajes!" first performed by Lucha Reyes at the obligatory cockfight, and then again with Negrete and other cast members in a cantina. The artists offer different interpretations of the song; Reyes provides a strong and raw solo performance, which exemplifies the estilo bravío, while Negrete's is a polished musical spectacle featuring the Trio Los Río, mariachi with trumpets, and communal singing from the surrounding charros and chinas poblanas. The song is ultimately a glorification of Jalisco, but as embodied in the charro figure. As a result, Jalisco and the charro become synonymous: if the charro is Jalisco and Jalisco is Mexico, then the charro becomes Mexico:

> Oh Jalisco, don't backslide!
> Your men are machos and are honorable,
> Brave, surly, and committed
> They don't accept rivals in things concerning love.[86]

Negrete's charro representation and apotheosis of machismo become a crucial fixture in his acting career and an important model for future comedias rancheras. The singing charro comes from an orphaned background, which enables him to hide behind a mask of pride and confidence and not seek help if needed; to receive help without asking would be considered an insult. The singing charro also exercises all practices of charrería and completes each task so well that he consistently wins competitions, all of which offer a

---

[85] Serna, *Jorge el bueno*, 49.
[86] Kuri-Aldana and Mendoza Martínez, *Cancionero popular mexicano*, 1:364.

cash award. He will claim a woman as his own and not only demonstrate his machismo through sharp talking, fist fights, and tequila drinking but also through musical performances at the cantina (confrontational music) and at his girlfriend's gated window (romantic music). The singing charro is also a loyal figure and will not abandon his girlfriend, will avenge the death of his parents, and will never lie. He is a figure of strength, talent, and admiration.

Machismo, the Performance of Gringo-ness, and Strategic Underscoring in *Los Tres García* (1946)

After the German attacks on the Mexican oil tanks SS Potrero del Llano and SS Faja de Oro in May 1942, then President Manuel Ávila Camacho allied with the neighbors to the north and entered the Second World War. This new alliance with the United States affected Mexico's industrial and agricultural development, as the United States exploited Mexican resources and labor for its own gain. This also led to the further modernization and development of Mexico's film industry.

The Office for the Coordinator of Inter-American Affairs (OCIAA), headed by Nelson Rockefeller, was responsible for the cultural and economic relations between Latin America and the United States during the war. Rockefeller intervened in Mexican film production, attempting to push forward Good Neighbor policies, but for the gain of Hollywood: "the initial rationale for Hollywood intervention in the Mexican film industry had less to do with preventing pro-Axis Mexican movie production than with formulating a transnational mode of entertainment production to serve U.S. ideological interests."[87] U.S. aid supplied new machinery and equipment, a consolidation of studios, and the training of new, national technicians in order to keep close control of the industry and to develop strong pan-American relationships.[88] Hollywood, it was hoped, could now maintain

---

[87] Seth Fein, "Myths of Cultural Imperialism and Nationalism in Golden Age Mexican Cinema," in *Fragments of a Golden Age: The Politics of Culture in Mexico Since 1940*, ed. Gilbert M. Joseph, Anne Rubenstein, and Eric Zolov (Durham, NC: Duke University Press, 2001), 164.

[88] Fein, "Myths of Cultural Imperialism and Nationalism," 171. For more information on Mexico–U.S. relations in cinema during World War II, see also Seth Fein, "Hollywood and United States–Mexican Relations in the Golden Age of Mexican Cinema," PhD diss., University of Texas at Austin, 1999; Francisco Peredo Castro, *Cine y propaganda para Latinoamérica: México y Estados Unidos en los años cuarenta*, 2nd ed. (Mexico City: Universidad Nacional Autónoma de México, 2011).

control of the Latin American audience after failing to fund its own Spanish-speaking industry back home.[89]

In compliance with the Good Neighbor policy, Hollywood studios attempted to portray positive depictions of Mexicans, and by extension Latin Americans, to reverse past decades of negative representations. In this process, men received more focused treatment. Since the silent period, Hollywood constructions of non-Western masculinities relied on derogatory stereotypes; Hollywood continuously portrayed the Other in a submissive and negative role as a strategy to elevate images of self-representation:

> While a heterogeneous range of masculine identities is emphasized for the dominant culture, the representation of the identity of non-Western males stands out for its singular and homogeneous economy, resting entirely within the negative side of the masculine equation.[90]

Because of Mexico's proximity to the United States, Mexicans were portrayed unfavorably in Hollywood cinema. The reconstruction of masculine identity was divided into categories that were associated with specific historical contexts. Mexican males were represented as conquistadors (extremely violent and reckless), "Indians" (bloodthirsty Aztecs) and, specific for the twentieth century, greasers (violent revolutionaries à la Pancho Villa), Latin lovers (sexually promiscuous), and gang members (a fusion of the above attributes).[91] Owing to the armed struggle of the Revolution, U.S. Americans labored under the misconception that all Mexicans were violent and unruly, capable of revolting at any moment.[92] The charro in Hollywood films, depicted with a dark moustache and wearing a fitted traje

---

[89] Fein points out that Mexico once held the leading place in the production of Spanish-language films. At the time, the coveted role went to the Argentinian film industry, but to prevent the industry from becoming a direct or indirect source of Axis propaganda, the United States cut off the exportation of film stock, a monopolized commodity in the United States, thereby crippling Argentina's film industry. See ibid., 166–67. For more information on the Argentine film industry, see Tamara L. Falicov, *The Cinematic Tango: Contemporary Argentine Film* (London: Wallflower, 2007) and her chapter "Latin America: How Mexico and Argentina Cope and Cooperate with the Behemoth of the North," in *The Contemporary Hollywood Film Industry*, ed. Paul MacDonald and Janet Wasko (Oxford: Wiley-Blackwell, 2008), 264–76.

[90] Rosa Linda Fregoso, *The Bronze Screen: Chicana and Chicano Film Culture* (Minneapolis: University of Minnesota Press, 1993), 29.

[91] Ibid.

[92] This belief arose as a result of actuality-style films focusing on Pancho Villa in battle. These films were produced by the American Mutoscope and Biograph Company and include *Life of Villa* (1912) and *The Life of General Villa* (1913). The Tropical Film Company also produced a film starring Villa: *Following the Flag in Mexico* (1916).

de charro, became the villain of choice, the kidnapper and rapist of innocent white women, and the thief who took advantage of decent, law-abiding
U.S. citizens.[93]

Mexicans did not accept these reconstructions kindly. Since Hollywood's
films were distributed to numerous theaters in Mexico, screenings of these
negative representations were shown to national audiences. In order to protect the public from the damaging images of the Mexican national, a censorship committee rejected those Hollywood films that strongly challenged
a positive Mexican identity. The Mexican industry, therefore, acquired the
difficult task of repairing the national image. During this cinematic reconstruction, which included receiving foreign aid from the United States,
several directors, including Arcady Boytler, Fernando de Fuentes, Emilio
Fernández, and Ismael Rodríguez, incorporated into their films an Anglo
American male character as a result of Hollywood's past portrayals.[94] The
character is an articulation of a stereotyped Anglo American male, or as
what I have termed a performance of gringo-ness, best demonstrated in
the comedia ranchera, Los tres García (The Three Garcías; 1947, dir. Ismael
Rodríguez) (figure 4.4).

Los tres García focuses on three feuding cousins, José Luis (Abel Salazar),
Luis Antonio (Pedro Infante), and Luis Manuel (Victor Manuel Mendoza),
who compete for the attention of their visiting blond Mexican American
cousin, Lupita Smith García (Marga López) (figure 4.5). The García cousins
continue a longstanding family tradition of fighting, much to the chagrin
and annoyance of their black-clothed, cigar-smoking grandmother (Sara
García), the only authority figure the men listen to and respect. The three
cousins represent different facets of Mexican machismo, forming a diverse
archetype that a single charro could not personify. Luis Manuel García is

---

[93] Some prominent silent films that follow this storyline include The Life of Villa (1913, dir. Christy
Cabanne and Raoul Walsh), An Arizona Wooing (1915, dir. Tom Mix), Along the Border (1916, dir.
Tom Mix), Heart of the Sunset (1918, dir. Frank Powell), and The Bad Man (1923, dir. Edwin Carewe).
Hollywood sound films that feature a charro character include Viva Villa! (1934, dir. John Conway),
Song of the Gringo (1936, dir John P. McCarthy), Border G-Man (1938, dir. David Howard), Durango
Valley Raiders (1938, dir. Sam Newfield), In Old México (1938, dir. Edward D. Venturini), and South
of the Border (1939, dir. George Sherman). See David R. Maciel, El bandolero, el pocho y la raza
(Mexico City: Consejo Nacional de la Cultura y las Artes, 2000), 26–78.

[94] Some films that include an Anglo/gringo archetype are La mujer del puerto (1933, dir. Arcady
Boytler), Allá en el Rancho Grande (1936, dir. Fernando de Fuentes), La golondrina (The Swallow;
1938, dir. Miguel Contreras Torres), Mala yerba (Bad Plant; 1940, dir. Gabriel Soria), Rancho Alegre
(Cheerful Ranch; 1941, dir. Rolando Aguilar), and Salón México (1949, dir. Emilio Fernández).

Figure 4.4 Advertisement for *Los tres García*, as it appeared in *El Univerisal*,
August 1947.

the well-dressed businessman whose sole preoccupation is money.[95] He is
able to turn off his ruthless business nature and get in touch with his sentimental side through his poetry. José Luis García represents the pride and

[95] Jorge Ayala Blanco, *La aventurera del cine mexicano: En la época de oro y déspues* (Mexico
City: Grijalbo, 1993), 61. Luis Manuel dons the charro suit after meeting Lupe. At their first meeting,
Lupe comments on how he does not look like he belongs in the town because he is wearing a flashy,
double-breasted business suit. He remarks that only tourists expect Mexican townsmen to always
wear a charro suit. Lupe expresses her admiration for the attire, exclaiming that it is very beautiful
and macho. After this encounter, Luis Manuel dresses as a charro for the remainder of the film.

Figure 4.5 Lupita (Marga López) picks a charro cousin to love in *Los tres García* (1947). Photo courtesy of Mil Nubes-Foto.

independent nature of the macho male. He refuses to work for fear of being exploited for pay, and is easily offended. Although living in poverty, his pride will not allow him to ask for help; he represents the triumphant dignity of the macho mexicano. He is also overly sensitive and on a quest for self-discovery, evident through the titles of his reading material: *How to Find Yourself* and *Masculine Pride*.

The last García, Luis Antonio, receives the most critical attention because he is played by the highly popular Pedro Infante, Mexican cinema's other embodiment of the macho singing charro. Luis Antonio is consistently described as "a happy womanizing cheater, dirty talker, a drunk, and sentimental."[96] Exhibiting the most machismo of the three, his pattern of womanizing is evident in his numerous wall portraits of his conquests and in the collection of earrings, which he strategically obtains after he kisses or sucks the lady's ear. Luis Antonio's machismo is solidified in his self-descriptive performance of Esperón's "Dicen que soy mujereigo" ("They say I am a Womanizer"),

[96] Ibid.

which he performs with a full mariachi at his grandmother's birthday party. While a song describing his sexual conquests may seem inappropriate at his grandmother's birthday, the crowd, especially his grandmother and several women, enjoy the performance and applaud Luis Antonio enthusiastically. His macho act is not only accepted, it is also rewarded.

According to *El Cine Gráfico*, *Los tres García* is "a film without grand pretensions that nevertheless captures the public's heart because it has all the necessary characteristics to be successful."[97] Much like other comedia rancheras, *Los tres García* features performances that showcase the folkloric and the national with music written by the Esperón-Cortázar duo. The diegetic, foregrounded use of mariachi and small brass bands at the grandmother's house, including a serenade of the traditional "Cielito lindo," and the brandish show-off performances of the three cousins at the jaripeo, are all intended to seduce the lovely Lupita.

Aside from the performed rancheras and the serenades, Esperón's orchestral underscoring helps to further establish a strong foundation of machismo for the charro characters. In several scenes involving Lupita's father, blandly named John Smith (Clifford Carr), and the self-identity–searching José Luis, Esperón sneaks in a quotation of the U.S popular song "The Turkey in the Straw." The first cue sounds in an early scene involving John and Lupe, who pull up in a convertible car, and José Luis, who rides on horseback. Here, John's performance of gringo-ness conveys his Anglo American Otherness, lack of machismo, and imprudence when he calls out in English, "Hey, boy!" to José Luis. Not knowing that she is speaking with her Mexican cousin, Lupe politely asks in fluent Spanish where they can find the village of San Luis de la Paz. After José Luis cheerfully points them in the right direction, John attempts to give José Luis a tip for his trouble. José Luis takes offense at this gesture and swiftly turns away from them, insulted and annoyed. In the scene's underscoring, upper woodwinds and strings quote the "The Turkey and the Straw" in an almost mocking manner, fastening a cultural synchresis to John's embarrassing and clumsy behavior.

The song quotation is not an isolated event; it occurs two more times during the film's narrative. Despite being family, the García cousins have no intention of meeting or knowing their U.S. American relations. This becomes clear in a scene when their grandmother introduces John to the trio as "the uncle they hate and they never wanted to meet" and Lupita as the

---

[97] "Enorme Éxito se Anotan Los Tres García," *El Cine Gráfico*, August 17, 1947.

one they call "rata blanca" ("white rat") because she was not born in Mexico, indicating that any ties with the United States are unwanted and ultimately out of the question. John slowly and bashfully explains that none of the Garcías went to his wedding because he was from the United States. During his explanation, "The Turkey and the Straw" sounds in a varied form, then is fully quoted in the upper strings when he is done, poking fun at his hurt feelings and emphasizing the charros' immediate dislike and distrust for him and his daughter. "The Turkey and the Straw" is articulated one more time at the grandmother's house. John and Lupita approach José Luis to apologize for offending him earlier, but he chooses to ignore them. As José Luis takes out his book on masculine pride, "The Turkey and the Straw" sounds again in strings and upper woodwinds, reenforcing his macho stance against the American visitors.

Why has this song been incorporated into the film's underscoring? Film scoring is about strategy on the part of the composer when the film is in its postproduction phase. During the film's spotting session, Esperón may have recognized the imprudence on the part of the gringo stereotype to the un-spoken yet understood charro rules of social conduct, gradually established through the trajectory of the comedia ranchera.[98] The inclusion of "The Turkey and the Straw" instills a cultural synchresis that parallels George Lipsitz's concept of "strategizing anti-essentialism." Borrowing from Gayarti Spivak's "strategic essentialism," a concept applied to a group that shares a common history and interests, but ignores the heterogeneity of the group in order to build unity based on common needs and desires, Lipsitz uncovers a "particular disguise" selected by an individual based on his "ability to high-light, underscore, and augment an aspect of one's identity that one cannot express directly."[99] It is the adoption or adaption of a cultural form from a different culture, which is then used to help shape a conception of the self.[100] For the case of Los tres García, the incorporation of a visual and aural

---

[98] By the time *Los tres García* premiered, Esperón had worked on several comedia rancheras, in-cluding: *¡Ay Jalisco, no te rajes!* (1941, dir. Joselito Rodríguez), *La liga de las canciones* (*The League of Songs*; 1941, dir. Chano Ureta), *Adios mi chaparrita* (*Goodbye My Small Girl*; 1943, dir. René Cardona), *Hasta que perdió Jalisco* (*Until Jalisco Loses*; 1945, dir. Fernando de Fuentes), *No basta ser charro* (*It is Not Enough to Be a Charro*; 1946, dir. Juan Bustillo Oro), *El tigre de Jalisco* (*The Tiger of Jalisco*; 1947, dir. René Cardona), *Si me han de matar mañana* (*If You Have to Kill Me Tomorrow*; 1947, dir Miguel Zacarías), and *Soy charro de Rancho Grande* (*I am a Charro of Rancho Grande*; 1947, dir. Joaquín Párdave). Esperón was aware of machismo signifiers in the charro figure.

[99] George Lipsitz, *Dangerous Crossroads: Popular Music, Postmodernism, and the Poetics of Place* (London: Verso, 1994), 62. See also Gayatri Chakravorty Spivak, *Outside in the Teaching Machine* (New York: Routledge, 1993), 3–4.

[100] Lipsitz, *Dangerous Crossroads*, 62.

representation of an Anglo American male, or the construction of a gringo archetype, is strategically incorporated not only to showcase (or mock) relations between the United States and Mexico but also to further augment the macho characteristics of the Mexican charro. Mexican cinema experimented with the construction of the Anglo American male characters in the 1936 version of *Allá en el Rancho Grande* with the secondary character Pete from Denver.[101] From the outset, Pete is molded as a buffoon; he is clumsy, oafish, and anti-macho all demonstrated in his inability to reproduce the grito or to successfully defend himself when confronted by other charros.[102] In *Los tres García*, the performance of the gringo John culturally synchretized to "The Turkey and the Straw" speaks both to the self-perception of Mexican machismo and to perceived notions of Anglo American masculinity. First known as "Zip Coon," "The Turkey and the Straw" is a minstrel song used by white performers performing in blackface.[103] According to Charles Hamm, the lyrics of "Zip Coon" were written in a specific way, intended to portray an African American male as a "comical, illiterate, almost subhuman being."[104] While the lyrics of the song are not sung in the film, the popular melody is associated with the presence of Anglo American culture in the form of John and his blundering interactions with the charros, transferring the negative connotations of the song to the Anglo American male. Esperón borrows "The Turkey and the Straw" in order to further emphasize the Otherness of the gringo archetype and to uphold the macho Mexican charro in a seemingly blatant and even sarcastic rejection of pan-Americanism.[105] This

[101] This depiction was also portrayed in the remake of *Allá en el Rancho Grande* from 1949, starring Jorge Negrete.

[102] It is important to note here that Clifford Carr plays both Pete from Denver in *Allá en el Rancho Grande* and John Smith in *Los tres García*.

[103] U.S. American composer Carl Breil borrowed twenty-six popular tunes for his original score for D. W. Griffith's monumental and racist film *The Birth of a Nation* (1918). Included in that list is "Zip Coon," which accompanies a particularly controversial scene at the plantation. For more information and analysis on Carl Breil's score for *The Birth of a Nation*, see Martin Miller Marks, *Music and the Silent Film: Contexts and Case Studies, 1895–1924* (New York: Oxford University Press, 1997).

[104] Charles Hamm, *Music in the New World* (New York: W.W. Norton, 1983), 163–64. For more information on "The Turkey and the Straw" and minstrel music see Carle Frederick Wikke, *Tambo and Bones: A History of the American Minstrel Stage* (Durham, NC: Duke University Press, 1930).

[105] Esperón's use of "The Turkey and the Straw" hints at silent-film music compilation practice. The cue sheets for silents consistently provided music, albeit stereotypical music, of ethnicities and nationalities in order for the audience to understand the change of character and/or location on screen. While the song is a part of the minstrel tradition and is anchored with racist connotations, after a necessary title change that occurred during the turn of the century, the song became an important part of U.S. popular song. Composer and silent film music compiler Erno Rapeé includes "The Turkey in the Straw" in his *Encyclopedia of Music for Pictures* under the category of American "Southern" songs; see Erno Rapeé, *Encyclopedia of Music for Pictures* (New York: Belwin, 1925), 65. For synchronized, animated films, such as Walt Disney's *Steamboat Willie* (1928), "The Turkey and

strategic underscoring also implies that a single charro by himself cannot fulfill the machismo role (as evidenced by the division of machismo characteristics among the three cousins) and necessitates assistance from the gringo archetype with essentialist music. All of these elements, when taken together, elevate the conception of the singing charro to new heights.

Conclusion

The charro in the comedia ranchera has been idolized as a national symbol and an ambassador of Mexicanidad. The figure, however, has undergone a series of interpretations along its journey as a horseman and ranch hand, as a popular figure absorbed by the urban culture into the theater, as an actor in silent films, and as a singer-actor in recorded, synchronized sound films. Through each representation, the charro adds varying characteristics based on specific sociocultural and sociopolitical contexts that allow him to still be recognizable to the popular, urban audience. In the theater, the charro became a crucial fixture for revistas set in the countryside, while in early sound cinema, he became an important symbol of Mexican masculinity and nationalism through his ability to sing the canción mexicana and the canción ranchera. In *Allá en el Rancho Grande*, his constructions in sound cinema became an important blueprint for the Mexican industry, through which it could challenge notions of conservatism during the Cárdenas administration. Throughout the 1940s, the singing charro was attached to members of the rising star system, especially Jorge Negrete in *¡Ay Jalisco, no te rajes!*, who provided the appropriate look and sound of the Mexican charro, with the help of the Esperón-Cortázar duo. In *Los tres García*, the charro is divided into three representations and is placed side by side with an Anglo American stereotype that turns the portrayals of Mexican men in Hollywood cinema on its head in order to bolster the conception of the macho charro and Mexican masculinity in general.

Throughout this examination, music, whether functioning diegetically or non-diegetically, has played a powerful role in facilitating a positive yet problematic representation of the charro for Mexican audiences through its romantic serenades, confrontational coplas, and strategic underscoring.

the Straw" became a prominent tune for onscreen, synchronized dancing. Although having a highly racist historical context, "The Turkey and the Straw" is considered a lighthearted and lively dance tune, becoming a sound embodiment for U.S. culture and parody.

Music's role in the comedia ranchera can be construed as crucial to the narrative, since the representation of the charro without music would be incomplete. In an interview with *Novedades*, Manuel Esperón affirms that the music has allowed the charro to exemplify several characteristics crucial to the construction of his cultural identity in cinema: "The music is an essential part, a character as important as the protagonists in the film."[106]

---

[106] María Luisa Velez, "Por los costos, sacrifican la música en el cine: Esperón," *Novedades*, December 9, 1989.

5

The Strains of the Revolution

Musicalizing the Soldadera in the Revolutionary Melodrama

What is definitive is the way a song can evoke an ambience of love and loss, becoming the emblematic seal of daily life in the revolution.
—Carlos Monsiváis[1]

After the silent-film period, the Mexican Revolution (1910–ca. 1920) became a major focal point for the developing film industry. The political conflict, which began as an uprising against the Porfirian dictatorship, led to the most violent and aggressive conflicts experienced on national soil since Independence. In Mexican popular culture, the Revolution has been continuously shaped and reshaped in the imaginations of visual artists, such as in the colorful and monumental murals of the Mexican muralist school, completed during the 1920s and 1930s, or detailed in prose by authors such as Mariano Azuela in his pivotal book *Los de abajo* (*The Underdogs*; 1915). On celluloid, the Mexican Revolution stands out as the first documented civil war, offering a fascinating moving, visual archive of people and events. In the midst of the fighting, exhibitors, cameraman, and directors filmed the armed conflicts and screened the footage throughout Mexico.[2] Because of the severity of the images—and the need to develop a unified front—the state encouraged the production of films that provided more positive and less violent representations, which limited the focus on

---

[1] Carlos Monsiváis, "Foreword: When Gender Can't Be Seen Amid the Symbols: Women and the Mexican Revolution," in *Sex in Revolution: Gender, Politics, and Power in Modern Mexico*, ed. Mary Kay Vaughan, Jocelyn Olcott, and Gabriela Cano (Durham, NC: Duke University Press, 2006), 6.

[2] For more information on the films and newsreels made during the Revolution, see Rielle Navitski, *Public Spectacles of Violence: Sensational Cinema and Journalism in Early Twentieth-Century Mexico and Brazil* (Durham, NC: Duke University Press, 2017).

the Revolution in Mexican productions from the end of the 1910s and the 1920s. By the 1930s, however, the Revolution was reexamined and critiqued by a new generation of filmmakers, a shift spurred on by the simultaneous advent of recorded, synchronized sound film. Films such as ¡*Vámonos con Pancho Villa!* (*Let's Go with Pancho Villa!*; 1935, dir. Fernando de Fuentes), *La Adelita* (1938; dir. Guillermo Hernández Gómez), and *Enamorada* (*Woman in Love*; 1946, dir. Emilio Fernández) provided audiences with diverse readings of the armed struggle—readings that would have lasting consequences on not just the national film industry but also the national— and international—imagination.

As a film genre, the revolutionary melodrama emphasizes the struggles, the heroism, and the triumphs, and even the failures, of revolutionary soldiers.[3] These films have augmented the visual construction of these men, often depicting the revolutionary in the form of a *ranchero* (a person who farms or works on a ranch) or the charro, whose virility, machismo, and patriotism intensified their role in the armed struggle. In the visual arts and literature, depictions of the Revolution focused on this demonstration of masculinity, while women received only marginal and limited recognition. Although women held major, substantial roles in Mexican film during the *época de oro*, when it came to the Revolution, national cinema provided a narrow and limited understanding of their contribution. Cinematically speaking, women featured in portrayals of the armed struggle were frequently shown as *soldaderas*—the women who followed male soldiers as they traveled from region to region during the struggle, providing food, medical attention, and other provisions. Revolutionary melodramas from the *época de oro* typically feature a soldadera as the principal female character, yet in each film, she is treated in differing ways. These divergent portrayals draw heavily from visual and musical cues that carried strong social and cultural significance.

The visual presentation of the soldadera is based on specific imagery or, rather, a specific image. The visual archives documenting the Revolution, discussed in the works of film scholar Zuzanna Pick and graphic historian John Mraz, provided much of the photographic evidence regarding women's involvement during the war, focusing on soldaderas making food, riding

---

[3] The revolutionary soldiers refer to those fighting the rebellion, particularly the Zapatistas, the Villistas, and the Carrancitas, against the Federalistas, who fought for the interests of the state and the Church. Mexican cinema's *época de oro* specifically exhibited the armed struggle from this perspective. It wasn't until much later that national cinema featured the perspective of the Federalistas.

trains, and standing next to disheveled soldiers.[4] One significant figure was the soldadera, Adelita. While Adelita's real identity is up for speculation, her visage has been erroneously applied to a photograph that was included in the monumental *Historia gráfica de México*. The photo, supposedly taken by Agustín V. Casasola in 1910, depicts a woman leaning forward from the handrails of a train and peering out, with a concentrated brow, to her left. She is flanked by other women who look directly at the camera, but it is this woman's leaning image that has been foregrounded. Mraz asserts that this photo became "the paradigmatic image of the *soldadera,* the Mexican's soldier faithful companion."[5] And the title of the photo, "Adelita-la-*soldadera*," became one of most crucial symbols of Mexican womanhood during the Revolution.

Adelita is also the protagonist in an anonymous hybrid corrido-canción by the same name from 1910. Over the course of several stanzas, a Revolutionary soldier pleads with his love interest Adelita to not leave him for another man and to wait for him until the fighting is over. This song of love and loss circulated extensively during the decade of fighting and became more popular in the post-Revolutionary years, becoming an unofficial anthem for the armed struggle, as described in the quote by Carlos Monsiváis that begins this chapter.

My aim in this chapter is not to reveal the discrepancies in Mexican cinema's representation of women during the Revolution but, rather, to examine how the soldadera was shaped in the national discourse on Mexican history, in popular culture, and on the silver screen, and how music was a major factor in constructing this role. As interpretations of the Revolution changed during the *época de oro*, the musical construction of the soldadera remained constant: she was synthesized with songs such as "La Adelita," "La Valentina," and "La Rielera"—corrido-canciones that feature a soldadera, but that are really about the men who love them. Using existing scholarship on the revolutionary melodrama as a foundation for analysis and the aforementioned films as case studies, I contend that the soldadera is positioned in a contested space where the visual archive affirms and praises her actions during the Revolution, but only as providing relief to and for male soldiers. Music, in this case the corrido-canciones, works in tandem with this moving image, constructing a recognizable cultural synchresis for audiences: the

---

[4] See Zuzana M. Pick, *Constructing the Image of the Mexican Revolution: Cinema and the Archive* (Austin: University of Texas Press, 2010); and John Mraz, *Looking for Mexico: Modern Visual Culture and National Identity* (Durham, NC: Duke University Press, 2009).

[5] Ibid., 233.

recycled music in these films set during the Revolution works to sculpt the female character into the soldadera.

The Revolution and Mexican Womanhood

The Mexican Revolution, as a singular event and a concept, has been interpreted and reconstructed numerous times, either for reasons of political and national cohesion, or for artistic and performative criticism, and/or for historical revision. The armed struggle involved disparate factions primarily drawn from the lower- and working-class populations, who fought for a variety of objectives that were not clearly identified at the time. During the 1920s after the violence ended, government officials and the cultural elite molded the Revolution to be seen not only as a struggle fought in the name of widespread, unified goals but also as a vehicle to promote national solidarity. The heroes of the Revolution—specifically male revolutionaries such as Pancho Villa and Emiliano Zapata—served as the conduits for national unity and were consistently exploited and placed on a pedestal. Women, however, were virtually ignored. Monsiváis states:

> The Mexican Revolution has been unified in order to be understood as a whole (a trap that facilitates the assimilation of history and the creation of institutions) and has been characterized however the regime pleases, which prohibits understanding its complexity. Yet, even within the realm of generalities, one thing is notorious: women (the gender, the groups, and the enormously dynamic individuals) mean very little in political and social terms and practically nothing when set before the deity of those times: History, an exclusively masculine territory.[6]

In the collective retelling of the Revolution, while events and ideologies were up for reinterpretation and even reimagining, the roles and contributions of women were typically not included in the reshaped historical narrative.

The activities and roles of women before, during, and after the armed struggle took on various forms, particularly in the social and political spheres. María Consuelo Guerrero has pointed out that it wasn't until recently that research has shown those women's roles to have been quite numerous and

---

[6] Carlos Monsiváis, "Foreword," 4.

diverse. Their contributions included feminist and political activism, seen in the works of Eliva Carrillo Puerto (1878–1968) and Hermila Galindo Acosta y Topete (1896–1954), and feminist criticism, exemplified in the writings of Laureana Wright Gonzaléz (1847–96), whose works became popular during and after the Revolution. Consuelo Guerrero also details the numerous political action groups that were organized and led by women prior to the armed struggle, including El Socialismo Mexicano (Mexican Socialism, 1908) and La Liga Femenina de Propaganda Política (The Feminine League of Political Propaganda, 1909), which impacted women's roles in modern Mexican society.[7] This short summary only scratches the surface.

While women participated in literary and political revolutionary discourse, the ultimate signifiers for women during the Revolution were the soldadera and the guerrilla fighter, two types who have been conflated together by visual artists, authors, composers, and filmmakers. These were the figures labeled "Adelitas, Valentinas, and Marietas," all named after popular songs that painted soldaderas with an affectionate and idealized light. There were, however, differences between the two roles. The soldadera is defined as a "camp follower," referring to women, typically of indigenous or mestizo descent, of the working or lower class, who, rather than be left alone, followed their partners into battle. Shirlene Soto specifies, "When their men were conscripted or kidnapped by the army, these women took their children and joined the march."[8] In retrospect, this is often interpreted as a sign of loyalty and devotion, but as many historians and scholars have revealed, these women left with their partners because they either could not afford to be on their own or because they were "recruited" as well.[9] Although many soldaderas followed their male partners, others were not attached but would accompany any regiment, as it offered employment regardless of political belief. These latter women, however, found far more hardship and received much less in payment than did the women who were partnered with men.

The Revolution lasted between ten and eleven years, beginning with the overthrow of dictator Porfirio Díaz in 1910 and carrying through to the end of warfare with the ascendency of Venustiano Carranza as president.[10]

---

[7] María Consuelo Guerrero, "La revolucionaria en el cine mexicano," *Hispania* 95, no. 1 (2012): 39.

[8] Shirlene Soto, *Emergence of the Modern Mexican Woman: Her Participation in Revolution and Struggle for Equality, 1900–1940* (Denver: Arden Press, 1990), 44.

[9] Ibid.

[10] Carranza's presidency lasted from 1917 to 1920. He opted not to run for president again, endorsing Ignacio Bonillas rather than General Álvaro Obregón. Obregón used his influence with

Andrés Fuentes notes that soldaderas were their most useful in 1913, as the military campaigns took the regiments farther from home and broke up into fragmented army units. Because these units were crossing unknown territory, the ability to push on while also attending to the wounded, without diverting attention away from battle, became imperative: "the soldadera emerged as the backbone for this type of military organization."[11] These armies eventually came to depend on the women's labor, but as Fuentes elucidates, their roles typically changed during their travels. The armies that most utilized the commissary abilities of the soldaderas were the Federalistas, the Villistas, and the Carranistas, particularly after 1913, when the fighting spread across the countryside.[12] Although the soldaderas did not follow the Zapatistas, this regiment also depended on the labor of women, although predominantly by force. Fuentes states: "The southern army thus flourished in symbiosis with the people of Morelos. It was an army that relied, so to speak, on long distance commissariat and cooking services. Women did not need to be in the military camps; for the most part they remained in the towns and pueblos."[13] Armies that used cavalry, particularly the Villistas, considered soldaderas as too burdensome and so they were not included in the regiment. According to General Juan F. Azcárate, the image of soldaderas accompanying revolutionary troops was a creation of the film industry.[14] Regiments that traveled primarily by train, such as other branches of the Villistas and the Federalistas, did include groups of soldaderas who, at stops along the way, would quickly disembark and begin to forage for food and other supplies.[15] Soldaderas typically did not fight, but the women guerrilla fighters did perform combat roles.

The soldaderas were perceived as indispensable yet they were also cast aside. As Monsiváis notes, soldaderas were not romantic figures and as such they should not be idealized: "The soldaderas suffered rape, rejection, and victimization to such a degree that in 1925, Secretary of Defense General

government officials, yet was convinced Carranza would not leave peacefully. On his way to Veracruz, Carranza was killed. Historians have debated whether Carranza was assassinated or if he committed suicide. See Enrique Krauze, *Mexico Biography of Power: A History of Modern Mexico, 1810–1996* (New York: HarperCollins, 1997).

[11] Andrés Reséndez Fuentes, "Battleground Women: Soldaderas and Female Soldiers in the Mexican Revolution," *The Americas* 51, no. 4 (1995): 552.

[12] The Villistas, armies led by Pancho Villa, and the Carranistas, were armies organized under Venustiano Carranza and were the regiments fighting in the north of Mexico, gaining more recognition in 1913.

[13] Reséndez Fuentes, "Battleground Women," 534.

[14] Elizabeth Salas, *Soldaderas in the Mexican Military* (Austin: University of Texas Press, 1990), 44.

[15] Ibid., 537.

Joaquín Amaro called them 'the main cause of vices, diseases, crime, and disorder', and ordered them expelled from the barracks."[16] Monsiváis astutely notes that these women suffered at the hands of the revolutionaries yet they are blamed for their suffering. At the end of the armed struggle, many women could not return home. Instead, they had to make their own way, with little or no assistance from the government. Some assumed the roles they had previously, in a sense solidifying the argument that the Revolution did not resolve or accomplish anything particularly for women. But, as Mary Kay Vaughan observes, the Revolution was born in a transnational context, and was accompanied in part by North American ideals of progressivism. She adds that the role of women in modern Mexican society was changing then: "the revolution was not just an attack on property, social hierarchy, and exclusion; it assaulted the Victorian morality and rules of sexual repression and brought women into public space in unprecedented ways."[17] Thus, the cinema became a crucial conduit for the portrayal of gender roles, as evidenced in the prostitute melodrama of the 1930s and the cabareteras of the 1940s. This portrayal of women, however, was fairly restricted, and when representation of the Revolution was concerned, their roles both on and off screen were limited.

The Soldadera in Popular Culture

[T]he *soldaderas* have become stock characters in literature, *corridos*, art, and films.

—Elizabeth Salas[18]

Alongside Pancho Villa and Emiliano Zapata, the soldadera has maintained an esteemed position as the sole representative of women in Revolutionary iconography, an archetype that personifies all women who participated in the armed struggle, regardless of occupation or position.[19] It is this role

---

[16] Monsiváis, "Foreword," 9.

[17] Mary Kay Vaughan, "Introduction: Pancho Villa, the Daughters of Mary and the Modern Woman: Gender in the Long Mexican Revolution," in *Sex in Revolution: Gender Politics, and Power in Modern Mexico*, ed. by Jocelyn Olcott, Mary Kay Vaughan, and Gabriela Cano (Durham, NC: Duke University Press, 2006), 25.

[18] Salas, *Soldaderas in the Mexican Military*, 82.

[19] There is not a specific identified woman placed alongside these men as a Revolutionary leader but, rather, a visual construction of what a typical soldadera would look like. Shirlene Soto notes

that, although patronized and barely tolerated during the period, has been especially glorified during the post-Revolutionary years. As previously mentioned, one of the reasons for this adoration comes from the extensive visual archive, specifically photographs, that were accumulated during the Revolution, which serve as a "highly mediated cultural product."[20] The images that carry the most cultural weight are those collected by the Casasola family for the *Historia gráfica de la Revolución Mexicana*, which appeared in 1942. According to John Mraz, the Casasolas "were the first to systematically explore the uses of and demand for printed visual history."[21] This collection of photographs amounted to an astounding number of volumes, but as Mraz astutely points out, the numerous images "appear together with a dry and conservative recitation of the 'facts.'"[22]

No historians were involved in the process; instead, a group of all-male politicians, lawyers, journalists, and generals provided their own feedback and commentary. When it came to the representation of women, Mraz notes that any mention of women was limited to the role of soldadera, adding that the utilization of images featuring women represented a touch of the exotic.[23] He further elucidates that "almost all the published pictures are posed in the Mexico City train station, where the women appear next to the federal soldiers they accompany, emphasizing their role as camp followers."[24]

Such photographic material of women during the Revolution has prompted several discussions regarding the place of women in history. Andrea Noble asserts that while women's roles during the Revolution have been "amply stated in the photographic record," *really seeing*—or understanding—the women in these materials is far from straightforward.[25] Discussing and inserting women into the historical narrative has proven to be problematic, as male agency often eclipses any female agency. Thus, the position of women is ultimately interpreted and understood in relation to men, who may or may not be present in the photographs, but who nevertheless maintain the dominant and hegemonic presence in the discourse. In her book on the illustrated

that while many soldaderas remained anonymous, a few received some recognition, including Margarita Neri, María Aguirre, and María Luisa Escobar. See Soto, *Emergence of the Modern Mexican Woman*, 45–46.

[20] Andrea Noble, *Photography and Memory in Mexico: Icons of Revolution* (Manchester: Manchester University Press, 2010), 103.

[21] Mraz, *Looking for Mexico*, 192.

[22] Ibid., 193.

[23] Ibid., 232.

[24] Ibid., 196.

[25] Noble, *Photography and Memory in Mexico*, 102.

history of Mexico, Julia Tuñón states that these photographs captured the images of the soldaderas completing "feminine" functions, carrying food and walking next to the cavalry. But by the end of the armed struggle, a new interpretation had surfaced: "Then comes the idealization; dirt and blood are romanticized; the Revolution becomes an auspicious scene for singing songs, for demonstrating value and to decorate oneself, as if it were really decoration."[26] Photos of soldaderas sitting in groups with soldiers, hanging from the side of trains, cooking food or carrying children, adorned with bandoliers and braids have graced the history books on the Mexican Revolution and even commercial merchandise, such as postcards, posters, and calendars.[27]

The idea of the soldadera as a crucial Revolutionary icon has been heavily constructed through visual representation. Music, however, has also played a significant role, in a sense mirroring the indexical readings of the photographs. Music composed and performed during the Revolution represented a wide variety of genres, many specific to different regions of the country, such as the son traditions from Jalisco, Michoacán, and Veracruz, and brass bands that played marches, polkas, and waltzes, as well as arrangements of nineteenth-century works from the Western art canon. In Mexico City, popular theaters featured the latest dance crazes, as did the rising dance hall culture that was discussed in chapter 1.

Amid this rich and vibrant expression of musical innovation and circulation, the *corrido* became the main aural signifier of the Revolution. Corridos are strophic, narrative songs or ballads that consist of a series of stanzas detailing a story, typically about the exploits of specific soldiers or important armed events of the Revolution, such as the victors (and the non-victors) of certain battles. The corrido's final stanza or strophe often included a moral or lesson, so that listeners would be informed and become more educated. As the armed struggle continued, the corridos were embellished, made longer with performance times that ranged from a few minutes to half an hour. While serving as a source of entertainment, the corridos also were a communication tool, articulated by traveling minstrels or troubadours through the oral tradition and, as the histories have indicated, passed from region to region. In effect, the corridos "spread the word" about the Revolution and its major participants, who were predominantly male.

---

[26] Julia Tuñón, *Mujeres: Entre la imagen y la acción* (Mexico City: Debate, 2015), 205.
[27] Several of these photographs are also included in Aurelio de los Reyes, *Con Villa en México: Testimonios sobre camarógrafos norteamericanos en la revolución, 1911–1915* (Mexico City: Universidad Nacional Autónoma de México, 2010).

Scholars such as Vicente T. Mendoza and María Herrera-Sobek have pointed to select Revolutionary corridos that shaped a specific under-standing of womanhood that aligned strongly with the soldadera. The most well-known of these songs, which are about specific women, however, are not strictly corridos; rather, they relate more with another prominent song tradition of the period, the *canción mexicana*. Leonora Saavedra notes that composer Manuel M. Ponce wrote about the phenomenon of the canción mexicana in popular culture, proposing his own model of the song form that consists of slightly chromatic harmonies and light textures. In terms of content, the songs describe the love between two people that "Ponce believed would redeem the suffering life of Mexican men."[28] Love and pas-sion, specifically conveyed by the male voice, comes with particular musical constructs: "The circular pendulum of passionate illusion and resigned disil-lusion, positioned like a trait of the Mexican soul, is expressed in the canción through a series of characteristics that eventually convert into Mexican mu-sical archetypes: melodies in arch forms, the formal structures displayed in a pendular movement, descending cadential melodic formulas, etc."[29] During the 1910s, several composers in addition to Ponce provided their own arrangements of popular canciones, including José de Jesús Martínez, who in 1915 and 1916 published versions of Revolutionary canciones: "La Cucaracha," "La Valentina," and "La Adelita."[30] These songs and their circu-lation, as Herrera-Sobek has observed, influenced the construction of the soldadera in the national imagination: "the great popularity of the songs helped imprint the image of the soldadera in the public mind, thus validating and cementing in Mexican culture the soldadera archetype."[31]

There is no question that these songs have narrative and descriptive qual-ities, but strictly speaking, they do not follow the formal structure of the corrido, which relies on patterned storytelling devices. Rather, they repre-sent a generic hybrid. The lyrics declare love for a soldadera, its romanticized nature aligning more with the canción mexicana tradition, while the strophic structure of the song fits with the corrido, transforming the songs that follow this particular pattern into a hybrid corrido-canción:

---

[28] Leonora Saavedra, "Manuel M. Ponce y los músicos populares." *Heteronfonía* 143 (July-December 2010): 53.

[29] Ibid.

[30] Ibid.

[31] María Herrera-Sobek, *The Mexican Corrido: A Feminist Analysis* (Bloomington: Indiana University Press, 1990), 108

The transposing of the soldadera into a love object became problematic for the troubadour since he or she could not employ the classic form of the heroic corrido; a more flexible structure, a more lyrical framework, had to be employed to fit the romantic contents of the ballad. . . . The love songs resemble more the canción's structure and style. Nonetheless, most corrido collections, recorded versions of these ballads, anthologies, and the people themselves generally classify these songs as corridos.[32]

Historically, and even culturally speaking, in spite of their aesthetic difference these songs are still popularly labeled as corridos and are treated mainly as revolutionary corridos: musical signifiers of the period that are continuously rearticulated whenever the Revolution is referenced.[33]

"La Adelita"

"La Adelita" remains the Revolutionary song that is most recognized by domestic audiences, associated with both the armed struggle and the soldadera. In his monumental collection on the Mexican corrido, Mendoza matter of factly categorizes "La Adelita" as a "corrido formado por cuatro semiperiodos o sean dos frases" ("corrido formed in four semi-periods or of two phrases").[34] The notated melody in his study is in G Major and written in a bouncy duple meter with voices moving primarily in parallel thirds. The text, written from the male's perspective, describes the overwhelming affection he feels for his sweetheart Adelita, whom he must leave behind so that he may fight in battle.

In her feminist analysis of the Mexican corrido, Herrera-Sobek has gone further in concentrating on the shaping of the soldier archetype in corridos, focusing on how "La Adelita" is an example of "the idealized, beautiful, and valiant soldadera type in its romanticized manifestation."[35] However, this

---

[32] Ibid., 104.

[33] Soldaderas and other female participants in the Revolution were in fact common in many traditionally labeled corridos. These corridos narrate specific stories about these women and offer a more intricate view of how they contributed to the war effort. We may wonder why these particular corridos were not used in cinema. The songs didn't circulate as widely as the corrido-canciones and didn't penetrate the popular culture bubble during and after the Revolution. See for example, Herrera-Sobek's chapter entitled "The Soldier Archetype," in *The Mexican Corrido*, 84–116.

[34]. Vicente T. Mendoza, *Romance español y el corrido mexicano* (Mexico City: Ediciones de Universidad Nacional Autónoma de México, 1939), 634.

[35] Herrera-Sobek, *The Mexican Corrido*, 108.

interpretation depends on which version of "La Adelita" one is examining. Following in the tradition of corridos, while the music would remain strophic, the lyrics of the strophes were often changed or new strophes added. Herrera-Sobek examines two versions of "La Adelita" in her study. The first example leaves Adelita's position in the Revolution ambiguous and is constructed mainly from the perspective of the soldier, who appears to view her as an extension of his masculinity and wants to show her off:

> If Adelita would be my wife
> If Adelita would be my woman,
> I would buy her a silk dress
> To take her dancing to the barracks.[36]

Her position is not quite solidified: "We do not know whether she is a soldadera living in the barracks already or whether she lives elsewhere and her boyfriend will bring her to his military quarters."[37] In the second, later version, Adelita is described as a soldadera with a valiant character and a willingness to follow a sergeant.[38] Both versions, however, exhibit the persistent fear felt by the male soldier that Adelita, having a wandering eye and being fickle, will reject and leave him for another man. This scenario rarely paralleled reality as, as previously mentioned, soldaderas were consistently abandoned. Because of this song, "La Adelita" has become a powerful signifier not *for* women but *of* women in the history of the Revolution. According to Alicia Arrizon, "The performative functionality of "La Adelita" lies in its enactment of real—albeit contested—history. As a text within a text, the ballad is useful analytically because it helps expose the performance of gender relations rooted in the upheaval of social transformation."[39] The idealization of the soldadera and fear of abandonment by the soldier shape this song as not an anthem for the strength of Revolutionary women but, rather, as a sign and symptom of the struggles to regain masculinity during the uprising. The song was especially popular with Pancho Villa's regiment: soldaderas became

---

[36] Ibid.

[37] Ibid., 105.

[38] The first stanza of this second version supports this description: "In the high sierras / Camped were the soldiers / And a young woman who valiantly followed / Madly in love with the sergeant / Popular among the troops was Adelita / The woman the sergeant adored / Because she was not only valiant but beautiful / So that even the colonel respected her." For the full second version and English translation of "La Adelita," see Herrera-Sobek, *The Mexican Corrido*, 107.

[39] Alicia Arrizon, *Latina Performance: Transversing the Stage* (Bloomington: Indiana University Press, 1999), 52.

known as "adelitas" among Villa's troops, while the soldaderas of the federal army were pejoratively called "gauchas" ("mannish women").[40]

As discussed in the previous section, the realities of the soldadera during the armed struggle were shaped by their roles as care workers and laborers. Women were responsible for making the regiments battle ready. These women experienced a great deal of oppression and abuse, and they were often cast aside by the men they followed and the government they served. "La Adelita," however, does not convey any of this, but instead constructs a perspective shaped by romantic love and sentimentality.

"La Valentina" and "La Rielera"

"La Adelita" was not the only corrido-canción that shaped the soldadera as a national archetype. Others, such as "La Valentina" and "La Rielera," aided in constructing interpretations that the film industry exploited. "La Valentina" operates similarly to "La Adelita," presenting another idealistic reading of the soldadera that is romantically tied to a male soldier. Monsiváis notes, "the primordial condition of indebtedness on the part of the survivor who carries memories from the battlefields, of the companion who bears witness to an honorable death, is consigned (in a manner of speaking) through the song 'La Valentina'":

> Valentina, Valentina
> Exhausted, I am at your feet.
> If they must kill me tomorrow
> Let them kill me now.[41]

Much like "La Adelita," Valentina is placed in a romanticized role by a dominant male voice. In the lyrics, she is described as a combat fighter; the song, however, only positions her in a role of love and adoration, and not on the battlefield, denying her any recognition for her involvement in the actual fighting. Although the identity of the real Adelita was never determined, Herrera-Sobek observes that "La Valentina" is based on Valentina Gatica,

---

[40] Reséndez Fuentes, "Battleground Women," 540n73.

[41] Monsiváis, "Foreword," 7. Lyrics of "La Valentina" are also quoted in Herrera-Sobek, *The Mexican Corrido*, 109.

who was a soldadera with the Obregón regime. Her biography indicates that she had a harsh upbringing, and was left an orphan when her father died in combat. She joined the Obregón forces as a soldadera: "She was brave, daring, beautiful and attractive. She attracted attention with her military type clothing, her two cartridge belts slung across her chest, and her rifle hanging on her shoulder."[42] Although this imagery constructs a noble image, the real Valentina, like many soldaderas, gained hardly any benefits from the end of the Revolution and was living with a small pension by herself.

The corrido-canción "La Rielera" continues the romance between a woman and a soldier, but is now described from her perspective:

> I am the train rider and I have my Juan,
> He is my life and I'm his love
> When they tell me that the train is leaving
> Goodbye my train rider there goes your Juan.[43]

The imagery illustrated in the strophes emphasizes the crucial symbolism associated with the train. As mentioned in chapter 1, trains, which connected the countryside to the city and served as a symbol of modernization during the Porfiriato, were also key signifiers of the Revolution, allowing regiments to move from region to region. They were also prone to attacks, however. The train was the primary mode for transporting the regiments and camp followers. The soldaderas rode on top or inside the railcars, rather than following behind the horseback-riding revolutionary soldiers on foot.

Another significant element in this corrido-canción is the reference to the soldier as "mi Juan" ("my John"): "Juan" becomes synonymous with a nameless revolutionary soldier. There is also no clear indication in this song that "La Rielera" is a soldadera; her possession of pistols and her declamatory manner align her more with the combat fighters than with the camp followers:

> I have my pair of pistols,
> To go for a walk with me.
> One is for my love,
> The other is for my rival.

[42] Romero Aceves, as quoted in Herrera-Sobek, *The Mexican Corrido*, 109.
[43] Ibid.

The Corrido-Canciones on the Stage

The aforementioned corrido-canciones construct a venerated representation of the soldadera, existing predominately as the object of affection for soldiers; she was the glorified female camp follower who became the potential lover, girlfriend, or wife of combat soldiers. Although the songs feature women, men ultimately claim the center of attention; it is their feelings, their manhood, and their needs that are conveyed in the lyrics.

Although the Revolution ceased to be a film backdrop for a short period, the Revolution remained an important fixture in the revistas, which served as an experimental space that shaped early conceptions of the soldadera for the urban audience.[44] During the 1910s and 1920s, "La Adelita" became a vital addition to the popular stage and was featured satirically in several productions. Armando de María y Campos notes that by 1914, the song was already popular in the north with the Villistas. By the time it arrived in Mexico City, parodies of the song had circulated in one of the main centers for teatro frívolo the Teatro María Guerrero, with the following changed lyrics:

> If Carranza marries Zapata
> Pancho Villa with Álvaro Obregón
> Adelita will marry me
> And the Revolution will be over.[45]

According to de María y Campos, a soldadera character was the protagonist for the 1903 Mexican zarzuela *La sargenta* (*The Female Sargent*), which featured a libretto by Aurelio González Carrasco and music by the popular Rafael Gascón. De María y Campos states that González Carrasco was the first Mexican author to construct this representation of Mexican womanhood for the theatrical stage, which was then later recycled during the Revolution in other revistas, particularly those featuring performances of "La Adelita" and "La Valentina."[46] During the post-Revolutionary

---

[44] The influence of the revistas on Mexican cinema is discussed in chapters 1, 2, and 4 of this book.
[45] "Si Carranza se casa con Zapata / Pancho Villa con Álvaro Obregón / Adelita se casa conmigo / Y termina la Revolución." See Armando de María y Campos, *El teatro de género chico en la revolución mexicana* (Mexico City: Biblioteca del Instituto Nacional de Estudios Históricos de la Revolución Mexicana, 1956), 163.
[46] Ibid., 38.

years, these corrido-canciones gained wider circulation: they were taught to schoolchildren and quickly became regular fixtures in popular culture. For the film industry that sought to create new interpretations of the Revolution, these songs were recycled to provide audiences with a soundscape they would immediately recognize. Their inclusion in these films had varying functions and messages that reinforced specific gendered ideologies of Mexican cultural nationalism, which I discuss in the following sections.

The Soldadera in ¡*Vámonos con Pancho Villa!* (1936)

In July of 1994, the popular magazine *Somos* celebrated its 100th edition with a special issue entitled "The 100 Best Films in Mexican Cinema," compiled by twenty-five experts in the industry, including critics, historians, directors, and actors. The 1936 production ¡*Vámonos con Pancho Villa!* was allotted the number-one spot. This film marks a period that brought the Revolution back into the national spotlight, but did not follow the currents of national discourse. This focus was neither heroic, nor inspirational, nor even optimistic. ¡*Vámonos con Pancho Villa!* is the third film in director Fernando de Fuentes's Revolution trilogy, which includes the controversial *El prisionero 13* (*Prisoner 13*; 1933) and *El compadre Mendoza* (*The Godfather Mendoza*; 1934). While each of these films takes on a distinct conception of the Revolution and none of them glorify this period, ¡*Vámonos con Pancho Villa!* is the only film in the trilogy to feature one of the armed struggle's most revered players: Pancho Villa.

Based on two chapters from the 1931 novel by Rafael F. Muñoz, the film focuses on a group of six *campesinos* (farmers) known as Los Leones de San Pablo (The Lions of San Pablo), or simply Los Leones (The Lions), from the northern region of Mexico, who join Villa's forces and, one by one, succumb to violent deaths. The sole survivor is the group's leader, Tiburcio, the protagonist of the novel, whose final task for Villa is to kill and set fire to a member of his group who had contracted smallpox. During and after each death, the dwindling members, at first enthusiastic about joining the Villistas, soon grow weary, frustrated, and fed up with the futility of battle, all resting on one question: "Why?"

The Contemporáneos poet Xavier Villaurrutia (1903–1950) adapted Muñoz's novel for the screenplay, and this adaptation, much like the novel, offers a scathing commentary on the Revolution that questions the contemporary national discourse.[47] Rather than pursuing the Revolution as a catalyst for positive change for the country, Villaurrutia adamantly focuses on and exploits the hypocrisy and confusion that the armed struggle instilled. Building upon several examples from the visual archive, director Fernando de Fuentes introduces a film reading of the Revolution that questions the official histories or master narratives concocted and manipulated by different factions. As Zuzana Pick argues, much of the film's visual construction centers on the railroad, a symbol of modernization stemming from the defunct Porfiriato, and the tradition of charrería, the equestrian practices of the lower-middle-class male that, during the 1920s, became a crucial symbol of Mexican nationalism and which had recently become linked to the post-Revolutionary state, and the figure of the charro (see chapter 4). All became imperative for the Revolution's iconography on the silver screen (figure 5.1).

While Muñoz's novel and de Fuentes's film present new avenues of criticism for the Revolution that move against the grain of national discourse, there is one area in which both the novel and the film exemplify nationalist rhetoric: machismo. According to Max Parra, Muñoz's narrative focuses on the redeeming qualities of machismo in the lower- and working-class men during the Porfiriato who attempted to regain their masculinity through their revolt against the corrupt administration. He states, "The revolution's assault on the caste system became a vehicle of social empowerment whereby lower-class men recovered their manhood by destroying an oppressive order."[48] Revolutionary conflict thus became the ultimate spectacle and demonstration of masculinity. Parra also indicates that Muñoz's depiction of Villa is bleak, a depiction that appears to be based primarily on the corridos written about the revolutionary leader that depict him as a leader of limitless cruelty.[49] Muñoz's depiction works against Villa's own efforts to construct his legacy. Wanting to appear as a monumental leader and hero, Villa becomes his greatest promoter and relies on "oral culture and popular belief to manipulate and spread the myth of his own immortality."[50] Muñoz's novel and de

---

[47] Los Contemporáneos were a group of modernist poets and authors active during the 1920s and early 1930s who sought to provide a more cosmopolitan approach to literature. See Guillermo Sheridan, *Los Contemporáneos de ayer* (Mexico City: Fonda de Cultura Económica, 2003).

[48] Max Parra, *Writing Pancho Villa's Revolution: Rebels in the Literary Imagination of Mexico* (Austin: University of Texas, 2005), 107.

[49] Ibid., 114.

[50] Ibid., 115.

Figure 5.1 Title screen in *¡Vámonos con Pancho Villa!* (1935). Screen capture from film.

Fuentes's subsequent film signal a significant contradiction in the national rhetoric about the Revolution.

Although the novel focuses on the actions of Los Leones de San Pablo and their devotion, and later repulsion, of Villa, Muñoz also provides descriptions of a wartorn soundscape that includes the sounds of battle, with gunfire, shouts, and explosions. He also references music. Unlike the detailed musical descriptions in Federico Gamboa's *Santa* (1903), however, Muñoz provides only scant allusions, vaguely mentioning "war songs" and battle cries. There is one quick reference to a line from the corrido-canción "La Valentina," sung by three members of Los Leones, but it is not repeated for the remainder of the novel. In the film adaptation, music in the form of popular songs and orchestral underscoring feature prominently. While the film visually transforms the Revolution into a moving canvas of violence and degradation, the musical track, functioning both diegetically and non-diegetically, recreates the period and shapes a carefully constructed aural atmosphere of the Revolution.

As one of the major sound films of the 1930s, *¡Vámonos con Pancho Villa!* features music composed by modernist composer Silvestre Revueltas (1899–1940), who held a significant position in the national film industry, supplying the orchestral underscoring to Paul Strand's experimental and social realist inspired film *Redes* (1935), which is briefly discussed in chapter 3.[51] It is not clear why Revueltas was chosen as this film's composer, since de Fuentes utilized different composers for the other two films of the trilogy,[52] but his close ties at the time with screenwriter Villaurrutía could have secured the position.[53] As a modernist composer, Revueltas exhibited a diverse and eclectic approach to his compositional style, incorporating a wide array of dissonance, heterophonic collages, and vibrant tone colors. In the film, the Revueltian approach is audible in the film's underscoring.

¡Vámonos con Pancho Villa! boasts a violent and dramatic narrative, yet the film begins musically with a lively interpretation of Pancho Villa's favorite corrido-canción, "Las tres pelonas" ("The Three Short-Haired Women"), performed by the Orquesta Nacional de México. This corrido-canción is about three young women with short haircuts sitting together and yelling out the names of their favorite Revolutionary leaders, not committing any allegiance to any side.[54] According to Francisco Torres, whenever Villa wanted to hear this song, he would hold up three fingers in front of his troop's band and they would play it. Villa would, apparently, begin dancing.[55] It is not known whether Revueltas knew this particular story, but he did know that Villa was partial to this song. In his interpretation of "Las tres pelonas," Revueltas utilizes the full orchestra and mimics the sounds of a military brass band, with forceful interjections by the trumpet and rapid sixteenth-note patterns articulated by the trombone. He does not, however, fully quote the

---

[51] For more information on the music in *Redes*, see Eduardo Contreras Soto, *Silvestre Revueltas en escena y en pantalla: La música del compositor en el cine, el teatro y la danza* (Mexico City: Consejo Nacional para la Cultural y las Artes, Instituto Nacional de Bellas Artes, 2012); José Luis Castillo and Roberto Kolb, eds. *Silvestre Revueltas edición crítica: Redes (1935)* (Mexico City: Universidad Nacional Autónoma de México, 2009); Jacqueline Avila, "The Influence of the Cinematic in the Music of Silvestre Revueltas," master's thesis, University of California, Riverside, 2007.

[52] *El prisoniero trece* features music by Guillermo A. Posadas, while *El compadre Mendoza* uses music composed by prominent revista composer Manuel Castro Padilla.

[53] Revueltas and Villaurrutia also worked on stage works, including *Upa u Apa y Mexicana*. See Contreras Soto, *Silvestre Revueltas en escena y en pantalla*, 181.

[54] These women are popularly known as *pelonas*, a trend that was synonymous with modern Mexican woman of the 1920s. For more information, see Joanne Hershfield, *Imagining la chica moderna: Woman, Nation, and Visual Culture in Mexico, 1917–1936* (Durham, NC: Duke University Press, 2008); and Laura Isabel Serna, *Cinelandia: American Films and Mexican Film Culture Before the Golden Age* (Durham, NC: Duke University Press, 2014).

[55] For a full discussion on the origins of this song, consult Francisco Torres, "Las tres pelonas," *Centauro del Norte*, January 8, 2012, https://centaurodelnorte.com/las-tres-pelonas/

melody; rather, in his distinct Revueltian style, he fragments it, splitting the beginning motive into polyrhythmic figures and jarring dissonances passed around the orchestra.

Accompanying this opening cue are select drawings of Revolutionary symbols, such as a gun, a bandolier, a saddle, and an acoustic guitar, all-important icons for the charro, which are positioned behind the beginning credits (see figure 5.1). These symbols and the accompanying corrido-canción illustrate a synthesis with not just Pancho Villa but also with, as Pick points out, the visual motifs of charrería. "Las tres pelonas" is also audible in the underscoring in one of the first scenes of battle, accompanying the death of one of Los Leones, Máximo. In this early scene, Los Leones are ordered to retrieve a machine gun in order for the troops to advance. A few members distract the Federalistas, calling them *pelones* (skin or bald heads or tough guys), while another, Máximo, lassos the gun and drags it behind him as he rides away in a haze of gunfire. As he performs this move, the corrido theme returns in a declamatory manner, accompanying Máximo's charrería skills, synthesizing this specific music with the action. The theme, however, quickly vanishes when the gun is successfully delivered to Villa, rescripting the corrido to associate it with Los Leones rather than their leader (figure 5.2).

In addition to Revueltas's original underscoring, the film includes a compiled song list, mainly performed diegetically, which includes: "La Valentina," "La Joaquinta," "Tierra blanca," "La Adelita," and "La cucaracha," all performed in varying locations, such as a cantina, on the street, and at a railway station.[56] In addition to the Revueltian interpretation of "Las tres pelonas," Los Leones have another corrido-canción attached to them, which becomes a self-espoused theme song for their group; some of the group's members sing a very short excerpt from "La Valentina." As previously mentioned, two lines of verse from "La Valentina" are sung by members of Los Leones in the original novel. The film recycles this musical moment, but focuses on a different verse. Muñoz's novel quotes two lines from the first verse: "Una pasión me domina, y es la que me hizo venir" ("a passion dominates me, and it is this passion that made me come").[57] As the lyrics convey, this verse focuses on the desire felt by the first-person soldier for his Valentina. The verse used in the film, however, creates a more tragic connotation: "Si me han de matar mañana / que me maten una vez" ("If they have

---

[56] Contreras Soto, *Silvestre Revueltas en escena y en pantalla*, 185.

[57] Rafael F. Muñoz, *¡Vámonos con Pancho Villa!* (Mexico City: Factoría Ediciones, 2010), 48.

Figure 5.2 Pancho Villa (Domingo Soler) with his regiment, in ¡*Vámonos con Pancho Villa!* (1935). Photo courtesy of Mil Nubes-Foto.

to kill me tomorrow / let them kill me now"). This selection of lyric functions almost as a premonition for the members of Los Leones, who will come to their own brutal and violent ends. Although this corrido-canción centers on the figure of Valentina, it in no way references or is associated with any female characters, only Los Leones.

The most significant musical scene in the film features the corrido-canción "La Adelita," which accompanies an everyday scene at a Villista campsite next to a stationary train, insinuating that this regiment was aboard the train, then disembarked to rest and to gather supplies.[58] It is here that we are introduced to the farmers turned Revolutionary soldiers and their daily activities, which include different charrería practices and target

[58] De María y Campos mentions that ¡*Vámonos con Pancho Villa!* was made into a revista by Roberto Soto's famous company and starred Joaquín Pardavé. He provides a cast list of the main players, all men. For the women in the production, he indicates that this was limited to the characterization of Adela or La Adelita, played by Consuelo Quiroz. According to de María y Campos, Quiroz sang the most popular version of the song that had been performed in the theater. See de María y Campos, *El teatro de género chico en la revolución mexicana*, 320.

shooting with their pistols. Musical performance is also crucial here, as we see a small ensemble with one member visually strumming the guitar, sitting at the edge of the train car. The music we hear and the music they appear to be performing are not the same; the music we hear in this scene is not synchronized to the visual performance. As the gaze provides several images of the goings-on at the campsite, the corrido-canción sounds. Here, women are visibly present for the first time, performing their daily tasks, such as grinding masa and handing out food, all against the backdrop of the train. At one point, we see one woman sitting off to the side of an open train car, repeatedly rejecting the sexual advances of a tactile soldier. He continues to try to grab her hand, despite her obvious refusal, depicting, however momentarily, the aggressive treatment the soldaderas had to endure from soldiers. Acting anempathetically, the diegetic corrido-canción functions as reinforcement of the Revolutionary vernacular soundscape, allowing us in the audience to visually and aurally "pass through" the varying features of the landscape (figure 5.3).

Figure 5.3 An "Adelita" at the campsite, in *¡Vámonos con Pancho Villa!* (1935). Screen capture from film.

This sonic presence of "La Adelita" provides the first instance in sound film in which the corrido-canción accompanies the moving image of soldaderas. The presence of women is relatively scant, serving only to showcase more of the male activities in the regiment, but the little that is shown of women's contributions adds to the construction of the soldadera in a surprisingly accurate way. In this short moment, their duties are restricted to that of providing and cooking food—one of their more crucial jobs for the Villista regiment. Equally intriguing is the moment focusing on the soldadera rejecting advances from the soldier. This moment is brief, yet it is significant for a cultural understanding of soldaderas and their position within the armed struggle.

Revueltas's score for ¡Vámonos con Pancho Villa! introduced a new musical paradigm for future composers of the Revolutionary melodrama during the 1930s, interweaving popular corrido-canciones with orchestral underscoring. The film, however, was not well received in Mexico or in the diasporic Mexican communities in the United States. Rather than continue with the Revolutionary backdrop for his later films, de Fuentes transitioned to a nostalgic rendering of the countryside with the revista-inspired charro singing comedia ranchera, Allá en el Rancho Grande (Over on the Big Ranch) from 1936, starring Tito Guízar and Ester Fernández (discussed in chapter 4), which was hugely successful both in Mexico and among Mexican audiences in the United States.

As mentioned in the previous chapter, Allá en el Rancho Grande marked a significant transition for the film industry that moved its focus onto a folkloric representation of the countryside and portrayed the utopian atmosphere of the hacienda system through a utopian lens. Charros and hacendados worked together peacefully and performed songs that reinforced this sense of harmony, and the film thus promoted an atmosphere of nostalgia for a period that never took place. The Revolution, however, was not abandoned by filmmakers during the época de oro. Rather, filmmakers just moved away from the blatant criticism depicted in de Fuentes's trilogy and transplanted revolutionary themes into the popular comedia ranchera structure.

Popularizing the Myth: La Adelita (1938)

While the presence of women participants in the Revolution was only minimally depicted in de Fuentes's ¡Vámonos con Pancho Villa!, it did not take the film industry long to bring the Revolutionary women into the limelight, particularly the figure of La Adelita. In 1938, director Guillermo Hernández Gómez premiered a new film that aided in her popularization, simply entitled *La Adelita*. The film's title suggests that this may be a biographical film, but the film's first intertitle provides a more romantic and even nostalgic interpretation:

> The version that has been interpreted for this film about the life and actions of Adelita, the heroine of the Revolution of the North, does not pretend to be historically authentic; it is an interpretation about this interesting figure, a symbol of Mexican womanhood, made for abnegation and heroism.[59]

Premiering two years after *Allá en el Rancho Grande*, Hernández Gómez's *La Adelita* recycles many narrative elements and structural components from the former box office success. Although not considered one of the more important or even compelling examples of the revolutionary melodrama during the 1930s, *La Adelita* highlights several elements that shape the imagery of the soldadera on the big screen, synthesized with the corrido-canción. The film not only concentrates on constructing an aural and visual representation of Adelita but also elucidates the contradictions of social mores and the construction of gender in Mexican society. "La Adelita," performed in varying forms, is made audible in several scenes that form the character/figure of Adelita from predominantly a male perspective.

Musically speaking, *La Adelita* features underscoring and diegetic music composed and arranged by Lorenzo Barcelata, coming off his successful onscreen performance (both musically and dramatically) in *Allá en el Rancho Grande*. Because of the film's popularity, Barcelata and orchestral director Manuel Esperón transferred many of the musical formulas employed in *Allá en el Rancho Grande* to *La Adelita*. The result was a hybrid film that illuminated the Revolution in a significantly less abrasive way than de Fuentes's trilogy—meaning that this film fuses characteristics of the revolutionary melodrama with the popular comedia ranchera. Musically, this includes the diegetic performance of trios: *La Adelita* features performances by Trío Calaveras and Los Tres Murciélagos, the latter of which appeared in *Allá en el Rancho Grande*. The presence of signifiers from the comedia

---

[59] Intertitle from the opening credits of *La Adelita* (1938). See Guillermo Hernández Gomez, dir., *La Adelita*, DVD (1939; Houston, TX: Union Telecom Texas, LLC, no date).

ranchera—specifically *Allá en el Rancho Grande*—serves as a cultural bridge, providing a more contemporary soundscape to the historical backdrop.[60] In fact, the film's protagonist is played by Ester Fernández, who at the time was shaping her reputation as the essential country girl with braids and rebozo, which she recycled from *Allá en el Rancho Grande* into *La Adelita*.

In 1914, four years into the Revolution, the orphan Adela or Adelita (Esther Fernández) is taken in as a house maid at the hacienda Cuatro Ríos (Four Rivers). There, she meets and falls in love with Sabino (Pedro Armendáriz), the head charro of Don Leandro, and the son of the chambermaid Doña Carmelita. Don Leandro's son, Manolo, comes back to the hacienda after a brief and scandalous sojourn in Mexico City and becomes infatuated with Adelita. She rejects his advances consistently, but has become the subject of gossip among the maids, particularly Tecla (Margarita Cortés) and her outspoken mother, Nicanora (Emma Roldán, in effect reprising her role from *Allá en el Rancho Grande*). After a party, Manolo sneaks into Adelita's room and tries to rape her. Sabino, who, along with his friend Canuto (Leopoldo Ortín),[61] witness the struggle between Adelita and Manolo. Sabino breaks through the window and wrestles Manolo to the ground. He shoots Manolo in the arm and flees the scene. Because of the gossip surrounding Adelita, Sabino believes that she is to blame for the situation, concluding that she brought it on herself. This sentiment is shared by the other maids and Don Leandro, who throws her out of the house. With nowhere to go, Adelita and her friend Catalina (Emma Duval), who is Canuto's love interest, unintentionally join the Villistas and travel north while Sabino and Canuto join the troop of the revolutionary captain Vargas.

At this point in the film, several musical selections have been performed, highlighting the atmosphere of a location or event, such as a party scene or a serenade scene taking place outside Catalina's window. Because the Revolution has only been referred to by the characters and not seen, the corrido-canción has yet to be a part of the dominant musical track. A hint of the melody, however, is heard during the attempted rape scene. When Adelita

---

[60] The music in the film also contains songs heard in popular revistas, including "Mi querido Capitán" and "Soy una flor."

[61] Ortín was a famous comedian and theater performer before he turned to film acting in the 1930s. Born in Lima, Peru, in 1893, he relocated to Mexico to study in Puebla. At the break of the Revolution, he joined the Villista forces and was a profound admirer of Villa, during and after the Revolution. His participation in this film and his politics are rarely discussed in Mexican film history and criticism, but his involvement here as a secondary character and not the protagonist suggests perhaps an emotional and sentimental tie to the production.

is in her room, she walks near the large window, knowing that Sabino and Caputo are waiting outside, watching her. Manolo abruptly enters with clear and forceful intentions. As he looks at Adelita with desire in his eyes, Adelita gazes back with fear and apprehension. When he advances toward her, the "La Adelita" melody momentarily enters in the underscoring, played in a minor key in the upper strings. The significance of its quotation here, during the beginning of a moment of sexual violence rather than revolutionary-based violence, places Adelita in a transitory position; this is the impetus that will lead her to join the Villistas. She doesn't join for revolutionary motivation or to follow her soldier partner; she joins because she has no other option. Much like the character Cruz in *Allá en el Rancho Grande*, Adelita's behavior on the hacienda is timid, yet she catches the eye of powerful men, who believe her to be easily snared. Because of all the attention, Adelita is considered by the other housemaids to have "impure character" and be a flirt. She is rejected for her supposed "bad" character by everyone she has befriended on the hacienda and is thrown out of the house. The quotation of the melody acts as a foreshadowing of her future role as soldadera.

The encounter with Manolo is not the only instance Adelita fights off unwanted sexual advancements. Building from ¡*Vámonos con Pancho Villa!*, the film features multiple occasions in which women, specifically Adelita and Catalina, are accosted by revolutionaries from their own regiment. These moments, however, are more explicit than those moments which focus on women being accosted in ¡*Vámonos con Pancho Villa!* After Adelita and Catalina situate themselves at a train station, both women are accused of being Federalista spies by a nameless Villista revolutionary. They are later taken to an isolated space at a camp and are ridiculed, harassed, and molested by a group of seven men. Because there are only two women for seven men, the group decides to play dice to "raffle them off" to the top two players. After the game, the two winners attempt to collect "their prizes." Adelita and Catalina fight the two men back by hitting and kicking them, while the other soldiers look on with amusement. Two other high-ranking officers eventually intervene, and Catalina begs the officers to help them because they are "muchachas buenas" ("good women").

Adelita and Catalina soon become integral parts of the regiment, working with other soldaderas to care for the soldiers. During a scene of combat with the Federalistas, Adelita sits nearby at a makeshift camp where the soldaderas are making food, taking care of the wounded, or rejecting the advances of other soldiers. The battle consists of Federalistas firing machine guns at the

Villistas on horseback. Adelita hears that the other side continues to push back against the Villistas, and she decides to act. She grabs Catalina and tells her to follow her on horseback. Adelita's transition from camp follower to combat fighter occurs here, as she leads a group of men into the line of fire, yelling "¡Viva la revolución!" Her command pushes the Villistas forward and leads the Federalistas to retreat. On the way, she and Catalina dismount to help a wounded soldier. Here, for the first time in the film, Adelita executes several important roles: essential soldadera, aggressive combat fighter, and brave regimental leader.

It is only after Adelita has established herself in these roles that the corrido-canción is heard. After her quick response on the battlefield, Adelita is next seen in her campsite tent, folding clothes and longing for Sabino. A captain walks in, declaring that he loves her and feels a great deal of passion for her. He forcefully kisses her and she pushes him away. Looking at him with contempt and disgust, she wipes her mouth, then grabs a whip and beats him repeatedly. Here, Adelita exhibits determination and confidence as she defends herself. Still not taking the beating as rejection, the captain persists in grabbing her. Thinking quickly, Adelita snatches a rifle and threatens to shoot him, causing the captain to leave the tent cautiously.

After this unpleasant encounter, Adelita walks through the camp with a wounded colonel until they meet El Pelón Ochoa, a traveling musician, strumming his guitar. El Pelón tells them that he composed a song about a young woman whom the whole regiment adores. It is at this moment that the corrido-canción "La Adelita" is "born." He begins with a slow and rubato introduction, before beginning to sing with a clear falsetto and with vibrato.

> If Adelita left with another
> I would follow her trail relentlessly
> If by sea, then in a warship
> If by land, then by military train.
>
> And if I die in battle
> And my body stays in the mountain range
> Adelita, for the love of God, I beg you
> With your eyes you will cry for me.[62]

---

[62] Hernández Gomez, *La Adelita*.

El Pelón performs the fourth and sixth strophes from the version of "La Adelita" that, according to Herrera-Sobek, makes little mention of her involvement in battle, but focuses on the specific fear felt by the men. She states, "The fourth strophe . . . introduces another traditional theme dear to Mexicans: the neurotic fear men have of being abandoned by their women. (Ironically, empirical studies demonstrate that the opposite is the rule: it is the Mexican male who frequently abandons the woman)."[63] The abandonment of the woman is exactly the case here, since Sabino left Adelita to fend for herself after the failed rape. The inclusion of the sixth strophe fixates on death and the strong possibility that the soldier will die: "Perhaps using his precarious position as a soldier to convince Adelita that life is short and they should take advantage of the moment for tomorrow may be too late, the poet-lover introduces the possibility of being mortally wounded in combat. . . . His pathetic last request would be for Adelita to cry at his grave."[64] Ultimately, the corrido-canción does not illustrate a soldadera in battle but, rather, depicts a sad and worried soldier pleading for his love to remain faithful to him while he is fighting. The onscreen Adelita poses no argument or objection to this song. In fact, we do not know how she feels; the camera's gaze is focused completely on El Pelón, smiling and singing, rather than Adelita.

The next scene also removes Adelita from the performance of the corrido-canción. In a cantina, Sabino and Caputo are enjoying an evening of dancing to "Mi querido Capitán" on the pianola, and drinking with other revolutionary fighters. Pancho Villa's esteemed group Los Dorados de Villa enter through the swinging doors and are met with cheers and gritos. In order to entertain the customers and instill an atmosphere of comradery, "La Adelita" is requested by several of the revolutionaries. El Pelón, now traveling with Los Dorados, appears with his guitar and begins to sing. Rather than articulate the verse he sang in the previous sequence at the Villista camp, here he delves into other strophes of the corrido-canción that still represent a lovelorn soldier pleading with his love to not leave him:

> If, Adelita, you would be my wife,
> If, Adelita, you will be my woman
> You place that rose on your chest
> And I will take you to dance in the barracks.[65]

---

[63] Herrera-Sobek, *The Mexican Corrido*, 106.
[64] Ibid.
[65] Hernández Gomez, *La Adelita*.

Figure 5.4   Adelita (Ester Fernández) superimposed with images of the Revolution, in *La Adelita* (1938). Screen capture from film.

El Pelón sings one strophe with guitar accompaniment, but the subsequent strophes are complemented by a full orchestra, playing in lush, dramatic, contrapuntal lines. El Pelón's voice is then taken over by a choir of mixed voices, moving the song away from the intimacy of the cantina and to another space where Adelita and several moving images of the Revolution exist on a simultaneous plane: an image of Adelita is superimposed on other relevant images, such as a moving train, galloping horses, and fighting. This synthesis takes place for a moment, then her image is exchanged for those of men fighting, images in which women are not present, but the music continues (figure 5.4).

This montage of images of the armed struggle against another image of Adelita, aurally accompanied with an orchestral and choral arrangement of the corrido-canción, constructs a specific cultural synchresis of imagery, sound, and meaning. The fact that the corrido-canción was requested by many Revolutionaries in the bar suggests it had already circulated regionally, a fair assumption given that the corrido proper was diffused orally at the beginning of the twentieth century and that with each performance its popularity spread. The montage shapes Adelita as a nostalgic myth or legend who these revolutionaries admire. The corrido-canción functions here as an anthem and is presented in a monumental way that promotes the Revolution as a nationalist event and Adelita as a revered participant . . . but only for a moment. The male revolutionaries dominate the screen, moving the focus away from Adelita as a significant figure of the armed struggle and to the anonymous men who are fighting, emphasizing the important role that masculinity maintains, even in this musical sequence.

"La Adelita" fails to return throughout the remainder of the film. In the end, Sabino and Adelita are reunited at the hacienda and Doña Carmelita, now sick and bed-ridden, apologizes to Adelita for treating her so badly. Manolo, who has admitted to his mistake of coming on to another man's girlfriend, attempts to purchase medicine for Doña Carmelita in town, but is captured by the revolutionaries and placed before a firing squad. He is quickly saved by Adelita, who stands defiantly in front of the firing squad, which prevents them from firing. Because of her bravery and assertiveness with the revolutionaries, she is raised onto the men's shoulders and carried away victoriously to begin her relationship with Sabino.

The Adelita in the film and the Adelita in the song are two different representations. The cinematic Adelita was thrown from the house after an attempted rape that she was blamed for, and she was insulted by those close to her, which led to her escape to the north and into battle. She pined for her love even though he rejected her. All, however, is ultimately forgiven. In the song, the soldier fears for Adelita's faithfulness to him; she eventually becomes a soldadera, but only because she followed him, not because she was shunned at home after a sexual assault. While in a sense idealizing Adelita, the film provides a divergent interpretation of women and soldaderas that emphasizes their struggles against male dominance and patriarchy, which contrasts with the song's lyrics.

"Taming" the Soldadera: *Enamorada* (1946)

Two human factors contributed to making *Enamorada* the most beautiful and emotive film in all of Mexican cinema: our María Félix

in the fullness of her beauty and talent and the great producer Emilio
Fernández.

—Roberto Browning[66]

During the 1940s, the cinematic interpretation of the Revolution developed
into a more melodramatic account of love, rather than just the ideological
contradictions of the armed struggle. One of more captivating examples is
Emilio Fernández's 1946 film *Enamorada*, starring María Félix and Pedro
Armendariz, two of the most acclaimed actors in Mexican cinema's star
system. Loosely based on William Shakespeare's *The Taming of the Shrew*,
Enamorada narrates the developing romance between the revolutionary general and Zapatista José Juan Reyes (Pedro Armendáriz) and the daughter of
an aristocrat, Beatriz Peñafiel (María Félix), a woman needing to be "tamed."
After taking over the city of Cholula, Beatriz's father is taken into custody by
the revolutionaries, who all report to José Juan, a Robin Hood–like figure
who forcefully takes from the rich and gives to the poor. One day, José Juan
encounters Beatriz outside and sees one of her calves when a gust of wind
blows her skirt slightly up. José Juan then remarks that he would gladly receive a slap from her if he could see the other calf. She obliges by slapping
him, and continues to do so throughout the film. José Juan, smitten, vows
to make Beatriz his wife and proceeds to try to win her over during their
various encounters. Beatriz, who is engaged to an American businessman,
resorts to pranks, physical violence, and name-calling to humiliate the general. Once the regiment begins its return to battle, however, Beatriz realizes
that she is quite in love and devoted to José Juan. In the end, she leaves her
own civil wedding to join a group of soldaderas and follow him into battle.

The shaping of masculinity and femininity in *Enamorada* has received focused attention by scholars, marking the film as an important example of
gender construction as it pertains to cultural nationalism during the *época
de oro*. Jean Franco examines the film from a patriarchal standpoint—
specifically the mandatory taming of Beatriz as an attempt to refeminize the
aggressive and assertive, albeit "masculinized" woman[67] (figure 5.5). Beatriz
continuously rejects José Juan on a several grounds: he captured her father,

---

[66] Roberto Browning, "*Enamorada*, el Film de México," *Cinema Reporter*, January 4, 1947, p. 25.
[67] Jean Franco, *Plotting Women: Gender & Representation in Mexico* (New York: Columbia
University Press, 1989), 150.

Figure 5.5 The enigmatic Beatriz (María Felix), in *Enamorada* (1947). Photo courtesy of Mil Nubes-Foto.

he is of a lower class, he is a revolutionary with power. In repeatedly denying him, she finds herself drawn to him. In the end, she follows, almost dutifully, behind her man. Dolores Tierney carries out an alternative reading, which focuses how the film proposes other understandings of masculinity and how this "attempts to go against the grain of cultural nationalism."[68] She closely examines José Juan, whose pursuit and love of Beatriz propels the melodrama, but acts contrary to established conceptions of machismo, both during the Revolutionary period and during the 1940s. Tierney argues the film follows in gender paradigms shaped by the Hollywood screwball comedy genre and positions José Juan to be a weaker character than the protagonist Beatriz, who throughout the film is much more emphatic and confident. The film therefore highlights the transition, or taming, of José Juan by

[68] Dolores Tierney, *Emilio Fernández: Pictures in the Margins* (Manchester: Manchester University Press, 2007), 107.

Beatriz. She states, "In his case, the transformation is brought about through Beatriz. Such an interpretation makes the film seem ultimately more concerned with his taming, rather than the taming of Beatriz—a taming which is achieved through love.[69] Both characters, I would argue, undergo a considerable transformation that moves against the grain of gender construction and even the social mores of the period. Intriguingly, music plays a pivotal role in this transitional process, but is geared more toward the eventual conversion of Beatriz, from upper-class woman to soldadera.

Enamorada offers a rich compilation of music functioning both diegetically and non-diegetically. The film's underscoring was composed by Eduardo Hernández Moncada, characterized by Pablo Capitan from *Cinema Reporter* as: "A very Mexican composer for a very Mexican film." The author also suggests that Hernández Moncada was up to the challenge of "portraying the soul of our people."[70] His orchestral underscoring is brought into the foreground during the opening credits of the film, which consist of a visual montage of revolutionaries fighting the Federalistas in the countryside, and the eventual impact on the city of Cholula. While the non-diegetic music provides an emotive atmosphere during scenes of war and even romantic interludes, it is the diegetic music that forms the cultural synchresis to and for Beatriz.

Music becomes a key mediator in the romantic and dramatic exchanges between José Juan and Beatriz. In an attempt to woo her, José Juan serenades her from beneath her balcony. José Juan, however, does not perform; instead, he speaks up to Beatriz's window, accompanied by the Trio Calaveras, one of Mexican cinema's most prestigious interpreters of popular music in film. They perform an arrangement of "La Malagueña," (or "Malagueña Salerosa"), a romantic son huasteco, or huapango, that is repeatedly performed in Mexican cinema.[71] The lyrics of the son parallel specific moments in this suggestive scene: the male protagonist describes to his love interest how beautiful she is,

---

[69] Ibid., 116.

[70] Pablo Capitan, "Primeros Planos: Música para 'Enamoranda,'" *Cinema Reporter*, October 12, 1946, p. 29.

[71] The title translates to "The Woman from Malaga." This song is credited to Elpidio Ramírez and Pedro Galindo, and was published by Peer International in 1947. However, there is a Decca recording covered by Los Rancheros in 1939 of the son, making direct authorship ambiguous. It is performed in two subsequent films from the *época de oro*: *La Malagueña* (1947, dir. Agustín Delgado) and *Al son del mambo* (*From Son to Mambo*; 1950, dir. Chano Ureta). The song is also performed during the beginning credits of *Once Upon a Time in Mexico* (2003, dir. Robert Rodriguez).

focusing attention on her eyes, and how he understands that she rejects him because of his low social status:

> Your eyes are so pretty
> Below those two eye lashes
> Below those two eye lashes
> Your eyes are so pretty.

In his declaration, José Juan pleads with her to forgive him. Since her balcony doors are closed, he says that his words cannot reach her ears; instead, he employs other voices to carry his message. Musically speaking, this song highlights the unique stylistic qualities of the trio, particularly of the lead singer whose high falsetto carries the lyrics and sustains a high pitch on the vowel "e" when declaring "Malagueña."[72] Led by guitars, the trio provides a soft and gentle atmosphere for the poetic declaration of the lyrics. Highlighting a sense of Otherness, as León F. García Corona notes, "the melody outlines the Andalusian progression popular in many Latin American music genres: VII—VI—V—I."[73]

The performance of "La Malagueña" by the trio is anachronistic for the Revolutionary period; it appeals to more contemporary tastes and reflects the more popular currents of musical practice, particularly concerning new interpretations of romantic music of the 1940s.[74] This was a common practice for films during this period, historically based or not.[75] The scene has received ample attention from scholars who note that the lyrics of the son, especially the first verse (quoted earlier), is synthesized with the extreme close-up of Beatriz's eyes slowly fluttering open. Franco labels this sequence a "play of looks," stating that "the camera cut(s) between the General, Beatriz, and the singers, whose falsetto seems to mime the softening of the male under

---

[72] This high falsetto became emblematic for the Trio Calaveras, and it was executed by Raul Prado, the founder of the Trio Calaveras and the second husband to María Felix. This sound helped shape the style of the group and was later imitated by others during the 1940s and 1950s. See "Raul Prado, fundador de Trío Calavera," El País, April 11, 1989, https://elpais.com/diario/1989/04/11/agenda/608248804_850215.html.

[73] León F. García Corona, "Mexico's Broken Heart: Music, Politics, and Sentimentalism," PhD diss., University of California, Los Angeles, 2015, p. 74.

[74] For a discussion of the development of the trios and their impact on Mexican cinema, see García Corona, "Mexico's Broken Heart."

[75] See for example Flor Silvestre (Wild Flower; 1943, dir. Emilio Fernández), which features music performed by the Trío Calaveras and Si Adelita se fuera con otro (1948; dir. Chano Ureta), which features music composed by Manuel Esperón and performances by Jorge Negrete.

the influence of love."[76] While highlighting this "play of looks," this music functions as a tool of persuasion, seducing Beatriz into recognizing that her animosity toward José Juan is, perhaps, love. At the beginning of the scene, José Juan tries to persuade her to come out onto the balcony, but Beatriz remains hidden, determined not to show herself. She listens to the strains of the music, sitting up in her bed cross-legged in a defiant stance, away from the window. When she gets up the nerve to look at (or for) him, however, he leaves. Franco further asserts that this moment "indicates a misrecognition which makes us, the audience, wish for an exchange of looks between the two."[77] Beatriz's hesitancy to look out the window at José Juan, followed by her brief glance at her bedside portrait of her fiancée, imply that she questions her feelings. The music coupled with these moving images augments her growing affection for José Juan, yet accentuates her persistent defiance to come to terms, or acknowledge, these feelings.

It is not only the serenade that persuades Beatriz to favor José Juan; the corrido-canciones "La Adelita" and "La Rielera" do as well, but both operate differently and do so referencing the soldadera. "La Adelita" is audible in two crucial scenes, both of which do not place women visually in the foreground. This first utterance takes place early in the narrative when José Juan, after taking control over Cholula, demands that the richest men in the town be taken to him, including Beatriz's father. In this intense scene, José Juan confronts a crooked shopkeeper who has been profiting from the Revolution and Cholula residents. Having no patience and little pity for the man, José Juan orders his prompt execution, despite his desperate pleas for mercy. This act instantly constructs José Juan as a harsh and unforgiving general, which leads many to fear him. As Tierney notes, "General José Juan is forceful and severe in his decisions, although he presents himself as being righteous too, a quality that is also portrayed as masculine."[78] When the schoolteacher approaches, he tells José Juan the school has been closed for an extended period and he has not been paid in several weeks. Seeing the unjust nature of the situation and the importance of education, José Juan instructs the teacher to open the school again and doubles his pay. As the teacher leaves the room, he whistles the melody from "La Adelita." This is a short, but significant musical moment. As previously mentioned, "La Adelita" spread throughout

---

[76] Franco, *Plotting Women*, 151.
[77] Ibid.
[78] Tierney, *Emilio Fernández*, 109.

Figure 5.6 Little Adela with José Juan (Pedro Armendáriz), in *Enamorada* (1947). Screen capture from film.

the north of Mexico and became intricately linked to Pancho Villa and the Villistas. By the time it reached Mexico City, it was being performed on the stage with satirical lyrics. A schoolteacher from the region controlled by the Zapatistas whistling the melody reveals that not only had this corrido-canción been shared widely and traveled from the north to Cholula but also that the song was well-known outside the regiments.[79] Its utterance here by a schoolteacher also insinuates what position this song has in public education; these corrido-canciones were taught and performed by schoolchildren as early as the 1920s.

This short melody also constructs a cultural synchresis to a character in this scene. Sitting next to José Juan on the desk is a little girl who is quietly sucking on a candy (figure 5.6). She is dressed in a long skirt and a long-sleeved blouse, her hair fashioned back into two braids with a small

[79] "La Adelita" has also remained steadfast as perhaps the most popular Revolutionary tune during the *época de oro*.

sombrero on her head. She watches the intense exchanges between the men with little interest. The priest and childhood friend of José Juan, Father Rafael Sierra (Fernando Fernández), throws concerned looks at the little girl but says nothing until she is ordered to leave by José Juan. When pressed, José Juan indicates that he adopted the little girl after her parents, a soldier and soldadera, died in a train accident. The girl, named Adelita, became his adopted daughter and follows him everywhere, posing as a mini version of the soldadera Adelita. Tierney reads José Juan's acceptance of an adopted daughter as a crack in his macho image, which he spent ample time executing earlier in this scene. This portrays him a man who can at once make a show of inherently masculine prowess while also conveying a gentler side, implying some depth and complexity in his character.[80] Women, on the other hand, are not necessarily given this consideration. Although the melody does not sound when Adelita is visually on screen, the connection between her and the song is made after José Juan audibly introduces her to the priest, and by extension the audience: there is no other role for women other than soldadera, even as young girls.

The melody of "La Adelita" is more discernible in a later scene that involves Beatriz when she is not visually present. When Beatriz learns of José Juan's feelings for her, she immediately rebukes him and tells him repeatedly to go back to his soldaderas, which she conflates with prostitutes.[81] José Juan, submissive up until that moment, rushes to their defense. Franco states, "The taunt provokes the General intro praising soldaderas as the supreme example of womanhood, and when Beatriz responds by slapping him, he strikes her in turn."[82] The highest position for women in José Juan's opinion is as soldaderas, working alongside the soldiers to make sure they are equipped for battle. In claiming early on that she will be his wife, it seems likely that his goal (intentional or not intentional) was to convert her into his soldadera. After Beatriz rejects José Juan again, he takes solace in a cantina, where he drinks tequila and carves Beatriz's name into a table, thinking of her and visually heartbroken. During this scene, an older soldier approaches José Juan to try and console him, but José Juan snaps back, forcing the older man to

---

[80] Ibid., 110.

[81] In this scene, Beatriz tells José Juan to go with his "mujerzuelas" or soldaderas. Mujerzuelas is a popular term meaning tart or prostitute. It conflates *mujer* (woman) with the word *zarzuela*, the staged entertainment popular in Mexico City, which were common looked down on by members of the upper class. Actresses in zarzuela performances and other staged performances were not regarded as part of a decent social circle. See chapter 2 for a discussion of this.

[82] Franco, *Plotting Women*, 150.

return to the bar while the other soldiers look at José Juan with deep sympathy. Compellingly, the music performed in the cantina does not consist of melancholy melodies for drinking, such as rancheras, but instead a potpourri of "La Adelita" and "La Rielera" played as lively polkas on an unseen piano and without the lyrics. Couples dance in a separate room in the background while the music is momentarily foregrounded. The general's focus on Beatriz's name, combined with the music, creates an intimate synchresis: his being a revolutionary soldier and a man of lower social standing, the only acceptable manner for her to be with him is to become a soldadera, which, for Beatriz, is a considerable transition. In a sense, the music foreshadows Beatriz eventual decision, helping to interpellate her into a soldadera before she even realizes what she is going to do.

The inclusion of "La Rielera" provides another provocative reading. As previously mentioned, "La Rielera" is interpreted through the perspective of a woman—who may or may not be a soldadera—and who follows her love "Juan" by train, carrying two pistols. In the film, the melody of "La Adelita" transitions into an arrangement of "La Rielera." This synthesis of the two songs in a sense parallels Beatriz's situation. While "La Adelita" fulfills José Juan's desire and love for Beatriz, "La Rielera" conforms more to Beatriz's personality: she is aggressive and will take care of her man, following him while also ready to battle any rival. The lyrics to the corrido-canciones are not sung, but the melodies are firmly articulated on the piano. These songs were so well known by the 1940s that the associations of the music to the soldadera and the Revolution were, by that point, already complete

In the end, Beatriz realizes that she loves José Juan and, just as she is about to sign the marriage document/certificate, she leaves her wedding party to join the group of women following the cavalry back onto the battlefield: "Shrew no more, Beatriz ultimately embraces her destiny as a humble and self-sacrificing *soldadera* devoted to her man, encouraging spectators, too, to sacrifice any hint of a potentially critical gaze in the name of national unity."[83] She trails behind José Juan, clutching the side of saddle with a proud stance, mimicking the other soldaderas following their soldiers (figure 5.7). Tierney defines this last scene as mirroring the conventions of the screwball comedy, as both characters, realizing they could no longer

---

[83] Elena Lahr-Vivaz, *Mexican Melodrama: Film and Nation from the Golden Age to the New Wave* (Tucson: University of Arizona Press, 2016), 42.

Figure 5.7 Beatriz (María Felix) as soldadera to her José Juan (Pedro Armendaríz), in *Enamorada* (1947). Screen capture from film.

stay in that present society as a couple or as individuals must go. She states, "this departure, rather than being interpreted as her submission to the 'virile' male and the requirements of the Revolution, can now be seen as a mutual escape from a world in which they do not belong."[84] Beatriz is not submissive to José Juan, but moves into the only position that would be allowable for her to remain with him: soldadera. Along with the Casasola photograph of the mistaken Adelita soldadera, leaning from the side of a train, this traveling shot has crystallized the image and the meaning of the soldadera in the Mexican imagination, something that would last for decades to come.

---

[84] Tierney, *Emilio Fernández*, 117–18.

Conclusion

The Mexican film industry's portrayal of soldaderas and women during the Revolution is not wholly accurate. According to Herrera-Sobek, "The industry's interpretation of the saga of these heroic figures, however, generally does not provide a realistic historical perspective of women soldiers in the Revolution."[85] Building on the cultural narratives constructed by the photographs and the corrido-canciones from the Revolution, the film industry constructed a concept of womanhood during the Revolution that ultimately focuses not on the women but, rather, on the men. In examining the visual material from the revolutionary period, Andrea Noble astutely points out that any reading of visual sources about women during the Revolution is done in reference to men and is sexually coded. The same can be said for the corrido-canciones that these films feature. Vicente Mendoza's anthologies catalog hundreds of corridos and revolutionary songs from the 1910s, yet it is the corrido-canciones about the romance between a soldier and soldadera that have become the musical signifiers of the Revolution. These corrido-canciones have proven to be malleable and have exhibited the sound of the Revolution. In these select examples of the revolutionary melodrama, we can see and hear how the soldadera was shaped and understood by the film industry. In ¡Vámonos con Pancho Villa!, soldaderas made a momentary visual appearance but played no part in the narrative, their presence only obvious through iterations of the corrido-canciones performed by and relating to the revolutionaries on screen. In La Adelita, the mythology surrounding the most well-known corrido-canción, "La Adelita," is imagined. Functioning as a hybrid of the comedia ranchera and revolutionary melodrama, La Adelita depicts the downfall of the protagonist Adelita after an attempted rape, who is then redeemed through her participation as a soldadera in the Villista regiment. While the song is performed in the film, it is not directly associated with her, as the gaze focuses on the male performer and the male revolutionaries, rather than on her and her position in the armed struggle. These two films constructed an idea of the soldadera that continued to perpetuate machismo ideology. In Enamorada, the corrido-canciones "La Adelita" and "La Rielera" are used to transform the assertive Beatriz into the role of soldadera so she could be with her revolutionary love interest. This furthers the contention

---

[85] Herrera-Sobek, The Mexican Corrido, 115.

that even though the gender roles do not conform with post-Revolutionary ideologies (as both characters challenge perceptions of masculinity and femininity in the film), women continued to be categorized as a soldadera whenever the Revolution is concerned. In each of these films, the visual and musical representations of the soldaderas become synthesized with the male characters, who appear in every performance. The soldadera as a protagonist is present but only connected to the man she will eventually follow.

Epilogue

After the *Época de Oro*

It is difficult to determine exactly when the *época de oro* ended, but many events that took place during the middle to end of the 1950s contributed to a period of crisis and the film industry's eventual decline and period of crisis. The deaths of both Jorge Negrete (d. 1953) and Pedro Infante (d. 1959), the film industry's leading male voices, plunged the country into national mourning.[1] Toward the end of the 1950s, Mexican film production experienced a severe crisis as a result of several developments. Emilio García Riera has noted several specific events, both national and international, that had a profound impact on the industry. After World War II, Mexico no longer received financial and technological support from the United States; the Cuban Revolution of 1958 closed a significant market for films, as Cuba looked to making more national films rather than co-productions; several studios closed; there was an overall decline in box office sales and considerable losses in investments and cuts in budgets; and several reputable directors left the country to film elsewhere, or died. The loss of these directors, it was widely believed, created a huge gap in cinematic creativity.[2]

In the decades following the *época de oro*, film production continued in Mexico, although at a slower pace. The industry began to resort to formulaic films that were cheaper to produce. Many of the actors and actressses from the illustrious star system continued to work in new film endeavors, but they never quite achieved the same notoriety or recognition. New genres that reflected a cosmopolitan modernization recycled many of the successful elements and conventions of older genres, but operated within new contexts and different consumer cultures. This included, but was not limited to, music and musical performance.

---

[1] Jorge Negrete died from complications due to hepatitis C and Pedro Infante died in a plane crash.

[2] Emilio García Riera, *Historia del cine mexicano* (Mexico City: Consejo Nacional de Fomento Educativo, 1986), 221. See also Ignacio M. Sánchez Prado, "The Golden Age Otherwise: Mexican Cinema and the Mediations of Capitalist Modernity in the 1940s and 1950s," in *Cosmopolitan Film Cultures in Latin America 1896–1960*, ed. Rielle Navitski and Nicholas Poppe (Bloomington: University of Indiana Press, 2017), 242.

Diegetic musical performances continued to be a significant feature in comedic films, particularly those of Germán Valdés ("Tin Tan"), famous for his role as a pachuco. Since his beginnings in cinema in the 1940s, particularly with the film *El rey del barrio* (*The King of the Neighborhood*; 1950, dir. Gilberto Martínez Solares), Valdés had exploited his ability to sing and dance in a wide variety of genres, often performing with rumberas in cabaret backdrops. Valdés's filmic contributions during the 1950s and well into the 1960s confronted the nationalist representation that the film industry had constructed with the other genres discussed earlier in this book. According to Ignacio Sánchez Prado, these films illustrated that Mexican cinema was not only "a machine for the construction of social identities but also was part of the mediation of capitalist modernity."[3] Films such as *El Fantasma de la opereta* (*The Phantom of the Operetta*; 1960, dir. Fernando Cortés) reinterpreted examples of European literature, adapting the story for a Mexicanized context and audience and filling it with musical numbers from a wide variety of international sources.[4]

Another significant genre was the *cine de luchadores* (cinema of wrestlers), a hybrid genre that concentrated on the crime-solving capabilities and wrestling talents of the masked wrestler Santo, a crucial figure in Mexican popular culture. According to Rafael Aviña, the cine de luchadores derived from the tradition of *lucha libre* (free-wrestling), popularized in Mexico City during the 1930s; but as a film genre, it became an essential feature of cultural nationalism and popular folklore. Built upon super-hero comics and serials featuring masked characters such as Batman, the cine de luchadores depicts the age-old fight between good and evil, in which the masked wrestler, always concealing his identity, signifies the good. As Aviña asserts, the genre conveys the slippery slope of national cinema's "exploiting the image of the vigilante hidden under a mask that faces mad scientists, monsters, aliens, sorceresses, thugs, and more, in a funny register between involuntary humor, fantastic horror, police suspense, and melee combat."[5] Santo, according to film historian Carl Mora, became "the king of kitsch and unintentional humor ... and

---

[3] Sánchez Prado, "The Golden Age Otherwise," 242.

[4] For an analysis of the music in *El Fantasma de la opereta*, see Jacqueline Avila, "*El Fantasma* and Tin Tan: Genre Hybridity and Musial Nostalgia in Fernando Cortés's *El Fantasma de la opereta* (1959)," *Opera Quarterly* 34, nos. 2–3 (2018): 187–200.

[5] Rafael Aviña, *Una mirada insolita: temas y géneros del cine mexicano* (Mexico City: Editorial Océano de México, S.A. de C.V., 2004), 196.

a wholesome camp figure with a huge following among children and adults."[6] Generally viewed as an example of kitsch, the cine de luchadores offered the best in genre hybridity and camp entertainment, synthesizing several popular elements of cinema from the *época de oro* with more contemporary and cosmopolitan currents. Although not consistent, musical performances alternate with sequences of Santo wrestling, suspending the narrative to showcase these different forms of popular entertainment.[7]

Throughout the 1970s and 1980s, particularly during the turbulent sexenios of Luis Echeverría (1970–1976) and José López Portillo (1976–1982), one of the most popular genres was the cine de ficheras, a subgenre that built on the conventions of the earlier prostitute melodrama. Sergio de la Mora states, "The hybrid *fichera* subgenre draws from the prostitute melodrama, vaudeville-like sketches, and soft-core pornography, although its immediate antecedents are the cabaretera films of the 1940s and '50s."[8] The genre exhibited representations of sexuality and elements of popular culture in an exploitative way, focusing on female nudity, stripteases, profanity and albures, and sex scenes.[9] Much like the rumbera in the cabaretera, the fichera features scantily dressed or semi-nude *vedettes* (showgirls) who work in nightclubs entertaining an audience of predominantly men. Miguel M. Delgado's *Bellas de noche* (*Beauties of the Night,* 1975), starring the controversial Sasha Montenegro,[10] inaugurated the genre. It featured a complicated narrative that revolves around sex, comedy, and musical performance. The musical models of the cabareteras were transferred to the ficheras and featured a variety of dance music from across Latin America so as to accentuate the sexuality and seductive nature of the vedettes.

Other prominent genres from the *época de oro*, such as the revolutionary melodrama, continued to be made, but were readapted to fit new currents of cosmopolitanism and hybridity. Music still maintained a crucial role in each

---

[6] Carl Mora, *Mexican Cinema: Reflections of a Society, 1896–2004,* 3rd edition (London: McFarland, 2005), 148.

[7] See, for instance, *Santo vs. el estrangulador* (*Santo vs. the Strangler;* 1964, dir. René Cardona) and the sequel, *Santo vs. el espectro del estrangulador* (*Santo vs. the Spectre of the Strangler;* 1966, dir. René Cardona).

[8] Sergio de la Mora, *Cinemachismo: Masculinities and Sexuality in Mexican Film* (Austin: University of Texas Press, 2006), 110.

[9] Ibid., 111.

[10] Montenegro became popular in the 1970s with her work as a vedette. Most of the controversy surrounding her had to do with her relationship with the former President José López Portillo during the 1980s. The 2016 documentary *Bellas de noche* (dir. María José Cuevas) describes the culture of the vedettes during the 1970s and 1980s. The film stars Olga Breeskin, Lyn May, Rossy Mendoza, Wanda Seux, and Princesa Yamal.

one, utilized to highlight specific features of the narrative and of character development, but throughout the decades, these precise functions would change to mirror contemporary sociocultural landscapes.

Remembering the *Época de Oro*

The significant place that the *época de oro* occupies in Mexican culture cannot be ignored, or even argued. Through the strategic planning undertaken by leading institutions such as the Cineteca Nacional, Filmoteca UNAM, IMCINE, and CONACULTA, numerous events, including photographic exhibitions, special screenings, book presentations, and specialized lectures have been held during the last two decades, highlighting the important influence that Mexican cinema from this period still has on national culture.[11] Special events include the International Film Festival in Morelia, which in 2014 featured a photographic installation of Mexican film noir from the late 1940s and 1950s.[12]

Popular artists have provided new interpretations of some of Mexican cinema's more revered songs, compiling albums in homage to composers of the period, as well as the period itself. In 2009, singer Eugenia León displayed her vocal and stylistic versatility in the album *Cine*, which features twenty-two tracks of songs performed in or written for prominent Mexican films in the twentieth century, many from the *época de oro*, including "Vendo Placer" ("I Sell Pleasure") from *La mujer del puerto* (1933) and "Santa" from the 1931 film that bears this name. One of Mexico's leading pop-rock performers, Natalia Lafourade, premiered a tribute album in 2012 entitled *Mujer Divina: Homenaje a Agustía Lara* (*Divine Woman: Homage to Agustín Lara*), featuring several songs that were included in musical tracks of earlier films, including "Aventurera," the theme song for the prostitute melodrama from 1950 by the same name, and "Farolito" ("Little Street Light"), a charming canción vals performed in the 1948 prostitute melodrama *Revancha* (*Revenge*). In September 2017, the Los Angeles Philharmonic, conducted by Gustavo Dudamel, initiated a concert cycle entitled "CDMX–Music of

---

[11] The Cineteca Nacional features special lectures and screenings by leading scholars and critics on Mexican cinema during the *época de oro*.

[12] This has been a major focus of investigative research by one of the leading scholars and historians of Mexican cinema, Rafael Aviña. See Rafael Aviña, *Mex Noir: cine mexicano policiaco* (Mexico City: Cineteca Nacional, 2018).

the City of Mexico. One night was dedicated to the music from Mexican cinema. Labeled "Noche de cine" ("An Evening of Film"), the program included "a diverse retrospective of Mexican film music spanning the Golden Age to the present day" with film clips. The program featured songs made famous by Pedro Infante and Jorge Negrete, "La malagueña" from *Enamorada*, "Nereidas" from *Salón México* (1949, dir. Emilio Fernández), selections from *Amores Perros* (*Love's a Bitch;* 2000, dir. Alejandro G. Iñárritu), and a clip from a new work by director Carlos Reygadas with music by Gabriela Ortiz.[13]

The *época de oro* maintains an extraordinary position in the national memory. De la Mora astutely states, "Film in Mexico remains a crucial source of cultural capital and international prestige and is an influential partner in circulating images of *mexicanidad* in the new millennium."[14] Although many tropes, archetypes, and musical conventions utilized during the *época de oro* have been reused in later filmmaking, Mexico's new wave of filmmakers, from the end of the twentieth century into the beginnings of the twenty-first century, have looked back on the era in several intriguing ways, and have produced remakes of canonical films. The remake of Emilio Fernández's 1949 cabaretera *Salón México* (1996, dir. José Luis García Agraz) continues the fascination with cabaret culture and the romantic interpretation of prostitutes. The film focuses on the strains and movements of the danzón and the tumultuous relationship between the prostitute Mercedes (María Rojo) and her pimp/boyfriend Paco (Alberto Estrella).

Arturo Ripstein's *La mujer del puerto* (1991) is a new interpretation of Arcady Boytler's 1933 version of the same name, which details the melodramatic story of a prostitute who commits suicide after finding out she (accidently) spent the night with her brother. In the 1933 film, Manuel Esperón's ballad "Vendo Placer" accompanies an image of the prostitute Rosario (Andrea Palma) leaning seductively against a lamppost smoking a cigarette before entering a cabaret.[15] Ripstein's adaptation features a new arrangement and function of the ballad. Its performance in the film signals a change in context; the pianist Carmelo (Alejandro Parodi) performs the song on an upright piano while the female protagonist Perla (Evangelina Sosa)

---

[13] "LA Phil Presents Noche de Cine, an Evening of Mexican Film Music," *ZayZay.com*, September 26, 2017, https://zayzay.com/news/la-phil-presents-noche-de-cine-an-evening-of-mexican-film-music/

[14] De la Mora, *Cinemachismo*, 170.

[15] For an analysis of this song in the 1933 version of *La mujer del puerto*, see Jacqueline Avila, "Musicalizando la muerte en el cine mexicano durante los 1930s," *Balajú: Revista de Cultura y Comunicación* 3, no. 2 (2016): 48–60; and her "Arcady Boytler: *La mujer del puerto* (1933)," in *Clásicos del cine mexicano*, ed. Christian Wehr (Frankfurt: Editorial Vervuert, 2015), 57–70.

performs fellatio on El Marro (Damián Alcázar) behind a projected sheet on stage. As part of "el acto internacional" ("the international act"), Perla and Carmelo are in competition with each other, "the latter attempting to hold a note for longer than it takes Perla to make her client reach his climax."[16] Little do they know that Perla and El Marro are siblings now involved in an incestuous relationship that will continue to the film's end.

The conventions of the cabaretera genre are recycled in *Danzón* (1991, dir. María Novaro), starring María Rojo as the protagonist Julia Solórzano, a telephone operator who also loves to dance the danzón. When her dance partner Carmelo (Daniel Regis) mysteriously disappears, she travels to Veracruz, one of the major port cities of danzón performance, to locate him. Danzón and cabaret culture play central roles in this travel film, harkening back to the *época de oro*, yet providing new settings and characters. This is best exemplified with the character Suzy (Tito Vasconcelos), a drag queen and cabaret performer who helps Julia with her search and who serves as a conduit for gay male culture. Elissa Rashkin has observed that the conventions of the cabaretera, particularly the privileged place of the danzón in the urban Mexicanidad, are still recognized in the narrative.[17] The prevalence of these conventions in new settings and time periods incorporates elements of the *época de oro* with contemporary practices, in a sense reviving the values of Mexicanidad in a new and inclusive cultural context.

Biographical films have utilized several tropes from this era within their own film narratives, linking the past and the present, and forming alliances with new interpretations of nationalist symbolism. *El fantástico mundo de Juan Orol* (*The Fantastic World of Juan Orol*; 2009, dir. Sebastian del Amo) features a melodramatic narrative about the life of director Juan Orol (Roberto Sosa), whose rise to cinematic fame during and after the *época de oro* included films principally about gangsters and rumberas. He has been recognized by many as one of Mexico's most significant directors of film noir. The film operates on the conventions of the cabaretera and gangster films, filmed in black and white and featuring mambos by Dámaso Pérez Prado to accompany the noiresque cinematography and narrative. Del Amo's next film *Cantinflas* (2012) retells the monumental career of Mario Moreno ("Cantinflas"), the actor who began his comedic career as a pelado in the

[16] Andrea Noble, *Mexican National Cinema* (New York: Routledge, 2005), 25.
[17] Elissa Rashkin, *Women Filmmakers in Mexico: The Country of Which We Dream* (Austin: University of Texas Press, 2001), 169.

carpas, then became a national and cultural icon. While the film tells the story of his position in Mexican national cinema, a major narrative focus is on Moreno's role as Passepartout in *Around the World in Eighty Days* (1956, dir. Michael Anderson), a role that won Moreno a Golden Globe for Best Comedy Actor. Intriguingly, the film provides a vibrant interpretation of national cinema and its star system during the *época de oro*, including Moreno's work in the carpas and in the revistas.

The *época de oro* and its music have also penetrated more recent fictional features, providing new functions for music from the past. Alonso Ruizpalacios's road film *Güeros* (2014) follows four youthful protagonists—the brothers Sombra (Tenoch Huerta) and Tomás (Sebastián Aguirre), the student activist Ana (Ilse Salas), and Sombra's roommate Santos (Leonardo Ortizgris)—as they navigate several neighborhoods in Mexico City, avoiding the student protest taking place at UNAM and attempting to find a famous rock performer from their childhood, whose music occupies a privileged and monumental position in their collective memory. Built on the memories and experiences of Ruizpalacios during the UNAM strike that took place in 1999, *Güeros* is a nostalgic interpretation of Mexico City, filmed in black and white and in 4:3 format. This nostalgia is aurally emphasized as well, utilizing songs by Agustín Lara, either performed by himself or by Toña la Negra, a prominent interpreter of Lara's music from the *época de oro*. The synthesis of musical nostalgia and the *época de oro* take place as the group drives toward a party for a film premiere. As Sombra and Ana make fun of specific elements from national cinema—including mimicking the accent and manner of speaking of the character Jaibo (Roberto Cobo) from Luis Buñuel's hallmark film *Los olvidados* (*The Young and the Damned*; 1950)—Lara's canción vals "Farolito" plays. This scene is at once satirical and quite revealing as these university-educated youths mock the somewhat dated practice of using this accent. The moment evokes a shared longing for Mexican cinema of the past (not necessarily *their* cinematic past), bringing back specific sound practices of the *época de oro*.

In the preceding chapters, I have discussed and analyzed the development of five film genres through the roles and functions of music and sound, both on and off the screen. Each genre exhibited and shaped several different representations of national signs and symbols that were not necessarily created or initiated by the film industry, but were continuously modified to fit specific narrative structures in the films and to achieve specific sociocultural objectives. These films produced unique and significant interpretations of Mexican society; they were emblematic of and even consequential to the search for national identity in Mexico during several periods of social, cultural, and political instability.[18] The music featured in these films operated as a significant and provocative layer of discourse, acting as a necessary aural stamp of association with the moving images.

In his groundbreaking study of the formation of cultural identities in a modern age, Stuart Hall astutely declared that identity is constantly in flux.[19] Mexican national cinema, from its early construction in the silent period to its development of recorded, synchronized sound film, juxtaposed and reorganized the character types, backdrops, narratives, and music that formed those genres now popular to Mexican audiences, conveying particular beliefs and practices that were prominent in this changing contemporary culture. As Joanne Hershfield notes, cinema "gave narrative form and visual confirmation to real-life experience."[20] Music and sound grafted meanings onto these experiences in a persuasive manner. In this way, music performs on equal levels with other components of film to solidify meaning and connect with the audience's experience. For Mexican cinema, this process functions as *cinesonidos*, the unique sonic fabric that crystalizes those distinct and diverse representations of perceived national identities on screen. As studies on the Mexican film industry during the twentieth and twenty-first centuries burgeon to include examinations of race, gender, class, nationalism, and transnationalism, it will be imperative to address how and why the music utilized in these films solidifies those representations and constructions on screen. This work seeks to augment those readings and contributes to those studies by looking at film music as a catalyst for exploring larger issues of cultural identity. In the concatenation of sight and sound, or synchresis, and its attendant cultural associations, Mexican film music becomes a locus for the contestation of ideology and identity.

[18] Joanne Hershfield, *Mexican Cinema/Mexican Woman, 1940–1950* (Tucson: University of Arizona, 1996), 133.
[19] Stuart Hall, *Questions of Cultural Identity* (London: Sage, 1996), 1.
[20] Hershfield, *Mexican Cinema/Mexican Woman*, 133.

Bibliography

Works Consulted

Agrasanchez, Rogelio, Jr. *Mexican Movies in the United States: A History of the Films, Theaters, and Audiences, 1920–1960*. Jefferson, NC: McFarland, 2006.

Agustín, José. *Tragicomedia mexicana I: La vida en México de 1940 a 1970*. 2nd ed. Mexico City: Editorial Planeta Mexicana, S.A. de C.V., 2007.

Alfaro, Francisco H., and Alejando Ochoa. *La república de los cines*. Mexico City: Clío, 1998.

Altman, Rick. *Film/Genre*. London: British Film Institute, 1999.

Altman, Rick. "Moving Lips: Cinema as Ventriloquism." *Yale French Studies–Cinema/Sound* 60 (1980): 67–79.

Altman, Rick, ed. *Silent Film Sound*. New York: Columbia University Press, 2004.

Altman, Rick, ed. *Sound Theory/Sound Practice*. London: Routledge, 1994.

Alvardo, Manuel, Ana M. López, and John King, eds. *Mediating Two Worlds: Cinematic Encounters in Latin America*. London: British Film Institute, 1993.

Álvarez, Lucía. "El compositor en el cine y teatro." *Cuadernos de Estudios Cinematográficos* 4 (2005): 55–66.

Alvear Acevedo, Carlos. *Lázaro Cárdenas: El hombre y el mito*. Mexico City: Ediciones Promesa S.A., 1986.

Amira, John, and Steven Cornelius. *The Music of Santería: Traditional Rhythms of the Batá Drums*. Tempe, AZ: White Cliffs Media, 1991.

Anderson, Benedict. *Imagined Communities: Reflections on the Origin and Spread of Nationalism*. 2nd ed. London: Verso, 2006.

Anguiano, Arturo. "Cárdenas and the Masses." In *The Mexico Reader: History, Culture, Politics*, edited by Gilbert M. Joseph and Timothy J. Henderson, 458. Durham, NC: Duke University Press, 2002.

Antonio Alcaraz, José. "La noche de los mayas." *Cuadernos de Estudios Cinematográficos* 4 (2005): 95–100.

Arrizon, Alicia. *Latina Performance: Transversing the Stage*. Bloomington: Indiana University Press, 1999.

Avila, Jacqueline. "Arcady Boytler: *La mujer del puerto* (1933)." In *Clásicos de cine mexicano: 31 películas emblemáticas desde la Época de Oro hasta el presente*, edited by Christian Wehr, 57–70. Frankfurt: Editorial Vervuert, 2015.

Avila, Jacqueline. "*Chin Chun Chan*: The Zarzuela as an Ethnic and Technological Farce." In *Oxford Research Encyclopedia for Latin American History*, edited by William Beezely. February 2018, https://oxfordre.com/latinamericanhistory/view/10.1093/acrefore/9780199366439.001.0001/acrefore-9780199366439-e-514

Avila, Jacqueline. "*El Fantasma* and Tin Tan: Genre Hybridity and Musical Nostalgia in Fernando Cortés's *El Fantasma de la Opereta* (1959)." *Opera Quarterly* 34, nos. 2–3 (2018): 187–200.

Avila, Jacqueline. "The Influence of the Cinematic in the Music of Silvestre Revueltas." Master's thesis, University of California, Riverside, 2007.

Avila, Jacqueline. "Juxtaposing *teatro de revista* and *cine*: Music in 1930s *comedia ranchera*." *Journal of Film Music* 5, nos. 1–2 (2012): 119–24.

Avila, Jacqueline. "*México de mis inventos*: Salon Music, Lyric Theater, and Nostalgia in *Cine de añoranza porfiriana*." *Latin American Music Review/Revista de Música Latino Americana* 38, no. 1 (2017): 1–27.

Avila, Jacqueline."Musicalizando la muerte en el cine mexicano durante los 1930s." *Balajú: Revista de Cultura y Comunicación* 3, no. 2 (2016): 48–60.

Avila, Jacqueline. "Using Latin American and Iberian Film Music: Classroom Methodologies." *Journal of Music History Pedagogy* 7, no. 2 (2017): 112–23.

Avila, Jacqueline, and Sergio de la Mora. "Fernando de Fuentes: *Allá en el Rancho Grande* (1936)." In *Clásicos del cine mexicano: 31 películas emblemáticas desde la Época de Oro hasta el presente*, edited by Christian Wehr, 123–58. Frankfurt: Editorial Vervuert, 2015.

Avila, Jacqueline, and Oswaldo Mejía Mendiola. "Dance, Desire, and Cosmopolitanism: Early Danzón Performances in the 1930s Prostitute Melodrama." In *Routledge Companion to the Music and Sound of World Cinema from the First 'Talkies' to the 1940s*, edited by Jeremy Barham. New York: Routledge, in press.

Aviña, Rafael. *Mex Noir: cine mexicano policiaco*. Mexico City: Cineteca Nacional, 2018.

Aviña, Rafael. *Una mirada insólita: Temas y géneros del cine mexicano*. Mexico City: Editorial Océano de México, S.A. de C.V., 2004.

Aviña, Rafael, Ana Vigne-Pacheco, and Patrick Lebre. "Los ritmos populares de cine mexicano / Les Rythmes Populaires dans la Cinéma Mexicain." *Cinémas D'Amérique Latine*, no. 8 (2000): 41–55.

Ayala Blanco, Jorge. *La aventurera del cine mexicano: En la época de oro y después*. Mexico City: Grijalbo, 1993.

Ayala Blanco, Jorge. *La condición del cine mexicano*. Mexico City: Posada, 1986.

Bailey, David C. *Viva Cristo Rey: The Cristero Rebellion and the Church-State Conflict in Mexico*. Austin: University of Texas Press, 1974.

Balbas, Manuel. *Recuerdos del Yaqui: Principales episodios durante la campaña de 1899 a 1901*. Mexico City: Sociedad de Edición y Librería Franco Americana, 1927.

Beals, Carleton. "*Las Carpas*: Mexican Street Theatres." *Theater Arts Monthly* 7, no. 2 (1928): 99–108.

Beezley, William H. *Judas at the Jockey Club and Other Episodes of Porfirian Mexico*. Lincoln: University of Nebraska Press, 1987.

Bellman, Jonathan, ed. *The Exotic in Western Music*. Boston: Northeastern University Press, 1998.

Belton, John, and Elisabeth Wise, eds. *Film Sound: Theory and Practice*. New York: Columbia University Press, 1985.

Bethell, Leslie, ed. *Mexico Since Independence*. Cambridge: Cambridge University Press, 1991.

Bhabha, Homi K. *The Location of Culture*. London: Routledge, 1994.

Blanco Moheno, Roberto. *Cardenismo*. Mexico City: Libro Mex Editores, 1963.

Bliss, Katherine E. *Compromised Positions: Prostitution, Public Health, and Gender Politics in Revolutionary Mexico City*. University Park: Pennsylvania State University Press, 2001.

Bonfil Batalla, Guillermo. *México profundo: Una civilización negrada*. 3rd ed. Mexico City: Random House Mondadori, S.A. de C.V., 2008.

Born, Georgina, and David Hesmondhalgh, eds. *Western Music and Its Others: Difference, Representation, and Appropriation in Music.* Berkeley: University of California Press, 2000.

Bracho, Julio, dir. *¡Ay qué tiempos señor don Simón!* 1941. DVD. Mexico City: Televisa S.A. de C.V., 2008.

Brooks, Peter. *The Melodramatic Imagination. Balzac, Henry James: Melodrama and the Mode of Excess.* New Haven, CT: Yale University Press, 1976.

Bryan, Susan E. "Teatro popular y sociedad durante el Porfiriato." *Historia Mexicana* 33, no. 1 (July–September 1983): 130–69.

Bunker, Steve. *Creating Mexican Consumer Culture in the Age of Porfirio Díaz.* Albuquerque: University of New Mexico Press, 2012.

Buñuel, Luis. *Mi último suspiro.* Madrid: Debolsillo Poc Edition, 2012.

Bustillo Oro, Juan, dir. *En tiempos de don Porfirio.* 1939. DVD. Mexico City: Laguna Films, 2007.

Bustillo Oro, Juan, dir. *México de mis recuerdos.* 1944. DVD. Mexico City: Zima Entertainment, 2008.

Bustillo Oro, Juan. *Vida cinematográfia.* Mexico City: Cineteca Nacional, 1984.

Calleja, Rafael. *Las bribonas: Zarzuela in One Act.* Madrid: Madrid Instituto Compultense de Ciencias Musicales, 2007. Originally published in 1908.

Cano, Gabriela, Jocelyn Olcott, and Mary Kay Vaughan, eds. *Sex in Revolution: Gender, Politics, and Power in Modern Mexico.* Durham, NC: Duke University Press, 2006.

Carmona, Gloria. *La música de México: Periodo de la independencia a la revolución (1810 a 1910).* Edited by Julio Estrada. Mexico City: Universidad Nacional Autónoma de México, 1984.

Caro Cocotle, Guadalupe. "La música de las pelonas. Nuevas identidades femeninas del México moderno, 1920–1930." PhD dissertation, Universidad Nacional Autónoma de México.

Carrasco Vázquez, Jorge. *Joaquín Pardavé: Un actor vuelto leyenda.* Mexico City: Grupo Editorial Tomo, S.A. de C.V., 2004.

Carrasco Vázquez, Jorge. *Pedro Infante, estrella de cine.* Mexico City: Grupo Editorial Tomo, S.A. de C.V., 2005.

Carreño King, Tania. *El charro: La constucción de un estereotipo nacional 1920–1940.* Mexico City: Instituto Nacional de Estudios Historicos de la Revolución Mexicana, 2000.

Carreño King, Tania. "I Am Mexican, I Come from an Untamed Land." In *Artes de México: Charrería*, edited by Margarita de Orellana, 89–93. Mexico City: Artes de México, 2000.

Carvajal, Teresa. "La obra de Manuel Esperón en el cine mexicano." *Bibliomúsica* 39 (Spring/Summer 1992): 39.

Casado Navarro, Arturo. *Gerardo Murillo, el Dr. Atl.* Mexico City: Universidad Nacional Autónoma de México, 1984.

Casares Rodicio, Emilio, ed. *Diccionario de Cine Iberoamericano.* Madrid: Sociedad General de Autores y Editores, 2011.

Cashion, Susan. "The Mexican Danzón: Restrained Sensuality." In *Dancing Across Borders: Danzas y Bailes Mexicanos*, edited by Olga Nájera-Ramírez, Norma E. Cantú, and Brenda M. Romero, 237–55. Urbana: University of Illinois Press, 2009.

Caso, Alfonso. *La comunidad indígena.* Mexico City: Secretaría de Educación Pública, 1971.

Caso, Alfonso. "Definición del indio y lo indio." *América Indigena* 8, no. 4 (October 1948): 238–47.

Caso, Alfonso. *Indigenismo*. Mexico City: Instituto Nacional Indigenista, 1958.

Caso, Alfonso. "La protección de las Artes Populares." *América Indigena* 2, no. 3 (July 1942): 25–29.

Castillo Debra A. *Easy Women: Sex and Gender in Modern Mexican Fiction.* Minneapolis: University of Minnesota Press, 1998.

Ceballos, Edgar. "Las abuelitas de las rumberas." *Somos: Las rumberas del cine mexicano* 10, no. 189 (November 1999): 82–85.

Cecilia Frost, Elsa. *Las categorías de la cultural mexicana.* Mexico City: Fondo de Cultura Económica, 2009.

Châteauvert, Jean, and André Gaudreault. "The Noises of Spectators, or the Spectator as Additive to the Spectacle." In *The Sounds of Early Cinema*, edited by Richard Abel and Rick Altman, 183–91. Bloomington: Indiana University Press, 2001.

Chatman, Seymour. "What Novels Can Do that Films Can't (and Vice Versa)." In *On Narrative*, edited by W. J. T. Mitchell, 117–36. Chicago: University of Chicago Press, 1980.

Chávez, Alex E. *Sounds of Crossing: Music, Migration, and the Aural Poetics of Huapango Arribeño.* Durham, NC: Duke University Press, 2017.

Chávez, Octavio. *La charrería: Tradición mexicana.* Mexico City: Instituto Mexiquense de Cultura, 1991.

Chevalier, Francois. *La formación de los latifundios en México.* Mexico City: Fondo de Cultura Económica, 1976. Originally published in 1956.

Chion, Michel. *Audio-Vision: Sound on Screen.* New York: Columbia University Press, 1994.

Chion, Michel. *La música en el cine.* Mexico City: Paidós, 1997.

Chion, Michel. *The Voice of Cinema.* New York: Columbia University Press, 1999.

Cisneros, José. *Riders Across the Centuries: Horsemen of the Spanish Borderlands.* El Paso: Texas Western Press, 1984.

Ciuk, Perla. *Diccionario de directores de cine mexicano 657 realizadores: Biografías, testimonies y fotografías.* Mexico City: Consejo Nacional para la Cultura y las Artes, 2009.

Clark, Walter Aaron, ed. *From Tejano to Tango.* New York: Routledge, 2002.

Consuelo Guerrero, María. "La revolucionaria en el cine mexicano." *Hispania* 95, no. 1 (2012): 37–52.

Contreras Soto, Eduardo. *Silvestre Revueltas: Baile, duelo y son.* Mexico City: Consejo Nacional para la Cultura y las Artes, Instituto Nacional de Bellas Artes, 2000.

Contreras Soto, Eduardo. *Silvestre Revueltas en escena y en pantalla: La música del compositor en el cine, el teatro y la danza.* Mexico City: Consejo Nacional para la Cultural y las Artes, Instituto Nacional de Bellas Artes, 2012.

Contreras Soto, Jaime. "El cine de ambiente porfiriano." In *Revista Filmoteca: El cine y la revolución mexicana*, edited by Manuel Gonzáles Casanova, 40–47. Mexico City: Filmoteca Universidad Nacional Autónoma de México, 1989.

Coria, José Felipe. *Taller de cinefilia.* Mexico City: Paidós, 2006.

Cortés, Ana María. "Cara e'foca y otros demonios." *Somos: Las rumberas del cine mexicano* 10, no. 189 (November 1999): 96–98.

Cortés González, Alma Rosa. *60 Aniversario de la Escuela Nacional de Danza Nellie y Gloria Campobello.* Mexico City: Instituto Nacional de Bellas Artes, 1992.

Cros Sandoval, Mercedes. *Worldview, the Orichas, and Santería: Africa to Cuba and Beyond.* Gainesville: University Press of Florida, 2006.

Dallal, Alberto. *El "dancing" mexicano.* Mexico City: Ediciones Oásis, S.A., 1982.

Dallal, Alberto. *La danza en México: Cuarta Parte, el dancing mexicano.* Mexico City: Universidad Nacional Autónoma de México, 2010.

Dávalos Orozco, Federico. *Albores del cine mexicano.* Mexico City: Clío, 1996.

Dávalos Orozco, Federico, and Carlos Arturo Flores Villela, eds. *Historia del cine mexicano (1896–1929): Edición facsimilar de las crónicas de José María Sánchez García.* Mexico City: Universidad Nacional Autónoma de México, 2013.

Deeds, Susan M., Michael C. Meyer, and William L. Sherman. *The Course of Mexican History.* 7th ed. Oxford: Oxford University Press, 2003.

de Fuentes, Fernando, dir. *Allá en el Rancho Grande.* 1936. DVD. Mexico City: Cinemateca, 2007.

de la Mora, Sergio. *Cinemachismo: Masculinities and Sexuality in Mexican Film.* Austin: University of Texas Press, 2006.

de la Vega Alfaro, Eduardo. *Del muro a la pantalla: S.M. Eisenstein y el arte pictórico mexicano.* Mexico City: Instituto Mexicano de Cinematografía, 1997.

de la Vega Alfaro, Eduardo and Claire Pallier. "El otro cine musical mexicano: semblanzas fílmicas de compositores e intérpretes / L'autre Cinéma Musical Mexicain: Évocations Filmées de Compositeurs et Interprètes." *Cinémas D'Amérique Latine,* no. 8 (2000): 56–67.

del Carmen de la Peza Casares, María. *El bolero y la educación sentimental en México.* Mexico City: Universidad Autónoma Metropolitana-Xochimilco, 2001.

Delgado Martínez, César, and Julio C. Villalva Jiménez. *Yol-Izma: La danzarina de las leyendas.* Mexico City: Escenología A.C., 1996.

de los Reyes, Aurelio. *Cine y sociedad en México 1896–1930: Vivir de sueños.* Mexico City: Universidad Nacional de Autónoma de México, 1981.

de los Reyes, Aurelio. *Con Villa en México: Testimonios sobre camarógrafos norteamericanos en la revolución, 1911–1915.* Mexico City: Universidad Nacional Autónoma de México, 2010. Originally published in 1985.

de los Reyes, Aurelio. "El nacionalismo en el cine 1920–1930: Búsqueda de una nueva simbología." In *El nacionalismo y el arte mexicano (IX Coloquio de Historia del Arte),* edited by Instituto de Investigaciones Estéticas. 271–95. Mexico City: Universidad Nacional Autónoma de México, 1986.

de los Reyes, Aurelio. *El nacimiento de ¡Que viva México!* Mexico City: Universidad Nacional Autónoma de México, 2006.

de los Reyes, Aurelio. *Filmografía del cine mudo mexicano 1896–1920.* Mexico City: Filmoteca Nacional, 1984.

de los Reyes, Aurelio. *Filmografía del cine mudo mexicano. Vol. 2: 1920–1924.* Mexico City: Filmoteca Universidad Nacional Autónoma de México, 1994.

de los Reyes, Aurelio. *Filmografía del cine mudo mexicano. Vol. 3: 1924–1931.* Mexico City: Filmoteca Universidad Nacional Autónoma de México, 2000.

de los Reyes, Aurelio. *Historia de la vida cotidiana en México: Siglo XX, Campo y ciudad.* Mexico City: Fondo de Cultural Económica, 2006.

de los Reyes, Aurelio. "Luis Márquez y el cine." *Alquimia* 4, no. 10 (2000): 33–41.

de los Reyes, Aurelio. *Medio siglo de cine mexicano (1896–1947).* Mexico City: Editorial Trillas S.A. de C.V., 1987.

de los Reyes, Aurelio. "La música para cine mudo en México." In *La música de México I: Historia, 4: Periodo nacionalista (1910 a 1958)*, edited by Julio Estrada, 4: 85–117. Mexico City: Universidad Nacional Autónoma de México, 1984.

de los Reyes, Aurelio. *Los orígenes del cine en México (1896–1900)*. Mexico City: Fondo de Cultura Económica, 2013. Originally published in 1983.

Delpar, Helen. *The Enormous Vogue of Things Mexican: Cultural Relations Between the U.S. and Mexico, 1920–1935*. Tuscaloosa: University of Alabama Press, 1992.

de Luna, Andrés. *La batalla y su sombra: La revolución en el cine mexicano*. Mexico City: Universidad Autónoma Metropolitana Unidad Xochimilco, 1984.

de María y Campos, Armando. *Angela Perlata: un ruiseñor mexicano*. Mexico City: Ediciones Xochitl, 1944.

de María y Campos, Armando. *Crónicas de teatro de "Hoy."* Mexico City: Ediciones Botas, 1941.

de María y Campos, Armando. *El teatro de género chico en la revolución mexicana*. Mexico City: Biblioteca del Instituto Nacional de Estudios Históricos de la Revolución Mexicana, 1956.

de María y Campos, Armando. *Frivolerías*. Mexico CIty: Imprenta Nacional, 1919.

de María y Campos, Armando. *Las Tandas del Principal*. Mexico City: Editorial Diana, 1989.

Derr, Virginia B. "The Rise of the Middle-Class Tradition in Mexican Art." *Journal of Inter-American Studies* 3, no. 3 (1961): 385–409.

de Van, Gilles. "Fin de Siècle Exoticism and the Meaning of Far Away." *Opera Quarterly* 11, no. 3 (1995): 77–94.

Díaz Covarrubias, Juan. *Obras completas*. Mexico City: Universidad Nacional Autónoma de México, 1959.

Díaz López, Marina. "El folclore invade el imaginario de la ciudad: Determinaciones regionales en el cine mexicano de los trienta." *Archivos de la Filmoteca: Revista de estudios históricos sobre la imagen, segunda época* 41 (June 2002): 10–31.

D'Lugo, Marvin. "Luis Alcoriza; or A Certain Antimelodramatic Tendency in Mexican Cinema." In *Latin American Melodrama: Passion, Pathos, and Entertainment*, edited by Darlene J. Sadlier, 110–29. Urbana: University of Illinois Press, 2009.

Domínguez, Francisco. *Album musical de Michoacán*. Mexico City: Secretaria de Educación Pública, 1923.

Dueñas, Pablo. *Bolero: Historica grafica y documental*. Mexico City: Asociación Mexicana de Estudios Fonográficos, A.C., 2005.

Dueñas, Pablo. "El trovador de sotavento: Lorenzo Barcelata." *Relatos e historias en México* 2, no. 18 (2010): 68–69.

Dueñas, Pablo. *Las divas en el teatro de revista mexicana*. Mexico City: Asociación Mexicana de Estudios Fonográficos, A.C., 1994.

Dueñas, Pablo, and Jesús Flores y Escalante. *Bicentenario 200 años de la historia de la música en México*. Mexico City: Sony Music Entertainment México S.A. de C.V., 2010.

Dumond, Don E. *The Machete and the Cross: Campesino Rebellion in Yucatan*. Lincoln: University of Nebraska Press, 1997.

Dyer, Richard. *Only Entertainment*. London: Routledge, 1992.

Eisenstein, Sergei. "Rough Outline of the Mexican Picture." In *Sergei Eisenstein and Upton Sinclair: The Making and Unmaking of Que Viva Mexico!*, edited by Harry M. Geduld and Ronald Gottesman, xxvii–xxix. Bloomington: Indiana University Press, 1970.

Eisenstein, Sergei. *The Film Sense*. New York: Harcourt Brace Jovanovich, 1947.

Elena Franco, María. "Charrería, Recurso Turístico de México." Master's thesis, Autonomous University of Nayarit, Mexico, 1990.

Espejo, Beatriz. *Dr. Atl: El paisaje como pasión.* Mexico City: Fondo Editorial de la Plástica Mexicana, 1994.

Estrada, Josefina. *Joaquín Pardavé: El señor del espectáculo. Vols. I–III.* Mexico City: Clío, 1996.

Fabio Sánchez, Fernando, and Gerardo García Muñoz. *La luz y la Guerra: El cine de la Revolución Mexicana.* Mexico City: Consejo Nacional para la Cultural y las Artes, 2010.

Fajardo Estrada, Ramón. *Rita Montaner: Testimonio de una epocá.* Havana: Fondo Editorial Casa de las Américas, 1997.

Falicov, Tamara L. *The Cinematic Tango: Contemporary Argentine Film.* London: Wallflower, 2007.

Falicov, Tamara L. "Latin America: How Mexico and Argentina Cope and Cooperate with the Behemoth of the North." In *The Contemporary Hollywood Film Industry,* edited by Paul MacDonald and Janet Wasko, 264–76. Oxford: Wiley-Blackwell, 2008.

Fein, Seth. "Hollywood and United States-Mexico Relations in the Golden Age of Mexican Cinema." PhD dissertation, University of Texas at Austin, 1996.

Fein, Seth. "Myths of Cultural Imperialism and Nationalism in Golden Age Mexican Cinema." In *Fragments of a Golden Age: The Politics of Culture in Mexico Since 1940,* edited by Gilbert M. Joseph, Anne Rubenstein, and Eric Zolov, 159–98. Durham, NC: Duke University Press, 2001.

Felski, Rita. *The Gender of Modernity.* Cambridge, MA: Harvard University Press, 1995.

Fernández, Adela. *El Indio Fernández: Vida y Mito.* 3rd ed. Mexico City: Panorama Editorial, S.A., 1986.

Fernández, Emilio, dir. *María Candelaria.* 1944. DVD. Mexico City: Alter Films, Televisa, 2004.

Fernández, Emilio, dir. *Victimas del pecado.* 1950. DVD. Mexico City: Zima Entertainment, 2006.

Fernández Ros, Antonio. "1910." In *Cine y Revolución: La Revolución Mexicana vista a través del cine,* edited by Roberto Garza Iturbide and Hugo Lara Chávez, 123. Mexico City: Instituto Mexicano de Cinematografía, 2010.

Flandrau, Charles. *Viva Mexico!* London: Elan, 1982.

Flores y Escalante, Jesús. "La Liga de la Decencia." *Relatos e Historias en México* 1, no. 11 (2009): 71–76.

Flores y Escalante, Jesús. *Salón México: Historica documental y gráfica del danzón en México.* Mexico City: Asociación Mexicana de Estudios Fonográficos, A.C., 2006.

Franco, Jean. *Plotting Women: Gender & Representation in Mexico.* New York: Columbia University Press, 1989.

Franco, María Elena. "Charrería, Recurso Turístico de México." Master's thesis, Autonomous University of Nayarit, Mexico, 1990.

Fregoso, Rosa Linda. *The Bronze Screen: Chicana and Chicano Film Culture.* Minneapolis: University of Minnesota Press, 1993.

Gamboa, Federico. *Mi diario tomo VII (1920–1939).* Mexico City: Consejo Nacional para la Cultura y las Artes, 1996.

Gamboa, Federico. *Santa.* Mexico City: Fondo de Cultura Económico, 2003. First published in 1903.

Gamio, Manual. "Calificación de características culturales de los grupos indígenas." *América Indígena* 2, no. 4 (October 1942): 19–22.

Gamio, Manuel. *Forjando Patria*. 2nd ed. Mexico City: Editorial Porrua, S.A.,1960. First published in 1916.

García, David F. "The Afro-Cuban soundscape of Mexico City: Authenticating Spaces of Violence and Immorality in *Salón México* and *Víctimas del pecado*." In *Screening Songs in Hispanic and Lusophone Cinema*, edited by Lisa Shaw, 167–88. Manchester: Manchester University Press, 2012.

García, Gustavo. *Viendo la luz … Salas de cine en la literature mexicana*. Mexico City: Uva Tinta Ediciones, 2013.

García, Gustavo, and David R. Macial, eds. *El cine mexicano a través de la crítica*. Mexico City: Dirección General de Actividades Cinematográficas, Universidad Nacional Autónoma de México, 2001.

Garcia Canclini, Nestor. *Consumidores y ciudadanos: Conflictos multiculturales de la globalización*. Mexico City: Debolsillo, 2009.

Garcia Canclini, Nestor. *Hybrid Cultures: Strategies for Entering and Leaving Modernity*. Minneapolis: University of Minnesota Press, 1995.

Garcia Canclini, Nestor. *Los nuevos espectadores: Cine, televisión, y video en México*. Mexico City: Instituto Mexicano de Cinematografía, Consejo Nacional para la Cultura y las Artes, 1994.

Garcia Canclini, Nestor. *Transforming Modernity: Popular Culture in Mexico*. Austin: University of Texas Press, 1993.

García Carretero, Emilio. *Historia del teatro de la zarzuela de Madrid*. Madrid: Fundación de la Zarzuela Española, 2003–2005.

García Corona, León F. "Mexico's Broken Heart: Music, Politics, and Sentimentalism." PhD dissertation, University of California, Los Angeles, 2015.

García Miranda, Guadalupe, ed. *Artes de México: Los dos volcanes: Popocatépetl e Iztaccíhuatl*. 73. Mexico City: Artes de México, 2006.

García Riera, Emilio. *Breve historia del cine mexicano, primer siglo, 1897–1997*. Mexico City: Instituto Mexico de Cinematografía., 1998.

García Riera, Emilio. *Emilio Fernández, 1904–1986*. Guadalajara: Universidad de Guadalajara, Centro de Investigaciones e Enseñanza Cinematográficas, 1987.

García Riera, Emilio. *Fernando de Fuentes (1894–1958)*. Mexico City: Cineteca Nacional, 1984.

García Riera, Emilio. *Historia del cine mexicano*. Mexico City: Consejo Nacional de Fomento Educativo, 1986.

García Riera, Emilio. *Historia documental del cine mexicano*. Vols. 1–12. Guadalajara: Univeridad de Guadalajara, 1993.

Garrido, Juan S. *Historia de la música popular en México*. Mexico City: Editorial Extemporaneos, 1974.

Gaytán Apáez, Leopoldo. "Lo negro de lo negro: La negritud a través de sus imagines Cinematográficas." *Antropología: Boletín oficial del Instituto de Antropología e Historia* 89 (2011): 85–90.

Geduld Harry M., and Ronald Gottesman, eds. *Sergei Eisenstein and Upton Sinclair: The Making and Unmaking of Que viva Mexico!* Bloomington: Indiana University Press, 1970.

Gellner, Ernest. *Nations and Nationalism*. Oxford: Blackwell, 1983.

Gómez Villanueva, Augusto. *Nacionalismo revolucionario: Orígenes socioeconómicos de la doctrina internacional de la Revolución mexicana*. Mexico City: Miguel Ángel Porrúa, 2009.

Gonzáles Casanova, Manuel, ed. *Revista Filmoteca: El cine y la revolución mexicana.* Mexico City: Filmoteca Universidad Nacional Autónoma de México, 1989.

González Navarro, Moisés. *Sociedad y cultura en el porfiriato.* Mexico City: Consejo Nacional para la Cultural y las Artes, 1994.

Gonzalez Rubio I, Javier, and Hugo Lara Chávez. *Cine antropológico mexicano.* Mexico City: Instituto Nacional de Antropología e Historia, 2009.

Gonzalez-Wippler, Migene. *Santería: African Magic in Latin America.* New York: Julien Press, 1973.

Gorbman, Claudia. "Narrative Film Music." *Yale French Studies–Cinema/Sound* 60 (1980): 117–36.

Gorbman, Claudia. "Scoring the Indian: Music in the Liberal Western." In *Western Music and Its Others: Difference, Representation, and Appropriation in Music,* edited by Georgina Born and David Hesmondhalgh, 234–53. Berkeley: University of California Press, 2000.

Gorbman, Claudia. *Unheard Melodies: Narrative Film Music.* Bloomington: Indiana University Press, 1987.

Gradante, William. "'El Hijo del Pueblo': José Alfredo Jiménez and the Mexican *Canción Ranchera.*" *Latin American Music Review/Revista de Música Latino Americana* 3, no. 1 (1982): 36–59.

Graham, Richard, ed. *The Idea of Race in Latin American, 1870–1940.* Austin: University of Texas Press, 1990.

Granados, Pedro. *Carpas de México: Leyendas, anécdotas e historia del Teatro Popular.* Mexico City: Editorial Universo, 1984.

"Gringo." *Urban Dictionary,* March 5, 2005, https://www.urbandictionary.com/define. php?term=gringo.

Gutierrez, Laura. *Performing Mexicanidad: Vendidas y cabareteras on the Transnational Stage.* Austin: University of Texas Press, 2010.

GW Law Logs: *Music Copyright Infringement Resource,* Marks v. Stasny 1 F.R.D. 720 (SDNY), https://blogs.law.gwu.edu/mcir/case/marks-v-stasny/

Hagedorn, Katherine J. *Divine Utterances: The Performance of Afro-Cuban Santeria.* Washington, DC: Smithsonian Institution Press, 2001.

Hall, Stuart. *Questions of Cultural Identity.* London: Sage, 1996.

Hamilton, Nora. *The Limits of State Autonomy: Post-Revolutionary Mexico.* Princeton, NJ: Princeton University Press, 1982.

Hamm, Charles. *Music in the New World.* New York: W.W. Norton, 1983.

Harrison, Michelle. *King Sugar: Jamaica, the Caribbean, and the World Sugar Economy.* London: Latin American Bureau, 2001.

Hayes, Joy Elizabeth. *Radio Nation: Communication, Popular Culture, and Nationalism in Mexico, 1920–1950.* Tucson: University of Arizona Press, 2000.

Hayward, Susan. *Cinema Studies: The Key Concepts.* 3rd ed. New York: Routledge, 2006.

Hernández Gomez, Guillermo, dir. *La Adelita.* 1939. DVD. Houston, TX: Union Telecom Texas, LLC, No date.

Herrera-Sobek, María. *The Mexican Corrido: A Feminist Analysis.* Bloomington: Indiana University Press, 1990.

Hershfield, Joanne. *Imagining la chica moderna: Woman, Nation, and Visual Culture in Mexico, 1917–1936.* Durham, NC: Duke University Press, 2008.

Hershfield, Joanne. *Mexican Cinema/Mexican Woman, 1940–1950.* Tucson: University of Arizona Press, 1996.

Hershfield, Joanne. "Race and Ethnicity in the Classical Cinema." In *Mexico's Cinema: A Century of Film and Filmmakers*, edited by Joanne Hershfield and David R. Maciel, 81–100. Wilmington: SR Books, 1999.

Herzog, Amy. *Dreams of Difference, Songs of the Same: The Musical Moment in Film*. Minneapolis: University of Minnesota Press, 2010.

Higgins, Ceri. *Gabriel Figueroa: Nuevas perspectivas*. Mexico City: Consejo Nacional para la Cultura y las Artes, 2008.

Hjort, Mette, and Scott Mackenzie, eds. *Cinema & Nation*. London: Routledge, 2000.

Hobsbawm, Eric. "Introduction: Inventing Traditions." In *The Invention of Tradition*, edited Eric Hobsbawm and Terence Ranger, 1–14. Cambridge: Canto, 1992.

Hobsbawm Eric, and Terrence Ranger, eds. *The Invention of Traditon*. Cambridge: Cambridge University Press, 1983.

Hunter, Mary. "The *Alla Turca* Style in the Late Eighteenth Century: Race and Gender in the Symphony and the Seraglio." In *The Exotic in Western Music*, edited by Jonathan Bellman, 43–73. Boston: Northeastern University Press, 1998.

Ibarra, Jesús. *Los Bracho: Tres generaciones de cine mexicano*. Mexico City: Universidad Nacional Autónoma de México, 2006.

Inclán, Luis. *Astucias*. Mexico City: Imprenta Universitaria, 1945.

Inclán, Luis. *El libro de las charrerías*. Mexico City: Librería Porrúa, 1940.

Jablonsja, Aleksandra, and Juan Felipe Leal. *La Revolución Mexicana en el cine nacional filmografía 1911–1917*. Mexico City: Universidad Pedagógica Nacional, 1991.

Jáuregui, Jesúz. *El mariachi: Símbolo musical de México*. Mexico City: Santillana Ediciones Generales, S.A. de C.V., 2007.

Jiménez, Armando. *Cabarets de antes y de ahora en la ciudad de México*. Mexico City: Plaza y Valdés Editores, 1991.

Johns, Michael. *The City of Mexico in the Age of Díaz*. Austin: University of Texas Press, 1997.

Joseph, Gilbert M., ed. *Everyday Forms of State Formation: Revolution and the Negotiation of Rule in Modern Mexico*. Durham, NC: Duke University Press, 1994.

Joseph, Gilbert M., Anne Rubenstein, and Eric Zolov, eds. *Fragments of a Golden Age: The Politics of Culture in Mexico Since 1940*. Durham, NC: Duke University Press, 2001.

Joseph, Gilbert M. and Timothy J. Henderson. *The Mexico Reader: History, Culture, and Politics*. Durham, NC: Duke University Press, 2002.

Kalinak, Kathryn. *Settling the Score: Music and the Classical Hollywood Film*. Madison: University of Wisconsin Press, 1992.

Katz, Friedrich. "The Liberal Republic and the Porfiriato, 1867–1910." In *Mexico Since Independence*, edited by Leslie Bethell, 49–124. Cambridge: Cambridge University Press, 1991.

Knight, Alan. "Racism, Revolution, and *Indigenismo*: Mexico, 1910–1940." In *The Idea of Race in Latin America, 1870–1940*, edited by Richard Graham, 71–113. Austin: University of Texas Press, 1990.

Knight, Alan. "The Rise and Fall of Cardenismo, c. 1940–1946." In *Mexico Since Independence*, edited by Leslie Bethell, 241–320. Cambridge: Cambridge University Press, 1991.

Kolb Neuhaus, Roberto. "*Janitzio*, ¿música de tarjeta postal? La retórica de un albur musical de Silvestre Revueltas." Mexico City: Universidad Nacional Autónoma de México. Working paper. 2006.

Krafft Vera, Federico and Elena Tamargo Cordero. *Bolero: Clave del corazón.* Mexico City: Fundación Ongenerio Alejo Peralta y Díaz Ceballos, IBP, 2004.

Krauze, Enrique. *El sexenio de Lázaro Cárdenas.* Mexico City: Clío, 2000.

Krauze, Enrique. *Mexico Biography of Power: A History of Modern Mexico, 1810–1996.* New York: Harper Collins, 1997.

Krauze, Enrique. *Plutarco E. Calles: Reformar desde el origen.* Mexico City: Fondo de Cultura Económica, 1987.

Kripper James, and Alfonso Morales Carrillo. *Paul Strand in Mexico.* New York: Aperture, 2010.

Kuri-Aldana, Mario, and Vicente Mendoza Martínez. *Cancionero popular mexicano*, 2 vols. 2nd ed. Mexico City: Consejo Nacional para la Cultura y las Artes, 1992–2001.

Lahr-Vivaz, Elena. *Mexican Melodrama: Film and Nation from the Golden Age to the New Wave.* Tucson: University of Arizona Press, 2016.

Lane, Jill. *Blackface Cuba.* Philadelphia: University of Pennsylvania Press, 2005.

Lara y Prado, Luis. *La Prostitución en México.* Mexico City: Librería de la viuda de Ch. Bouret, 1908.

Leal, Juan Felipe, Carlos Arturo Flores, and Eduardo Barraza. *Anales del cine en México, 1895–1911.* Vols. 1–6. 2nd ed. Mexico City: D.R. Voyeur, 2006.

Lerner, Neil. "Preface: Listening to Fear/Listening with Fear." In *Music in the Horror Film: Listening to Fear,* edited by Neil Lerner, viii–xi. New York: Routledge, 2010.

Lilia Roura, Alma. *Dr. Atl: Paisaje de hielo y fuego.* Mexico City: Consejo Nacional para la Cultura y las Artes, 1999.

Lipsitz, George. *Dangerous Crossroads: Popular Music, Postmodernism, and the Poetics of Place.* London: Verso, 1994.

LoBrutto, Vincent. *Sound on Film: Interviews with Creators of Film Sound.* Westport, CT: Praeger, 1994.

Lomax, John, and Alan Lomax. *American Ballads and Folks Songs.* New York: Macmillan, 1934.

López, Ana M. "Early Cinema and Modernity in Latin America." *Cinema Journal* 40, no. 1 (2000): 48–78.

López, Ana M. "Mexico." In *The International Film Musical,* edited by Corey K.Creekmur, and Linda Y. Mokdad, 121–40. Edinburgh: Edinburgh University Press, 2012.

López, Ana M.. "Of Rhythms and Borders." In *Everynight Life: Culture and Dance in Latin/o America,* edited by Celese Fraser Delgado and José Esteban Muñoz, 310–42. Durham, NC: Duke University Press, 1997.

López, Ana M.. "Tears and Desire: Women and Melodrama in the 'Old' Mexican Cinema." In *Mediating Two Worlds: Cinematic Encounters in Latin America,* edited by Manuel Alvarado, Ana M. López, and John King, 147–63. London: British Film Institute, 1993.

López, Rick A. "The Noche Mexicana and Popular Arts." In *The Eagle and the Virgin: Nation and Cultural Revolution in Mexico, 1920–1940,* edited by Mary Kay Vaughan and Stephen E. Lewis, 23–42. Durham, NC: Duke University Press, 2006.

Lucie-Smith, Edward. *Latin American Art of the 20th Century.* 2nd ed. New York: Thames & Hudson, 2004.

Luis Castillo, José, and Roberto Kolb Neuhaus, eds. *Silvestre Revueltas edición crítica: Redes (1935).* Mexico City: Universidad Nacional Autónoma de México, 2009.

Maciel, David R. *El bandolero, el pocho y la raza.* Mexico City: Consejo Nacional de la Cultura y las Artes, 2000.

Madrid, Alejandro L. *Music in Mexico: Experiencing Music, Expressing Culture.* New York: Oxford University Press, 2013.

Madrid, Alejandro L. *Sounds of the Modern Nation: Music, Culture, and Ideas in Post-Revolutionary Mexico.* Philadelphia: Temple University Press, 1998.

Madrid, Alejandro L. "The Sounds of the Nation: Visions of Modernity and Tradition in Mexico's First National Congress." *Hispanic American Historical Review* 86, no. 4 (2006): 681–706.

Madrid Alejandro L., and Robin Moore. *Danzón: Circum-Caribbean Dialogues in Music and Dance.* New York: Oxford University Press, 2013.

Magaña Esquivel, Antonio. *Medio siglo de teatro mexicano (1900–1961).* Mexico City: Instituto Nacional de Bellas Artes, 1964.

Mangan, Timothy, and Irene Hermann, eds. *Paul Bowles on Music.* Berkeley: University of California Press, 2003.

Mañón, Manuel. *Historia de Teatro Principal de México.* Mexico City: Editorial Cultura, 2009. Originally published in 1932.

Manuel, Peter. *Caribbean Currents: Caribbean Music from Rumba to Reggae.* Philadelphia: Temple University Press, 1995.

Marks, Martin Miller. *Music and the Silent Film: Contexts and Case Studies, 1895–1924.* New York: Oxford University Press, 1997.

Martín, Enrique, and Álvaro Vega. "La canción yucateca." In *La música en México: Panorama del siglo XX,* edited by Aurelio Tello, 253–90. Mexico City: Fondo de Cultura Económica, 2010.

Martín-Barbero, Jesús. *Communication, Culture and Hegemony: From the Media to Mediations.* London: Sage, 1993.

McClary, Susan. *Georges Bizet Carmen.* Cambridge: Cambridge University Press, 1992.

Medina, Rafeal, and José F. Elizondo. *Chin Chun Chan: Conflicto chino en un acto.* Mexico City: Medina y Comp. Impresores, 1904.

Mendoza, Vicente T. *Romance español y el corrido mexicano.* Mexico City: Ediciones de Universidad Nacional Autónoma de México, 1939.

Mercer, John, and Martin Shingler. *Melodrama: Genre, Style, Sensibility.* London: Wallflower, 2004.

Meyer, Eugenia. *Cuadernos de la Cineteca Nacional: Testimonios para la historia del cine mexicano,* Vol 1–5. Mexico City: Cineteca Nacional, 1976.

Michaels, Albert L. "The Crisis of Cardenismo." *Journal of Latin American Studies* 2, no. 1 (May 1970): 51–79.

Michel, Manuel, and Neal Oxenhandler. "Mexican Cinema: A Panoramic View." *Film Quarterly* 18, no. 4 (1965): 46–55.

Miguel, Ángel. *Acercamientos al cine silente mexicano.* Cuernavaca: Universidad Autónoma del Estado de Morelos, 2006.

Miguel, Ángel, ed. *La ficción de la historia: El siglo XIX en el cine mexicano.* Mexico City: Cineteca Nacional, 2010.

Miguel, Ángel. *Mimí Derba.* Mexico City: Filmoteca Universidad Nacional Autónoma de México, 2000.

Miller, Marilyn. "'The Soul Has No Color' but the Skin Does: *Angelitos Negros* and the Uses of Blackface on the Mexican Silver Screen, ca. 1950." In *Global Soundtrack: Worlds of Film Music,* edited by Mark Slobin, 241–58. Middletown, CT: Wesleyan University Press, 2008.

Miller, Patrick. "Music and the Silent Film." *Perspectives of New Music* 21, no. 1 (1982): 582–84.

Miranda, Ricardo. "La seducción y sus pautas." *Artes de México: Música de la Independencia a la Revolución* 97 (2010): 14–25.

Mitchell, Tim. *Intoxicating Identities: Alcohol's Power in Mexican History and Culture.* New York: Routledge, 2004.

Moitt, Bernard. *Sugar, Slavery, and Society: Perspectives on the Caribbean, India, the Mascarenes, and the United States.* Gainesville: University Press of Florida, 2004.

Molina Enríquez, Andrés. *Los grandes problemas nacionales y otros textos (1911–1919).* Mexico City: Ediciones Era. 1978. First published in 1909.

Monsiváis, Carlos. *A través del espejo: El cine mexicano y su público.* Mexico City: Ediciones El Milagro/Instituto Mexicano de Cinematografía, 1994.

Monsiváis, Carlos. *Aires de familia: Cultura y sociedad en América Latina.* Barcelona: Editorial Anagrama, 2000.

Monsiváis, Carlos. "All the People Came and Did Not Fit onto the Screen: Notes on the Cinema Audience in Mexico." In *Mexican Cinema*, edited by Paulo Antonio Paranaguá, 145–51. London: British Film Institute, 1995.

Monsiváis, Carlos. *Amor Perdido.* Mexico City: Ediciones Era, 1977.

Monsiváis, Carlos. "Foreword: When Gender Can't Be Seen Amid the Symbols: Women and the Mexican Revolution." In *Sex in Revolution: Gender, Politics, and Power in Modern Mexico*, edited by Mary Kay Vaughan, Jocelyn Olcott, and Gabriela Cano, 1–20. Durham, NC: Duke University Press, 2006.

Monsiváis, Carlos. "Mexican Cinema: Of Myths and Demystifications." In *Mediating Two Worlds: Cinematic Encounters in Latin America*, edited by John King, Ana M. Lopez, and Manuel Alvarado, 139–46. London: British Film Institute, 1993.

Monsiváis, Carlos. *Mexican Postcards.* London: Verso, 1997.

Monsiváis, Carlos. "Mythologies." In *Mexican Cinema*, edited by by Paulo Antonio Paranaguá, 117–27. London: British Film Institute/Instituto Mexicano de Cinematografía/Consejo Nacional para la Cultura y las Artes de México, 1995.

Monsiváis, Carlos. "Notas sobre la cultura mexicano en siglo XX." In *Historia general de México*, edited by Centro de Estudio Históricos, 957–1076. Mexico City: El Colegio de México, A.C., 2000.

Monsiváis, Carlos. *Pedro Infante: Las leyes del querer.* Mexico City: Santillana Ediciones Generales, S.A. de C.V., 2008.

Moore, Robin D. *Nationalizing Blackness: Afrocubanismo and Artistic Revolution in Havana, 1920–1940.* Pittsburgh, PA: University of Pittsburgh Press, 1997.

Mora, Carl J. *Mexican Cinema: Reflections of a Society, 1896–2004.* 3rd ed. London: McFarland, 2005.

Moreno, Antonio, dir. *Santa.* 1932. DVD, Mexico City: Filmoteca Universidad Nacional Autónoma de México, 1994.

Moreno Rivas, Yolanda. *Historia de la música popular mexicana.* Mexico City: Editorial Océano de México, 2003.

Moreno Rivas, Yolanda. "Los estilos nacionalistas en la música culta: aculturación de las formas populares." In *El nacionalismo y el arte mexicano (IX Coloquio de historia del arte)*, edited by Instituto de Investigaciones Estéticas, 35–70. Mexico City: Universidad Nacional Autónoma de México, 1986.

Moreno Rivas, Yolanda. *Rostros del nacionalismo en la música mexicana: un ensayo de Interpretación.* Mexico City: Fondo de Cultura Económica, 1989.

Moss, Arthur. *Cancan and Barcarolle: The Life and Times of Jacques Offenbach*. Westport, CT: Greenwood Press, 1975.

Mraz, John. *Looking for Mexico: Modern Visual Culture and National Identity*. Durham, NC: Duke University Press, 2009.

Mullen Sands, Kathleen. *Charrería mexicana: An Equestrian Folk Tradition*. Tucson: University of Arizona Press, 1993.

Muñoz, Rafael F. *¡Vámonos con Pancho Villa!* Mexico City: Factoría Ediciones, 2010. First published in 1931.

Muñoz Castillo, Fernando. *Las reinas del trópico*. Mexico City: Azabache, 1993.

Murch, Walter. "Foreword." In Michel Chion, *Audio/Vision*. New York: Columbia University Press, vii–xxiv, 1990.

Murillo, Gerardo. *Las artes populares en México*. Mexico City: Secretaría de Industria, Comercio y Trabajo, 1922.

Nájera-Ramírez, Olga. "Engendering Nationalism: Identity, Discourse, and the Mexican Charro." *Anthropology Quarterly* 67, no. 1 (1994): 1–14.

Nájera-Ramírez, Olga, Norma E. Cantú, and Brenda M. Romero, ed. *Dancing Across Borders: Danzas y Bailes Mexicanos*. Urbana: University of Illinois Press, 2009.

Navarro, Carlos, dir. *Janitzio*. 1934. VHS. Harlingen, TX: Agrasánchez Film Archive, 2000.

Navitski, Rielle. *Public Spectacles of Violence: Sensational Cinema and Journalism in Early Twentieth-Century Mexico and Brazil*. Durham, NC: Duke University Press, 2017.

Niblo, Stephen R. *México en los cuarenta: Modernidad y corrupción*. Mexico City: Editorial Océano de México, 2008.

Noble, Andera. *Mexican National Cinema*. London: Routledge, 2005.

Noble, Andrea. *Photography and Memory in Mexico: Icons of Revolution*. Manchester: Manchester University Press, 2010.

Nomland, John. *Teatro mexicano contemporáneo 1900–1950*. Mexico City: Ediciones del Instituto Nacional de Bellas Artes, Departamento de Literatura, 1967.

Noriega, Chon A., and Steven Ricci, eds. *The Mexican Cinema Project*. Los Angeles: UCLA Film and Television Archive, 1994.

Norman, James. *Charro: Mexican Horsemen*. New York: G.P. Putnam's Sons, 1969.

Novo, Salvador. *La vida en México en el periodo presidencial de Lázaro Cárdenas*. Mexico City: Empresas Editoriales, S.A., 1964.

Obscura Gutierrez, Siboney. "La comedia ranchera y la construcción del estereotipo del charro cantante en el cine mexicano de los treinta e inicio de los cuarenta." Master's thesis, Universidad Nacional Autónoma de México, 2003.

Ochs, Anna. "Opera in Contention: Social Conflict in Late Nineteenth Century Mexico City." PhD dissertation, University of North Carolina, Chapel Hill, 2011.

Olguín, David, ed. *Un siglo de teatro en México*. Mexico City: Fondo de Cultura Económica, 2011.

Olsson, Tore C. *Agrarian Crossings: Reformers and the Remaking of the U.S. and Mexican Countryside*. Princeton, NJ: Princeton University Press, 2017.

Ortiz, Fernando. *La música afro-cubana*. Madrid: Ediciones Jucar, 1974.

Ortiz Bullé Goyri, Alejandro. "Orígenes y desarollo del teatro de revistas en México (1896–1953)." In *Un siglo de teatro en México*, edited by David Olguín, 40–53. Mexico City: Fondo de Cultura Económica, 2011.

Ortiz Garza, José Luis. *La Guerra de las ondas*. Mexico City: Editorial Planeta Mexicana, 1992.

Ortiz Monasterio, Pablo, ed. *Fragmentos: Narración cinematográfica compilada y arreglada por Salvador Toscano, 1900–1930.* Mexico City: Instituto Mexicano de Cinematografía, 2010.

O'Shaughnessy, Edith. *Diplomatic Days.* New York: Harper and Brothers, 1911.

El país de las tandas: teatro de revista, 1900–1940. Mexico City: Mueso Nacional de Culturas Populares, 1984.

Paranaguá, Paulo Antonio, ed. *Mexican Cinema.* Translated by Ana M. López. London: British Film Institute/Instituto Mexicano de Cinematografía/Consejo Nacional Para la Cultura y las Artes de México, 1995.

Pareyón, Gabriel. *Diccionario enciclopédico de música en México.* Vol. 1. Guadalajara: Secretaría de Cultura de Jalisco, 1995.

Parker, Robert. "Revueltas, the Chicago Years." *Latin American Music Review/Revista de Música Latino Americana* 25, no. 2 (2004): 180–94.

Parker, Robert. "Revueltas in San Antonio and Mobile." *Latin American Music Review/Revista de Música Latino Americana* 23, no. 1 (2002): 114–30.

Parra, Max. *Writing Pancho Villa's Revolution: Rebels in the Literary Imagination of Mexico.* Austin: University of Texas Press, 2005.

Paz, Octavio. *The Labyrinth of Solitude and Other Essays.* New York: Grove Press, 1985. First published in 1961.

Pedelty, Mark. "The Bolero: The Birth, Life, and Decline of Mexican Modernity." *Latin American Music Review/Revista de Música Latino Americana* 20, no. 1 (Spring-Summer 1999): 30–58.

Pedelty, Mark. *Musical Ritual in Mexico City: From the Aztec to NAFTA.* Austin: University of Texas Press, 2004.

Peñaloza Méndez, Ernesto. "De luces y sombra." *Luna Córnea* 32 (2008): 211–32.

Peredo Castro, Francisco. *Cine y propaganda para Latinoamérica: México y Estados Unidos en los años cuarenta.* 2nd ed. Mexico City: Universidad Nacional Autónoma de México, 2011.

Pérez Montfort, Ricardo. *Estampas de nacionalismo popular mexicano: Ensayos sobre cultura popular y nacionalismo.* Mexico City: Centro de Investigaciones y Estudios Superiores en Antropología Social, 1994.

Pérez Montfort, Ricardo, Pablo Picatto, and Alberto del Castillo. *Hábitos, normas y escándalo: Prensa, criminalidad y drogas durante el porfiriato tardío.* Mexico City: Plaza y Valdés, S.A de C.V., 1997.

Pick, Zuzana M. *Constructing the Image of the Mexican Revolution: Cinema and the Archive.* Austin: University of Texas Press, 2010.

Pisani, Michael V. "'I'm an Indian too': Creating Native American Identities in Nineteenth and Early Twentieth-Century Music." In *The Exotic in Western Music,* edited by Jonathan Bellman, 218–57. Boston: Northeastern University Press, 1998.

Powrie, Phil. *Music in Contemporary French Cinema: The Crystal-Song.* London: Palgrave Macmillan, 2017.

Price, David. *Cancan!* London: Cygnus Arts, 1998.

Prida Santacilla, Pablo. *Y se levanta el telon: Mi vida dentro del teatro.* Mexico City: Ediciones Botas, 1960.

Pulido Llano, Gabriela. "Empresarias y tandas." *Bicentenario* 2, no. 6 (2009): 14–21.

Pulido Llano, Gabriela. *Mulatas y negros cubanos en la escena Mexicana, 1920–1950.* Mexico City: Instituto Nacional de Antropología e Historia, 2010.

Radano, Ronald, and Philip V. Bohlman, eds. *Music and the Racial Imagination.* Chicago: University of Chicago Press, 2000.

Ramirez, Fausto. *Modernización y modernismo en el arte mexicano.* Mexico City: Universidad de Autónoma de México, 2008.

Ramírez Berg, Charles. *The Classical Mexican Cinema: The Poetics of the Exceptional Golden Age Films.* Austin: University of Texas Press, 2015.

Ramos, Samuel. *Profile of Man and Culture in Mexico.* Rev. ed. Austin: University of Texas Press, 1962. First published in 1934.

Ramos Smith, Maya. *Teatro musical y danza en el México de la belle époque (1867–1910).* Mexico City: Universidad Autónoma Metropolitana y Grupo Editorial Gaceta, 1995.

Rapeé, Erno. *Encyclopedia of Music for Pictures.* New York: Belwin, 1925.

Rashkin, Elissa J. *The Stridentist Movement in Mexico: The Avant-Garde and Cultural Change in the 1920s.* Lanham, MD: Lexington, 2009.

Rashkin, Elissa J.. *Women Filmmakers in Mexico: The Country of Which We Dream.* Austin: University of Texas Press, 2001.

"Raul Prado, fundador de Trío Calavera." *El País,* April 11, 1989, https://elpais.com/diario/1989/04/11/agenda/608248804_850215.html.

Reed, Nelson. *The Caste War of Yucatán.* Stanford, CA: Stanford University Press, 1964.

Reséndez Fuentes, Andrés. "Battleground Women: Soldaderas and Female Soldiers in the Mexican Revolution." *The Americas* 51, no. 4 (1995): 525–53.

Reyes de la Maza, Luis. *Circo, maroma y teatro, 1819–1910.* Mexico City: Universidad Nacional Autónoma de México, 1985.

Reyes de la Maza, Luis. *El teatro en México durante el porfirismo, vol. I-III.* Mexico City: Universidad Nacional Autonóma de México, 1968.

Reyes Nevares, Beatriz. *Trece directores del cine mexicano.* Mexico City: Secretaría de Educación Pública, 1974.

Rico, Elena. "Anatomía de un éxito loco: *Allá en el Rancho Grande.*" *Contenido* 157 (June 1976): 20–56.

Rincón Gallardo, Alfonso. "En la hacienda de antaño." In *Artes de México: Charrería,* edited by Margarita de Orellana, 29–31. Mexico City: Artes de México, 2000.

Rincón Gallardo, D. Carlos. *El libro del charro mexicano.* 3rd ed. Mexico City: Editorial Porrua, S.A., 1960. First published in 1939.

Rodríguez, Ismael. *Los tres García.* 1947. DVD. Burbank, CA: Warner Home Video, 2009.

Rodríguez, José Antonio. "Modernas sombras fugitivas: Las construcciones visuales de Gabriel Figueroa." *Luna Córnea* 32 (2008): 233–89.

Rodríguez, Joselito. *¡Ay Jalisco, no te rajes!* 1941. DVD. Mexico City: Películas Rodríguez S.A. de C.V., 2000.

Rosen, Philip. "Adorno and Film Music: Theoretical Notes on Composing for Films." *Yale French Studies–Cinema/Sound* 60 (1980): 157–82.

Roy, Maya. *Cuban Music: From Son and Rumba to the Buena Vista Social Club and Timba Cubana.* London: Latin American Bureau, 1998.

Rubenstein, Anne. "Bodies, Cities, Cinema: Pedro Infante's Death as Political Spectacle." In *Fragments of a Golden Age: The Politics of Culture in Mexico Since 1940,* edited by Gilbert M. Joseph, Anne Rubenstein, and Eric Zolov, 199–233. Durham, NC: Duke University Press, 2001.

Rubestein, Anne. "Mass Media and Popular Culture in the Post Revolutionary Era." In *The Oxford History of Mexico,* edited by M. C. Meyer and W. H. Beezley, 65. New York: Oxford University Press, 2000.

Rubenstein, Anne. "The War on *Las Pelonas:* Modern Women and Their Enemies, Mexico City, 1924." In *Sex in Revolution: Gender, Politics, and Power in Modern Mexico,* edited by Jocelyn Olcott, Mary Kay Vaughan, and Gabriela Cano, 57–80. Durham, NC: Duke University Press, 2006.

Saavedra, Leonora. "Manuel M. Ponce y los músicos populares." *Heterofonía* 143 (July–December 2010): 51–84.

Saavedra, Leonora. "Of Selves and Others: Historiography, Ideology, and the Politics of Modern Mexican Music." PhD dissertation, University of Pittsburgh, 2001.

Saavedra, Leonora. "Urban Music in the Mexican Revolution." Paper read at the National Meeting for the Society of Ethnomusicology, Columbus, OH, 2007.

Sadlier, Darlene J., ed. *Latin American Melodrama: Passion, Pathos, and Entertainment.* Urbana: University of Illinois Press, 2009.

Sagredo Baeza, Rafael. *Maria Villa (a) La Chiquita, no. 4002: Un parásito social del Porfiriato.* Mexico City: Cal y Arena, 1996.

Said, Edward. *Orientalism.* New York: Random House, 1978.

Salas, Elizabeth. *Soldaderas in the Mexican Military.* Austin: University of Texas Press, 1990.

Saldavar, Gabriel. *El jarabe: Baile popular mexicano.* Puebla: Lecturas Históricas de Puebla, 1987.

Sánchez Prado, Ignacio. "The Golden Age Otherwise: Mexican Cinema and the Mediations of Capitalist Modernity in the 1940s and 1950s." In *Cosmopolitan Film Culturesin Latin America 1896–1960,* edited by Rielle Navitski and Nicholas Poppe, 241–66. Bloomington: University of Indiana Press, 2017.

Sánchez Prado, Ignacio. *Screening Neoliberalism: Transforming Mexican Cinema, 1988–2012.* Nashville, TN: Vanderbilt University Press, 2015.

Sánchez, Alberto Ruy, ed. *Artes de México: Revision del Cine Mexicano: Edición Especial 10.* Mexico City: Artes de México, 2001.

Sánchez, Alberto Ruy and Margarita de Orellana, eds. *Artes de México: Música de la Independencia a la Revolución.* 97. Mexico City: Artes de México, 2010.

Semo, Enrique. *Historia de la cuestión agraria mexicana. Vol. 1: El siglo de la hacienda 1800–1900.* Mexico City: Siglo XXI-CEHAM, 1988.

Serna, Enrique. *Jorge el bueno: La vida de Jorge Negrete.* 2 vols. Mexico City: Clío,1993.

Serna, Laura Isabel. *Cinelandia: American Films and Mexican Film Culture Before the Golden Age.* Durham, NC: Duke University Press, 2014.

Schneider, Luis M., ed. *El estridentismo: México 1921–1927.* Mexico City: Insitituto de Investigaciones Estéticas, Universidad Nacional Autónoma de México, 1985.

Schwartz, Perla, ed. *Vanidad de vanidades: Moda femenina en México, siglos XIX y XX.* Mexico City: Uva Tinta Ediciones, 2013.

Sheehy, Daniel. *Mariachi Music in America: Expressing Music, Expressing Culture.* New York: Oxford University Press, 2006.

Sheridan, Guillermo. *Los Contemporáneos de ayer.* Mexico City: Fonda de Cultura Econónmica, 2003. First published in 1985.

Silva Cázares, Carlos. *Plutarco Elías Calles.* Mexico City: Planeta, 2005.

Singer, Ben. *Melodrama and Modernity: Early Sensational Cinema and Its Contexts.* New York: Columbia University Press, 2001.

Slobin, Mark, ed. *Global Soundtracks: Worlds of Film Music.* Middletown, CT: Wesleyan University Press, 2008.

Smith, Anthony D. "Images of the Nation: Cinema, Art and National Identity." In *Cinema & Nation*, edited by Mette Hjort and Scott Mackenzie, 45–60. London: Routledge, 2000.

Smith, Anthony D. *Myths and Memories of the Nation*. Oxford: Oxford University Press, 2000.

Somos: Las rumberas del cine mexicano 10, no. 189 (November 1999).

Soto, Shirlene. *Emergence of the Modern Mexican Woman: Her Participation in Revolution and Struggle for Equality, 1900–1940*. Denver: Arden, 1990.

Spivak, Gayatri Chakravorty. *Outside in the Teaching Machine*. New York: Routledge, 1993.

Stilwell, Robynn J. "The Fantastical Gap between Diegetic and Nondiegetic." In *Beyond the Soundtrack: Representing Music in Cinema*, edited by Daniel Goldmark, Lawrence Kramer, and Richard Leppert, 184–202. Berkeley: University of California Press, 2007.

Sturman, Janet L. *The Course of Mexican Music*. New York: Routledge, 2016.

Sturman, Janet L. *Zarzuela: Spanish Operetta, American Stage*. Urbana: University of Illinois Press, 2000.

Sublette, Ned. *Cuba and Its Music: From the First Drums to the Mambo*. Chicago: Chicago Review Press, 2004.

Taibo I, Paco I. *La música de Agustín Lara en el cine*. Mexico City: Universidad Nacional Autónoma de México, 1984.

Talavera, Mario. *Miguel Lerdo de Tejada: su vida pintoresca y anecdótica*. Mexico City: Editoral Compas, 1942.

Tannenbaum, Frank. *Mexico: The Struggle for Peace and Bread*. New York: Alfred Knopf, 1956.

Tapia Colman, Simón. *Música y musicos en México*. Mexico City: Panorama Editorial, 1991.

Tello, Aurelio. "Francisco Domínguez." In *Diccionario del Cine Iberoamericano*, vol. 3, edited by Emilio Casares Rodicio, 320. Madrid: Sociedad General de Autores y Editores, 2011.

Terán, Luis. "La rubia con piernas de oro." *Somos: las rumberas del cine mexicano* 10, no. 189 (November 1999): 60–67.

Thomas, Susan. *Cuban Zarzuela: Performing Race and Gender on Havana's Lyric Stage*. Urbana: University of Illinois Press, 2009.

Tierney, Dolores. *Emilio Fernández: Pictures on the Margins*. Manchester: Manchester University Press, 2007.

Tierney, Dolores. "Silver Sling-backs and Mexican Melodrama: *Danzón* and *Salón México*." *Screen* 38, no. 4 (Winter 1997): 360–71.

Torres, George. "The *Bolero romántico*: From Cuban Dance to International Popular Song." In *From Tejano to Tango*, edited by Walter Clark, 151–71. New York: Routledge, 2002.

Torres, Francisco. "Las tres pelonas." *Centauro del Norte*, January 8, 2012, https://centaurodelnorte.com/las-tres-pelonas/.

Tortajada Quiroz, Margarita. *Danza y poder*. Mexico City: Instituto Nacional de Bellas Artes, 1995.

Tovar y de Teresa, Rafael. *El último brindis de don Porfirio 1910: Los festejos del Centenario*. Mexico City: Santillana Ediciones Generales, S.A. de C.V., 2012.

Tuñón, Julia. *Mujeres de luz y sombra en el cine mexicano: La construcción de una imagen, 1939–1952*. Mexico City: El Colegio de México A.C./Instituto Mexicano de Cinematografía, 1998.

Tuñón, Julia. *Mujeres: Entre la imagen y la acción*. Mexico City: Debate, 2015.

Turner, John Kenneth. *Barbarous Mexico*. Austin: University of Texas Press, 1969.

Valero Silva, José. *El libro de la charrería.* Mexico City: Gráficas Montealbán, 1989.

Vanderwood, Paul J. *Los rurales mexicanos.* Mexico City: Fondo de Cultura Económica, 1981.

Vasconcelos, José. *The Cosmic Race.* Baltimore, MD: John Hopkins University Press, 1976.

Vaughan, Mary Kay. "Introduction: Pancho Villa, the Daughters of Mary and the Modern Woman: Gender in the Long Mexican Revolution." In *Sex in Revolution: Gender Politics, and Power in Modern Mexico,* edited by Jocelyn Olcott, Mary Kay Vaughan, and Gabriela Cano, 21–34. Durham, NC: Duke University Press, 2006.

Vaughan, Mary Kay. "Nationalizing the Countryside: Schools and Rural Communities in the 1930s." In *The Eagle and the Virgin: Nation and Cultural Revolution in Mexico, 1920–1940,* edited by Mary Kay Vaughan and Stephan E. Lewis, 157–75. Durham, NC: Duke University Press, 2006.

Vaughan, Mary Kay, and Stephan E. Lewis, eds. *The Eagle and the Virgin: Nation and Cultural Revolution in Mexico, 1920–1940.* Durham, NC: Duke University Press, 2000.

Vázquez Mantecón, Álvaro. *Orígenes literarios de un arquetipo fílmico: Adaptciones cinematográficas a Santa de Federico Gamboa.* Mexico City: Biblioteca de Ciencias Sociales y Humanidades, 2005.

von Wobeser, Giselia. *La formación de la hacienda en la época colonial.* Mexico City: Institutio de Investigaciones Históricas, Universidad Nacional Autónoma de México, 1989.

Webber, Christopher. "The alcalde, the negro and *la bribona: género ínfirmo* zarzuela, 1900–1910." In *De la zarzuela al cine: Los medios de comunicación populares y su traducción de la voz marginal,* edited by Max Doppelbauer and Kathrin Sartingen, 71–73. Múnchen: Martin Meidenbauer, 2010.

Webber, Christopher. *The Zarzuela Companion.* Lanham, MD: Scarecrow, 2002.

Wierzbicki, James. *Film Music: A History.* London: Routledge, 2009.

Wikke, Carle Frederick. *Tambo and Bones: A History of the American Minstrel Stage.* Durham, NC: Duke University Press, 1930.

Wood, Andrew Grant. *Agustín Lara: A Cultural Biography.* New York: Oxford University Press, 2014.

Zamecnik, J.S. *Sam Fox Moving Picture Music, vol. 1.* Cleveland, OH: Sam Fox Publishing Company, 1914.

Archives Consulted

Archivo General de la Nación, Mexico City

Archivo Mil Nubes Cine, Mexico City

Biblioteca Lerdo de Tejada, Mexico City

Biblioteca de las Artes, Centro Nacional de las Artes, Mexico City

Centro de Documentación, Cineteca Nacional, Mexico City

Filmoteca Universidad Nacional Autónoma de México, Mexico City

Hermeoteca Nacional Universidad Nacional Autónoma de México, Mexico CIty

Latin American and Iberian Archival Collections, University of New Mexico

Margaret Herrick Library, Academy of Motion Pictures, Arts, and Sciences, Beverly Hills, California

Permanencia Voluntaria Archivo Cinematográfico, Tepoztlán

Newspapers and Magazines Consulted

Cahiers du Cinéma
Cinema Reporter
Cine Mundial
Contenido
El Cine Gráfico
El Mundo Ilustrado
El Nacional
El Sol de México
Esto
El Universal
El Universal Ilustrado
Excélsior
Hoy
Imagen Diario
La Opinión
La Prensa
La Semana Ilustrada
Mañana
New York Times
Novedades
Proceso
Revista de Revistas
Variety

Index

Figures are indicated by *f* following the page number.

1910 (Fernández Ros), 1–3, 2n2–3

Acosta y Topete, Hermila Galindo, 197
African identity, 62, 62n126, 63*f*
Alavés, José López
  Allá en el Rancho Grande, 166–167
  childhood, 167, 167n52
Alba, Luz, 48
Alemán, Miguel, 50, 109
Allá en el Rancho Grande (film, de
    Fuentes), 9, 12, 19, 151–152,
    160–178, 215
  audience, intended, 177–178
  "cancioneros del alma nacional,"
    169–170
  "Canción Mixteca," 159, 166–167, 168
  canción ranchera, 161, 180
  cantina music, machismo and,
    172–178, 174*f*
  coplas de huapango, 176
  hispanismo, 164–165
  historical era and rural setting, 161–162
  huapango retachado, 170, 175–176, 182
  jarabe tapatío, 171–173, 171*f*
  "Lucha María," 170
  "Amanecer ranchero," 168
  masculinity, 161
  mestizaje, music as, 165–166
  Mexicanidad, 161, 172, 178
  "Presumida," 170
  at Rancho Grande, 162–166, 163*f*
  serenades and accolades, 168–172, 170*f*
  "Sobre las olas," 169
  success, first Mexican film industry,
    160–161
"Allá en el Rancho Grande" (song), 173–174,
    173n66, 174*f*
  Alavés, José López (composer),
    166–167

Barcelata, Lorenzo (composer), 166
"Altiva" (Castellot Jr. and de Rocca),
    83, 86, 87
Álvarez, Sofía, 7
"Amanecer ranchero," 168
Amaro, Joaquín, 199
"Amor de Ciego" (Villegas), 40n60
Anderson, Benedict, 4
Anguiano, Arturo, 75
anti-essentializing, strategizing, 189
Así es mi tierra (Boytler), 179
Atl, Dr., 118, 119, 119n23
Aventurera (Sevilla), 51, 64n130
ávilacamachismo, 92
Aviña, Rafael, 151
Ayala Blanco, Jorge, 70–71, 81, 186n96
¡Ay Jalisco, no te rajes!
    (Negrete), 178–191
  canción ranchera, 180–181
  Esperón and Cortázar (composers),
    179–182
  lead actors, 179
  rural setting and story, 179–180
¡Ay, qué tiempos señor don Simón!
    (Bracho), 90, 93–99, 96*f*, 109
Azcárate, Juan F., 198
Azuela, Mariano, *Los de abajo*, 193

Barbarous Mexico (Turner), 73
Barcelata, Lorenzo, 174–175
  Allá en el Rancho Grande, 166
  success, 166
Barranca trágica (de la Bandera),
    156, 156n17
battement, 94, 94n72
Beezely, William H., 74
Bellas de noche (Delgado), 236
Benítez, Francisco, *En tiempos de don
    Porfirio*, 78

Berg, Charles Ramírez, 6
Bicentenario, 1–2, 1n1
"Bienvenida," 34
Bliss, Katherine, 25–27
bolero, 9
    cabaretera film, 53
    estilo yucateco, 41
    Lara, Agustín, 38
    Santa, 40n60, 40–44, 41*f*, 41n63,
        43*f*, 48, 67
Bon Bernard, Claude Ferdinand, 77
bongocero, 62–63
"Boston," 35, 35n42
botao, 64, 64*f*
Bowles, Paul, 10, 10n21
Boytler, Arcady, 7
    Así es mi tierra, 179
    La mujer del puerto, 49, 238
Bracho, Julio, *¡Ay, qué tiempos señor don
    Simón!*, 90, 93–99, 96*f*, 109
Breil, Carl, *The Birth of a Nation*, 190n103
Brooks, Peter, 12–13
Bunker, Steve, 74
Buñuel, Luis
    Los Olvidados, 7, 240
    in Mexico, 7n15
Bustillo Oro, Juan
    En tiempos de don Porfirio, 68, 71, 80–
        91, 86*f* (see also *En tiempos de don
        Porfirio* [Bustillo Oro])
    México de mis recuerdos, 5, 96–102,
        101*f*, 105–109, 106*f*, 108*f*

Caballero, Manuel Fernández, *La
    viejecita*, 100
cabaretera, 8, 17, 20, 50, 52, 53. *See also*
    prostitute melodrama; *specific films*
    Afro-Cuban music and dance, 9
    Aventurera, 51, 64n130
    conventions, 239
    cultural synchresis, 23
    exoticism, 51–53, 52n99
    exoticization, 58n118
    mambos, 55n112
    mid-1900s, 50–51
    rumbera, 96, 236
    Salón México, 51, 54, 238
    social and economic instabilities, 9

Víctimas del pecado, 17, 23, 54–66, 57*f*,
    60*f*, 63*f*–64*f*
cabarets
    El dancing and modern woman, 26–30
    shimmy, 27–28
Calderón, Felipe, 2
Camacho, Manuel Ávila, 50, 81, 91–92,
    92n69, 138
Camus, Germán, 31, 31n30, 33
cancan, 93, 97n75
    ¡Ay, qué tiempos señor don Simón!,
        93–97, 96*f*
    battement, 94, 94n72
    En tiempos de don Porfirio, 90–91
    gallop, 94
    rond de jambe, 94, 94n72
canción mexicana, 159–160, 202, 203
    Allá en el Rancho Grande, 168
    "Altiva," 83, 86, 87
    ¡Ay Jalisco, no te rajes!, 181
    Lara, Agustín, 38, 83, 86, 87
    masculinity, 160
    Ponce on, 127n49
    regional performance styles, 38
"Canción Mixteca" (Alavés), 159,
    166–167, 168
canción ranchera, 158–160, 191
    Allá en el Rancho Grande, 161, 180
    ¡Ay Jalisco, no te rajes!, 180–181
    estilo bravío, 159–160
canción romántica, 40
Canclini, Nestor García, 152
cantina, music and machismo in,
    172–178, 174*f*
Cantinflas (del Amo), 239
Cárdenas, Lázaro, 75–76, 75n21, 117
Carmen (Bizet), 53
"Carmen," 99, 99n81
carpas, 13
Carrancitas, 194n3
Carranza, Venustiano, 197
Carrasco, González, 207
Carrillo, Julián, 127
Casasola, Agustín V., 195, 231
Casasola family, 200
Caso, Alfonso, 18, 114, 116–117, 117n16
Castellot Jr., L., "Altiva," 83, 86, 87
Castro, Ricardo, *Vals capricho*, 100

Centenario, 1–2, 1n1
"Changó," 56–58, 57*f*
charro, singing, 18–19, 18n43, 150–192.
    See also *specific movies*
    1920s films, 156, 156nn17–21
    Allá en el Rancho Grande, 9, 12, 19,
       151–152, 160–178
    Así es mi tierra, 179
    attire, 153–154
    ¡Ay Jalisco, no te rajes!, 178
    Barranca trágica, 156, 156n17
    conservative responses, politics, 152
    Cortázar, Ernesto (composer), 180–182
    definition, 164
    El caporal, 156
    estilo bravío, 159–160, 182
    as fighter, Revolution, 155
    gritos, 172
    Guadalajara, 179
    hacienda, 154, 154n10
    Hollywood and Mexican silent film,
       155–156
    Los tres García, 19, 183–191,
       187*f*, 189n99
    machismo, 152, 153, 190
    masculinity, 152, 164, 179, 191
    Mexicanidad, 161, 172, 178, 191
    in Mexican viceroyalty,
       150–151, 150n1
    mexiquitos, 151
    Negrete archetype, 179
    origins to 20th century, 153–157
    regional folkloric genre, 150–151
    after Revolution, 155
    symbolism, 152, 153–154
    teatro de revistas, canción mexicana,
       and canción ranchera, 157–160
Chávez, Carlos, 133, 133n70
chica moderna, la, 29
Chin Chun Chan (Medina and Elizondo),
    102, 104*f*
Chion, Michel, 15
cine campirano
    backdrop, 150
    charro, 150–151
cine de añoranza porfiriana, 8, 18, 68–109
    ¡Ay, qué tiempos señor don Simón!, 90,
       93–99, 96*f*, 109

corruption, modernization, and
    cosmopolitanism, 71–76
El globo de Cantolla, 109
En tiempos de don Porfirio, 68, 71, 80–91,
    86*f* (see also *En tiempos de don Porfirio*
    [Bustillo Oro])
female roles, 103, 103n92
genre, 81
Porfiriato, 1940s, 91–109 (*see also*
    Porfiriato [Porfirio Díaz])
Porfiriato, genre, 68–70
stage and silent screen, 76–79
Teatro Principal, 98, 102, 102n87, 103,
    105, 106
utopian escape, 28, 71, 97, 108, 150
Yo bailé con don Porfirio, 103n93, 109
cine de ficheras, 20
cine de luchadores, 20, 235
cinema. See also *specific topics*
    cultural nationalism and
       cosmopolitanism, 5
    as learning tool, 5
    weekly movie going ritual, 5
cinemachismo, 16
cinesonidos, 16, 241
cine mexicano, 5–6
Cineteca Nacional, 1
"Cine y Revolución: La Revolución
    Mexicana vista a través del cine," 2–3
cinquillo rhythm, 41, 41*f*
Club Changoo cabaret
    mambos and boleros, 54
    Pérez Prado, Dámaso and Pérez Prado
       Orchestra, 55–56, 58, 59–60, 60*f*, 239
    Víctimas del pecado, 54–66 (see also
       Víctimas del pecado [Fernández])
comedia ranchera, 7, 18–19, 18n43. See
    also *specific movies*
    Allá en el Rancho Grande, 9, 12, 19,
       151–152, 160–178
    charro, singing, 150–192 (*see also*
       charro, singing)
    Negrete, Jorge, 180
    setting, 111
    teatro de revista, 156, 157–159
CONACULTA, 237
Contemporáneos, Los, 208–209, 209n47
Contreras Soto, Jaime, 81

Contreras Torres, Miguel, *El caporal*, 156
coplas de huapango, 176
Corona, Jesús, 83
Corona, León F. García, 226
corrido, 2, 207
  definition, 19
  "La Adelita," 203–205
  Mexican Revolution, 201–203,
    210, 231
corrido-canciones, 2, 207–231
  Enamorada, 222–227, 224f
  hybrid form, 202
  La Adelita (film), 215–222, 221f
  "La Adelita," 203–205
  "La Rielera," 205, 206–207, 227,
    230, 231f
  "Las tres pelonas," 211–212
  "La Valentina," 205–206, 212
  representation, 207–208
  Revolution in, 207–208
  ¡Vámonos con Pancho Villa!, 208–215,
    210f, 213f, 214f
Cortázar, Ernesto
  ¡Ay Jalisco, no te rajes!, 178–192
  Los tres García, 178–192
Cristero rebellion, 138, 138n81
Cuadernos de estudios cinematográficos, 11
cuadros, 78
cultural synchresis, 12–16

Dallal, Alberto, *El "dancing" mexicano*, 28
danza mexicana, "Bienvenida," 34
  "Adíos....!," 88
  En tiempos de don Porfirio, 81, 82
danzón, 9
  cabaretera and prostitute melodrama, 9,
    15, 17, 27, 53
  cabaretera film, 53
  cinquillo rhythm, 41, 41f
  dance style, 45–48, 48f
  Danzón, 238
  estribrillo, 46
  La mancha de sangre, 49
  La mujer del puerto, 49
  origins and adaptation, 45
  popularity, 44, 83
  Salón México, 238
  Santa, 37, 40, 44–49, 45n74, 48f, 67

in teatro de revista, 45n74
  Víctimas del Pecado, 67
Danzón (Novaro), 239
*Danzón: Circum-Caribbean Dialogues
    in Music and Dance* (Madrid and
    Moore), 46
Davalos Orozco, Federico, 32, 32n35
de Ega, Juan, 28–29
de Fuentes, Fernando. See also
    specific films
  Allá en el Rancho Grande (see *Allá en el
    Rancho Grande*)
  El compadre Mendoza, 208
  El prisionero 13, 208
  Enamorada, 19, 194, 222–227, 224f
  ¡Vámonos con Pancho Villa!, 19, 194
de Ibarra, José, 119
de Jesús Martínez, José, 202–203
del Amo, Sebastian
  Cantinflas, 239
  El Fantástico mundo de Juan Orol, 239
de la Mora, Sergio, 16, 31, 58, 89, 165,
    236, 238
de la Vega, Ricardo, 84
de la Vez, Francisco Martínez, 76
Delgado, Miguel M., *Bellas de noche*, 236
de los Reyes, Aurelio, 120
  Medio siglo de cine mexicano, 12,
    32nn34–35
  ¡Que viva México!, 120
del Río, Dolores, 131n61
  in Hollywood, 141n62, 165n46
  María Candelaria, 139–147, 140f,
    144f (see also *María Candelaria*
    [Fernández])
Derba, Mimi, 101, 101–102n84
de Rocca, A., "Altiva," 83, 86, 87
d'Harcourt, René and Marguerite, *La
    Musique des Incas et ses survivances*,
    133–134
Díaz López, Marina, 9
Díaz, Porfirio. See Porfiriato
    (Porfirio Díaz)
Díaz López, Marina, 9
Diccionario del Cine Iberoamericano
    (Tello), 11
D'Lugo, Marvin, 13
domesticity, modern, 29

Domínguez, Francisco, 18, 113, 124–129
  Janitzio, 128–129, 132–137, 148
  María Candelaria, 141–145, 148–149
Draper, Jack, 7
Dueñas, Pablo, 102

Echeverría, Luis, 236
Eisenstein, Sergei, 7, 120
  indigenismo, 113
  in Mexico, 7n15
  ¡Que viva México!, 120–124 (see also
    ¡Que viva México! [Eisenstein])
El caporal (Contreras Torres), 156
El compadre Mendoza (de Fuentes), 208
el dancing, 28–29
El "dancing" mexicano (Dallal), 28
el estilo lariano, 39
El Fantasma de la opereta (Cortés), 235
El Fantástico mundo de Juan Orol (del
    Amo), 239
"El gálan incógnito," 84–88, 86f
El globo de Cantolla (Martínez), 109
Elizondo, José F., *Chin Chun Chan*,
    102, 104f
El prisionero 13 (de Fuentes), 208
El rey del barrio (Solares), 235
El Salón México (Copland), 10, 10n21
El Teatro mexicano del murciélago
    (Quintanilla, González, and Bartolo),
    126, 126n44
"El tren," 66
Enamorada (de Fuentes), 19, 194,
    222–227, 224f
  "La Malagueña," 225, 226, 238
  Moncada, Eduardo Hernández
    (composer), 225
Eniso, Jorge, 118
Enríquez Molina, Andrés, 114
En tiempos de don Porfirio (Bustillo Oro),
    68, 71, 80–91, 86f
  comedic relief, 83–84
  "El gálan incógnito," 84–88, 86f
  locations, musical performances, 89
  música culta, 82–83
  música de salón, 82–83
  narrative, 92–93
  orchestral sound, 87–88
  Porfiriato cultural activity after, 90–91

romance scenes, 83
storyline, 80–81, 88–89
success, 89–90
time, showcasing, 81–82
Urban's danzas and waltzes,
    82–83, 82n46
En tiempos de don Porfirio (Ortega, Prida,
    and Benítez), 78–79
Entierro de un obrero (Siqueiro), 122
época de oro, 1, 6, 17, 20. See also *specific
    films and topics*
  after, 234–237
  remembering, 237–241
Esperón, Manuel, 11, 49, 192
  ¡Ay Jalisco, no te rajes!, 180–182
  Los tres García, 188
  "Vendo Placer," 238
estilo bravío, 159–160, 182
estilo yucateco bolero, 41
estribrillo, 46
Estridentismo, 126, 126n44
evolucionistas, 127
exoticism, cabaretera films,
    51–53, 52n99

"fallen woman" narrative. See prostitute
    melodrama
Felski, Rita, 70–71, 104
Fernández, Emilio, 53, 54, 129, 130f, 131.
    See also *Janitzio* (Navarro); *María
    Candelaria* (Fernández); *Víctimas del
    pecado* (Fernández)
  Salón México, 51, 54–55, 238
Fernández Ros, Antonio, *1910*, 1–3, 2n2–3
fichera, 20, 27, 27n14, 28, 49, 58, 236
Figueroa, Gabriel, 53, 139. See also *María
    Candelaria* (Fernández)
  Víctimas del pecado, 53, 61 (see also
    Víctimas del pecado)
Forjando Patria (Gamio), 114–115
Fuentes, Andrés Reséndez, 198

Gamboa, Federico, 21
  Santa (see *Santa* [Gamboa])
  Vázquez Mantecón on, 30–32, 30n26
Gamio, Manuel, 18, 114, 117
  Forjando Patria, 114–115
García, David L., 56–57

García Riera, Emilio, 90, 162, 173–174, 234
  Historia documental del cine mexicano, 10, 10n23
Gatica, Valentina, 205–206
gauchas, 205
Gellner, Ernest, 4
Gorbman, Claudia, 14
Gómez, Humberto, *En tiempos de don Porfirio*, 80. See also *En tiempos de don Porfirio* (Bustillo Oro)
Gonzalez, Laureana Wright, 197
González, Manuel, 72
Gonzaléz Navarro, Moisés, 73
Gorbman, Claudia, 132, 132n68
gringo archetype, 189–191
gringo-ness, performance, 185–191, 185n95, 186f, 187f
gritos, 172
Grovas, Jesús, 80
Guadalajara (Jiménez), 179
guaguancó, 63–65, 64f
Güeros (Ruizpalacios), 240
Guerrero, María Consuelo, 196
güiro, 56, 56–57n116
Guízar, Tito, 174–175

hacienda, 154, 154n10
Hall, Stuart, 241
Hamilton, Nora, 76
Hernández Gómez, Guillermo, *La Adelita*, 19, 194, 195, 216–220, 221f
Hernández Moncada, Eduardo, 225
Herrera-Sobek, María, 202, 203, 204
Hershfield, Joanne, 9, 12, 13, 29, 50, 164
Herzog, Amy, 14
hispanismo, *Allá en el Rancho Grande*, 164–165
Historia de la música popular mexicana (Rivas), 9
Historia documental del cine mexicano (Riera), 10, 10n23
Hobsbawm, Eric, 4
Hollywood
  charro, singing, 155–156
  del Río, Dolores, 141n62, 165n46
  features, 5
  film score, classical, 10, 10–11n24

Los tres García, 183–184
  portrayals of Mexicans, 184–185
huapango, 225
  coplas de, 176
  "La Malagueña," 225, 226, 238
huapango retachado, 170, 175–176, 182
Huerta, Efraín, 146–147
Humanidad (Maugard), 165
Hurtado, Elías, 26, 26n12

Icaza, René, 164
imagined community, 4
IMCINE, 1, 237
"Indian," 116, 116n12
indigenismo/indigenista films, 8, 18, 18n43, 111–149
  actor roles, white- *vs.* darker skin, 164–165
  Cárdenas, Lázaro, 117
  Caso, Alfonso, 114, 116–117, 117n16
  collective property, 115, 115n9
  Domínguez, Francisco, 18, 113, 124–129, 132–137, 141–145, 148–149
  Eisenstein, Sergei, 113
  Eisenstein, Sergei, *¡Que viva México!*, 120–124
  Enríquez Molina, Andrés, 114
  Gamio, Manuel, 114–115, 117
  "Indian," 116, 116n12
  integrating indigenous, 113–117
  Janitzio, 129–138, 130f, 135f (see also *Janitzio*)
  María Candelaria, 138–147, 140f, 144f
  mestizaje, 111, 114–115
  musicalizing indigenous communities, 112–113
  representing indigenous, 112, 117–120
  setting, 111
  Vasconcelos, José, 114, 118
Infante, Pedro, 179, 234
Instituto Mexicano de Cinematografía (IMCINE), 1, 237
invented traditions, 4
Iztaccíhuatl, 131, 131n60

Janitzio (Navarro), 18, 113, 129–138, 135f
  basis, Romay's narrative accounts, 130–131

Domínguez, Francisco (composer),
   128–129, 132–137, 148–149
   ethnographic approach, 130, 134–138
   Fernández, Emilio, 129, 130f, 131
   music, Indian style, 132–134
   music, role, 131–132
   musical theme, 132, 134–137
   pentatonic paradigm, 132–134
   pirékua, 137
   story, 129, 130f
jarabe tapatío, 171f, 172–173
Johns, Michael, 74
José, D., 27
Junco, Alfonso, 91

Korngold, Erich, 10

La Adelita (film, Hernández Gómez), 19,
   194, 195, 216–222, 221f
"La Adelita" (song), 19, 195–196, 203–205,
   212–214, 214f, 216–218, 219–220,
   222, 227, 229–230
la chica moderna, 29
"La cocaleca," 59–60, 60f
"La Malagueña," 225–226, 238
La mancha de sangre (Maugard), 49
"La maquinista del amor," 105, 106f
Lamarque, Libertad, 7
La mujer del puerto (Boytler), 49, 237
La Musique des Incas et ses survivances
   (d'Harcourt), 133–134
Landero, Gómez, 82
Lara, Agustín, 37
   boleros, 39
   effeminate lyrics and sounds, 160
   fame and popularity, 37–39
   family and background, 37
   Güeros, 240
   laraismo, 39
   Mujer Divina: Homenaje a Agustín
      Lara, 237
   Santa, bolero, 40–44, 41f, 41n63,
      43f, 67
   Santa, danzón, 48
   Santa, myth, 36–39, 67
laraismo, 39
"La Rielera," 205, 206–207, 227, 230, 231f
La Sargenta (Carrasco and Gascón), 207

Las fiestas del Centenario, 77, 79
las pelonas, 40n61
"Las tres pelonas," 211–212
"La Valentina," 205–206, 212
La viejecita (Caballero), 100
Leal, Juan Felipe, 77
Leblanc, Oscar, 39
Lerdo de Tejada, Miguel
   Orquesta Típica "Lerdo," 33–34,
      33n39
   Santa music, 33n39, 37
Lerner, Neil, 16
Liga de la decencia, 53, 97
liminal space, 87
Lipsitz, George, 189
López, Ana M., 7–8
López, Rafael, 27–28
Los Contemporáneos, 208–209, 209n47
Los de Abajo (Azuela), 193
Los Olvidados (Buñuel), 7, 240
Los tres García (Rodríguez), 19, 183–191,
   187f, 189n99
   Cortázar, 178–192
   Esperón and Cortázar, 188–189
   gringo-ness, performance, 185–191,
      186f, 187f
   Hollywood intervention, Mexican film
      industry, 183–184
   Hollywood portrayals of Mexicans,
      184–185
   masculinity and machismo, 190
   storyline, 185–188, 186f, 187f
   "The Turkey and the Straw," 188–190
"los tres grandes" (muralists), 118–119,
   118n22, 119, 119n23
Los Trovadores Tamaulipecos, 170
lucha libre, 235
"Lucha María," 170
Lumière brothers, 76–77

machismo
   ávilacamachismo, 92
   cantina music, 172–178, 174f
   charro, 152, 153, 190
   cinemachismo, 16
   definition, 16
   huapango retachado, 176
   Los tres García, 190

machismo (*cont.*)
  Negrete's charro, *¡Ay Jalisco, no te rajes!*, 182–183
Madero, Francisco I., 75
Madrid, Alejandro L.
  Danzón: Circum-Caribbean Dialogues in Music and Dance, 46
  Music in Mexico: Experience Music, Expressing Culture, 41
Magdaleno, Mauricio, 53, 139, 139n82. See also *María Candelaria* (Fernández); *Víctimas del pecado*
"Malagueña Salerosa," 225, 226, 238
mambo, 55, 55n112
  "La cocaleca," 59–60, 60*f*
María Candelaria (Fernández), 18, 113, 138–147
  critics on, 146–147
  Domínguez's music and theme, 141–145, 148–149
  historical setting and Cristero rebellion, 138–139, 138n81
  hostility and persecution, 141
  Magdaleno, Mauricio (screenwriter), 139, 139n82
  masculinity, 139
  Mexicanidad representation, 139, 139n83
  story, 139–141, 140*f*, 143–145, 144*f*
María y Campos, Armando de, 207, 213n58
Martín-Barbero, Jesús, 13–14
masculinity
  Allá en el Rancho Grande, 161
  ávilacamachismo, 92
  canción mexicana, 160
  charro and comedia ranchera, 152, 164, 179, 191
  cinemachismo, 16
  Los tres García, 183, 190
  María Candelaria, 139
  Mexicanidad, 65
  revolutionary melodrama, 89
  ¡Vámonos con Pancho Villa!, 215
Más fuerte que el deber (Sevilla), 36
Maugard, Adolfo Best
  Humanidad, 165
  La mancha de sangre, 49

McClary, Susan, 53
Medina, Rafael, *Chin Chun Chan*, 102, 104*f*
Medio siglo de cine mexicano (de los Reyes), 12, 33
Méliès, Georges, 32
melodrama. See also *specific types*
  cultural synchresis and, 12–16
  definition, 12
  European, early, 12–13
  scholars on, 12–13
Memorias de un mexicano (Toscano), 69–70
Mendoza, Vicente, 202, 203, 232
mestizo
  audience, urban/modern, 111, 113, 118, 148
  charro, 153
  cultural, 114
  culture and music, 165–166
  hacienda on, 154
  populace, 113
  representations, 114
  vs. self-identification, 116
  soldaderas, 197–198
mestizoizing, 111
Mexicanidad, 3, 6, 14, 16, 17, 19
  Allá en el Rancho Grande, 161, 172, 178
  charro, 161, 172, 178, 191
  danzón, 239
  época de oro, 238
  masculinity, 65
Mexican Revolution, 1–3, 193. See also *specific films, individuals, and topics*
  Enamorada, 19, 194
  films, 193–194
  Mexican Mural School, 193
  Mexican womanhood and, 196–199
  soldadera, 193–233
  urban music, 78n32
  ¡Vámonos con Pancho Villa!, 19, 194
México de mis recuerdos (Bustillo Oro), 96–102, 101*f*, 105–109, 106*f*, 108*f*
  "La maquinista del amor," 105, 106*f*
  Las bribonas, 5
Mitchell, Tim, 176–177
Mixteca, 167
modern domesticity, 29

Monsiváis, Carlos, 5, 19, 39, 41, 119, 139, 173, 179, 195–197, 198–199, 205–206
Montenegro, Roberto, 118, 119
Monterrey, Jimmy, 62, 62n126, 63f
Moore, Robin D.
   Danzón: Circum-Caribbean Dialogues in Music and Dance, 46
   Nationalizing Blackness: Afrocubanismo and Artistic Revolution in Havana, 45, 52n100, 65
Mora, Carl, 235–236
Moreno, Antonio, 7
   Santa, 7, 21–23 (see also *Santa* [Gamboa])
Moreno Rivas, Yolanda, 9, 82–83, 170, 179
Moriones, Hermanas, 102
moving memory, 69
Mraz, John, 194–195, 200
Mujer Divina: Homenaje a Agustín Lara (Lafourcade), 237
Muñoz, Rafael F., 209–210, 212–213
muralists, Mexican
   on Eisenstein, 120, 122n34
   ideologies of the Revolution, 118
   "los tres grandes," 118–119, 118n22, 119, 119n23
   Mexican Revolution, 193
Murillo, Fidel, 178–179
música culta, 82–83
música de fondo, 10
música de salón, 18
   En tiempos de don Porfirio, 82–83
música tropical, la, 9
Music in Mexico: Experience Music, Expressing Culture (Madrid), 41

Nájera-Ramírez, Olga, 154
nationalism, 4–8
Nationalizing Blackness: Afrocubanismo and Artistic Revolution in Havana (Moore), 45, 52n100, 65
Negrete, Jorge, 179
   ¡Ay Jalisco, no te rajes!, 178–183, 179–183
   death of, 234, 234n1
   on rancheras, 180
   on rancheras, popularity from, 179–181
Noble, Andrea, 69, 200, 232

Noche Mexicana, 126, 126n45
Nomland, John, 78–79
nostalgia, 70–71
Novo, Salvador, 25, 147

Orega, Carlos, *En tiempos de don Porfirio*, 78–79
orisha, 55, 55n109
Orquesta Típica "Lerdo," 33–34, 33n39
ostinati, repetitive percussive, 132, 132n69
Oudrid, Cristóbal, 84

pachuco, 58–59
Padilla, Manuel Castro, 45n74, 82, 211n52
   En tiempos de don Porfirio, 78
Pallares, Eduardo, 26
Pardavé, Joaquín, 84
Parra, Max, 209
pelonas, 211, 211n54
pelonas, las, 40n61
Peredo, Luis G., 31–33
Peréz Montfort, Ricardo, 117, 123–124
Pérez Prado, Dámaso, 55–56, 58, 59–60, 60f, 239
Pérez Prado Orchestra, 56, 58, 59–60, 60f
Pick, Zuzana, 194–195, 209, 212
pirékua, 137
Ponce, Manual M., 202
Porfiriato (Porfirio Díaz), 2–3, 22, 22n3, 24–26, 24n7, 9, 25n11, 68, 91–109
   ¡Ay, qué tiempos señor don Simón!, 90, 93–99, 96f, 109
   Camacho and ávilacamachismo, 91–92, 92n69
   Chin Chun Chan, 102, 104f
   corruption, modernization, and cosmopolitanism, 71–76
   Díaz's celebrity, 76–77
   En tiempos de don Porfirio, 68, 71, 80–91, 86f (see also *En tiempos de don Porfirio* [Bustillo Oro])
   on female bourgeoisie and nostalgia, 70–71
   function, 70
   genre, 68–70
   Las fiestas del Centenario, 77
   México de mis recuerdos, 96–102, 101f, 105–109, 106f, 108f

Porfiriato (Porfirio Díaz) *(cont.)*
  music, 82
  nostalgia, 70
  Porfirian spectacle, 79
  Reglamento para el ejercicio de la
    prostitución, 24, 24n7
  rurales and *pax porfiriana*, 73
  stage and silent screen, 76–79
  teatro de revistas, 78, 78n32
  theatrical spectacles, 93
  Villanueva, Felipe, "Vals poético," 68,
    69f, 83
  zonas de tolerancia, 24–25
Portillo, José López, 236
Powrie, Phil, 14
Presidents, Mexico. See also *specific
    individuals*
  1920s and 1930s, 75, 75n21
"Presumida," 170
Prida, Pablo, *En tiempos de don
    Porfirio*, 78–79
prostitute melodrama, 21–67. *See also*
    cabaretera; *specific films*
  cabaret dance music, 15
  cabarets, El dancing, and modern
    woman, 26–30
  danzón for Santita, 44–49, 48f
  history, 23, 67
  La mujer del puerto, 49, 237
  modernization, exoticism, and
    rumbera, 49–53
  popularity, 23
  Porfiriato and spaces of "sin," 24–26
  prostitute symbolism, 22
  Revancha, 237
  Santa, 12, 17, 21–23
  Santa, Lara's bolero, 40–44, 41f, 41n63,
    43f, 67
  Santa, silent, Gamboa's aural
    environment and, 30–35
  Santa, sound in, and Agustín Lara
    myth, 36–39
  Víctimas del pecado, prostitute as
    rumbera, 62–67, 62n126, 63f
Puerto, Elvia Carrillo, 197

¡Que viva México! (Eisenstein), 120–124
  camera use, experimental, 124

  categorization and filming techniques,
    122–123
  "Conquest," 122
  epilogue, 122
  "Fiesta," 122
  imagery and folkloric stereotypes,
    123–124
  "Maguey," 122
  prologue, 122
  "Sandunga," 122
  "Soldadera," 122

Rabasa, Emilio, 30
rancheros, 165, 194. See also *specific films*
Rashkin, Elissa, 126
Redes (Gómez Muriel), 124
Redes (Strand), 145, 145–146n87,
    211, 211n51
red-light districts, 24–25
repetitive percussive ostinati, 132, 132n69
Revancha, 237
revista mexicana (Mimi Derba), 101,
    101–102n84
revistas de evocación, *En tiempos de don
    Porfirio*, 78–79, 79n35
revolutionary melodrama, 8, 19,
    68–69, 111
  male archetypes, 89
  setting, 111
revolutionary melodrama, musicalizing
    soldadera in, 193–233
  corrido-canciones, 207–231 (*see also*
    corrido-canciones)
  genre, rancheros, and soldaderas, 194
  La Adelita (film), 19, 194, 195,
    216–222, 221f
  "La Adelita" (song), 19, 195–196, 203–205,
    212–214, 214f, 216–218, 219–220, 222,
    227, 229–230
  "La Rielera," 205, 206–207, 227, 230, 231f
  "La Valentina," 205–206, 212
  Mexican womanhood, Revolution and,
    196–199
  soldadera, in popular culture, 199–203
Revueltas, Silvestre, 9–10, 9n19,
    211–213, 215
Rivas, Yolanda Moreno, *Historia de la
    música popular mexicana*, 9

Rodríguez brothers, 36
Romay, Luis Márquez, 130
rond de jambe, 94, 94n72
Rosas, Juventino, "Carmen," 99, 99n81
Rouskaya, Norka, 32, 32n35
Ruíz, Federico, *En tiempos de don Porfirio*, 78
rumba, 52, 53
    guaguancó, 63–65, 64*f*
    Víctimas del pecado, 62–67, 62n126, 63*f*, 64*f*
rumbera, 52–53, 52n100, 65, 67, 107–108.
    See also *Víctimas del pecado*

Saavedra, Leonora, 127, 132n69, 133, 133n71
Salón México (Fernández), 51, 54–55, 238
Santa (Gamboa), 12, 17, 21–23, 30, 210
    "Bienvenida," danza mexicana, 34
    bolero, Lara's, 40–44, 41*f*, 41n63, 43*f*, 67
    bolero, Villegas', 40n60
    Camus silent film adaptation and Peredo's production, 31–32
    danzas and danzones, 34–35
    gender constructions, 22
    Mexico City nightlife, 22–23
    Orquesta Típica "Lerdo," 33–34, 33n39
    silent, Gamboa's aural environment and, 30–35
    sound, and Agustín Lara myth, 36–39
    waltz, "Boston" style, 35, 35n42
scholarly challenge, 8–12
Scotch snap, 132, 132n69
self, 4
self-identification, 116
señoras decentes, 22
Serna, Enrique, 179
Sevilla, Ninón
    Aventurera, 51, 64n130
    Víctimas del pecado, 17, 23, 54–66, 57*f*, 60*f*, 62n126, 63*f*–64*f* (see also *Víctimas del pecado*)
shimmy, 27–28
silent film period, Mexican, 31, 31n31
singing charro. *See* charro, singing
Siqueiros, David Alfaro, *Entierro de un obrero*, 122
Slobin, Mark, 112, 148

Smith, Maya Ramos, 97
"Sobre las olas" (Rosa), 169
soldadera
    Carrancitas, 194n3
    mestizo, 197–198
    popular culture, 199–203
    Villistas, 194n3, 198, 198n12
    Zapatistas, 194, 194n3, 198, 228
soldadera, revolutionary melodrama, 19, 193–233. *See also* revolutionary melodrama, musicalizing soldadera in
    corrido-canciones, representation, 207–208
    imagery, 194–195
    La Adelita (film), 19, 194, 195, 216–222, 221*f*
    "La Adelita" (song), 19, 195–196, 203–205, 212–214, 214*f*, 216–218, 219–220, 222, 228, 229–230
    meaning, 194n4
    ¡Vámonos con Pancho Villa!, 208–215, 210*f*, 213*f*, 214*f*
"Soldadera," 122
Soto, Shirlene, 197
sound-on-disc method, 36, 36n43
    The Jazz Singer, 36
    Más fuerte que el deber, 36
spectacles, Porfiriato, 93
Spivak, Gayartri, 189
Stein, Max, 10
Stilwell, Robynn J., 87
Strand, Paul, 7, 7n15
strategic essentialism, 189
stridentism, 126, 126n44
synchresis
    cultural, 12–16
    definition, 15

teatro culto, 78
teatro de revista, 9, 13, 78n32
    comedia ranchera, 156, 157–159
    danzón, 45n74
    definition and origins, 157
    Lara, piano playing, 9, 137
    Porfiriato backdrop, 78, 78nn32–33
teatro de revistas, 13, 78, 78n32, 157
teatro frivolo, 207

Teatro Lírico, 79, 79n36
Teatro María Guerrero, 207
Teatro mexicano del murciélago, El
    (Quintanilla, González, Barolo),
    126, 126n44
teatro popular, 78, 78n33
Teatro Principal, 98, 102, 102n87, 103,
    105, 106
Tello, Aurelio, Diccionario del Cine
    Iberoamericano, 11
theatrical spectacles, Porfiriato, 93
"The Turkey and the Straw," 188–190
Tierney, Dolores, 56, 62, 130, 146, 227–230
Tierney, Joanne, 9
Torres, Francisco, 211
Toscano, Carmen, Memorias de un
    mexicano, 69–70
Toscano, Salvador, 70
tradicionalistas, 127
trio, musical, 169–171
Trio Garnica-Ascencio, 170
Trio Murciélago, 170–171
Trio Tariácuri, 169–170
Tuñón, Julia, 201
Turner, John Kenneth, Barbarous
    Mexico, 73

UNAM, 32, 237, 250
unheard melody, 14
Urban, Max, 82–83, 82n46

Valenzuela, Sánchez, 32
Villaurrutia, Xavier, 209
Vals capricho (Castro, Ricardo), 100
"Vals poético" (Villanueva), 68, 69f, 83
¡Vámonos con Pancho Villa!, 19, 194
    soldaderas, 208–215, 210f, 213f, 214f
    women, 215
Vasconcelos, José, 114, 118
Vaughan, May Kay, 199
Vázquez Mantecón, Álvaro, 30–32, 30n26
"Vendo Placer," 238
Vera, José, 175
Veyre, Gabriel, 77
Víctimas del pecado (Fernández), 17,
    23, 54–66
    botao, 64, 64f
    "Changó," 56–58, 57f

Club Changoo cabaret in, 54–56
"El tren," 66
La Máquina Loca, 61–66
mambo, "La cocaleca," 59–60, 60f
Perez Prado Orchestra, 56, 58, 59–60, 60f
rumba, guaguancó, 63–65, 64f
rumba, Jimmy Monterrey, 62–63,
    62n126, 63f
story, 54
swing dance and pachuco
    fashion, 58–59
Vigilanti Cura (Vatican), 97
Villa, Pancho, 155, 198n12, 212
Villanueva, Felipe, "Vals poético," 68,
    69f, 83
Villaurrutia, Xavier, 209
Villegas, Juan Alberto, "Amor de
    ciego," 40n60
Villistas, 194n3, 198, 198n12
Vitaphone sound-on-disc method,
    36, 36n43

waltzes
    En tiempos de don Porfirio, 82–83
    México de mis recuerdos, 98
    México de mis recuerdos "Carmen,"
        99, 99n81
    Santa, "Boston" style, 35, 35n42
    Vals capricho, 100
womanhood, Mexican, 196–199

Yo bailé con don Porfirio (Solares),
    103n93, 109

Zapata, Emiliano, 155
Zapatistas, 194, 194n3, 198, 228
zarzuela, 13, 18
    de género chico, 102, 102n85
    de género grande, 102n86
    "El gálan incógnito," 84–88, 86f
    La Sargenta, 207
    Las bribonas, 5
    La viejecita, 100
    popularity, Porfiriato, 101–102
    structure, 102n85
"Zip Coon," 190, 190n103
Zola, Èmile, 30
zonas de tolerancia, 24–25